Elvis Presley

Write a review to receive any **FREE** eBook from our Catalogue - $99 Value!

If you recently bought this book we would love to hear from you! Benefit from receiving a free eBook from our catalogue at http://www.emereo.org/ if you write a review on Amazon (or the online store where you purchased this book) about your last purchase!

How does it work?

To post a review on Amazon, just log in to your account and click on the Create your own review button (under Customer Reviews) of the relevant product page. You can find examples of product reviews in Amazon. If you purchased from another online store, simply follow their procedures.

What happens when I submit my review?

Once you have submitted your review, send us an email at review@emereo.org with the link to your review, and the eBook you would like as our thank you from http://www.emereo.org/. Pick any book you like from the catalogue, up to $99 RRP. You will receive an email with your eBook as download link. It is that simple!

Complete Guide to Elvis Presley.

Get the information you need--fast! This comprehensive guide offers a thorough view of key knowledge and detailed insight. It's all you need.

There is absolutely nothing that isn't thoroughly covered in the book. It is straightforward, and does an excellent job of explaining all about Elvis Presley in key topics and material.

There is no reason to invest in any other materials to learn about Elvis Presley. You'll understand it all.

Contents

Elvis Presley

Elvis Presley

Elvis Presley

Publicity photo for Jailhouse Rock (1957)
Background information
Birth name Elvis Aaron Presley
Born January 8, 1935
Tupelo, Mississippi, U. S.
Died August 16, 1977 (aged 42)
Memphis, Tennessee, U. S.
Genres Rock and roll, pop, rockabilly, country, blues, gospel, R&B
Occupations Musician, actor
Instruments Vocals, guitar, piano
Years active 1953–77
Labels Sun, RCA Victor
Associated acts The Blue Moon Boys, The Jordanaires, The Imperials
Website elvis. com
Elvis Aaron Presley (January 8, 1935 – August 16, 1977) was one of the most popular American singers of the 20th century. A cultural icon, he is commonly known by the single name Elvis. He is often referred to as the "King of Rock and Roll" or simply "the King".

Born in Tupelo, Mississippi, Presley moved to Memphis, Tennessee, with his family at the age of 13. He began his career there in 1954, working with Sun Records owner Sam Phillips, who wanted to bring the sound of African American music to a wider audience. Accompanied by guitarist Scotty Moore and bassist Bill Black, Presley was the most important popularizer of rockabilly, an uptempo, backbeat-driven fusion of country and rhythm and blues. RCA Victor acquired his contract in a deal arranged by Colonel Tom Parker, who went on to manage the singer for over two decades. Presley's first RCA single, "Heartbreak Hotel", released in January 1956, was a number-one hit. He became the leading figure of the newly popular sound of rock and roll with a series of network television appearances and chart-topping records. His energized interpretations of songs, many from African

American sources, and his uninhibited performance style made him enormously popular—and controversial. In November 1956, he made his film debut in Love Me Tender.

Drafted into military service in 1958, Presley relaunched his recording career two years later with some of his most commercially successful work. He staged few concerts however, and guided by Parker, proceeded to devote much of the 1960s to making Hollywood movies and soundtrack albums, most of them critically derided. In 1968, after seven years away from the stage, he returned to live performance in a celebrated comeback television special that led to an extended Las Vegas concert residency and a string of profitable tours. In 1973 Presley staged the first concert broadcast globally via satellite, Aloha from Hawaii. Prescription drug abuse severely compromised his health, and he died suddenly in 1977 at the age of 42.

Presley is regarded as one of the most important figures of 20th-century popular culture. He had a versatile voice and unusually wide success encompassing many genres, including country, pop ballads, gospel, and blues. He is the best-selling solo artist in the history of popular music. Nominated for 14 competitive Grammys, he won three, and received the Grammy Lifetime Achievement Award at age 36. He has been inducted into multiple music halls of fame.

Life and career

Early years (1935–53)

Childhood in Tupelo

Elvis Presley was born on January 8, 1935, in Tupelo, Mississippi, to 18-year-old Vernon Elvis and 22-year-old Gladys Love Presley, in the two-room shotgun house built by his father in readiness for the birth. Jesse Garon Presley, his identical twin brother, was delivered 35 minutes before him, stillborn. As an only child, Presley became close to both parents and formed an unusually tight bond with his mother. The family attended an Assembly of God church where he found his initial musical inspiration.

Presley's ancestry was primarily a Western European mix: On his mother's side, he was Scots-Irish, with some French Norman; one of Gladys's great-great-grandmothers was Cherokee. His father's forebears were of Scottish or German origin. Gladys was regarded by relatives and friends as the dominant member of the small family. Vernon moved from one odd job to the next, evidencing little ambition. The family often relied on help from neighbors and government food assistance. In 1938, they lost their home after Vernon was found guilty of altering a check written by the landowner. He was jailed for eight months, and Gladys and Elvis moved in with relatives.

In September 1941, Presley entered first grade at East Tupelo Consolidated, where his instructors regarded him as "average". He was encouraged to enter a singing contest after impressing his schoolteacher with a rendition of Red Foley's country song "Old Shep" during morning prayers. The contest, held at the Mississippi-Alabama Fair and Dairy Show on October 3, 1945, saw his first public performance: dressed as a cowboy, the ten-year-old Presley stood on a chair to reach the microphone and sang "Old Shep". He recalled placing fifth. A few months later, Presley received his first guitar for his birthday; he had hoped for something else—by different accounts, either a bicycle or a rifle. Over the following year, he received basic guitar lessons from two of his uncles and the new pastor at the family's church. Presley recalled, "I took the guitar, and I watched people, and I learned to play a little bit. But I would never sing in public. I was very shy about it. "

Entering a new school, Milam, for sixth grade in September 1946, Presley was regarded as a loner. The following year, he began bringing his guitar in on a daily basis. He played and sang during lunchtime, and was often teased as a "trashy" kid who played hillbilly music. The family was by then living in a largely African-American neighborhood. A devotee of Mississippi Slim's show on the Tupelo radio station WELO, Presley was described as "crazy about music" by Slim's younger brother, a classmate of Presley's, who often took him in to the station. Slim supplemented Presley's guitar tuition by demonstrating chord techniques. When his protégé was 12 years old, Slim scheduled him for two on-air performances. Presley was overcome by stage fright the first time, but succeeded in performing the following week.

Teenage life in Memphis

In November 1948, the family moved to Memphis, Tennessee. After residing for nearly a year in rooming houses, they were granted a two-bedroom apartment in the public housing complex known as the Courts. Enrolled at Humes High School, Presley received only a C in music in eighth grade. When his music teacher told him he had no aptitude for singing, he brought in his guitar the next day and sang a recent hit, "Keep Them Cold Icy Fingers Off Me", in an effort to prove otherwise. A classmate later recalled that the teacher "agreed that Elvis was right when he said that she didn't appreciate his kind of singing. " He was generally too shy to perform openly, and was occasionally bullied by classmates who viewed him as a "mama's boy". In 1950, he began practicing guitar regularly under the tutelage of Jesse Lee Denson, a neighbor two-and-a-half years his senior. They and three other boys—including two future rockabilly pioneers, brothers Dorsey and Johnny Burnette—formed a loose musical collective that played frequently around the Courts. That September, he began ushering at Loew's State Theater. Other jobs followed during his school years: Precision Tool, Loew's again, and MARL Metal Products.

During his junior year, Presley began to stand out more among his classmates, largely because of his appearance: he grew out his sideburns and styled his hair with rose oil and Vaseline. On his own time, he would head down to Beale Street, the heart of Memphis's thriving blues scene, and gaze longingly at the wild, flashy clothes in the windows of Lansky Brothers. By his senior year, he was wearing them. Overcoming his reticence about performing outside the Courts, he competed in Humes's Annual "Minstrel" show in April 1953. Singing and playing guitar, he opened with "Till I Waltz Again with You", a recent hit for Teresa Brewer. Presley recalled that the performance did much for his reputation: "I wasn't popular in school . . . I failed music—only thing I ever failed. And then they entered me in this talent show . . . when I came onstage I heard people kind of rumbling and whispering and so forth, 'cause nobody knew I even sang. It was amazing how popular I became after that. "

Presley, who never received formal music training or learned to read music, studied and played by ear. He frequented record stores with jukeboxes and listening booths. He knew all of Hank Snow's songs and he loved records by other country singers such as Roy Acuff, Ernest Tubb, Ted Daffan, Jimmie Rodgers, Jimmie Davis, and Bob Wills. The Southern Gospel singer Jake Hess, one of his favorite performers, was a significant influence on his ballad-singing style. He was a regular audience member at the monthly All-Night Singings downtown, where many of the white gospel groups that performed reflected the influence of African-American spiritual music. He adored the music of black gospel singer Sister Rosetta Tharpe. Like some of his peers, he may have attended blues venues—of necessity, in the segregated South, only on nights designated for exclusively white audiences. He certainly listened to the regional radio stations that played "race records": spirituals, blues, and the modern, backbeat-heavy sound of rhythm and blues. Many of his future recordings were inspired by local African-American musicians such as Arthur Crudup and Rufus Thomas. B. B. King recalled that he knew Presley before he was popular when they both used to frequent Beale Street. By the time he graduated from high school in June 1953, Presley had already singled out music as his future.

First recordings (1953–55)

Sam Phillips and Sun Records

In August 1953, Presley walked into the offices of Sun Records. He aimed to pay for a few minutes of studio time to record a two-sided acetate disc: "My Happiness" and "That's When Your Heartaches Begin". He would later claim he intended the record as a gift for his mother, or was merely interested in what he "sounded like", though there was a much cheaper, amateur record-making service at a nearby general store. Biographer Peter Guralnick argues that he chose Sun in the hope of being discovered. Asked by receptionist Marion Keisker what kind of singer he was, Presley responded, "I sing all kinds. " When she pressed him on whom he sounded like, he repeatedly answered, "I don't sound like nobody. " After he recorded, Sun boss Sam Phillips asked Keisker to note down the young man's name, which she did along with her own commentary: "Good ballad singer. Hold. " Presley cut a second acetate in January 1954—"I'll Never Stand In Your Way" and "It Wouldn't Be the Same Without You"—but again nothing came of it.

Not long after, he failed an audition for a local vocal quartet, the Songfellows. He explained to his father, "They told me I couldn't sing. " Songfellow Jim Hamill later claimed that he was turned down because he did not demonstrate an ear for harmony at the time. In April, Presley began working for the Crown Electric company as a truck driver. His friend Ronnie Smith, after playing a few local gigs with him, suggested he contact Eddie Bond, leader of Smith's professional band, which had an opening for a vocalist. Bond rejected him after a tryout, advising Presley to stick to truck driving "because you're never going to make it as a singer. "

Phillips, meanwhile, was always on the lookout for someone who could bring to a broader audience the sound of the black musicians on whom Sun focused. As Keisker reported, "Over and over I remember Sam saying, 'If I could find a white man who had the Negro sound and the Negro feel, I could make a billion dollars. '" In June, he acquired a demo recording of a ballad, "Without You", that he thought might suit the teenaged singer. Presley came by the studio, but was unable to do it justice. Despite this, Phillips asked Presley to sing as many numbers as he knew. He was sufficiently affected by what he heard to invite two local musicians, guitarist Winfield "Scotty" Moore and upright bass player Bill Black, to work something up with Presley for a recording session.

The session, held the evening of July 5, proved entirely unfruitful until late in the night. As they were about to give up and go home, Presley took his guitar and launched into a 1946 blues number, Arthur Crudup's "That's All Right". Moore recalled, "All of a sudden, Elvis just started singing this song, jumping around and acting the fool, and then Bill picked up his bass, and he started acting the fool, too, and I started playing with them. Sam, I think, had the door to the control booth open . . . he stuck his head out and said, 'What are you doing?' And we said, 'We don't know. ' 'Well, back up,' he said, 'try to find a place to start, and do it again. '" Phillips quickly began taping; this was the sound he had been looking for. Three days later, popular Memphis DJ Dewey Phillips played "That's All Right" on his Red, Hot, and Blue show. Listeners began phoning in, eager to find out who the singer was. The interest was such that Phillips played the record repeatedly during the last two hours of his show. Interviewing Presley on-air, Phillips asked him what high school he attended in order to clarify his color for the many callers who had assumed he was black. During the next few days, the trio recorded a bluegrass number, Bill Monroe's "Blue Moon of Kentucky", again in a distinctive style and employing a jury-rigged echo effect that Sam Phillips dubbed "slapback". A single was pressed with "That's All Right" on the A side and "Blue Moon of Kentucky" on the reverse.

Early live performances and signing to RCA

The trio played publicly for the first time on July 17 at the Bon Air club—Presley still sporting his child-size guitar. At the end of the month, they appeared at the Overton Park Shell, with Slim Whitman headlining. A combination of his strong response to rhythm and nervousness at playing before a large crowd led Presley to shake his legs as he performed: his wide-cut pants emphasized his movements, causing young women in the audience to start screaming. Moore recalled, "During the instrumental parts he would back off from the mike and be playing and shaking, and the crowd would just go wild". Black, a natural showman, whooped and rode his bass, hitting double licks that Presley would later remember as "really a wild sound, like a jungle drum or something". Soon after, Moore and Black quit their old band to play with Presley regularly, and DJ and promoter Bob Neal became the trio's manager. From August through October, they played frequently at the Eagle's Nest club and returned to Sun Studio for more recording sessions, and Presley quickly grew more confident on stage. According to Moore, "His movement was a natural thing, but he was also very conscious of what got a reaction. He'd do something one time and then he would expand on it real quick. " Presley made what would be his only appearance on Nashville's Grand Ole Opry on October 2; after a polite audience response, Opry manager Jim Denny told Phillips that his singer was "not bad" but did not suit the program. Two weeks later, Presley was booked on Louisiana Hayride, the Opry's chief, and more adventurous, rival. The Shreveport-based show was broadcast to 198 radio stations in 28 states. Presley had another attack of nerves during the first set, which drew a muted reaction. A more composed and energetic second set inspired an enthusiastic response. House drummer D. J. Fontana brought a new element, complementing Presley's movements with accented beats that he had mastered playing in strip clubs. Soon after the show, the Hayride engaged Presley for a year's worth of Saturday-night appearances. Trading in his old guitar for $8 (and seeing it promptly dispatched to the garbage), he purchased a Martin instrument for $175, and his trio began playing in new locales including Houston, Texas, and Texarkana, Arkansas.

By early 1955, Presley's regular Hayride appearances, constant touring, and well-received record releases had made him a substantial regional star, from Tennessee to West Texas. In January, Neal signed a formal management contract with Presley and brought the singer to the attention of Colonel Tom Parker, whom he considered the best promoter in the music business. Parker—Dutch-born, though he claimed to be from West Virginia—had acquired an honorary colonel's commission from country singer turned Louisiana governor Jimmie Davis. Having successfully managed top country star Eddy Arnold, he was now working with the new number-one country singer, Hank Snow. Parker booked Presley on Snow's February tour. When the tour reached Odessa, Texas, a 19-year-old Roy Orbison saw Presley for the first time: "His energy was incredible, his instinct was just amazing. . . . I just didn't know what to make of it. There was just no reference point in the culture to compare it. " Presley made his television debut on March 3 on the KSLA-TV broadcast of Louisiana Hayride. Soon after, he failed an audition for Arthur Godfrey's Talent Scouts on the CBS television network. By August, Sun had released ten sides credited to "Elvis Presley, Scotty and Bill"; on the latest recordings, the trio were joined by a drummer. Some of the songs, like "That's All Right", were in what one Memphis journalist described as the "R&B idiom of negro field jazz"; others, like "Blue Moon of Kentucky", were "more in the country field", "but there was a curious blending of the two different musics in both". This blend of styles made it difficult for Presley's music to find radio airplay. According to Neal, many country-music disc jockeys would not play it because he sounded too much like a black artist and none of the rhythm-and-blues stations would touch him because "he sounded too much like a hillbilly. " The blend came to be known as rockabilly. At the time, Presley was variously billed as "The King of Western Bop", "The Hillbilly Cat", and "The Memphis Flash".

Presley renewed Neal's management contract in August 1955, simultaneously appointing Parker as his special adviser. The group maintained an extensive touring schedule throughout the second half of the year. Neal recalled, "It was almost frightening, the reaction that came to Elvis from the teenaged boys. So many of them, through some sort of jealousy, would practically hate him. There were occasions in some towns in Texas when we'd have to be sure to have a police guard because somebody'd always try to take a crack at him. They'd get a gang and try to waylay him or something. " The trio became a quartet when Hayride drummer Fontana joined as a full member. In mid-October, they played a few shows in support of Bill Haley, whose "Rock Around the Clock" had been a number-one hit the previous year. Haley observed that Presley had a natural feel for rhythm, and advised him to sing fewer ballads.

At the Country Disc Jockey Convention in early November, Presley was voted the year's most promising male artist. Several record companies had by now shown interest in signing him. After three major labels made offers of up to $25,000, Parker and Phillips struck a deal with RCA Victor on November 21 to acquire Presley's Sun contract for an unprecedented $40,000. Presley, at 20, was still a minor, so his father signed the contract. Parker arranged with the owners of Hill and Range Publishing, Jean and Julian Aberbach, to create two entities, Elvis Presley Music and Gladys Music, to handle all of the new material recorded by Presley. Songwriters were obliged to forego one third of their customary royalties in exchange for having him perform their compositions. By December, RCA had begun to heavily promote its new singer, and before month's end had reissued many of his Sun recordings.

Commercial breakout and controversy (1956–58)

First national TV appearances and debut album

On January 10, 1956, Presley made his first recordings for RCA in Nashville. Extending the singer's by now customary backup of Moore, Black, and Fontana, RCA enlisted pianist Floyd Cramer, guitarist Chet Atkins, and three background singers, including Gordon Stoker of the popular Jordanaires quartet, to fill out the sound. The session produced the moody, unusual "Heartbreak Hotel", released as a single on January 27. Parker finally brought Presley to national television, booking him on CBS's Stage Show for six appearances over two months. The program, produced in New York, was hosted on alternate weeks by big band leaders and brothers Tommy and Jimmy Dorsey. After his first appearance, on January 28, Presley stayed in town to record at RCA's New York studio. The sessions yielded eight songs, including a cover of Carl Perkins' rockabilly anthem "Blue Suede Shoes". In February, Presley's "I Forgot to Remember to Forget", a Sun recording initially released the previous August, reached the top of the Billboard country chart. Neal's contract was terminated and, on March 2, Parker became Presley's manager.

RCA Victor released Presley's self-titled debut album on March 23. Joined by five previously unreleased Sun recordings, its seven recently recorded tracks were of a broad variety. There were two country songs and a bouncy pop tune. The others would centrally define the evolving sound of rock and roll: "Blue Suede Shoes"—"an improvement over Perkins' in almost every way", according to critic Robert Hilburn—and three R&B numbers that had been part of Presley's stage repertoire for some time, covers of Little Richard, Ray Charles, and The Drifters. As described by Hilburn, these "were the most revealing of all. Unlike many white artists . . . who watered down the gritty edges of the original R&B versions of songs in the '50s, Presley reshaped them. He not only injected the tunes with his own vocal character but also made guitar, not piano, the lead instrument in all three cases. " It became the first rock-and-roll album to top the Billboard chart, a position it held for 10 weeks. While Presley was not an innovative instrumentalist like Moore or contemporary African American rockers Bo Diddley and Chuck Berry, cultural historian Gilbert B. Rodman argues that the album's cover image, "of Elvis having the time of his life on stage with a guitar in his hands played a crucial role in positioning the guitar. . . as the instrument that best captured the style and spirit of this new music. "

Milton Berle Show and "Hound Dog"

Presley made the first of two appearances on NBC's Milton Berle Show on April 3. His performance, on the deck of the USS Hancock in San Diego, prompted cheers and screams from an audience of sailors and their dates. A few days later, a flight taking Presley and his band to Nashville for a recording session left all three badly shaken when an engine died and the plane almost went down over Arkansas. Twelve weeks after its original release, "Heartbreak Hotel" became Presley's first number-one pop hit. In late April, Presley began a two-week residency at the New Frontier Hotel and Casino on the Las Vegas Strip. The shows were poorly received by the conservative, middle-aged hotel guests—"like a jug of corn liquor at a champagne party", wrote a critic for Newsweek. Amid his Vegas tenure, Presley, who had serious acting ambitions, signed a seven-year contract with Paramount Pictures. He began a tour of the Midwest in mid-May, taking in 15 cities in as many days. He had attended several shows by Freddie Bell and the Bellboys in Vegas, and was struck by their cover of "Hound Dog", a hit in 1953 for blues singer Big Mama Thornton by songwriters Jerry Leiber and Mike Stoller. It became the new closing number of his act. After a show in La Crosse, Wisconsin, an urgent message on the letterhead of the local Catholic diocese's newspaper was sent to FBI director J. Edgar Hoover. It warned that "Presley is a definite danger to the security of the United States. . . . [His] actions and motions were such as to rouse the sexual passions of teenaged youth. . . . After the show, more than 1,000 teenagers tried to gang into Presley's room at the auditorium. . . . Indications of the harm Presley did just in La Crosse were the two high school girls . . . whose abdomen and thigh had Presley's autograph. "

The second Milton Berle Show appearance came on June 5 at NBC's Hollywood studio, amid another hectic tour. Berle persuaded the singer to leave his guitar backstage, advising, "Let 'em see you, son. " During the performance, Presley abruptly halted an uptempo rendition of "Hound Dog" with a wave of his arm and launched into a slow, grinding version accentuated with energetic, exaggerated body movements. Presley's gyrations created a storm of controversy. Television critics were outraged: Jack Gould of The New York Times wrote, "Mr. Presley has no discernible singing ability. . . . His phrasing, if it can be called that, consists of the stereotyped variations that go with a beginner's aria in a bathtub. . . . His one specialty is an accented movement of the body . . . primarily identified with the repertoire of the blond bombshells of the burlesque runway. " Ben Gross of the New York Daily News opined that popular music "has reached its lowest depths in the 'grunt and groin' antics of one Elvis Presley. . . . Elvis, who rotates his pelvis . . . gave an exhibition that was suggestive and vulgar, tinged with the kind of animalism that should be confined to dives and bordellos". Ed Sullivan, whose own variety show was the nation's most popular, declared him "unfit for family viewing". To Presley's displeasure, he soon found himself being referred to as "Elvis the Pelvis", which he called "one of the most childish expressions I ever heard, comin' from an adult. "

Steve Allen Show and first Sullivan appearance

The Berle shows drew such high ratings that Presley was booked for a July 1 appearance on NBC's Steve Allen Show in New York. Allen, no fan of rock and roll, introduced a "new Elvis" in a white bow tie and black tails. Presley sang "Hound Dog" for less than a minute to a basset hound wearing a top hat and bow tie. As described by television historian Jake Austen, "Allen thought Presley was talentless and absurd. . . [he] set things up so that Presley would show his contrition". Allen, for his part, later wrote that he found Presley's "strange, gangly, country-boy charisma, his hard-to-define cuteness, and his charming eccentricity intriguing" and simply worked the singer into the customary "comedy fabric" of his program. Presley would refer back to the Allen show as the most ridiculous performance of his career. Later that night, he appeared on Hy Gardner Calling, a popular local TV show. Pressed on whether he had learned anything from the criticism to which he was being subjected, Presley responded, "No, I haven't, I don't feel like I'm doing anything wrong. . . . I don't see how any type of music would have any bad influence on people when it's only music. . . . I mean, how would rock 'n' roll music make anyone rebel against their parents?"

The next day, Presley recorded "Hound Dog", along with "Any Way You Want Me" and "Don't Be Cruel". The Jordanaires sang harmony, as they had on The Steve Allen Show; they would work with Presley through the 1960s. A few days later, the singer made an outdoor concert appearance in Memphis at which he announced, "You know, those people in New York are not gonna change me none. I'm gonna show you what the real Elvis is like tonight. " In August, a judge in Jacksonville, Florida, ordered Presley to tame his act. Throughout the following performance, he largely kept still, except for wiggling his little finger suggestively in mockery of the order. The single pairing "Don't Be Cruel" with "Hound Dog" ruled the top of the charts for 11 weeks—a mark that would not be surpassed for 36 years. Recording sessions for Presley's second album took place in Hollywood during the first week of September. Leiber and Stoller, the writers of "Hound Dog", contributed "Love Me".

Allen's show with Presley had, for the first time, beaten CBS's Ed Sullivan Show in the ratings. Sullivan, despite his June pronouncement, booked the singer for three appearances for an unprecedented $50,000. The first, on September 9, 1956, was seen by approximately 60 million viewers—a record 82. 6 percent of the television audience. Actor Charles Laughton hosted the show, filling in while Sullivan recuperated from a car accident. Presley appeared in two segments that night from CBS Television City in Los Angeles. According to Elvis legend, Presley was shot only from the waist up. Watching clips of the Allen and Berle shows with his producer, Sullivan had opined that Presley "got some kind of device hanging down below the crotch of his pants–so when he moves his legs back and forth you can see the outline of his cock. . . . I think it's a Coke bottle. . . . We just can't have this on a Sunday night. This is a family show!" Sullivan publicly told TV Guide, "As for his gyrations, the whole thing can be controlled with camera shots. " In fact, Presley was shown head-to-toe in the first and second shows. Though the camerawork was relatively discreet during his debut, with leg-concealing closeups when he danced, the studio audience reacted in customary style: screaming. Presley's performance of his forthcoming single, the ballad "Love Me Tender", prompted a record-shattering million advance orders. More than any other single event, it was this first appearance on

The Ed Sullivan Show that made Presley a national celebrity of barely precedented proportions.

Accompanying Presley's rise to fame, a cultural shift was taking place that he both helped inspire and came to symbolize. Igniting the "biggest pop craze since Glenn Miller and Frank Sinatra . . . Presley brought rock'n'roll into the mainstream of popular culture", writes historian Marty Jezer. "As Presley set the artistic pace, other artists followed. . . . Presley, more than anyone else, gave the young a belief in themselves as a distinct and somehow unified generation—the first in America ever to feel the power of an integrated youth culture. "

Crazed crowds and movie debut

The audience response at Presley's live shows became increasingly fevered. Moore recalled, "He'd start out, 'You ain't nothin' but a Hound Dog,' and they'd just go to pieces. They'd always react the same way. There'd be a riot every time. " At the two concerts he performed in September at the Mississippi-Alabama Fair and Dairy Show, 50 National Guardsmen were added to the police security to prevent crowd trouble. Elvis, Presley's second album, was released in October and quickly rose to number one. Assessing the musical and cultural impact of Presley's recordings from "That's All Right" through Elvis, rock critic Dave Marsh wrote that "these records, more than any others, contain the seeds of what rock & roll was, has been and most likely what it may foreseeably become. "

Presley returned to the Sullivan show at its main studio in New York, hosted this time by its namesake, on October 28. After the performance, crowds in Nashville and St. Louis burned him in effigy. His first motion picture, Love Me Tender, was released on November 21. Though he was not top billed, the film's original title—The Reno Brothers—was changed to capitalize on his latest number one record: "Love Me Tender" had hit the top of the charts earlier that month. To further take advantage of Presley's popularity, four musical numbers were added to what was originally a straight acting role. The movie was panned by the critics but did very well at the box office. Presley would receive top billing on every subsequent film he made.

On December 4, Presley dropped into Sun Records where Carl Perkins and Jerry Lee Lewis were recording and jammed with them. Though Phillips no longer had the right to release any

Presley material, he made sure the session was captured on tape. The results became legendary as the "Million Dollar Quartet" recordings—Johnny Cash was long thought to have played as well, but he was present only briefly at Phillips' instigation for a photo opportunity. The year ended with a front-page story in The Wall Street Journal reporting that Presley merchandise had brought in $22 million on top of his record sales, and Billboard's declaration that he had placed more songs in the top 100 than any other artist since records were first charted. In his first full year on RCA, one of the music industry's largest companies, Presley had accounted for over 50 percent of the label's singles sales.

Leiber and Stoller collaboration and draft notice

Presley made his third and final Ed Sullivan Show appearance on January 6, 1957—on this occasion indeed shot only down to the waist. Some commentators have claimed that Parker orchestrated an appearance of censorship to generate publicity. In any event, as critic Greil Marcus describes, Presley "did not tie himself down. Leaving behind the bland clothes he had worn on the first two shows, he stepped out in the outlandish costume of a pasha, if not a harem girl. From the make-up over his eyes, the hair falling in his face, the overwhelmingly sexual cast of his mouth, he was playing Rudolph Valentino in The Sheik, with all stops out. " To close, displaying his range and defying Sullivan's wishes, Presley sang a gentle black spiritual, "Peace in the Valley". At the end of the show, Sullivan declared Presley "a real decent, fine boy". Two days later, the Memphis draft board announced that Presley would be classified 1A and would probably be drafted sometime that year.

Each of the three Presley singles released in the first half of 1957 went to number one: "Too Much", "All Shook Up", and "(Let Me Be Your) Teddy Bear". Already an international star, he was attracting fans even where his music was not officially released. Under the headline "Presley Records a Craze in Soviet", The New York Times reported that pressings of his music on discarded X-ray plates were commanding high prices in Leningrad. Between film shoots and recording sessions, the singer also found time to purchase an 18-room mansion eight miles (13 km) south of downtown Memphis for himself and his parents: Graceland. Loving You—the soundtrack to his second film, released in July—was Presley's third straight number one album. The title track was written by Leiber and Stoller, who were then retained to write four of the six songs recorded at the sessions for Jailhouse Rock, Presley's next movie. The songwriting team effectively produced the Jailhouse sessions and developed a close working relationship with Presley, who came to regard them as his "good-luck charm". The title track was yet another number one hit, as was the Jailhouse Rock EP.

Presley undertook three brief tours during the year, continuing to generate a crazed audience response. A Detroit newspaper suggested that "the trouble with going to see Elvis Presley is that you're liable to get killed. " Villanova students pelted him with eggs in Philadelphia, and in Vancouver, the crowd rioted after the end of the show, destroying the stage. Frank Sinatra, who had famously inspired the swooning of teenaged girls in the 1940s, condemned the new musical phenomenon. In a magazine article, he decried rock and roll as "brutal, ugly, degenerate, vicious. . . . It fosters almost totally negative and destructive reactions in young people. It smells phoney and false. It is sung, played and written, for the most part, by cretinous goons. . . . This rancid-smelling aphrodisiac I deplore. " Asked for a response, Presley said, "I admire the man. He has a right to say what he wants to say. He is a great success and a fine actor, but I think he shouldn't have said it. . . . This is a trend, just the same as he faced when he started years ago. "

Leiber and Stoller were again in the studio for the recording of Elvis' Christmas Album. Toward the end of the session, they wrote a song on the spot at Presley's request: "Santa Claus Is Back In Town", an innuendo-laden blues. The holiday release stretched Presley's string of number one albums to four and would eventually become the best selling Christmas album of all time. After the session, Moore and Black—drawing only modest weekly salaries, sharing in none of Presley's massive financial success—resigned. Though they were brought back on a per diem basis a few weeks later, it was clear that they had not been part of Presley's inner circle for some time. On December 20, Presley received his draft notice. He was granted a deferment to finish the forthcoming King Creole, in which $350,000 had already been invested by Paramount and producer Hal Wallis. A couple of weeks into the new year, "Don't", another Leiber and Stoller tune, became Presley's tenth number one seller. It had been only 21 months since "Heartbreak Hotel" had brought him to the top for the first time. Recording sessions for the King Creole soundtrack were held in Hollywood mid-January. Leiber and Stoller provided three songs and were again on hand, but it would be the last time they worked closely with Presley. A studio session on February 1 marked another ending: it was the final occasion on which Black was to perform with Presley. He died in 1965.

Military service and mother's death (1958–60)

On March 24, Presley was inducted into the U. S. Army as a private at Fort Chaffee, near Fort Smith, Arkansas. His arrival was a major media event. Hundreds of people descended on Presley as he stepped from the bus; photographers then accompanied him into the base. Presley announced that he was looking forward to his military stint, saying he did not want to be treated any differently from anyone else: "The Army can do anything it wants with me. "

Soon after Presley commenced basic training at Fort Hood, Texas, he received a visit from Eddie Fadal, a businessman he had met on tour. According to Fadal, Presley had become convinced his career was finished—"He firmly believed that. " During a two-week leave in early June, Presley cut five sides in Nashville. In early August, his mother was diagnosed with hepatitis and her condition swiftly worsened. Presley, granted emergency leave to visit her, arrived in Memphis on August 12. Two days later, she died of heart failure, aged 46. Presley was devastated; their relationship had remained extremely close—even into his adulthood, they would use baby talk with each other and Presley would address her with pet names.

After training, Presley joined the 3rd Armored Division in Friedberg, Germany, on October 1. Introduced to amphetamines by a sergeant while on maneuvers, he became "practically evangelical about their benefits"—not only for energy, but for "strength" and weight loss, as well—and many of his friends in the outfit joined him in indulging. The Army also introduced Presley to karate, which he studied seriously, later including it in his live performances. Fellow soldiers have attested to Presley's wish to be seen as an able, ordinary soldier, despite his fame, and to his generosity. He donated his Army pay to charity, purchased TV sets for the base, and bought an extra set of fatigues for everyone in his outfit.

While in Friedberg, Presley met 14-year-old Priscilla Beaulieu. They would eventually marry after a seven-and-a-half-year courtship. In her autobiography, Priscilla says that despite his worries that it would ruin his career, Parker convinced Presley that to gain popular respect, he should serve his country as a regular soldier rather than in Special Services, where he would have been able to give some musical performances and remain in touch with the public. Media reports echoed Presley's concerns about his career, but RCA producer Steve Sholes and Freddy Bienstock of Hill and Range had carefully prepared for his two-year hiatus. Armed with a substantial amount of unreleased material, they kept up a regular stream of successful releases. Between his induction and discharge, Presley had ten top 40 hits, including "Wear My Ring Around Your Neck", the best-selling "Hard Headed Woman", and "One Night" in 1958, and "(Now and Then There's) A Fool Such as I" and the number one "A Big Hunk o' Love" in 1959. RCA also generated four albums compiling old material during this period, most successfully Elvis' Golden Records (1958), which hit number three on the LP chart.

Focus on movies (1960–67)

Elvis Is Back

Presley returned to the United States on March 2, 1960, and was honorably discharged with the rank of sergeant on March 5. The train that carried him from New Jersey to Tennessee was mobbed all the way, and Presley was called upon to appear at scheduled stops to please his fans. On the night of March 20, he entered RCA's Nashville studio to cut tracks for a new album along with a single—"Stuck on You" was rushed into release and swiftly became a number one hit. Another Nashville session two weeks later yielded a pair of his best-selling singles, the ballads "It's Now or Never" and "Are You Lonesome Tonight?", along with the rest of Elvis Is Back! The album features several songs described by Greil Marcus as full of Chicago blues "menace, driven by Presley's own super-miked acoustic guitar, brilliant playing by Scotty Moore, and demonic sax work from Boots Randolph. Elvis's singing wasn't sexy, it was pornographic. " As a whole, the record "conjured up the vision of a performer who could be all things", in the words of music historian John Robertson: "a flirtatious teenage idol with a heart of gold; a tempestuous, dangerous lover; a gutbucket blues singer; a sophisticated nightclub entertainer; [a] raucous rocker". Released only days after recording was complete, it reached number two on the album chart.

Presley returned to television on May 12 as a guest on The Frank Sinatra Timex Special—ironic for both stars, given Sinatra's not-so-distant excoriation of rock and roll. Also known as Welcome Home Elvis, the show had been taped in late March, the only time all year Presley performed in front of an audience. Parker secured an unheard-of $125,000 fee for eight minutes of singing. The broadcast drew an enormous viewership.

G. I. Blues, the soundtrack to Presley's first film since his return, was a number one album in October. His first LP of sacred material, His Hand in Mine, followed two months later. It reached number 13 on the U. S. pop chart and number 3 in Great Britain, remarkable figures for a gospel album. In February 1961, Presley performed two shows for a benefit event in Memphis, on behalf of 24 local charities. During a luncheon preceding the event, RCA presented him with a plaque certifying worldwide sales of over 75 million records. A 12-hour Nashville session in mid-March yielded nearly all of Presley's next studio album, Something for Everybody. As described by John Robertson, it exemplifies the Nashville sound, the restrained, cosmopolitan style that would define country music in the 1960s. Presaging much of what was to come from Presley himself over the next half-decade, the album is largely "a pleasant, unthreatening pastiche of the music that had once been Elvis's birthright. " It would be his sixth number one LP. Another benefit concert, raising money for a Pearl Harbor memorial, was staged on March 25, in Hawaii. It was to be Presley's last public performance for seven years.

Lost in Hollywood

Parker had by now pushed Presley into a heavy moviemaking schedule, focused on formulaic, modestly budgeted musical comedies. Presley at first insisted on pursuing more serious roles, but when two films in a more dramatic vein—Flaming Star (1960) and Wild in the Country (1961)—were less commercially successful, he reverted to the formula. Among the 27 movies he made during the 1960s, there were few further exceptions. His films were almost universally panned; one critic dismissed them as a "pantheon of bad taste". Nonetheless, they were virtually all profitable. Hal Wallis, who produced nine of them, declared, "A Presley picture is the only sure thing in Hollywood. "

Of Presley's films in the 1960s, 15 were accompanied by soundtrack albums and another 5 by soundtrack EPs. The movies' rapid production and release schedules—he frequently starred in three a year—affected his music. According to Jerry Leiber, the soundtrack formula was already evident before Presley left for the Army: "three ballads, one medium-tempo [number], one up-tempo, and one break blues boogie". As the decade wore on, the quality of the soundtrack songs grew "progressively worse". Julie

Parrish, who appeared in Paradise, Hawaiian Style (1966), says that he hated many of the songs chosen for his films. The Jordanaires' Gordon Stoker describes how Presley would retreat from the studio microphone: "The material was so bad that he felt like he couldn't sing it. " Most of the movie albums featured a song or two from respected writers such as the team of Doc Pomus and Mort Shuman. But by and large, according to biographer Jerry Hopkins, the numbers seemed to be "written on order by men who never really understood Elvis or rock and roll. " Regardless of the songs' quality, it has been argued that Presley generally sang them well, with commitment. Critic Dave Marsh heard the opposite: "Presley isn't trying, probably the wisest course in the face of material like 'No Room to Rumba in a Sports Car' and 'Rock-a-Hula Baby. '"

In the first half of the decade, three of Presley's soundtrack albums hit number one on the pop charts, and a few of his most popular songs came from his films, such as "Can't Help Falling in Love" (1961) and "Return to Sender" (1962). ("Viva Las Vegas", the title track to the 1964 film, was a minor hit as a B-side, and became truly popular only later.) But, as with artistic merit, the commercial returns steadily diminished. During a five-year span—1964 through 1968—Presley had only one top-ten hit: "Crying in the Chapel" (1965), a gospel number recorded back in 1960. As for non-movie albums, between the June 1962 release of Pot Luck and the November 1968 release of the soundtrack to the television special that signaled his comeback, only one LP of new material by Presley was issued: the gospel album How Great Thou Art (1967). It won him his first Grammy Award, for Best Sacred Performance. As Marsh described, Presley was "arguably the greatest white gospel singer of his time [and] really the last rock & roll artist to make gospel as vital a component of his musical personality as his secular songs. "

Shortly before Christmas 1966, more than seven years since they first met, Presley proposed to Priscilla Beaulieu. They were married on May 1, 1967, in a brief ceremony in their suite at the Aladdin Hotel in Las Vegas. The flow of formulaic movies and assembly-line soundtracks rolled on. It was not until October 1967, when the Clambake soundtrack LP registered record low sales for a new Presley album, that RCA executives recognized a problem. "By then, of course, the damage had been done", as historians Connie Kirchberg and Marc Hendrickx put it. "Elvis was viewed as a joke by serious music lovers and a has-been to all but his most loyal fans. "

Comeback (1968–73)

Elvis: the '68 Comeback Special

Elvis (1968 TV program)

Presley's only child, Lisa Marie, was born on February 1, 1968, during a period when he had grown deeply unhappy with his career. Of the eight Presley singles released between January 1967 and May 1968, only two charted in the top 40, and none higher than number 28. His forthcoming soundtrack album, Speedway, would die at number 82 on the Billboard chart. Parker had already shifted his plans to television, where Presley had not appeared since the Sinatra Timex show in 1960. He maneuvered a deal with NBC that committed the network to both finance a theatrical feature and broadcast a Christmas special.

Recorded in late June in Burbank, California, the special, called simply Elvis, aired on December 3, 1968. Later known as the '68 Comeback Special, the show featured lavishly staged studio productions as well as songs performed with a band in front of a small audience—Presley's first live performances since 1961. The live segments saw Presley clad in tight black leather, singing and playing guitar in an uninhibited style reminiscent of his early rock-and-roll days. Director and coproducer Steve Binder had worked hard to reassure the nervous singer and to produce a show that was far from the hour of Christmas songs Parker had originally planned. The show, NBC's highest rated that season, captured 42 percent of the total viewing audience. Jon Landau of Eye magazine remarked, "There is something magical about watching a man who has lost himself find his way back home. He sang with the kind of power people no longer expect of rock 'n' roll singers. He moved his body with a lack of pretension and effort that must have made Jim Morrison green with envy. " Dave Marsh calls the performance one of "emotional grandeur and historical resonance. "

By January 1969, the single "If I Can Dream", written for the special, reached number 12. The soundtrack album broke into the top ten. According to friend Jerry Schilling, the special reminded Presley of what "he had not been able to do for years, being able to choose the people; being able to choose what songs and not being told what had to be on the soundtrack. . . . He was out of prison, man. " Binder said of Presley's reaction, "I played Elvis the 60-minute show, and he told me in the screening room, 'Steve, it's the greatest thing

I've ever done in my life. I give you my word I will never sing a song I don't believe in. '"

From Elvis In Memphis and the International

Buoyed by the experience of the Comeback Special, Presley engaged in a prolific series of recording sessions at American Sound Studio, which led to the acclaimed From Elvis in Memphis. Released in June 1969, it was his first secular, non-soundtrack album from a dedicated period in the studio in eight years. As described by Dave Marsh, it is "a masterpiece in which Presley immediately catches up with pop music trends that had seemed to pass him by during the movie years. He sings country songs, soul songs and rockers with real conviction, a stunning achievement. " The album featured the hit single "In the Ghetto", issued in April, which reached number three on the pop chart—Presley's first non-gospel top ten hit since "Bossa Nova Baby" in 1963. Further hit singles were culled from the American Sound sessions: "Suspicious Minds", "Don't Cry Daddy", and "Kentucky Rain".

Presley was keen to resume regular live performing. Following the success of the Comeback Special, offers came in from around the world. The London Palladium offered Parker $28,000 for a one-week engagement. He responded, "That's fine for me, now how much can you get for Elvis?" In May, the brand new International Hotel in Las Vegas, boasting the largest showroom in the city, announced that it had booked Presley. He was scheduled to perform 57 shows over four weeks beginning July 31. Moore, Fontana, and the Jordanaires declined to participate, afraid of losing the lucrative session work they had in Nashville. Presley assembled new, top-notch accompaniment, led by guitarist James Burton and including two gospel groups, The Imperials and Sweet Inspirations. Nonetheless, he was nervous: his only previous Las Vegas engagement, in 1956, had been dismal. Parker, who intended to make Presley's return the show business event of the year, oversaw a major promotional push. For his part, hotel owner Kirk Kerkorian arranged to send his own plane to New York to fly in rock journalists for the debut performance.

Presley took to the stage without introduction. The audience of 2,200, including many celebrities, gave him a standing ovation before he sang a note and another after his performance. A third followed his encore, "Can't Help Falling in Love" (a song that would be his closing number for much of the 1970s). At a press conference after the show, when a journalist referred to him as "The King", Presley gestured toward Fats Domino, who was taking in the scene. "No," Presley said, "that's the real king of rock and roll. " The next day, Parker's negotiations with the hotel resulted in a five-year contract for Presley to play each February and August, at an annual salary of $1 million. Newsweek commented, "There are several unbelievable things about Elvis, but the most incredible is his staying power in a world where meteoric careers fade like shooting stars. " Rolling Stone called Presley "supernatural, his own resurrection. " In November, Presley's final non-concert movie, Change of Habit, opened. The double album From Memphis To Vegas/From Vegas To Memphis came out the same month; the first LP consisted of live performances from the International, the second of more cuts from the American Sound sessions. "Suspicious Minds" reached the top of the charts—Presley's first U. S. pop number one in over seven years, and his last.

Cassandra Peterson, later television's Elvira, met Presley during this period in Las Vegas, where she was working as showgirl. She recalls of their encounter, "He was so anti-drug when I met him. I mentioned to him that I smoked marijuana, and he was just appalled. He said, 'Don't ever do that again. '" Presley was not only deeply opposed to recreational drugs, he also rarely drank. Several of his family members had been alcoholics, a fate he intended to avoid.

Back on tour and meeting Nixon

Presley returned to the International early in 1970 for the first of the year's two month-long engagements, performing two shows a night. Recordings from these shows were issued on the album On Stage. In late February, Presley performed six attendance-record–breaking shows at the Houston Astrodome. In April, the single "The Wonder of You" was issued—a number one hit in Great Britain, it topped the U. S. adult contemporary chart, as well. MGM filmed rehearsal and concert footage at the International during August for the documentary Elvis: That's the Way It Is. Presley was by now performing in a jumpsuit, which would become a trademark of his live act. During this engagement, he was threatened with murder unless $50,000 was paid. Presley had been the target of many threats since the 1950s, often without his knowledge. The FBI took the threat seriously and security was stepped up for the next two shows. Presley went onstage with a Derringer in his right boot and a . 45 pistol in his waistband, but the concerts went off without incident.

The album That's the Way It Is, produced to accompany the documentary and featuring both studio and live recordings, marked a stylistic shift. As music historian John Robertson notes, "The authority of Presley's singing helped disguise the fact that the album stepped decisively away from the American-roots inspiration of the Memphis sessions towards a more middle-of-the-road sound. With country put on the back burner, and soul and R&B left in Memphis, what was left was very classy, very clean white pop—perfect for the Las Vegas crowd, but a definite retrograde step for Elvis. " After the end of his International engagement on September 7, Presley embarked on a week-long concert tour, largely of the South, his first since 1958. Another week-long tour, of the West Coast, followed in November.

On December 21, 1970, Presley engineered a meeting with President Richard Nixon at the White House, where he expressed his patriotism and his contempt for the hippie drug culture. He asked Nixon for a Bureau of Narcotics and Dangerous Drugs badge, to add to similar items he had begun collecting and to signify official sanction of his patriotic efforts. Nixon, who apparently found the encounter awkward, expressed a belief that Presley could send a positive message to young people and that it was therefore important he "retain his credibility". Presley told Nixon that The Beatles, whose songs he regularly performed in concert during the era, exemplified what he saw as a trend of anti-Americanism and drug abuse in popular culture. (Presley and his friends had had a four-hour get-together with The Beatles five years earlier.) On hearing reports of the meeting, Paul McCartney later said that he "felt a bit betrayed. . . . The great joke was that we were taking [illegal] drugs, and look what happened to him", a reference to Presley's death, hastened by prescription drug abuse.

The U. S. Junior Chamber of Commerce named Presley one of its annual Ten Most Outstanding Young Men of the Nation on January 16, 1971. Not long after, the City of Memphis named the stretch of Highway 51 South on which Graceland is located "Elvis Presley Boulevard". The same year, Presley became the first rock and roll singer to be awarded the Lifetime Achievement Award (then known as the Bing Crosby Award) by the National Academy of Recording Arts and Sciences, the Grammy Award organization. Three new, non-movie Presley studio albums were released in 1971, as many as had come out over the previous eight years.

Best received by critics was Elvis Country, a concept record that focused on genre standards. The biggest seller was Elvis Sings the Wonderful World of Christmas, "the truest statement of all", according to Greil Marcus. "In the midst of ten painfully genteel Christmas songs, every one sung with appalling sincerity and humility, one could find Elvis tom-catting his way through six blazing minutes of 'Merry Christmas, Baby,' a raunchy old Charles Brown blues. . . . If [Presley's] sin was his lifelessness, it was his sinfulness that brought him to life".

Marriage breakdown and Aloha from Hawaii

MGM again filmed Presley in April 1972, this time for Elvis on Tour, which went on to win the Golden Globe Award for Best Documentary Film that year. His gospel album He Touched Me, released that month, would earn him his second Grammy Award, for Best Inspirational Performance. A 14-date tour commenced with an unprecedented four consecutive sold-out shows at New York's Madison Square Garden. The evening concert on July 10 was recorded and issued in LP form a week later. Elvis: As Recorded at Madison Square Garden became one of Presley's biggest-selling albums. After the tour, the single "Burning Love" was released—Presley's last top ten hit on the U. S. pop chart. "The most exciting single Elvis has made since 'All Shook Up'", wrote rock critic Robert Christgau. "Who else could make 'It's coming closer, the flames are now licking my body' sound like an assignation with James Brown's backup band?"

Presley and his wife, meanwhile, had become increasingly distant, barely cohabiting. In 1971, an affair he had with Joyce Bova resulted—unbeknownst to him—in her pregnancy and an abortion. He often raised the possibility of her moving in to Graceland, saying that he was likely to leave Priscilla. The Presleys separated on February 23, 1972, after Priscilla disclosed her relationship with Mike Stone, a karate instructor Presley had recommended to her. Priscilla relates that when she told him, Presley "grabbed . . . and forcefully made love to" her, declaring, "This is how a real man makes love to his woman. " Five months later, Presley's new girlfriend, Linda Thompson, a songwriter and one-time Memphis beauty queen, moved in with him. Presley and his wife filed for divorce on August 18. According to Joe Moscheo of the Imperials, the failure of Presley's marriage "was a blow from which he never recovered. "

In January 1973, Presley performed two benefit concerts for the Kui Lee Cancer Fund in connection with a groundbreaking TV special, Aloha from Hawaii. The first show served as a practice run and backup should technical problems affect the live broadcast two days later. Aired as scheduled on January 14, Aloha from Hawaii was the first global concert satellite broadcast, reaching millions of viewers live and on tape delay. Presley's costume became the most recognized example of the elaborate concert garb with which his latter-day persona became closely associated. As described by Bobbie Ann Mason, "At the end of the show, when he spreads out his American Eagle cape, with the full stretched wings of the eagle studded on the back, he becomes a god figure. " The accompanying double album, released in February, went to number one and eventually sold over 5 million copies in the United States. It proved to be Presley's last U. S. number one pop album during his lifetime.

At a midnight show the same month, four men rushed onto the stage in an apparent attack. Security men leapt to Presley's defense, and the singer's karate instinct took over as he ejected one invader from the stage himself. Following the show, he became obsessed with the idea that the men had been sent by Mike Stone to kill him. Though they were shown to have been only overexuberant fans, he raged, "There's too much pain in me . . . Stone [must] die. " His outbursts continued with such intensity that a physician was unable to calm him, despite administering large doses of medication. After another two full days of raging, Red West, his friend and bodyguard, felt compelled to get a price for a contract killing and was relieved when Presley decided, "Aw hell, let's just leave it for now. Maybe it's a bit heavy. "

Health deterioration and death (1973–77)

Medical crises and last studio sessions

Presley's divorce took effect on October 9, 1973. He was now becoming increasingly unwell. Twice during the year he overdosed on barbiturates, spending three days in a coma in his hotel suite after the first incident. Toward the end of 1973, he was hospitalized, semicomatose from the effects of Demerol addiction. According to his main physician, Dr. George C. Nichopoulos, Presley "felt that by getting [drugs] from a doctor, he wasn't the common everyday junkie getting something off the street. " Since his comeback, he had staged more live shows with each passing year, and 1973 saw

168 concerts, his busiest schedule ever. Despite his failing health, in 1974 he undertook another intensive touring schedule.

Presley's condition declined precipitously in September. Keyboardist Tony Brown remembers the singer's arrival at a University of Maryland concert: "He fell out of the limousine, to his knees. People jumped to help, and he pushed them away like, 'Don't help me. ' He walked on stage and held onto the mike for the first thirty minutes like it was a post. Everybody's looking at each other like, Is the tour gonna happen?" Guitarist John Wilkinson recalled, "He was all gut. He was slurring. He was so fucked up. . . . It was obvious he was drugged. It was obvious there was something terribly wrong with his body. It was so bad the words to the songs were barely intelligible. . . . I remember crying. He could barely get through the introductions". Wilkinson recounted that a few nights later in Detroit, "I watched him in his dressing room, just draped over a chair, unable to move. So often I thought, 'Boss, why don't you just cancel this tour and take a year off. . . ?' I mentioned something once in a guarded moment. He patted me on the back and said, 'It'll be all right. Don't you worry about it. '" Presley continued to play to sellout crowds. As cultural critic Marjorie Garber describes, he was now widely seen as a garish pop crooner: "in effect he had become Liberace. Even his fans were now middle-aged matrons and blue-haired grandmothers. "

On July 13, 1976, Vernon Presley—who had become deeply involved in his son's financial affairs—fired "Memphis Mafia" bodyguards Red West (Presley's friend since the 1950s), Sonny West, and David Hebler, citing the need to "cut back on expenses". Presley was in Palm Springs at the time, and some suggest the singer was too cowardly to face the three himself. Another associate of Presley's, John O'Grady, argued that the bodyguards were dropped because their rough treatment of fans had prompted too many lawsuits. However, Presley's stepbrother David Stanley has claimed that the bodyguards were fired because they were becoming more outspoken about Presley's drug dependency. Presley and Linda Thompson split in November, and he took up with a new girlfriend, Ginger Alden. He proposed to Alden and gave her an engagement ring two months later, though several of his friends later claimed that he had no serious intention of marrying again.

RCA, which had enjoyed a steady stream of product from Presley for over a decade, grew anxious as his interest in spending time in the studio waned. After a December 1973 session that produced 18 songs, enough for almost two albums, he did not enter the studio in 1974. Parker sold RCA on another concert record, Elvis: As Recorded Live on Stage in Memphis. Recorded on March 20, it included a version of "How Great Thou Art" that would win Presley his third and final competitive Grammy Award. (All three of his competitive Grammy wins—out of 14 total nominations—were for gospel recordings.) Presley returned to the studio in Hollywood in March 1975, but Parker's attempts to arrange another session toward the end of the year were unsuccessful. In 1976, RCA sent a mobile studio to Graceland that made possible two full-scale recording sessions at Presley's home. Even in that comfortable context, the recording process was now a struggle for him.

For all the concerns of his label and manager, in studio sessions between July 1973 and October 1976, Presley recorded virtually the entire contents of six albums. Though he was no longer a major presence on the pop charts, five of those albums entered the top five of the country chart, and three went to number one: Promised Land (1975), From Elvis Presley Boulevard, Memphis, Tennessee (1976), and Moody Blue (1977). The story was similar with his singles—there were no major pop hits, but Presley was a significant force in not just the country market, but on adult contemporary radio as well. Eight studio singles from this period released during his lifetime were top ten hits on one or both charts, four in 1974 alone. "My Boy" was a number one AC hit in 1975, and "Moody Blue" topped the country chart and reached the second spot on the AC in 1976. Perhaps his most critically acclaimed recording of the era came that year, with what Greil Marcus described as his "apocalyptic attack" on the soul classic "Hurt". "If he felt the way he sounded", Dave Marsh wrote of Presley's performance, "the wonder isn't that he had only a year left to live but that he managed to survive that long. "

Final year and death

Journalist Tony Scherman writes that by early 1977, "Elvis Presley had become a grotesque caricature of his sleek, energetic former self. Hugely overweight, his mind dulled by the pharmacopoeia he daily ingested, he was barely able to pull himself through his abbreviated concerts. " In Alexandria, Louisiana, the singer was on stage for less than an hour and "was impossible to understand". Presley failed to appear in Baton Rouge; he was unable to get out of his hotel bed, and the rest of the tour was cancelled. Despite the accelerating deterioration of his health, he stuck to most touring commitments. In Rapid City, South Dakota, "he was so nervous on stage that he could hardly talk", according to Presley historian Samuel Roy, and unable to "perform any significant movement. " Guralnick relates that fans "were becoming increasingly voluble about their disappointment, but it all seemed to go right past Elvis, whose world was now confined almost entirely to his room and his spiritualism books. " A cousin, Billy Smith, recalled how Presley would sit in his room and chat for hours, sometimes recounting favorite Monty Python sketches and his own past escapades, but more often gripped by paranoid obsessions that reminded Smith of Howard Hughes. "Way Down", Presley's last single issued during his lifetime, came out on June 6. His final concert was held in Indianapolis at Market Square Arena, on June 26.

The book Elvis: What Happened?, cowritten by the three bodyguards fired the previous year, was published on August 1. It was the first exposé to detail Presley's years of drug misuse. He was devastated by the book and tried unsuccessfully to halt its release by offering money to the publishers. By this point, he suffered from multiple ailments: glaucoma, high blood pressure, liver damage, and an enlarged colon, each aggravated—and possibly caused—by drug abuse.

Presley was scheduled to fly out of Memphis on the evening of August 16, 1977, to begin another tour. That afternoon, Alden discovered him unresponsive on his bathroom floor. Attempts to revive him failed, and death was officially pronounced at 3:30 pm at Baptist Memorial Hospital.

President Jimmy Carter issued a statement that credited Presley with having "permanently changed the face of American popular culture". Thousands of people gathered outside Graceland to view the open casket. One of Presley's cousins, Billy Mann, accepted $18,000 to secretly photograph the corpse; the picture appeared on the cover of the National Enquirer's biggest-selling issue ever. Alden struck a $105,000 deal with the Enquirer for her story, but settled for less when she broke her exclusivity agreement. Presley left her nothing in his will.

Presley's funeral was held at Graceland, on Thursday, August 18. Outside the gates, a car plowed into a group of fans, killing two women and critically injuring a third. Approximately 80,000 people lined the processional route to Forest Hill Cemetery, where Presley was buried next to his mother. Within a few days, "Way Down" topped the country and UK pop charts.

Following an attempt to steal the singer's body in late August, the remains of both Elvis Presley and his mother were reburied in Graceland's Meditation Garden on October 2.

Since his death, there have been numerous alleged sightings of Elvis. A long-standing theory among some fans is that he faked his death. Fans have noted alleged discrepancies in the death certificate, reports of a wax dummy in his original coffin and numerous accounts of Presley planning a diversion so he could retire in peace.

Since 1977

Between 1977 and 1981, six posthumously released singles by Presley were top ten country hits. Graceland was opened to the public in 1982. Attracting over half a million visitors annually, it is the second most-visited home in the United States, after the White House. It was declared a National Historic Landmark in 2006.

Presley has been inducted into four music halls of fame: the Rock and Roll Hall of Fame (1986), the Country Music Hall of Fame (1998), the Gospel Music Hall of Fame (2001), and the Rockabilly Hall of Fame (2007). In 1984, he received the W. C. Handy Award from the Blues Foundation and the Academy of Country Music's first Golden Hat Award. In 1987, he received the American Music Awards' Award of Merit.

In 1994, a Golden Palm Star on the Palm Springs, California, Walk of Stars was dedicated to him.

A Junkie XL remix of Presley's "A Little Less Conversation" (credited as "Elvis Vs JXL") was used in a Nike advertising campaign during the 2002 FIFA World Cup. It topped the charts in over 20 countries, and was included in a compilation of Presley's number one hits, ELV1S, that was also an international success. In 2003, a remix of "Rubberneckin'", a 1969 recording of Presley's, topped the U. S. sales chart, as did a 50th-anniversary re-release of "That's All Right" the following year. The latter was an outright hit in Great Britain, reaching number three on the pop chart.

In 2005, another three reissued singles, "Jailhouse Rock", "One Night"/"I Got Stung", and "It's Now or Never", went to number one in the United Kingdom. A total of 17 Presley singles were reissued during the year; all made the British top five. For the fifth straight year, Forbes named Presley the top-earning deceased celebrity, with a gross income of $45 million. He placed second in 2006, returned to the top spot the next two years, and ranked fourth in 2009. The following year, he was ranked second, with his highest annual income ever—$60 million—spurred by the celebration of his 75th birthday and the launch of Cirque du Soleil's Viva Elvis show in Las Vegas. In November 2010, Viva Elvis: The Album was released, setting his voice to newly recorded instrumental tracks. As of mid-2011, there were an estimated 15,000 licensed Presley products. He was again the second-highest-earning deceased celebrity.

Presley holds the records for most songs charting in Billboard's top 40 and top 100: chart statistician Joel Whitburn calculates the respective totals as 104 and 151; Presley historian Adam Victor gives 114 and 138. Presley's rankings for top ten and number one hits vary depending on how the double-sided "Hound Dog/Don't Be Cruel" and "Don't/I Beg of You" singles, which precede the inception of Billboard's unified Hot 100 chart, are analyzed. According to Whitburn's analysis, Presley and Madonna share the record for most top ten hits with 38; per Billboard's current assessment, he ranks second with 36. Whitburn and Billboard concur that The Beatles hold the record for most number one hits with 20 and that Mariah Carey is second with 18. Whitburn has Presley also with 18 and thus tied for second; Billboard has him third with 17. Presley retains the record for cumulative weeks at number one: alone at 80, according to Whitburn and the Rock and Roll Hall of Fame; tied with Carey at 79, according to Billboard. He holds the records for most British number one hits, with 21, and top ten hits, with 76.

Musical style

Influences

Presley's earliest musical influence came from gospel. His mother recalled that from the age of two, at the Assembly of God church in Tupelo attended by the family, "he would slide down off my lap, run into the aisle and scramble up to the platform. There he would stand looking at the choir and trying to sing with them. " In Memphis, Presley frequently attended all-night gospel singings at the Ellis Auditorium, where groups such as the Statesmen Quartet led the music in a style that, Guralnick suggests, sowed the seeds of Presley's future stage act:

The Statesmen were an electric combination . . . featuring some of the most thrillingly emotive singing and daringly unconventional showmanship in the entertainment world . . . dressed in suits that might have come out of the window of Lansky's. . . . Bass singer Jim Wetherington, known universally as the Big Chief, maintained a steady bottom, ceaselessly jiggling first his left leg, then his right, with the material of the pants leg ballooning out and shimmering. "He went about as far as you could go in gospel music," said Jake Hess. "The women would jump up, just like they do for the pop shows. " Preachers frequently objected to the lewd movements . . . but audiences reacted with screams and swoons.
As a teenager, Presley's musical interests were wide-ranging, and he was deeply informed about African American musical idioms as well as white ones (see "Teenage life in Memphis"). Though he never had any formal training, he was blessed with a remarkable memory, and his musical knowledge was already considerable by the time he made his first professional recordings in 1954 at the age of 19. When Jerry Leiber and Mike Stoller met him two years later, they were astonished at his encyclopedic understanding of the blues. At a press conference the following year, he proudly declared, "I know practically every religious song that's ever been written. "

Genres

Presley was a central figure in the development of rockabilly, according to music historians. "Rockabilly crystallized into a recognizable style in 1954 with Elvis Presley's first release, on the Sun label", writes Craig Morrison. Paul Friedlander describes the defining elements of rockabilly, which he similarly characterizes as "essentially . . . an Elvis Presley construction": "the raw, emotive, and slurred vocal style and emphasis on rhythmic feeling [of] the blues with the string band and strummed rhythm guitar [of] country". In "That's All Right", the Presley trio's first record, Scotty Moore's guitar solo, "a combination of Merle Travis–style country finger-picking, double-stop slides from acoustic boogie, and blues-based bent-note, single-string work, is a microcosm of this fusion. "

At RCA, Presley's rock and roll sound grew distinct from rockabilly with group chorus vocals, more heavily amplified electric guitars and a tougher, more intense manner. While he was known for taking songs from various sources and giving them a rockabilly/rock and roll treatment, he also recorded songs in other genres from early in his career, from the pop standard "Blue Moon" at Sun to the country ballad "How's the World Treating You?" on his second LP to the blues of "Santa Claus Is Back In Town". In 1957, his first gospel record was released, the four-song EP Peace in the Valley. Certified as a million seller, it became the top-selling gospel EP in recording history. Presley would record gospel periodically for the rest of his life.

After his return from military service in 1960, Presley continued to perform rock and roll, but the characteristic style was substantially toned down. His first post-Army single, the number one hit "Stuck on You", is typical of this shift. RCA publicity materials referred to its "mild rock beat"; discographer Ernst Jorgensen calls it "upbeat pop". The modern blues/R&B sound captured so successfully on Elvis Is Back! was essentially abandoned for six years until such 1966–67 recordings as "Down in the Alley" and "Hi-Heel Sneakers". The singer's output during most of the 1960s emphasized pop music, often in the form of ballads such as "Are You Lonesome Tonight?", a number one in 1960. While that was a dramatic number, most of what Presley recorded for his movie soundtracks was in a much lighter vein.

While Presley performed several of his classic ballads for the '68 Comeback Special, the sound of the show was dominated by aggressive rock and roll. He would record few new straight-ahead rock and roll songs thereafter; as he explained, they were "hard to find". A significant exception was "Burning Love", his last major hit on the pop charts. Like his work of the 1950s, Presley's subsequent recordings reworked pop and country songs, but in markedly different permutations. His stylistic range now began to embrace a more contemporary rock sound as well as soul and funk. Much of Elvis In Memphis, as well as "Suspicious Minds", cut at the same sessions, reflected his new rock and soul fusion. In the mid-1970s, many of his singles found a home on country radio, the field where he first became a star.

Vocal style and range

Music critic Henry Pleasants observes that "Elvis Presley has been described variously as a baritone and a tenor. An extraordinary compass . . . and a very wide range of vocal color have something to do with this divergence of opinion. " He identifies Presley as a high baritone, calculating his range as two octaves and a third, "from the baritone low G to the tenor high B, with an upward extension in falsetto to at least a D-flat. Presley's best octave is in the middle, D-flat to D-flat, granting an extra full step up or down. " In Pleasants' view, his voice was "variable and unpredictable" at the bottom, "often brilliant" at the top, with the capacity for "full-voiced high Gs and As that an opera baritone might envy. " Scholar Lindsay Waters, who figures Presley's range as two and a quarter octaves, emphasizes that "his voice had an emotional range from tender whispers to sighs down to shouts, grunts, grumbles and sheer gruffness that could move the listener from calmness and surrender, to fear. His voice can not be measured in octaves, but in decibels; even that misses the problem of how to measure delicate whispers that are hardly audible at all. " Presley was always "able to duplicate the open, hoarse, ecstatic, screaming, shouting, wailing, reckless sound of the black rhythm-and-blues and gospel singers," writes Pleasants, and also demonstrated a remarkable ability to assimilate many other vocal styles.

Questions over cause of death

"Drug use was heavily implicated" in Presley's death, writes Guralnick. "No one ruled out the possibility of anaphylactic shock brought on by the codeine pills . . . to which he was known to have had a mild allergy. " A pair of lab reports filed two months later each strongly suggested that polypharmacy was the primary cause of death; one reported "fourteen drugs in Elvis' system, ten in significant quantity. " Forensic historian and pathologist Michael Baden views the situation as complicated: "Elvis had had an enlarged heart for a long time. That, together with his drug habit, caused his death. But he was difficult to diagnose; it was a judgment call. "

The competence and ethics of two of the centrally involved medical professionals were seriously questioned. Before the autopsy was complete and toxicology results known, medical examiner Dr. Jerry Francisco declared the cause of death as cardiac arrhythmia, a condition that can be determined only in someone who is still alive. Allegations of a cover-up were widespread. While Presley's main physician, Dr. Nichopoulos, was exonerated of criminal liability for the singer's death, the facts were startling: "In the first eight months of 1977 alone, he had [prescribed] more than 10,000 doses of sedatives, amphetamines and narcotics: all in

Elvis's name. " His license was suspended for three months. It was permanently revoked in the 1990s after the Tennessee Medical Board brought new charges of over-prescription.

Among other errors, the initial autopsy report listed Presley's weight as 170 pounds and that he was bald.

Amidst mounting pressure in 1994, the Presley autopsy was reopened. Coroner Dr. Joseph Davis declared, "There is nothing in any of the data that supports a death from drugs. In fact, everything points to a sudden, violent heart attack. " Whether or not combined drug intoxication was in fact the cause, there is little doubt that polypharmacy contributed significantly to Presley's premature death.

Racial issues

When Dewey Phillips first aired "That's All Right" on Memphis radio, many listeners who contacted the station by phone and telegram to ask for it again assumed that its singer was black. From the beginning of his national fame, Presley expressed respect for African American performers and their music, and disregard for the norms of segregation and racial prejudice then prevalent in the South. Interviewed in 1956, he recalled how in his childhood he would listen to blues musician Arthur Crudup—the originator of "That's All Right"—"bang his box the way I do now, and I said if I ever got to the place where I could feel all old Arthur felt, I'd be a music man like nobody ever saw. " The Memphis World, an African American newspaper, reported that Presley, "the rock 'n' roll phenomenon", "cracked Memphis's segregation laws" by attending the local amusement park on what was designated as its "colored night". Such statements and actions led Presley to be generally hailed in the black community during the early days of his stardom. By contrast, many white adults, according to Billboard's Arnold Shaw, "did not like him, and condemned him as depraved. Anti-negro prejudice doubtless figured in adult antagonism. Regardless of whether parents were aware of the Negro sexual origins of the phrase 'rock 'n' roll', Presley impressed them as the visual and aural embodiment of sex. "

Despite the largely positive view of Presley held by African Americans, a rumor spread in mid-1957 that he had at some point announced, "The only thing Negroes can do for me is buy my records and shine my shoes. " A journalist with the national African

American weekly Jet, Louie Robinson, pursued the story. On the set of Jailhouse Rock, Presley granted him an interview, though he was no longer dealing with the mainstream press. He denied making such a statement or holding in any way to its racist view. Robinson found no evidence that the remark had ever been made, and on the contrary elicited testimony from many individuals indicating that Presley was anything but racist. Blues singer Ivory Joe Hunter, who had heard the rumor before he visited Graceland one evening, reported of Presley, "He showed me every courtesy, and I think he's one of the greatest. " Though the rumored remark was wholly discredited at the time, it was still being used against Presley decades later. The identification of Presley with racism—either personally or symbolically—was expressed most famously in the lyrics of the 1989 rap hit "Fight the Power", by Public Enemy: "Elvis was a hero to most / But he never meant shit to me / Straight-up racist that sucker was / Simple and plain".

The persistence of such attitudes was fueled by resentment over the fact that Presley, whose musical and visual performance idiom owed much to African American sources, achieved the cultural acknowledgment and commercial success largely denied his black peers. Into the 21st century, the notion that Presley had "stolen" black music still found adherents. Notable among African American entertainers expressly rejecting this view was Jackie Wilson, who argued, "A lot of people have accused Elvis of stealing the black man's music, when in fact, almost every black solo entertainer copied his stage mannerisms from Elvis. " And throughout his career, Presley plainly acknowledged his debt. Addressing his '68 Comeback Special audience, he said, "Rock 'n' roll music is basically gospel or rhythm and blues, or it sprang from that. People have been adding to it, adding instruments to it, experimenting with it, but it all boils down to [that]. " Nine years earlier, he had said, "Rock 'n' roll has been around for many years. It used to be called rhythm and blues. "

Influence of Colonel Parker and others

Parker and the Aberbachs

Once he became Presley's manager, Colonel Tom Parker insisted on exceptionally tight control over his client's career. Early on, he and his Hill and Range allies, the brothers Jean and Julian Aberbach, perceived the close relationship that developed between Presley and songwriters Jerry Leiber and Mike Stoller as a serious threat to that control. Parker effectively ended the relationship, deliberately or not, with the new contract he sent Leiber in early 1958. Leiber thought there was a mistake—the sheet of paper was blank except for Parker's signature and a line on which to enter his. "There's no mistake, boy, just sign it and return it", Parker directed. "Don't worry, we'll fill it in later. " Leiber declined, and Presley's fruitful collaboration with the writing team was over. Other respected songwriters lost interest in or simply avoided writing for Presley because of the requirement that they surrender a third of their usual royalties.

By 1967, Parker's contracts with Presley gave him 50 percent of most of the singer's earnings from recordings, films, and merchandise. Beginning in February 1972, he took a third of the profit from live appearances; a January 1976 agreement entitled him to half of that as well. Priscilla Presley noted that "Elvis detested the business side of his career. He would sign a contract without even reading it. " Presley's friend Marty Lacker regarded Parker as a "hustler and a con artist. He was only interested in 'now money'—get the buck and get gone. "

Lacker was instrumental in convincing Presley to record with Memphis producer Chips Moman and his handpicked musicians at American Sound Studio in early 1969. The American Sound sessions represented a significant departure from the control customarily exerted by Hill and Range. Moman still had to deal with the publisher's staff on site, whose song suggestions he regarded as unacceptable. He was on the verge of quitting, until Presley ordered the Hill and Range personnel out of the studio. Although RCA executive Joan Deary was later full of praise for the producer's song choices and the quality of the recordings, Moman, to his fury, received neither credit on the records nor royalties for his work.

Throughout his entire career, Presley performed in only three venues outside the United States—all of them in Canada, during brief tours there in 1957. Rumors that he would play overseas for the first time were fueled in 1974 by a million-dollar bid for an Australian tour. Parker was uncharacteristically reluctant, prompting those close to Presley to speculate about the manager's past and the reasons for his apparent unwillingness to apply for a passport. Parker ultimately squelched any notions Presley had of working abroad, claiming that foreign security was poor and the venues unsuitable for a star of his magnitude.

Parker arguably exercised tightest control over Presley's movie career. In 1957, Robert Mitchum asked Presley to costar with him in Thunder Road, on which Mitchum was writer and producer. According to George Klein, one of his oldest friends, Presley was offered starring roles in West Side Story and Midnight Cowboy. In 1974, Barbra Streisand approached Presley to star with her in the remake of A Star is Born. In each case, any ambitions the singer may have had to play such parts were thwarted by his manager's negotiating demands or flat refusals. In Lacker's description, "The only thing that kept Elvis going after the early years was a new challenge. But Parker kept running everything into the ground. " The operative attitude may have been summed up best by the response Leiber and Stoller received when they brought a serious film project for Presley to Parker and the Hill and Range owners for their consideration. In Leiber's telling, Jean Aberbach warned them to never again "try to interfere with the business or artistic workings of the process known as Elvis Presley".

Memphis Mafia

Memphis Mafia

In the early 1960s, the circle of friends with whom Presley constantly surrounded himself until his death came to be known as the "Memphis Mafia". "Surrounded by the[ir] parasitic presence", as journalist John Harris puts it, "it was no wonder that as he slid into addiction and torpor, no-one raised the alarm: to them, Elvis was the bank, and it had to remain open. " Tony Brown, who played piano for Presley regularly in the last two years of the singer's life, observed his rapidly declining health and the urgent need to address it: "But we all knew it was hopeless because Elvis was surrounded by that little circle of people . . . all those so-called friends". In the Memphis Mafia's defense, Marty Lacker has said, "[Presley] was his own man. . . . If we hadn't been around, he would have been dead a lot earlier. "

Larry Geller became Presley's hairdresser in 1964. Unlike others in the Memphis Mafia, he was interested in spiritual questions and recalls how, from their first conversation, Presley revealed his secret thoughts and anxieties: "I mean there has to be a purpose. . . there's got to be a reason. . . why I was chosen to be Elvis Presley. . . . I swear to God, no one knows how lonely I get. And how empty I really feel. " Thereafter, Geller supplied him with books on religion and mysticism, which the singer read voraciously. Presley would be preoccupied by such matters for much of his life, taking trunkloads of books with him on tour.

Sex symbol

Presley's physical attractiveness and sexual appeal were widely acknowledged. "He was once beautiful, astonishingly beautiful", in the words of critic Mark Feeney. Television director Steve Binder, no fan of Presley's music before he oversaw the '68 Comeback Special, reported, "I'm straight as an arrow and I got to tell you, you stop, whether you're male or female, to look at him. He was that good looking. And if you never knew he was a superstar, it wouldn't make any difference; if he'd walked in the room, you'd know somebody special was in your presence. " His performance style, as much as his physical beauty, was responsible for Presley's eroticized image. Writing in 1970, critic George Melly described him as "the master of the sexual simile, treating his guitar as both phallus and girl. " In his Presley obituary, Lester Bangs credited him as "the man who brought overt blatant vulgar sexual frenzy to the popular arts in America. " Ed Sullivan's declaration that he perceived a soda bottle in Presley's trousers was echoed by rumors involving a similarly positioned toilet roll tube or lead bar.

While Presley was marketed as an icon of heterosexuality, some cultural critics have argued that his image was ambiguous. In 1959, Sight and Sound's Peter John Dyer described his onscreen persona as "aggressively bisexual in appeal". Brett Farmer places the "orgasmic gyrations" of the title dance sequence in Jailhouse Rock within a lineage of cinematic musical numbers that offer a "spectacular eroticization, if not homoeroticization, of the male image". In the analysis of Yvonne Tasker, "Elvis was an ambivalent figure who articulated a peculiar feminised, objectifying version of white working-class masculinity as aggressive sexual display. "

Reinforcing Presley's image as a sex symbol were the reports of his dalliances with various Hollywood stars and starlets, from Natalie Wood in the 1950s to Connie Stevens and Ann-Margret in the 1960s to Candice Bergen and Cybill Shepherd in the 1970s. June Juanico of Memphis, one of Presley's early girlfriends, later blamed Parker for encouraging him to choose his dating partners with publicity in mind. Presley, however, never grew comfortable with the Hollywood scene, and most of these relationships were insubstantial.

Legacy

I know he invented rock and roll, in a manner of speaking, but . . . that's not why he's worshiped as a god today. He's worshiped as a god today because in addition to inventing rock and roll he was the greatest ballad singer this side of Frank Sinatra—because the spiritual translucence and reined-in gut sexuality of his slow weeper and torchy pop blues still activate the hormones and slavish devotion of millions of female human beings worldwide.

Presley's rise to national attention in 1956 transformed the field of popular music and had a huge effect on the broader scope of popular culture. As the catalyst for the cultural revolution that was rock and roll, he was central not only to defining it as a musical genre but in making it a touchstone of youth culture and rebellious attitude. With its racially mixed origins—repeatedly affirmed by Presley—rock and roll's occupation of a central position in mainstream American culture facilitated a new acceptance and appreciation of black culture. In this regard, Little Richard said of Presley, "He was an integrator. Elvis was a blessing. They wouldn't let black music through. He opened the door for black music. " Al Green agreed: "He broke the ice for all of us. " President Jimmy Carter remarked on his legacy in 1977: "His music and his personality, fusing the styles of white country and black rhythm and blues, permanently changed the face of American popular culture. His following was immense, and he was a symbol to people the world over of the vitality, rebelliousness, and good humor of his country. " Presley also heralded the vastly expanded reach of celebrity in the era of mass communication: at the age of 21, within a year of his first appearance on American network television, he was one of the most famous people in the world.

Presley's name, image, and voice are instantly recognizable around the globe. He has inspired a legion of impersonators. In polls and surveys, he is recognized as one of the most important popular music artists and influential Americans. "Elvis Presley is the greatest cultural force in the twentieth century", said composer and conductor Leonard Bernstein. "He introduced the beat to everything and he changed everything—music, language, clothes. It's a whole new social revolution—the sixties came from it. " Bob Dylan described the sensation of first hearing Presley as "like busting out of jail".

A New York Times editorial on the 25th anniversary of Presley's death observed, "All the talentless impersonators and appalling black velvet paintings on display can make him seem little more than a perverse and distant memory. But before Elvis was camp, he was its opposite: a genuine cultural force. . . . Elvis's breakthroughs are underappreciated because in this rock-and-roll age, his hard-rocking music and sultry style have triumphed so completely. " Not only Presley's achievements, but his failings as well, are seen by some cultural observers as adding to the power of his legacy, as in this description by Greil Marcus:

Elvis Presley is a supreme figure in American life, one whose presence, no matter how banal or predictable, brooks no real comparisons. . . . The cultural range of his music has expanded to the point where it includes not only the hits of the day, but also patriotic recitals, pure country gospel, and really dirty blues. . . . Elvis has emerged as a great artist, a great rocker, a great purveyor of schlock, a great heart throb, a great bore, a great symbol of potency, a great ham, a great nice person, and, yes, a great American.

Discography

A vast number of recordings have been issued under Presley's name. The total number of his original master recordings has been variously calculated as 665 and 711. His career began and he was most successful during an era when singles were the primary commercial medium for pop music. In the case of his albums, the distinction between "official" studio records and other forms is often blurred. For most of the 1960s, his recording career focused on soundtrack albums. In the 1970s, his most heavily promoted and best-selling LP releases tended to be concert albums. This summary discography lists only the albums and singles that reached the top of one or more of the following charts: the main U. S. Billboard pop chart; the Billboard country chart, the genre chart with which he was most identified (there was no country album chart before 1964); and the official British pop chart. In the United States, Presley also had five or six number one R&B singles and seven number one adult contemporary singles; in 1964, his "Blue Christmas" topped the Christmas singles chart during a period when Billboard did not rank holiday singles in its primary pop chart. He also had number one hits in many countries beside the United States and United Kingdom.

Number one albums

Number one singles

Filmography

Elvis Presley filmography

(Ghost) Riders in the Sky: A Cowboy Legend

(Ghost) Riders in the Sky: A Cowboy Legend

"(Ghost) Riders in the Sky: A Cowboy Legend" is a country and cowboy-style song. It was written on June 5, 1948 by Stan Jones. A number of versions were crossover hits on the pop charts in 1949. The ASCAP database lists the song as "Riders in the Sky" (title code: 480028324), but the title has been written as "Ghost Riders", "Ghost Riders in the Sky", and "A Cowboy Legend".

The song tells a folk tale of a cowboy who has a vision of red-eyed, steel-hooved cattle thundering across the sky, being chased by the spirits of damned cowboys. One warns him that if he does not change his ways, he will be doomed to join them, forever "trying to catch the Devil's herd across these endless skies". Jones said that he had been told the story when he was 12 years old by an old cowboy friend. The story resembles the northern European mythic Wild Hunt.

More than 50 performers have recorded versions of the song. Charting versions were recorded by The Outlaws, Vaughn Monroe ("Riders in the Sky" with orchestra and vocal quartet), by Bing Crosby (with the Ken Darby Singers), Frankie Laine, Burl Ives (two different versions), Marty Robbins, The Ramrods and Johnny Cash. Other recordings were made by Peggy Lee (with the Jud Conlon Singers) and Spike Jones and his City Slickers. Gene Autry sang it in the 1949 movie, Riders in the Sky. Jones himself recorded it for his 1957 album Creakin' Leather. Children of Bodom, Impaled Nazarene and Die Apokalyptischen Reiter have also made covers.

The melody is based on the song "When Johnny Comes Marching Home. " According to Robby Krieger, it inspired the classic Doors song "Riders on the Storm. "

The song was also the inspiration for the Marvel Comics Western character "Ghost Rider" later renamed Phantom Rider (not to be confused with the later character named "Ghost Rider").

The chorus lines of this song are and have been since the 1960s a terrace song of the Aston Villa Football Club of England. The words have been modified to include the line "Holte Enders in the Sky", a reference to the occupants of the vast stand behind the goal at the southern end of the Villa Park stadium.

Recordings

The original version, by Burl Ives, was recorded on February 17, 1949 and released by Columbia Records as catalog number 38445. The recording first appeared on the Billboard charts on April 22, 1949, lasting 6 weeks and peaking at position #21.

Vaughn Monroe and His Orchestra. Vocalists: Vaughn Monroe and The Moon Men. Their version, the best-selling one, was recorded on March 14, 1949 and released by RCA Victor Records as catalog number 20-3411 (in USA) and by EMI on the His Master's Voice label as catalog numbers BD 1247, HN 3014, HQ 2071, IM 1425 and GY 878. The recording first appeared on the Billboard charts on April 15, 1949, lasting 22 weeks and peaking at position #1.

The Bing Crosby version was recorded on March 22, 1949 and released by Decca Records as catalog number 24618. The recording first appeared on the Billboard charts on May 6, 1949, lasting 6 weeks and peaking at position #14.

The Peggy Lee version was recorded on April 18, 1949 and released by Capitol Records as catalog number 57-608. It reached #2 in Billboard's Most Played By Disc Jockeys listing without appearing in the retail Top 30.

The Spike Jones version was recorded on May 24, 1949 and released by RCA Victor Records as catalog number 20-3741. Copies of the original release, containing lyrics ridiculing RCA stockholder Vaughn Monroe, are rare. The recording parodies the original Monroe recording, injecting much of Jones' quintessential humor along the way.

Another popular early version was recorded by the Sons of the Pioneers.

This song was then recorded by the Norman Luboff Choir and released in their album, "Songs of the Cowboy" in 1960.

The Brothers Four recorded a driven, up-tempo version (with edited lyrics and truncated to three stanzas) for their third LP, "B. M. O. C. : Best Music On/Off Campus," for Columbia Records in 1961.

A twangy guitar instrumental version by The Ramrods, which featured the spooky ghostly sounds of mooing cattle, broncos cheers, and sound of whips, made the Billboard Top 30 in 1961, as well as the Top 10 in the UK. This was covered by UK band The Scorpions (not the German rock band) on the "Parlophone" Label. Bob James recording as Bob James Trio included it as the last track on his very first album Bold Conceptions released in 1962. This may be a bonus track on the CD but it is consistent with the adventurous nature of the rest of the album.
Frankie Laine recorded a version of it on his 1963 album Wanderlust.
Daniel Amos recorded a Liver version of it on their Miracle Faith Telethon CD.
Dick Dale recorded a version in the surf style and released it on his second album, King of the Surf Guitar, in 1963. For a time it also accompanied a NASA montage as part of the preshow video on Space Mountain at Disneyland.
Davie Allan and the Arrows recorded two versions; one in 1967 on the Blues' Theme album (Tower Records) and one in 2008 on the Moving Right Along album (Spinout Records).
Duane Eddy brought his electrified "twangy guitar" sound along with a sax edition by Jim Horn to a 1996 version on an Curb Album "Ghost Rider. "
Recorded by Elvis Presley in June 1970 at MGM's soundstage in Culver City.
Recorded by Susan Christie in 1970, on her album Paint a Lady.
Riders in the Sky recorded this song on their debut album, Three on the Trail, in 1979, and on several of their subsequent albums.
Johnny Cash made a recording in 1979 which was faithful to the original. He also recorded it live with Willie Nelson for 1998's VH1 Storytellers. In that recording, Willie Nelson misses the start of the third verse because he forgets the text, and ends up switching the third and fourth verses.
The rock band Outlaws made a recording on their 1980 album Ghost Riders that left out the last verse. This version has often been mistakenly credited to The Marshall Tucker Band. They also released a live version of the song, recorded in 1982 at the King Biscuit Flower Hour, which appeared on Greatest Hits of The Outlaws. . . High Tides Forever
A version by The Shadows reached number 12 in the UK Singles Chart in 1980. This version was a semitone higher than the original.
Milton Nascimento recorded a version in Portuguese as "Cavaleiros Do Céu" on his 1981 album Caçador de Mim.
There is also a Sesame Street version called "The Dirtiest Town in The West" with altered lyrics. It was first aired in 1982.

Peter, Paul & Mary recorded a parody of the song entitled "Yuppies in the Sky" on their 1990 album "Flowers and Stones".
Impaled Nazarene recorded a black metal version of the song, which was released on the Sadogoat EP in 1993. Later it was included in the CD version of their bonus album Tol Cormpt Norz Norz Norz.
The Alberta Celtic rock group Captain Tractor recorded an unusual version for their 1994 album Land. New lyrics describe the frenzy of corruption in a prairie town at the climax of a real estate bubble. Rather than fire-and-brimstone Christian imagery, the warning takes the form of vaguely Zen lamentations—"The winds still blow / The rains still fall / The trees don't seem to care AT ALL!"
Ned Sublette included a merengue rendition on his Cowboy Rumba (1999).
The Blues Brothers performed the song in the movie Blues Brothers 2000. Similar to the "Rawhide" scene in the first movie, the band is mistakenly booked at a bluegrass festival (announced to the crowd as the "Bluegrass Brothers").
Dolan Ellis, Arizona's Official State Balladeer since 1966, included this as the only cover on his CD, "Tall Tales, Lost Trails & Heroes," released in 2000. He has sung the song throughout the nation and in 20 foreign countries, solo and as a member of the New Christy Minstrels, always telling the folk tale of Stan Jones, the Cochise County cowboy.
The heavy metal band Die Apokalyptischen Reiter recorded a version that was released on their 2006 single, "Friede Sei Mit Dir".
Me First and the Gimme Gimmes covered the song on their 2006 album Love Their Country.
Deborah Harry, lead singer of Blondie, recorded a trance version of the song which features on the soundtrack to the film Three Businessmen. The song (produced and arranged by Dan Wool and Pray for Rain) is available free on her website deborahharry. com.
The Ventures made a surf rock cover of the song.
Terry Scott Taylor and Daniel Amos recorded a version in 1990 that appeared on the "Miracle Faith Telethon" compilation album.
Same year 1990, French guitarist and singer Gill Dougherty recorded a half vocal, half instrumental version on his LP "Live In Bourges".
Pedro Vargas recorded a version called "Jinetes en el Cielo" in Spanish.
Raphael a Spanish singer in the 1970s performed this song, changing the lyrics talking about a cowboy doomed to ride for eternity for breaking a young girl's heart. The song ends happily when the girl saves him from that horrible destinity by crying and

praying for him, then letting a rose fall on his grave.
During his tour as "Giant Robot", Buckethead played a dub style version of the song.
During the credits of the 2007 movie Ghost Rider, a rock cover by the band Spiderbait is played. An instrumental version is also heard at points in the film.
Concrete Blonde recorded a version for their last album, 2004's Mojave.
Los Baby's, a famous 1960s band from Mexico, made the Spanish version called "Jinetes en el Cielo", which mean riders in the sky.
Former REO Speedwagon guitarist Gary Richrath quoted the melody of the song during his unaccompanied guitar solo on the band's 1977 live album, Live: You Get What You Play For.
The German "Western Metal" band Dezperadoz (featuring a member of Sodom) covered the song on their 2000 album The Dawn of Dying.
The Texan band Ghoultown recorded a version of this song on their album Tales from the Dead West
The Spotnicks, a Swedish instrumental rock band, covered this song and released it on The Spotnicks in London.
Finnish melodic death metal band Children of Bodom covered this song under the title 'Ghostriders in the Sky' and have released it on the special edition of their 2008 album Blooddrunk.
Adelaide, Australia band The Fabulaires did a cover version on their Apocalypso 12" E. P. circa 1980.
Baja Marimba Band recorded this song on the album "Watch Out!" in 1966.
Christopher Lee recorded a version of this song on the album "Devils, Rogues & Other Villains", released by Nikolas Schreck in 1998 on his Wolfslair label.
Art Greenhaw, Grammy Award-Winning guitarist, producer and leader of The Light Crust Doughboys, recorded a world music fusion version of this song on the album "Lone Star Sitar" and released in 2006 on the Greenhaw Records label.
Judy Collins, featuring the Nashville Rhythm Section and Ghost Riders Chorus, covered Ghost Riders In The Sky on her 2010 album Paradise.
Recordings have also been made by Mary McCaslin, The Tubes (masquerading as "Cowboy Fee & The Heifer's Dream"), Roy Clark, Marty Robbins, Dean Martin, Boston Pops, Lawrence Welk, R. E. M. , Dixie Chicks, Kaleidoscope, (Guy Vanderhoof), The All-American Boys Chorus, and the British gothic rock band Scary Bitches. There is a German language version of the song called "Geisterreiter" which, as early as 1949, was recorded by east German entertainer

Rita Paul & her Cornel-Trio. In the same year, a version was released by Gerhard Wendland. More than 20 versions of the German version are known. Most notably by Howard Carpendale and Karel Gott. There is a cover by the surf-punk-electro-band Mikrowelle as well as in 2008 by German TV-entertainer Götz Alsmann feat. Bela B (from Die Ärzte).

The Space Lady, Boston/San Francisco career street musician, did a cover of the song performed on a Casiotone MT-40 through a phase shifter, and vocals through a delay unit.
John Frusciante, Michael Rother, and Josh Klinghoffer performed a short instrumental version of the song live in 2004.

(Now and Then There's) A Fool Such as I

(Now and Then There's) A Fool Such as I

"(Now and Then There's) A Fool Such as I"
Single by Hank Snow
Released 1952
Format 1952
Writer(s) Bill Trader
Hank Snow singles chronology
"The Gal Who Invented Kissin'"
(1952) "(Now and Then There's) A Fool Such as I"
(1952) "Honeymoon on a Rocket Ship"
(1953)
"(Now and Then There's) A Fool Such as I"
B-side to "I Need Your Love Tonight" by Elvis Presley
Published 1952
Released March 10, 1959
Recorded June 10, 1958
Genre Rock and roll
Length 02:39
Label RCA
Writer Bill Trader
"Fool Such as I"
Single by Baillie & the Boys
from the album The Lights of Home
Released 1990
Genre Country
Length 2:50
Label RCA

Writer(s) Bill Trader
Producer Kyle Lehning
Baillie & the Boys singles chronology
"Perfect"
(1990) "Fool Such as I"
(1990) "Treat Me Like a Stranger"
(1991)

"(Now and Then There's) A Fool Such as I" is a popular song written by Bill Trader and was published in 1952. Performed by Hank Snow it peaked at number four on the country charts early in 1953.

Since the original Snow version, "Fool Such as I" — as the song is sometimes known — has been covered and released as singles several times, by artists as diverse as Jo Stafford, Elvis Presley, Bob Dylan and Baillie & the Boys.

Contents

Other versions

Tommy Edwards

This section is empty. You can help by adding to it.

Jo Stafford

The recording by Jo Stafford was released by Columbia Records as catalog number 39930. It reached the Billboard Best Seller chart on February 28, 1953 at number twenty, its only week on the chart.

Elvis Presley

A recording by Elvis Presley, initially released as b-side to "I Need Your Love Tonight", was an even bigger hit, reaching number one in the UK and number two in the USA (1959). The Elvis Presley version went to number sixteen on the R&B charts and featured backing vocals by The

Jordanaires.

Petula Clark

Petula Clark's French language version titled "Prends mon Cœur", was more successful in France (#9, 1960) than Elvis Presley's version.

Bob Dylan

In 1967, Bob Dylan recorded the song during the Basement Tape sessions. Although never officially released, the recording has been widely bootlegged. Dylan would go on to record the song again in April 1969; that version was released in 1973 by Columbia on the Dylan album.

Baillie & the Boys

In 1990, Baillie & the Boys released the song from its album The Lights of Home. This version, released under the title "Fool Such as I", would peak at No. 5 on the Billboard Hot Country Singles chart. It was the trio's last Top 10 hit on the country charts.

Chart performance

Release date Artist Chart Positions
US
Country U. S. CAN
Country FRA
1952 Hank Snow 3 — — —
1953 Tommy Edwards — 24 — —
1953 Jo Stafford — 16 — —
1959 Petula Clark — — — 9
1973 Mickey Gilley — 55 — —
1979 Rodney Crowell 90 — — —
1990 Baillie & the Boys 5 — 7 —

Elvis Presley

Chart (1959) Peak
position
U. S. Billboard Hot Singles 2
U. S. Hot Rhythm & Blues Singles 16
U. S. Cashbox Hot Singles 2
U. S. Cashbox Hot Country Singles 6
U. K. Singles Charts 1
Canadian Singles Charts 1
Australian Kent Singles Charts 1
Belgian Singles Charts 13

Dutch Singles Charts 15
Norway VG-Lista 5
South African Charts 1
Swedish Singles Charts 17
Chart (2005) Peak position
U. K. Singles Charts 2
European Singles Charts 6
Preceded by
"It Doesn't Matter Anymore" by Buddy Holly UK number one single
(Elvis Presley version)
"A Fool Such As I"/"I Need Your Love Tonight"
May 15, 1959 (for 5 weeks) Succeeded by
"Roulette" by Russ Conway

(You're the) Devil in Disguise

(You're the) Devil in Disguise

"(You're the) Devil in Disguise"

Single by Elvis Presley
B-side "Please Don't Drag That String Around"
Released 1963
Format 7"
Recorded May 26, 1963, RCA Studios, Nashville, Tennessee
Genre Rock and roll
Length 2:17
Label RCA
Writer(s) Bill Giant, Bernie Baum, Florence Kaye
Elvis Presley singles chronology
"One Broken Heart for Sale"
(1963) "(You're the) Devil in Disguise"
(1963) "Bossa Nova Baby"
(1963)
"(You're the) Devil in Disguise" is a UK number one single by Elvis Presley which was written by the songwriting team Giant, Baum and Kaye and published by Elvis Presley Music in 1963. It peaked at number three in the US on the Billboard singles chart and number nine on the Billboard Rhythm and Blues singles chart, becoming his last top ten single on the Rhythm and Blues charts. The single was

certified "Gold" by the RIAA for sales in excess of 1 000,000 units in the US. The song also topped Japan's Utamatic record chart in the fall of 1963.

In 1963, when the song was debuted to a British audience on the BBC television show Juke Box Jury, the celebrity guest John Lennon voted the song "a miss" stating on the new song that Elvis Presley was "like Bing Crosby now. "

Presley originally recorded the song May 26, 1963 at RCA Studios in Nashville. "(You're the) Devil in Disguise" and its flipside, "Please Don't Drag That String Around", was recorded for a full-length album that was scheduled for release in 1963, but RCA chose instead to release the album piecemeal on singles and as soundtrack album bonus tracks.

The song is noted for Presley's singing in a low register to represent the Devil with the repeated phrase "Oh, Yes, You Are", before the song's fade.

Uses in popular culture

The song was featured in Lilo & Stitch, a 2002 American animated feature produced by Walt Disney Feature Animation and released on June 21, 2002.

A cover version by Trisha Yearwood appears on Honeymoon in Vegas soundtrack, which consists mainly of covers of Presley songs.

The song was used in a 2010 TV commercial for the Nissan Altima.

English band Hollow Horse recorded a version entitled "Tory in Disguise" about former British prime minister Tony Blair.

The song featured in a 1993 television advertisement for the launch of the Volvo 850.

Werner Müller - You're The Devil In Disguise

2nd to None

2nd to None

For the album by Chemistry, see Second to None (Chemistry album)

ELVIIS: 2nd to None

Cover to the standard edition of the album

Greatest hits album by Elvis Presley

Released 2009 Blu-spec CD October 7, 2003

Recorded July 5, 1954-February 4, 1976
Genre Rock and roll
Length 78:39
Label RCA
Producer Ernst Mikael Jorgensen, Ray Bardani
Elvis Presley chronology
ELV1S: 30 #1 Hits
(September 2002) 2nd to None
(October 2003) Hitstory
(October 2005)
Alternative cover

Professional ratings
Review scores
Source Rating
Allmusic

ELVIIS: 2nd to None is a collection of songs by American rock and roll icon Elvis Presley. The album was released by on October 7, 2003 by RCA Records (see 2003 in music) as the sequel to the previous year's highly successful ELV1S: 30 #1 Hits.
The album included Elvis's #1 singles that did not appear on the previous release, other notable recordings by the artist, one previously unreleased recording—"I'm a Roustabout"—, and a remix of "Rubberneckin'" by Paul Oakenfold.
Although not as successful as its predecessor, 2nd to None made the top 10 in at least nine countries and received certifications in several regions.
Contents

Production, artwork and packaging

Unlike ELV1S, 2nd to None was not produced by David Bendeth but was instead produced by Ernst Mikael Jorgensen and Ray Bardani. Bardani also mixing many of the songs on the collection with the assistance of Matt Snedecor, while the tape transferring and mastering on the recordings were handled by Andreas Meyer and

Vic Anesini, respectively.

The artwork and design for the American and European releases of the album are different from one another. The American release's artwork is very similar to ELV1S having the art direction and design by the same person, Thomas Vasquez, and both had album covers that were both similar to 1 by The Beatles. The European release's artwork, however, was very different from either ELV1S or 1 with the album cover consisting of a picture of Elvis' head and the number 2 against a black background. The European release's art direction and design was handled by a different person, Mike Jurkovac.

Track listing

"That's All Right (Mama)"
"I Forgot to Remember to Forget"
"Blue Suede Shoes"
"I Want You, I Need You, I Love You"
"Love Me"
"Mean Woman Blues"
"Loving You"
"Treat Me Nice"
"Wear My Ring Around Your Neck"
"King Creole"
"Trouble"
"I Got Stung"
"I Need Your Love Tonight"
"A Mess of Blues"
"I Feel So Bad"
"Little Sister"
"Rock-A-Hula Baby"
"Bossa Nova Baby"
"Viva Las Vegas"
"If I Can Dream"
"Memories"
"Don't Cry Daddy"
"Kentucky Rain"
"You Don't Have to Say You Love Me"
"An American Trilogy"
"Always on My Mind"
"Promised Land"
"Moody Blue"
"I'm a Roustabout" (previously unreleased bonus track)
"Rubberneckin'" (Paul Oakenfold Remix - Radio Edit)

Bonus tracks
"Rubberneckin'" (Paul Oakenfold Remix) (12" version)
"Rubberneckin'" (Original version)

Charts and certifications

Chart (2003) Peak position
Australian Top 50 Albums 4
Austrian Top 75 Albums 5
Belgium (Flanders) 100 Albums 21
Belgium (Wallonia) 100 Albums 40
Canadian Albums Chart 3
Danish Top 40 Albums 11
Finnish Top 50 Albums 9
French Compilations 21
German Albums Chart 13
Irish Top 75 Albums 13
Netherlands Top 100 Albums 22
New Zealand Top 40 Albums 16
Norwegian Top 40 Albums 17
Polish Top 50 Albums 9
Swedish Top 60 Albums 5
Swiss Top 100 Albums 7
UK Albums Chart 4
US Billboard 200 3
Region Certification Sales/shipments
Australia (ARIA) Gold 35,000^
Austria (IFPI Austria) Platinum 30,000 or 50,000x
Denmark (IFPI Denmark) Gold 20,000^
Finland (Musiikkituottajat) Gold 17,716
New Zealand (RIANZ) Gold 7,500^
Sweden (GLF) Gold 30,000^
Switzerland (IFPI Switzerland) Gold 20,000x
United States (RIAA) Platinum 1,000,000^
^shipments figures based on certification alone
xunspecified figures based on certification alone

Promotion

Before Anyone Did Anything, Elvis Did Everything

Greatest hits album by Elvis Presley

Released 2003
Recorded July 5, 1954-February 4, 1976
Genre Rock and Roll
Length 25:32
Label BMG
Producer Various
Elvis Presley chronology
ELV1S: 30 #1 Hits
(2002) Before Anyone Did Anything, Elvis Did Everything
(2003) 2nd to None
(2003)
To promote the album in the United Kingdom, a compilation album titled Before Anyone Did Anything, Elvis Did Everything was released as a free covermount album in the British newspaper Daily Mail. The album contains a blue cover quite similar to that of 2nd to None and ELV1S and ten songs, although not all of these are from 2nd to None, as some are from 30 #1 Hits and various other releases like the Close Up box set.

Track listing

No. Title Length
1. "Heartbreak Hotel" (live track from the box set 'Close Up'. An updated sound version features on the album '30 #1 Hits' (CD sleeve notes).) 1:55
2. "Love Me Tender" (live track from the box set 'Close Up'. An updated sound version features on the album '30 #1 Hits' (CD sleeve notes).) 1:42
3. "Can't Help Falling In Love" (live track from the box set 'Close Up'. An updated sound version features on the album '30 #1 Hits' (CD sleeve notes). Note that this and the above two play gaplessly, presumably because they were recorded at the same concert.) 1:45
4. "Suspicious Minds" (Taken from the album '30 #1 Hits' (CD sleeve notes).) 4:32
5. "Love Me" (live track from the box set 'Close Up'. An updated sound version features on the album '2nd To None' (CD sleeve notes).) 1:49
6. "Burning Love" (Taken from the album '30 #1 Hits' (CD sleeve notes).) 2:56
7. "Have I Told You Lately That I Love You" (This track is an alternate take from the box set 'Close Up' (CD sleeve notes).) 2:34
8. "Kentucky Rain" (An updated sound version features on the

album '2nd To None' (CD sleeve notes).) 3:14
9. "Don't Cry Daddy" (An updated sound version features on the album '2nd To None' (CD sleeve notes).) 2:47
10. "I Want To Be Free" (This track is an alternate take from the box set 'Close Up' (CD sleeve notes).) 2:16

3rd Armored Division (United States)

3rd Armored Division (United States)

3rd Armored Division

3rd Armored Division shoulder sleeve insignia
Active 1941–1945
1947–1992
Country United States of America
Allegiance United States of America
Branch Armor Branch (United States)
Type Armored Division (Heavy)
Role Armored Attack/Exploitation
Size Typically 15,000+
Nickname Spearhead
Colors Blue, Red, Gold, Black
March Spearhead March
Engagements World War II
Gulf War
Commanders
Notable
commanders MG Maurice Rose
MG Gordon B. Rogers
MG Creighton Abrams
Insignia
Identification
symbol Armored Division Triangle

The 3rd Armored Division ("Spearhead") was an armored division of the United States Army. Nickamed the Third Herd, the division was first activated in 1941, and was active in the European Theater of World War II. The division was stationed in West Germany for much of the Cold War, and participated in the Persian Gulf War. On 17 January 1992 in Germany, the division ceased operations; in October 1992 it was formally deactivated as part of a general drawing down of forces at the end of the Cold War.

World War II

Order of battle

The Third Armored Division was organized as a "heavy" armored division, as was its counterpart, the Second Armored Division aka "Hell on Wheels". Later, higher-numbered U. S. armored divisions of World War II were smaller, with a higher ratio of armored infantry to tanks, based on lessons of the fighting in North Africa.

As a "heavy" division, the 3rd Armored possessed two armored regiments totaling four medium tank battalions and two of light tanks (18 companies) instead of three tank battalions containing both (12 companies), 232 medium tanks instead of the 168 allotted a light armored division, and with attached units numbered over 16,000 men, instead of the normal 12,000 found in the light armored divisions. Each division type had an infantry component of three mechanized infantry battalions.

The division's core units were the 36th Armored Infantry Regiment, the 32nd Armored Regiment, the 33rd Armored Regiment, the 23rd Armored Engineer Battalion, the 83rd Armored Reconnaissance Battalion, and the 143rd Armored Signal Company. During World War II, these were organized operationally into task forces known as Combat Commands A, B and R (Reserve), as in the light divisions.

In addition to the core units, a number of other units of various kinds were attached to the division during various operations. As with most American divisions in World War II, the 3rd Armored suffered heavy casualties, and by the end of the war replacement troops often outnumbered veterans in the line units.

During 1944 and 1945, the units comprising the Third Armored Division included:

Combat units:
32nd Armored Regiment
33rd Armored Regiment
36th Armored Infantry Regiment
54th Field Artillery Battalion
67th Field Artillery Battalion
391st Field Artillery Battalion

143rd Signal Battalion
23rd Armored Engineer Battalion
83rd Armored Reconnaissance Battalion
Headquarters units:
Headquarters Company, 3rd Armored Division
Service Company, 3rd Armored Division
Division Trains
Supply Battalion
45th Armored Medical Battalion
503rd Intelligence Corps
Attached units:
643rd Tank Destroyer Battalion (attached 22 December 1944 to 26 December 1944)
703rd Tank Destroyer Battalion (attached 25 June 1944 to 17 December 1944, 2 January 1945 to 9 May 1945)
803rd Tank Destroyer Battalion (attached 25 June 1944 to 2 July 1944)
413th AAA Gun Battalion (attached 7 July 1944 to 16 July 1944)
486th AAA Auto-Weapons Battalion (attached 25 June 1944 to 9 May 1945)
Training timeline

The division was activated on 15 April 1941 at Camp Beauregard, Louisiana. In June 1941, it moved to Camp Polk Louisiana (now Fort Polk). On 9 March 1942, it came under Army Ground Forces and was assigned to the II Armored Corps. In July 1942, it was transferred to Camp Young, CA and from August to October 1942, took part in maneuvers at the Desert Training Center. It left Camp Young in January 1943 and moved to the Indiantown Gap Military Reservation, Pennsylvania.

The 3rd AD arrived in the European Theatre on 15 September 1943, conducting pre-invasion training in the Liverpool and Bristol areas. It remained in Somerset, England until 24 June 1944, when it departed to partake in the Normandy operations.

Into battle

The first elements of the 3rd Armored in France saw combat on 29 June, with the division as a whole beginning combat operations on 9 July 1944. During this time, it was under the command of VII Corps and XVIII Airborne Corps for some time, and assigned to the First Army and the 12th Army Group for the duration of its career.

The division "spearheaded" the US First Army through Normandy, taking part in a number of engagements, notably including the Battle of Saint Lô, where it suffered significant casualties. After facing heavy fighting in the hedgerows, and developing methods to overcome the vast thickets of brush and earth that constrained its mobility, the unit broke out at Marigny, alongside the 1st Infantry Division, and swung south to Mayenne. The engineers and maintenance crews took the large I-Beam Invasion barriers from the beaches at Normandy and used the beams to weld large crossing rams on the front of the Sherman tanks. They would then hit the hedgerows at high speed, bursting through them without exposing the vulnerable underbellies of the tanks. Until this happened, they could not get across the hedgerows.

Ordered to help close the Falaise Gap and Argentan pocket which contained the German Seventh Army, the division finished the job near Putanges by 18 August. Six days later the outfit had sped through Courville and Chartres and was located at the banks of the Seine River. On the night of 25 August 1944 the crossing of the Seine by the division started; once over, the 3rd slugged its way across France, reaching Belgium on 2 September 1944.

Liberated in the path of the division were Meaux, Seissons, Laon, Marle, Mons, Charleroi, Namur and Liege. It was at Mons that the division cut off 40,000 Wehrmacht troops and captured 8,000 prisoners. "Then the division began the first invasion of Germany since the days of Napoleon" is a claim often repeated and derives from 1947 U. S. Army literature that ignored earlier acts such as the 5th Armored Division's reconnaissance into Germany on 11 September 1944, French troops entering the Saarland in September 1939 during the Saar Offensive, and the entry into Germany by imperial Russian troops in 1914.

Across the Rhine

On 10 September 1944 the Spearhead Division fired what it claimed was the first American field artillery shell of the war onto German soil. Two days later it passed the German border and soon breached the Siegfried Line, taking part in the Battle of Hurtgen Forest.

The 3rd Armored Division continued fighting during the Battle of Bulge, far north of the deepest German penetration. Countering

German attacks, it severed an important highway leading to St Vith. By late January 1945, the German offensive had been checked, and the division began pushing its way into Germany. Advancing at a little better than half a mile a day against stiff resistance, the 3rd captured ten towns in January 1945, took 2,149 prisoners and destroyed 61 armored vehicles.

Death of a general

The division began a thrust into the Rhineland of Germany on 7 February 1945. On 31 March, the commander of the division, Major General Maurice Rose, famed as one of few commanding generals to frequent the front lines during combat, rounded a corner in his jeep and found himself face to face with a German tank. As he withdrew his pistol to surrender, a young German tank commander, apparently misunderstanding Rose's intentions, shot the general.

After Rose's death, the division pushed east and swept into the key city of Cologne in March 1945. Beyond Cologne the division swept up Paderborn in its advance, to shut the back door to the Ruhr Pocket. In April, the division crossed the Saale River, north of Halle, and sped on toward the Elbe River.

On 11 April 1945, the 3rd Armored discovered the Dora-Mittelbau concentration camp. The division first arrived on the scene, reporting back to headquarters that it had uncovered a large concentration camp near the town of Nordhausen. Requesting help from the 104th Infantry Division, the 3rd immediately began transporting some 250 ill and starving prisoners to nearby hospital facilities.

The last major fighting in the war for the division was the Battle of Dessau, which the division captured on 23 April 1945 after three days of combat. Following the action at Dessau, the division moved into corps reserve at Sangerhausen. Occupational duty near Langen was given the division following V-E Day, a role it filled until inactivation on 10 November 1945.

Combat statistics

The 3rd Armored Division had 231 days of combat in World War II, with a total of 2,540 killed, 7,331 wounded, 95 missing, and 139 captured. Total battle and non-battle casualties came to 16,122.

The 3rd Armored Division lost more tanks in combat than any other U. S. division. Combat Command A lost more tanks than any other unit in the 3rd Armored Division.

Medals and awards earned by division soldiers

Distinguished Service Crosses – 17
Legions of Merit – 23
Silver Stars – 885
Soldiers Medal – 32
Bronze Stars – 3,884
Purple Hearts – in excess of 10,500
Air Medals – 138
Distinguished Flying Crosses – 3
Successive division commanders during World War II

Major General Alvin C. Gillem Jr. , April 1941 to January 1942
Major General Walton H. Walker, January 1941 to August 1942
Major General Leroy R. Watson, August 1942 to August 1944
Major General Maurice Rose, August 1944 to March 1945 KIA
Brigadier General Doyle O. Hickey, March to June 1945
Brigadier General Truman E. Boudinot, June & July 1945
Brigadier General Frank A. Allen, Jr. , July 1945
Major General Robert W. Grow, July 1945 until inactivation
The Cold War

The division was reactivated on 15 July 1947 at Fort Knox, Kentucky to act as training formation. In 1955 the 3d Armored Division was reorganized for combat and shipped to Germany the next year. It replaced the 4th Infantry Division under a program called Operation Gyroscope. The 3d Armored Division served in Cold War Germany from May 1956 to July 1992, with the exception of the time spent in Desert Storm.

The 3rd Armored's primary mission during this period was, in the event of war, to defend the Fulda Gap against numerically superior Warsaw Pact forces alongside other NATO elements. In June 1962 USAREUR maxed out its Cold War troop strength; that number was never achieved again. Also in June 1962 the nuclear warheads for the Davy Crocketts arrived in USAREUR (3rd AD combat maneuver battalions were issued Davy Crocketts). In late October 1962 during the Cuban Crisis there was no hotline between Washington and

Moscow; Soviet Forces, including those in the Group of Soviet Forces Germany, were placed on the highest alert level. At the peak of 1980s East/West tensions, as many as nineteen Soviet and East German divisions faced off against Spearhead soldiers. To prepare their defenses against an invasion, the division's units frequently conducted field training at Hohenfels, Bavaria and at Wildflecken and Grafenwöhr U. S. Army training areas, conducting exercises of live fire, movement and communications. The division would also frequently take to the German countryside for training maneuvers, including what became an annually staged war game Reforger, which simulated invasion of Western Europe by Warsaw Pact forces.

Throughout the Cold War, the division headquarters company, 503d Adjutant General Co. and 503d M. P. Co. were based on Drake Kaserne, with 143rd Signal Bn. and other support units stationed across the street at Edwards Kaserne in Frankfurt, West Germany. A number of its subunits were based in other Kasernes throughout the German state of Hessen, notably Ayers Kaserne (50° 28' 32. 44" N 8° 38' 29. 24" E) at Kirch-Goens and Schloss Kaserne at Butzbach (CCA/1st Brigade), Gelnhausen (CCB/2nd Brigade), Ray Barracks at Friedberg (CCC/3rd Brigade) and Fliegerhorst near Hanau (Combat Aviation Brigade/4th Avn Bde). The NCO Academy contained 2 companies: Co. 'A' was assigned to the medieval castle at Usingen-Kransburg, while Co. 'B' was located in Butzbach. The division itself comprised an average of 15,000 soldiers, organized into three combat commands (CC's) later renamed brigades (ROAD reorganization in 1963), organizations of comparable size to the World War II combat commands. These brigades were individually manned by at least one battalion each of infantry, armor, and artillery, and various supporting units, notably including medical, engineering, and aviation elements. The division was also assigned the dedicated 533rd Military Intelligence]]/CEWI (Combat Electronic Warfare and Intelligence) Battalion by 1980, replacing the 503rd MI Company that previously supported the division intelligence staff.

Most of the kasernes were located adjacent to or within German communities, leading to lively trade and interaction between soldiers and German civilians. A few, however, were somewhat remotely located, particularly Ayers Kaserne ("The Rock")(50° 28' 32. 44" N 8° 38' 29. 24" E), where the 1st Brigade was stationed, outside Kirch-Goens. The most famous soldier in the 3rd Armored Division during the 1950s was Elvis Presley, assigned to Company

A, 1st Medium Tank Battalion, 32nd Armor Regiment, Combat Command C at Ray Barracks in Friedberg. After his time in service, Presley made the movie G. I. Blues, in which he portrays a 3rd Armored Division tank crewman with little field duty but with a singing career. Colin Powell also served in this division. He was assigned to the 2d Armored Rifle Battalion, 48th Infantry, Combat Command B, Coleman Kaserne, Gelnhausen, between 1958 & 1960. It started out with his first command assignment, as an Infantry Platoon Leader.

By 1990, Communism in eastern Europe collapsed, the two German states reunited, and the Soviet Army was being withdrawn back to the Soviet Union. With these events, the Cold War came to a peaceful conclusion, freeing U. S. Army units in Europe for other deployments.

Desert Storm

In response to the changing cold war scenario, 3AD was instructed to begin selective standing down of various Division elements during the summer of 1990. Some units, for example 3-5 ADA Battalion had turned in equipment or cross-leveled with other 3AD units by August of 1990, when momentous events in the Middle East developed. That month, Iraq invaded Kuwait, and soon after, President George H. W. Bush committed U. S. troops to the theater, first to defend Saudi Arabia, and then to eject Iraqi troops from Kuwait. Deployment of advance elements of 3AD began in December, with the remaining deploying units arriving by January. Units that had drawn down were replaced or augmented back to full strength. As an example, 3-5 ADA was replaced by the 8th Infantry Division's 5-3 ADA Battalion. Other units were attached to 3AD to bring it up to, and even beyond full strength.

Redeployment and retraining

The 3rd Armored Division, then commanded by Major General Paul Funk, was one of four U. S. heavy divisions deployed with VII Corps. The division and its equipment were shifted from Germany to Saudi Arabia, with in some cases, Army National Guard and Army Reserve elements taking over some of their duties in Germany, while in others, kasernes were left virtually empty. This massive redeployment was possible only due to the Western victory in the Cold War, in which the 3rd AD helped to play an integral part by guarding the Fulda Gap.

After redeployment, the division acclimated to the desert climate, and its troops faced new challenges in mobility, tactics and maintenance in a sandy and hot climate. Various National Guard and Army Reserve units were then attached to the division for the duration of the conflict, swelling the division's size to over 20,000 troops – 25% larger than during its time in Germany.

The majority of the division's troops never received Desert Battle Dress Uniforms due to a shortage, and fought instead in lightweight summer "woodland pattern" uniforms, covered by tanker suits or chemical warfare protective MOPP suits.

Order of battle

1st Brigade:
Headquarters and Headquarters Company (HHC), 1st Brigade
4th Battalion, 32nd Armored Regiment
3rd Battalion, 5th Cavalry Regiment
5th Battalion, 5th Cavalry Regiment
2nd Brigade:
HHC, 2nd Brigade
3rd Battalion, 8th Cavalry Regiment
4th Battalion, 8th Cavalry Regiment
4th Battalion, 18th Infantry Regiment
3rd Brigade:
HHC, 3rd Brigade
2nd Battalion, 67th Armor Regiment
4th Battalion, 67th Armor Regiment
5th Battalion, 18th Infantry Regiment

Aviation Brigade:
HHC, Aviation Brigade
4th Squadron, 7th Cavalry Regiment
2nd Battalion, 227th Aviation Regiment (augmented with A Co. , 5-229 AVN just before ground war began)
3rd Battalion, 227th Aviation Regiment (detached and assigned to XVIII Airborne Corps prior to 3AD deployment)
9th Battalion, 227th Aviation Regiment
Task Force Viper
Division Artillery (DIVARTY):
Headquarters and Headquarters Battery (HHB), DIVARTY
A Battery, 40th Field Artillery Regiment

F Battery, 333rd Field Artillery Regiment
2nd Battalion, 3rd Field Artillery Regiment
2nd Battalion, 82nd Field Artillery Regiment
4th Battalion, 82nd Field Artillery Regiment
Division Support Command (DISCOM):
HHC, DISCOM
22nd Chemical Company
503rd Forward Support Battalion
54th Forward Support Battalion
45th Forward Support Battalion
122nd Main Support Battalion
Division Troops:
HHC, 3rd Armored Division
3rd Armored Division Band
503rd Military Police Company
23rd Engineer Battalion
143rd Signal Battalion
533rd Military Intelligence Battalion
3rd Battalion, 5th Air Defence Artillery Regiment
Attached Units:
302nd RAOC
323 Chemical Company
148th Public Affairs Detachment, IDARNG
369th Personnel Service Company
C Co. , 17th Signal Battalion
4th Battalion, 34th Armor Regiment
3rd Battalion, 20th Field Artillery Regiment
12th Engineer Battalion
Into battle

Finally, after months of training the division moved to the Line of Departure, alongside the 1st Armored Division on its left flank and the 2nd Armored Cavalry Regiment on its right flank. While the Iraqi Army concentrated much of its defenses in and around Kuwait itself, the 3rd AD and VII Corps launched a massive armored attack into Iraq, just to the west of Kuwait, taking the Iraqis completely by surprise.

Scouts from 2nd Brigade crossed on the afternoon of the 23 February 1991 just after 1500 hours. Less than two hours later, they had penetrated several miles into Iraq and managed to capture over 200 prisoners. On 24 February, the official first day of action, the division as a whole swung into action as part of a coordinated attack by hundreds of thousands of allied troops.

During the first day of battle, the Third Herd pushed 18 miles into Iraq, taking over 200 prisoners. By dawn of the second day, an additional 50 prisoners had been taken, with scouts reporting enemy reinforcements moving to meet the division.

The second day

At 1115 hours of the second day, all elements of the division were finally across the line of departure. The day was marked by hard pushing to penetrate deep and fast, striking for an objective south of Basra. In the course of its drive, various elements of the division engaged the enemy, taking prisoners, skirmishing, sometimes bypassing enemy strongholds to gain ground, other time engaging in full scale battle.

By nightfall of the second day, 3AD had driven 53 miles into Iraq, with dozens of enemy vehicles destroyed, hundreds of POWs captured, and was on the verge of achieving its first objective – an accomplishment that war planners had not anticipated.

The third day

On the third day of combat, 26 February, the division closed in upon its objective and faced for the first time the Iraqi Republican Guard, a much stronger foe than the forces the division had first engaged, and less inclined to retreat or surrender. Opposing forces included the highly touted Republican Guard "Tawakalna" Division, the Iraqi 52nd Armored Division and elements of the 17th and the 10th Armored Divisions. The division engaged in full scale tank battles for the first time since World War II, and as one of the division's veterans states "There was more than enough action for everyone".

Action continued after nightfall, and by 1840 hours, the ground and air elements of the 3rd AD could report over 20 tanks, 14 APCs, several trucks and some artillery pieces destroyed. Unfortunately, that same evening, the 4th Battalion, 32d Armor lost the division's first casualties in a Bradley Fighting Vehicle to 25mm cannon fire – with two soldiers killed and three wounded. During the night, both darkness and sandstorms hampered soldiers' visibility, but thermal sighting systems on board the M1A1 Abrams tanks and Bradleys allowed gunners to knock out Iraqi targets.

The fourth and fifth days

By the fourth day, the division reached its objective, and pursued its now retreating enemy. The division turned east, into Kuwait, continuing to inflict heavy casualties and capture troops as it rolled forward, often hitting new units whose defensive berms and foxholes faced south from their northern flank, rendering their defenses ineffective. By nightfall, forces facing 3AD had been virtually eliminated, with their remnants in full retreat.

By the fifth day of combat, the division had achieved all objectives and continued to push east to block Iraqi retreat from Kuwait, conducting mopping up operations. One hundred hours after the ground campaign started, President Bush declared a ceasefire.

Spearhead

At the height of the battle, the 3rd Armored Division included 32 battalions and 20,533 troops. It was the largest coalition division in the Gulf War and the largest U. S. armored division in history. In its moving arsenal were 360 Abrams main battle tanks, 340 Bradley Fighting Vehicles, 128 self-propelled 155 mm howitzers, 27 Apache attack helicopters, 9 multiple-launch rocket systems, and more.

Superior training, initiative and equipment had enabled the soldiers of the division to spearhead their way through the Iraqi Army, including opponents with Soviet-provided training and equipment. In the 100-hour Gulf War, 3rd AD destroyed hundreds of Iraqi tanks and vehicles, and captured more than 2,400 Iraqi prisoners. Fifteen troops of the 3rd AD were killed between December 1990 and late February 1991.

In 1991, Division Historian Dan Peterson, comparing the performance of the division in World War II and Desert Storm stated "History does always repeat itself. 3rd Armored Division was the Spearhead in both wars. "

Following the war, 3rd Armored Division was one of the first units rotated to Camp Doha, Kuwait, providing protection to Kuwait as it rebuilt.

Retirement

Following Desert Storm, a number of the division's units were transferred to the First Armored Division.

On 17 January 1992, the 3rd Armored Division officially ceased operations in Germany, with a ceremony in Frankfurt at Division Headquarters, Drake Kaserne.

"Sir, this is my final salute. Mission accomplished," said Maj. Gen. Jerry Rutherford, the division commander. Rutherford preceded the final salute to General Crosbie E. Saint, USAREUR Commander, with a loudly shouted "Spearhead!" The division colors were then returned to the United States, with the 3rd AD still officially active, since Army Regulations state that Divisional "Casing of Colors" cannot occur on foreign soil.

Official retirement took place at Fort Knox, on 17 October 1992. In attendance at the ceremony were several former Spearhead commanding generals, and division veterans from all eras. In a traditional ceremony, Command Sgt. Major Richard L. Ross, holding the division color with battle streamers, passed it to General Frederick M. Franks, Jr. , and with that, the official retirement of the "Third Herd" was complete, and the 3rd Armored Division was removed from the official force structure of the U. S. Army.

Reassignment

With the end of the Cold War, several of the division's overseas Kasernes were transferred to other units, particularly the 1st Armored Division. Over time, many were closed, fell into disrepair and were eventually demolished. Some 3rd Armored Units were also transferred to the 1st Armored, notably the 2nd Battalion, 3rd Field Artillery Regiment, later to become semi-famous as the unit portrayed in Gunner Palace.

The 1st Battalion, 32nd Armor Regiment now resides at Fort Campbell, Kentucky as part of the 101st Airborne Division (Air Assault). The unit was reorganized as the 1st Squadron, 32nd Cavalry Regiment, and is assigned to the 1st Brigade Combat Team of the 101st Airborne Division (Air Assault) as its organic Reconnaissance, Surveillance, and Target Acquisition (RSTA) element. The 1st Battalion, 33rd Armor Regiment is also calling Fort Campbell and the 101st Airborne Division (Air Assault) home. The 1st Battalion, 33rd Armor was reorganized as the 1st Squadron, 33rd Cavalry Regiment and is assigned to the 3rd Brigade Combat Team of the 101st Airborne Division (Air Assault). 4th Squadron, 7th

Cavalry is now part of 1st Brigade, 2nd Infantry Division.

The following units joined the 1st Cavalry Division:

1st Battalion, 5th Cavalry
2nd Battalion, 5th Cavalry
3rd Battalion, 8th Cavalry
2nd Battalion, 227th Aviation
3rd Battalion, 227th Aviation
Additionally, the lineage of the 122d Support Battalion (Main) from the Division Support Command was reactivated at Fort Bragg and assigned to the Combat Aviation Brigade, 82d Airborne Division as the 122d Support Battalion (Aviation). Also, the 54th Support Battalion (Main) was reactivated on 16 September 1994 as the 54th Support Battalion (Base) of the 80th Support Group (Area).

Commanders

The 3rd Armored Division had thirty-nine commanders over the course of its history, many of whom went on to four star rank.

In media and memory

Despite the division's impressive record and the important role it played during the war, it has been often overlooked by both historians and Hollywood, who have favored depictions and histories of units participating in D-Day, and in the siege of Bastogne during the Battle of the Bulge. Books, movies and other media that feature the Third Armored Division include:

The Tanks Are Coming (1951) – A typical WWII action movie of the time, only vaguely based on actual events
G. I. Blues (1960) – Elvis Presley, a real life 3AD tanker, stars as a 3rd AD Tanker with an off-post singing career and dreams of owning a nightclub
Cooper, Belton Y. (1998). Death Traps: The Survival of an American Armored Division in World War II. Navato, CA: Presidio Press. ISBN 0-89141-670-6. OCLC 38753044. A unique look at the war from a maintenance officer's perspective.
Rolling Thunder: The True Story of the Third Armored Division (2002) – A History Channel documentary detailing the history of the division from birth to the 1990s.
Man, Moment, Machine (season 1, episode 4): "Stormin' Norman and the Abrams Tank" – Featuring footage of the 3rd AD in the Gulf

War, and interviews with 3AD tankers.

50,000,000 Elvis Fans Can't Be Wrong

50,000,000 Elvis Fans Can't Be Wrong

Greatest hits album by Elvis Presley
Released November 13, 1959
Recorded September 1956 – June 1958
Genre Rock and roll
Label RCA Victor
Producer Steve Sholes
Elvis Presley chronology
A Date with Elvis
(1959) 50,000,000 Elvis Fans Can't Be Wrong
(1959) Elvis Is Back!
(1960)
Professional ratings
Review scores
Source Rating
Allmusic link
50,000,000 Elvis Fans Can't Be Wrong: Elvis' Gold Records - Volume 2 is the ninth album by Elvis Presley, issued on RCA Victor Records (LPM 2075) in November 1959. It is a compilation of hit singles released in 1958 and 1959 by Presley, from two recording sessions in June 1958 at RCA Studios in Nashville and three at Radio Recorders in Hollywood. The album peaked at #31 on the Billboard Top Pop Albums chart, and is considered to be one of the most successful and influential compilation albums of all time. It was certified Gold on 11/1/1966 and Platinum on 3/27/1992 by the R. I. A. A.
Contents

Content

Gold Records Vol. 2 comprises every single, both A-sides and B-sides, released by Presley during 1958 and 1959, with the exception of "Hard Headed Woman" backed with "Don't Ask Me Why," both of which having been previously issued on King Creole. The singles all made the Top Five on the Billboard Hot 100, and the b-sides all charted in the Top 40 independently of the hit sides. In the 1950s, a gold record awarded for a single referred to sales of one million units, different from the definition in use by the late 1970s for albums, where a gold record came to mean sales of 500,000 units. Exact sales figures from the RIAA for each record, however, are difficult to confirm.

The original 1984 compact disc issue in reprocessed (fake) stereo sound was quickly withdrawn and reissued in original monophonic. The July 15, 1997 reissue doubles the number of tracks to 20, adding the b-side "Playing for Keeps" from a single issued on Elvis' first singles compilation. The remaining bonus tracks derive from albums and EP singles released in the decade, with "Peace in the Valley" released on both EP and the Christmas LP. The bonus tracks are interspersed within the original tracks, with the running order to the album substantially altered. The album was reissued again with the bonus tracks removed and the original running order restored.

Although RCA executive Steve Sholes was the in-house A&R man for Presley, and nominally in charge of his recording sessions at RCA, accounts by Presley historian Peter Guralnick and Presley discographer Ernst Mikael Jorgensen indicate that Presley himself acted as the producer for his RCA sessions in the 1950s.

The unified Billboard Hot 100 singles chart was not created until August, 1958. Chart positions for records prior to this date would be taken from the Best Sellers In Stores chart, although early measurement of rock and roll records also came from the Most Played In Jukeboxes chart. Chart position for bonus album tracks taken from Billboard Top Pop Albums.

Homage

The famous cover photo, of multiple images of Elvis wearing the gold lamé suit designed by Nudie's of Hollywood, has been copied many times. Album covers so inspired include:

Phil Ochs' Greatest Hits album of 1970; not a "greatest hits" album at all but consisting of new original material, ironically subtitled "50 Phil Ochs Fans Can't Be Wrong!"

Mark E. Smith ponders the maths
The 1983 album by Rod Stewart, Body Wishes.
The Elvis Costello & The Attractions bootleg album of the same name from the 1980s.
Blues Traveler's more modest 1,000,000 People Can't Be Wrong of 1994.
Blumfeld's second studio album L'Etat Et Moi from 1995.
The Fall's compilation 50,000 Fall Fans Can't Be Wrong from 2004.
100,000,000 Bon Jovi Fans Can't Be Wrong, also from 2004.
50,000,000 Soulwax Fans Can't Be Wrong from 2005.
The meme has also been adopted to other media, such as:
The second album by the group Dread Zeppelin, which is fronted by an Elvis impersonator, from 1991 is titled 5,000,000 in reference to this album; the footnote says "Tortelvis Fans Can't Be Wrong. " The cover more obviously spoofs Led Zeppelin's fourth album.
The title used verbatim in the lyrics to "The Thanksgiving Song", by Adam Sandler in 1993.
The 1997 documentary by Joe Franklin 50,000,000 Joe Franklin Fans Can't Be Wrong.
Mindless Self Indulgence's song "You'll Rebel To Anything (As Long As It's Not Challenging)" from their 2005 album of the same name contains the lyrics, "you're telling me that 50,000,000 screaming fans are never wrong, I'm telling you that 50,000,000 screaming fans are fucking morons".
Die! Die! Die!'s self-titled debut features a song named "Franz (17 Die! Die! Die! Fans Can't Be Wrong)" in 2006.
Steven Pastis, author of comic strip Pearls Before Swine, released a collection in 2010 titled "50,000,000 Pearls Fans Can't Be Wrong. "

Title meanings

The cover to Welcome To New York, a 1970s Rolling Stones bootleg, is a cartoon by William Stout, showing the Stones against a grafitted wall which includes the phrase "50,000,000 flies can't be wrong - eat shit!"
The title is itself a reference to the hit song of 1927, "Fifty Million Frenchmen Can't Be Wrong", by Willie Raskin, Billy Rose, and Fred Fisher, most notably performed by Sophie Tucker. It is also supposed to be an estimate of the number of singles that Presley sold worldwide by late 1959.
Its evolution of the phrase into a snowclone - as expressed in the Simpsons pastiche "Fifty million smokers can't be wrong,"

for example - ironically ridicules argumentum ad populum, the misconception that popularity or consensus equals validity.

Track listing

Chart positions for LPs and EPs from Billboard Top Pop Albums chart; positions for singles from Billboard Pop Singles chart

Side one

Track Recorded Catalogue Release Date Chart Peak Song Title Writer(s) Time
1. 6/10/58 47-7506b 3/10/59 #4 I Need Your Love Tonight Bix Reichner and Sid Wayne 2:04
2. 9/6/57 47-7150 1/7/58 #1 Don't Jerry Leiber and Mike Stoller 2:48
3. 2/1/58 47-7240 4/1/58 #2 Wear My Ring Around Your Neck Bert Carroll and Moody Russell 2:13
4. 9/6/57 47-7600b 6/23/59 #12 My Wish Came True Ivory Joe Hunter 2:33
5. 6/11/58 47-7410b 10/21/58 #8 I Got Stung David Hill and Aaron Schroeder 1:49

Side two

Track Recorded Catalogue Release Date Chart Peak Song Title Writer(s) Time
1. 2/23/57 47-7410 10/21/58 #4 One Night Dave Bartholomew, Pearl King, Anita Steiman 2:29
2. 6/10/58 47-7600 6/23/59 #1 A Big Hunk O' Love Aaron Schroeder and Sidney Wyche 2:12
3. 2/23/57 47-7150b 1/7/58 #8 I Beg of You Rose Marie McCoy and Cliff Owens 1:50
4. 6/10/58 47-7506 3/10/59 #2 (Now And Then There's) A Fool Such As I Bill Trader 2:36
5. 2/1/58 47-7240b 4/1/58 #15 Doncha' Think It's Time Luther Dixon and Clyde Otis 1:54

1997 reissue with bonus tracks

Track Recorded Original LP/EP Issue Catalogue Release Date Chart Peak Song Title Writer(s) Time
1. 6/10/58 47-7600 6/23/59 #1 A Big Hunk O' Love Aaron Schroeder and Sidney Wyche 2:12
2. 9/6/57 47-7600b 6/23/59 #12 My Wish Came True Ivory Joe Hunter 2:33

3. 6/10/58 47-7506 3/10/59 #2 (Now And Then There's) A Fool Such As I Bill Trader 2:36
4. 6/10/58 47-7506b 3/10/59 #4 I Need Your Love Tonight Bix Reichner and Sid Wayne 2:04
5. 9/6/57 47-7150 1/7/58 #1 Don't Jerry Leiber and Mike Stoller 2:48
6. 2/23/57 47-7150b 1/7/58 #8 I Beg of You Rose Marie McCoy and Cliff Owens 1:50
7. 9/7/57 Elvis' Christmas Album LOC 1035 10/15/57 #1 Santa Bring My Baby Back (To Me) Aaron Schroeder and Claude DeMetrius 1:54
8. 9/7/57 Elvis' Christmas Album LOC 1035 10/15/57 #1 Santa Claus Is Back In Town Jerry Leiber and Mike Stoller 2:22
9. 1/57 Loving You LPM 1515 7/1/57 #1 Party Jessie Mae Robinson 1:26
10. 9/2/56 Elvis LPM 1382 10/19/56 #1 Paralyzed Otis Blackwell and Elvis Presley 2:23
11. 2/23/57 47-7410 10/21/58 #4 One Night Dave Bartholomew, Pearl King, Anita Steiman 2:29
12. 6/11/58 47-7410b 10/21/58 #8 I Got Stung David Hill and Aaron Schroeder 1:49
13. 1/23/58 King Creole LPM 1884 9/19/58 #2 King Creole Jerry Leiber and Mike Stoller 2:08
14. 2/1/58 47-7240 4/1/58 #2 Wear My Ring Around Your Neck Bert Carroll and Moody Russell 2:13
15. 2/1/58 47-7240b 4/1/58 #15 Don'cha Think It's Time Luther Dixon and Clyde Otis 1:54
16. 1/13/57 Loving You LPM 1515 7/1/57 #1 Mean Woman BluesClaude DeMetrius 2:15
17. 9/1/56 47-6800b 1/4/57 #21 Playing for Keeps Stan Kesler 2:50
18. 1/15/58 47-7280 6/10/58 #1 Hard Headed Woman Claude DeMetrius 1:53
19. 1/12/57 Loving You LPM 1515 7/1/57 #1 Got a Lot o' Livin' to Do Aaron Schroeder and Ben Weisman 2:31
20. 1/13/57 Peace in the Valley EPA 4054 4/57 #3 (There'll Be) Peace in the Valley (For Me) Thomas A. Dorsey 3:22

A Date with Elvis

A Date with Elvis

A Date with Elvis

Compilation album by Elvis Presley
Released July 24, 1959
Recorded June 1954-April 1957
Genre Rock
Length 22:58
Label RCA Victor
Elvis Presley chronology
For LP Fans Only
(1959) A Date with Elvis
(1959) Elvis' Gold Records - Volume 2
(1959)
Professional ratings
Review scores
Source Rating
Allmusic
A Date with Elvis is the eighth album by Elvis Presley, issued on RCA Victor Records (LPM 2011) in July 1959. It is a compilation of previously unreleased material from an August 1956 recording session at 20th Century Fox Stage One, two from Radio Recorders in Hollywood, and multiple sessions at Sun Studio. The album reached #32 on the Billboard Top Pop Albums chart. It is currently out of print.
Contents

Content

After Presley's induction into the army on March 24, 1958, RCA and his manager, Colonel Tom Parker, were faced with the prospect of keeping his name before the public for two years with no possibility of live performances, no movies, and with few unissued marketable recordings in the vault. A recording session was arranged for two days in June, which yielded enough items for five more single sides, singles being the commercial focus for rock and roll in the 1950s. Four of those tracks would be issued on 45s in 1958 and 1959 during his absence while doing military service.

Presley, however, also did well in the albums market, all but one of his previous seven LPs charting no lower than #3, and RCA wished to continue promoting albums by Presley given his sales record. Much of Presley's material had not been released on LP, and for this album RCA collected material previously unavailable on album. Like its predecessor For LP Fans Only, this album featured tracks that had been issued on Sun Records with limited release, and were almost impossible to locate beyond certain parts of the south. The remaining five tracks derived from three different EPs issued in 1956 and 1957.

Even by the standards of the late 1950s and early 1960s, where long-playing albums often ran to only about 35 minutes, this was a very short album at twenty-three minutes, and as such became the lowest charting Presley LP of the decade. RCA would squeeze one more album in 1959 out of previously issued material, the second singles collection, but it too would be a lower seller by previous standard. Presley would return from overseas in 1960 to commence proper recording again. this album also folds out to be a calendar for the year 1960.

A different version of the album, duplicating six tracks from the American release, but expanding the track list to a healthy fourteen, was issued in Australia on vinyl in September 1959. Compact Disc versions of the album by RCA have been done in several worldwide releases Reissue and bonus track (only Germany and Other Country in Eu but in US don't have bonus)And Australia (except For LP fans Only) on compact disc in 1989. Audiophile CD recordings are available on import in the United States, including the version from Japan in 2005.

Collective personnel

Elvis Presley – vocals, guitar, bass
Scotty Moore – guitar
Dudley Brooks – piano
Mike Stoller – piano, backing vocals
Bill Black – bass
D. J. Fontana – drums
Johnny Bernero – drums
The Jordanaires – backing vocals

Track listing

Chart positions for LPs and EPs from Billboard Top Pop Albums chart; peak position for EPA 4114 from EP chart commenced October 1957; positions for singles from Billboard Country & Western chart

Side one

Track Recorded Original EP Issue Catalogue Release Date Chart Peak Song Title Writer(s) Time

1. 7/5/54 Sun 209b 7/19/54 Blue Moon of Kentucky Bill Monroe 2:02
2. 4/30/57 Jailhouse Rock EPA 4114 10/57 Young And Beautiful Aaron Schroeder and Abner Silver 2:02
3. 4/30/57 Jailhouse Rock EPA 4114 10/57 R&B #14 (You're So Square) Baby I Don't Care Jerry Leiber and Mike Stoller 1:51
4. 11?12/54 Sun 215 12/28/54 Milkcow Blues Boogie Kokomo Arnold 2:38
5. 2/5/55 Sun 217 4/10/55 C&W #5 Baby Let's Play House Arthur Gunter 2:15

Side two

Track Recorded Original EP Issue Catalogue Release Date Chart Peak Song Title Writer(s) Time

1. 9/10/54 Sun 210 9/25/54 Good Rockin' Tonight Roy Brown 2:12
2. 1/19/57 Just For You EPA 4041 4/57 #16 Is It So Strange Faron Young 2:28
3. 8/24/56 Love Me Tender EPA 4006 11/56 We're Gonna Move Vera Matson and Elvis Presley 2:30
4. 4/30/57 Jailhouse Rock EPA 4114 10/57 I Want To Be Free Jerry Leiber and Mike Stoller 2:12
5. 7/11/55 Sun 223b 8/6/55 C&W #1 I Forgot to Remember to Forget Stan Kesler and Charlie Feathers 2:28

Australia And Germany Reissue And Bonus Track

Track Recorded Original LP Issue Catalogue Release Date Chart Peak Song Title Writer(s) Time

1. 7/5/54 Sun 209b 7/19/54 Blue Moon of Kentucky Bill Monroe 2:02
2. 11/12/54 Sun 215 12/28/54 Milkcow Blues

Boogie Kokomo Arnold 2:38
3. 2/5/55 Sun 217 4/10/55 C&W #5 Baby Let's Play House Arthur Gunter 2:15
4. 9/11/54 Sun 217b 3/5/55 I Don't Care If the Sun Don't Shine Mack David 2:27
5. 1/31/56 Elvis Presley LPM 1254 3/23/56 #1 Tutti Frutti Dorothy LaBostrie and Richard Penniman 1:58
6. 1/31/56 Elvis Presley LPM 1254 3/23/56 #1 I'm Gonna Sit Right Down and Cry (Over You) Howard Biggs and Joe Thomas 2:01
7. 1/10/56 Elvis Presley LPM 1254 3/23/56 #1 I Got A Woman Ray Charles and Renald Richard 2:23
8. 9/11/54 Sun 210 9/25/54 Good Rockin' Tonight Roy Brown 2:12
9. 1/19/57 Just For You EPA 4041 4/57 #16 Is It So Strange Faron Young 2:28
10. 8/24/56 Love Me Tender EPA 4006 11/56 #22 We're Gonna Move Vera Matson and Elvis Presley 2:30
11. 8/19/54 Elvis Presley LPM 1254 3/23/56 #1 Blue Moon Richard Rodgers and Lorenz Hart 2:31
12. 9/11/54 Elvis Presley LPM 1254 3/23/56 #1 Just Because Sydney Robin, Bob Shelton, Joe Shelton 2:32
13. 1/30/56 Elvis Presley LPM 1254 3/23/56 #1 One-Sided Love Affair Bill Campbell 2:09
14. 9/4/56 Love Me Tender EPA 4006 11/56 #22 Let Me Vera Matson and Elvis Presley 2:08

A Little Less Conversation

A Little Less Conversation

"A Little Less Conversation"

The original picture sleeve of the 1968 single.
Single by Elvis Presley
B-side "Almost in Love"
Released September 1968
Format 7" 45 RPM
Recorded 7 March 1968
Genre Rock
Length 2:28
Label RCA

Writer(s) Mac Davis, Billy Strange
Producer Elvis Presley
Elvis Presley singles chronology
"Let Yourself Go"
(1968) "A Little Less Conversation"
(1968) "If I Can Dream"
(1968)
"A Little Less Conversation" is a song written by Mac Davis and Billy Strange that was originally written for, and performed by, American rock and roll icon Elvis Presley for the 1968 film Live a Little, Love a Little. When the song was released as a single with "Almost in Love" as the B-side, it became a minor hit in the United States. A 2002 remix of the song by Junkie XL became a world-wide hit, topping the singles charts in nine countries and was awarded certifications in ten countries by 2003 (see chart positions and certifications sections below).

The song has made numerous appearances in popular culture and has been covered by several artists.

Original recordings

"A Little Less Conversation" was recorded on 7 March 1968 at Western Recorders in Hollywood, California. The song was not released on an LP until November 1970, when it was included on the RCA Camden budget label LP Almost in Love. There are several different takes that were made of the song in the session on 7 March. The single version used take 16, which was also used for the soundtrack of the film. The version released on the Almost In Love album is take 10, which is 1 second longer in duration.

The musicians on the 7 March recording session included Hal Blaine, drums; Al Casey, guitar; Larry Knechtel, bass; and Don Randi, piano.

Re-recording for 1968 television special

In June 1968, Elvis Presley re-recorded the song for the soundtrack of his 1968 comeback special, with the intent of performing it during the program, possibly as part of the show's medley of film songs featured. Ultimately, it was decided not to use this recording, and the song was dropped from the planned special. The newer version transposed the key of A major recording of three months earlier into E major and featured a vocal, now with heavy reverb, in which Elvis performed an octave leap between verses, with backup vocals from The Blossoms. This new version was not officially released by RCA until the 1990s.

Chart performance

Remakes and remixes

Junkie XL/JXL

Following the song's use in the 2001 film Ocean's Eleven, it was remixed by Junkie XL (also known as Tom Holkenborg). The techno remix featured Elvis with a lower voice, and added emphasis to the 1968 guitars, horns and a funky drums sound. Holkenborg is the first artist to receive authorization from the Elvis Presley Estate to remix an Elvis Presley song. The techno version of the song became a No. 1 hit in Britain in 2002. The song also became No. 1 in Japan and Australia.

In 2002, the TV special version of "A Little Less Conversation," remixed by Junkie XL was used for a 2002 World Cup advertising campaign. A single, credited to "Elvis vs. JXL," was issued and went on to become a Number 1 hit in over 20 countries.

At about the same time, a compilation of Presley's U. S. Number 1 chart hits, entitled ELV1S 30 No. 1 Hits, was being prepared for release. At the last minute, "A Little Less Conversation (Remix Version)" was added as the album's 31st track just before its release in October 2002. The full 6:09 version was edited slightly and extended to 6:22, and this version was featured on the US version of JXL's 2004 album Radio JXL: A Broadcast from the Computer Hell Cabin.

Covers and other versions

An uptempo eurodance remix was recorded by CJ Crew, appearing on the 2002 dance compilation Dancemania Speed 10. There are three very exclusive releases in Spanish, the film Live a Little, Love a Little and two mixes played by Marco T. , a Colombian Rockabilly musician. In addition, Dolph Lundgren performed this song at Melodifestivalen 2010. In Glee, Will Schuester (Matthew Morrison) sings a combination of a Spanish and English version of the song.

In popular culture

The song has made a generous impact on the popular culture of both the 20th and 21st centuries. The song has made appearances on at least four TV shows, two movie trailers, and eight films—the most notable being the 2001 remake of Ocean's Eleven.

The remix version by JXL subsequently appeared:

as the title song for the NBC TV series Las Vegas
in the films Jackass Number Two, Shark Tale, Lilo & Stitch 2: Stitch Has a Glitch, Percy Jackson & the Olympians: The Lightning Thief, Megamind, Super Bowlin' and Next.
in the Smallville episode "Heat" when Clark Kent is discovering how to use his heat vision
in the Everybody Loves Raymond episode "Robert's Wedding" for newlyweds Robert and Amy's first dance.
Presley's original "A Little Less Conversation" has been used in several political campaigns as a message of more accomplishment and less talk. The first time the song was used in political campaign was in 2003 by former Vermont Governor Howard Dean. In 2004, Democratic presidential nominee Senator John Kerry used the song during his campaign. George W. Bush also used the song as the anthem of his reelection campaign in 2004. Furthermore, in 2008 in Colorado Springs, Sarah Palin and John McCain emerged while "A Little Less Conversation" was playing in the background.

It has also been used in various advertisements, including the 2012 BMW ad, linked to BMW's sponsorship of the London 2012 Olympics.

Charts and certifications

Chart positions

Weekly charts

End of year charts

Chart (2002)	Peak position
Australian Top 100 Singles	3
Australian Dance Singles	1

End of decade positions

Certifications

Region	Certification	Sales/shipments
Australia (ARIA)	2× Platinum	140,000^
Austria (IFPI Austria)	Gold	15,000x
Belgium (BEA)	Gold	25,000*
France (SNEP)	Silver	125,000*
New Zealand (RIANZ)	Gold	7,500*
Norway (IFPI Norway)	2× Platinum	20,000*
Sweden (GLF)	Platinum	30,000x
Switzerland (IFPI Switzerland)	Platinum	40,000x
United Kingdom (BPI)	Platinum	600,000^
United States (RIAA)	Gold	500,000^

*sales figures based on certification alone
^shipments figures based on certification alone
xunspecified figures based on certification alone

A Star Is Born (1976 film)

A Star Is Born (1976 film)

A Star Is Born

VHS cover
Directed by Frank Pierson
Produced by Jon Peters
Barbra Streisand
Written by Frank Pierson
William A. Wellman
Robert Carson
John Gregory Dunne
Joan Didion
Starring Barbra Streisand
Kris Kristofferson
Gary Busey
Music by Kenny Ascher
Rupert Holmes
Roger Kellaway
Kenny Loggins
Leon Russell
Paul Williams
Barbra Streisand
Cinematography Robert Surtees

Distributed by Warner Bros.
Release date(s)
Running time 140 minutes
Country United States
Language English
Budget $6 million
Box office $80,000,000

A Star Is Born is a 1976 American rock music musical film telling the story of a young woman, played by Barbra Streisand who enters show business, and meets and falls in love with an established male star, played by Kris Kristofferson, only to find her career ascending while his goes into decline. It is a remake of two earlier versions – the 1937 version was a drama starring Janet Gaynor and Fredric March, and the 1954 version was a musical film starring Judy Garland and James Mason. This version was the highest-grossing of the three films.

Plot

Esther Hoffman, an aspiring female singer/songwriter meets John Norman Howard, a famous, successful and self-destructive male singer/songwriter, whom, after a series of coincidental meetings, she finally start dating. Believing in her talent, John gives her a helping hand and her career begins to eclipse his.

Writer and director Frank Pierson, in his New West magazine article "My Battles With Barbra and Jon" summarized it this way:

"An actress is a little more than a woman, an actor a little less than a man (Oscar Wilde) . . . The woman in our story is ambitious to become a star, but it is not necessary: it can make her happier and richer, but she could give it all away and not be a better or worse person. With stardom she is only a little more than a woman. For the man, his career is his defense against a self-destructive part of himself that has led him into outrageous bursts of drunkenness, drugs, love affairs, fights and adventures that have made him a legend. His career is also what gives him his sense of who he is. Without it, he is lost and confused; his demons eat him alive. That's why he is a little less than a man. And it is not that her success galls him, or that she wins over him; the tragedy is that all her love is not enough to keep alive a man who has lost what he measures his manhood with. "[this quote needs a citation]

And so the conclusion is measured by the theme. He takes his life in the mistaken belief that he will then not drag her down with him.

Cast

Barbra Streisand as Esther Hoffman
Kris Kristofferson as John Norman Howard
Gary Busey as Bobbie Ritchie
Oliver Clark as Gary Danziger
Venetta Fields as One (of the Oreos)
Clydie King as Two (of the Oreos)
Marta Heflin as Quentin
Bill Graham as Himself
Rita Coolidge as Herself
Tony Orlando as Himself
M. G. Kelly as DJ Bebe Jesus
Susan Richardson as Groupie
Production

Directed by Frank Pierson, the film updates the original story and screenplay of William A. Wellman and Robert Carson with additional contributions by Pierson, John Gregory Dunne and Joan Didion. It also features Gary Busey and Sally Kirkland. Venetta Fields and Clydie King perform as Streisand's backing vocalists "The Oreos". Kristofferson's wife Rita Coolidge and Tony Orlando appear briefly as themselves.

The earlier films had portrayed the behind-the-scenes world of Hollywood film making. However, this version adapted the story to the music business. For example, the 1937 and 1954 films each portrayed the lead female character winning an Academy Award, while the 1976 version depicted the heroine winning a Grammy Award instead.

A Star Is Born was co-produced by Streisand and her then-partner Jon Peters for Barwood Films and Warner Brothers with Peters as the main producer and Streisand as executive producer. Among the actors considered for the male lead were Neil Diamond and Marlon Brando. Both Streisand and Peters wanted Elvis Presley for the role: they met with Elvis and discussed the film, and he was interested in taking on the part, thinking it would revive his film career. Elvis' manager, Colonel Tom Parker, insisted that Elvis have top billing and asked for a substantial sum of money for the role, even though he had not had an acting role since 1969, and people were unsure of what kind of box office draw he would be, which essentially ended Elvis's involvement with the project. Parker also did not want to have Elvis portrayed as having a show business career that was in decline. This in fact was far from the truth, with Elvis playing to packed auditoriums wherever he toured in the States.

The film cost around $6 million to produce. Its soundtrack album was also an international success reaching number 1 in many countries and selling nearly 15 million copies worldwide. It featured the ballad "Evergreen (Love Theme from A Star Is Born)", which became one of the biggest hits of Streisand's career, spending three weeks at number one in the United States, and peaking at number three in the United Kingdom. The filming locations included many in Arizona such as downtown Tucson, Tucson Community Center, Sonoita and Tempe.

A costume note was that Streisand's character's (Esther Hoffman Howard) clothing used in the movie was straight out of Streisand's own closet. The film was choreographed by David Winters of West Side Story fame, who worked closely with Streisand to perfect the movie's dancing sequences.

Reception

Critical reception

A Star Is Born maintains a 38% "Rotten" rating on Rotten Tomatoes. Roger Ebert gave the film two and 1/2 stars.

Awards

The film won the Academy Award for Best Original Song for "Evergreen" with the award shared by its songwriters, Streisand and Paul Williams, and was also nominated in the categories of Best Cinematography (Robert Surtees), Best Sound (Robert Knudson, Dan Wallin, Robert Glass and Tom Overton) and Original Music Score (Roger Kellaway).

It won five Golden Globe Awards for Best Motion Picture – Musical or Comedy, Best Actress – Motion Picture Musical or Comedy (Streisand), Best Actor – Motion Picture Musical or Comedy (Kristofferson), Best Original Score (Paul Williams and Kenny Ascher) and Best Original Song, (Streisand and Williams for "Evergreen").

In the two previous versions, Gaynor and Garland were each depicted on screen as winning an Oscar, yet neither won for their film in real life (though both had won an Oscar before, as did Streisand). In this film, Streisand is instead depicted as winning a Grammy, and in real life the film's song "Evergreen" won her both a Grammy (for Song of the Year) and an Oscar.

According to at least one Streisand biography[vague], unhappy with a few of Frank Pierson's scenes, Streisand later directed them herself (a claim also made for 1979's "The Main Event"), adding to the rumours that she and Pierson clashed constantly during production.

Home media

In 2006, the Region 1 DVD was released in North America in 5. 1 dolby sound with extras which include, a full length commentary by Barbra Streisand, 16 minutes of never before seen and additional footage and original wardrobe test. In 2007 the Region 2 DVD with the same extras was released in Germany. In 2008 the Region 4 DVD was released in Australia, the content of which appears to be the same as the Region 1 edition. The DVD has yet to be released in any other region.

To date, Warner Bros. has no official plans for a Blu-Ray release of the film, despite rumors of Streisand's direct involvement in same.

Soundtrack

The soundtrack to the movie, performed by Barbra Streisand and Kris Kristofferson, was successful, reaching the number-one spot on the Billboard 200 chart for five weeks and eventually sold more than 4 million copies with a reported 10 million copies world wide. The import version of the CD adds the Spanish version of Evergreen as a bonus track.

The track listing of the album is as follows:

"Watch Closely Now" – 3:49
"Queen Bee" – 3:55
"Everything" – 3:50
"Lost Inside of You" – 2:54
"Hellacious Acres" – 2:58
"Evergreen (Love Theme from A Star Is Born)" – 3:04

"The Woman in the Moon" – 4:49
"I Believe in Love" – 3:13
"Crippled Crow" – 3:30
"Finale: With One More Look at You/Watch Closely Now" – 7:43
"Reprise: Evergreen (Love Theme from A Star Is Born)" – 1:46
"Evergreen (Love theme from A Star Is Born)"- (Spanish version)- 3:05-(Import version only)
It should be noted that the songs that appear on the soundtrack are in some cases alternate (live) and studio recordings that do not appear in the film.

Albert Goldman

Albert Goldman

For the Trotskyist and labor movement lawyer, see Albert Goldman (politician).
Albert Harry Goldman (April 15, 1927 – March 28, 1994) was an American professor and author.

Goldman wrote about the culture and personalities of the American music industry both in books and as a contributor to magazines. He is best known for his bestselling book on Lenny Bruce and his controversial biographies of Elvis Presley and John Lennon.

Early life

Goldman was born in Dormont, Pennsylvania and raised in Mount Lebanon, Pennsylvania.

Academic career

Goldman briefly studied theater at the Carnegie Institute of Technology before serving in the U. S. Navy from 1945-1946. Although he did not possess a bachelor's degree, he earned a master's degree in English from the University of Chicago in 1950. While enrolled in the doctoral program at Columbia University, Goldman taught literature courses at the City College of New York. He completed his Ph. D in 1961 with a dissertation on Thomas de Quincey. Goldman argued that de Quincey had plagiarized most of his acclaimed journalism from lesser-known writers; the dissertation was subsequently published by Southern

Illinois University Press in 1965. From 1963 to 1972, Goldman was an adjunct associate professor of English at Columbia; among his course offerings was the University's first class on popular culture.

Written work

Bestseller dealing with Lenny Bruce

Goldman's breakthrough bestseller, Ladies and Gentlemen - Lenny Bruce!!! won praise from the likes of Norman Mailer and Pauline Kael, who called the book "brilliant. " The book was largely positive in its appraisal of Bruce's talent, though it was attacked by many of Bruce's friends for allegedly distorting his character and for claims that Bruce had had homosexual experiences. Goldman had done legal work for Bruce before the latter's death.

Elvis Presley biography

Goldman's 1981 biography Elvis was much more controversial. In this book, Goldman drew on more than four years' research into Elvis Presley's life. But for many fans and some critics, his research was undermined by his intense personal dislike of Presley. For instance, Goldman dismissed Presley as a plagiarist who never did anything of note after his first records at Sun Records, insisting that he was inferior as an artist to Little Richard and other early rock'n'roll singers. He also portrayed Presley as nearly insane, using stories that some might see as innocuous (such as Presley taking his friends halfway across the country to buy them peanut-butter sandwiches) to "prove" that the singer had lost his grip on reality. On the other hand, the book includes several newly discovered facts. For instance, in the course of his research, Goldman discovered that Presley's manager, Colonel Tom Parker, was not a Southerner but a native of Holland. Parker had successfully covered this up to the degree that Presley himself allegedly never learned of it. (The book is harshest on Parker out of all the figures in Presley's life with whom it deals.) Furthermore, the book critically deals with the singer's weight problems, his diet, his choice of performing costumes, and his sexual appetites and peculiarities. The author even suggests that Presley's promiscuity masked latent homosexuality. Discussing Presley's personal life, Goldman concludes: "Elvis was a pervert, a voyeur. " Some critics found comments like these overly biased and judgmental.

In his review of the book in the Village Voice, rock critic and

Elvis Presley scholar Greil Marcus wrote: "The real significance of Goldman's 'Elvis' is its attempt at cultural genocide . . . The torrents of hate that drive this book are unrelieved. " He particularly objected to Goldman's constant slurs against Presley's background, including his characterization of Presley's parents as "the original Beverly Hillbillies" without bothering to include the explanatory context that the situation comedy was actually the story of suddenly rich innocents, as Presley's parents themselves were, who were trying to cope with the fear that even money and social access would never be enough to enable them to belong. "It is Goldman's purpose to entirely discredit Elvis Presley, the culture that produced him, and the culture he helped create — to altogether dismiss and condemn, in other words, not just Elvis Presley, but the white working-class South from which he came, and the pop world which emerged in his wake. " However, Marcus also admits that Goldman has significantly shown that "Elvis Presley built his own world. . . where the promise was that every fear, pain, doubt, and wish could be washed away with money, sex, drugs, and the bought approval of yes-men. . . " And the reviewer also admits that the book, "as no book on Elvis Presley before it, . . . has been taken seriously. Despite some partially negative or carping notices, the reviewing media have accepted the book as it presents itself—as the last book we will need about Elvis Presley. " In 2006, BLENDER Magazine called Elvis a "muckraking biography", stating that Goldman dealt with everything about Elvis Presley but his music.

Other critics liked the book. Jonathan Yardley of the Washington Post called it a "nasty book, written in spectacularly execrable prose, but the view of Presley that it expressed dovetailed in many instances with my own, and in spite of itself I found things in it to admire. "

According to Rolling Stone, October 21, 1981, Elvis "is a poignant book, the result of Goldman's winning the trust and confidence of hundreds of sources, including many of Elvis' closest friends. It is also an intimate look at a side of Elvis that few even suspected existed. Many people will find some of the revelations unpleasant and view them as a needless and harmful invasion of privacy. Yet, such revelations comprise a truth about modern American heroism and success. The fact is that somehow inherent in Elvis' great fame as an American ideal and idol is a contradiction that was the seed of destruction. "

Lamar Fike, the Presley insider and former member of the Memphis Mafia, who introduced Goldman to many of his sources, recalled: "The problem was Albert's personality. At first, he liked Elvis. But

later, he started disliking him. And by the end of (writing) the book, I think he hated him. I said, 'Albert, you can't do this. ' But I couldn't stop him. "
Defending himself against his critics, Goldman told an interviewer: "People were scandalized by my use of humor and ridicule in (the Elvis biography). Elvis was someone they were accustomed to taking in a very sentimental way. But I feel he was a figure of the most bizarre and grotesque character. . . . The humor is a mode of perception. Of making things vivid. "

Book on Bruce Lee

In 1982, Goldman wrote a very unflattering article on actor Bruce Lee which was divided into two parts for Penthouse Magazine (Jan, Feb 1983 issues).

Second book on Presley

In 1990, Goldman published a second book, entitled Elvis: The Last 24 Hours, on the circumstances and events of Presley's death, arguing that the singer had committed suicide. The book drew some attention for its sensational thesis but was largely ignored.

The Lives of John Lennon

Goldman's next biography arguably aroused even more controversy than the Elvis biography. In The Lives of John Lennon, a product of years of research and hundreds of interviews with many of Lennon's friends, acquaintances, servants and musicians, Goldman describes John Lennon as both talented and neurotic. The book reveals a very personal side of the musician who was prone to faults, such as anger, violence, drug abuse, adultery, and indecisiveness, but who was also a leader of "Peace and Love. " It deals with Lennon's childhood and the impact others had on the life of the sensitive little boy, among them his aunt, Mimi Smith, his father, Fred Lennon, and Johnny Dykins. The author implies that strong women ruined Lennon, starting with Smith, and that he was later being held prisoner by his wife, Yoko Ono. Centering on the mistakes or mean things the musician did, Goldman made many controversial allegations, among them the charge that he may have had something to do with the death of his friend Stuart Sutcliffe, an early member of The Beatles. The author also says that Lennon had a homosexual affair with The Beatles' manager, Brian Epstein, whom Goldman characterizes as a dishonest, incompetent businessman who hid behind the image of a "gentleman". Half of the book covers the personality of Lennon's wife, Yoko Ono, who is portrayed in a very bad light; Goldman alleges that, among other things, she hated Paul McCartney, neglected her children and brainwashed and pulled Lennon away from everyone who ever meant something to him. Goldman also alleged that the two carried on constant affairs throughout their marriage and he substantially revealed that no record exists of the phone calls Yoko Ono claims to have made to McCartney and Mimi Smith the night Lennon was murdered.

Concerning Goldman's account of Lennon's consumption of LSD, Luc Sante, in the New York Review of Books, said: "Goldman's background research was either slovenly or nonexistent. " The author replied:

What is the basis for this sweeping and defamatory assertion? Absolutely nothing save for my quoting only one book about LSD. Yet if Sante knew anything about drugs, he would recognize that the only serious problem about Lennon's consumption of LSD was one that has no literature; namely, the question of what effect this drug has upon a man who takes it every day, eating it 'like candy. '

Death

Goldman died on March 28, 1994 en route to London. He left unfinished a biography of Doors singer Jim Morrison.

Family

Goldman is survived by a daughter in her early thirties. Goldman never married the girl's mother (now deceased), who had no connection with their daughter.

In popular culture

U2 lead singer Bono referenced his disdain for Goldman in the song "God Part II" from the album Rattle and Hum:

"Don't believe in Goldman
His type [is] like a curse
Instant Karma's gonna get him
If I don't get him first"
The American television program Saturday Night Live had a season

14 sketch in which it was revealed that Albert Goldman, portrayed by Phil Hartman, was the fifth member of the Beatles, playing trompet, but the band, supported by Elvis Presley, decides to fire him, a task they leave to John, with Elvis backing him up, ostensibly fueling Goldmans lifelong hatred of the two.

Partial bibliography

The Mine and the Mint: Sources for the Writings of Thomas de Quincey (1965)
Freakshow;: The rocksoulbluesjazzsickjewblackhumorsexpoppsych gig and other scenes from the counter-culture (1971)
Ladies and Gentlemen – Lenny Bruce!! (1974)
Carnival in Rio (1978)
Grass Roots: Marijuana in America Today (1979)
Disco (1979)
Elvis (1981)
The Lives of John Lennon (1988)
Elvis: The Last 24 Hours (1990)
Sound Bites (1992)
Freakshow : Misadventures in the Counterculture, 1959–1971 (2001) – posthumous collection

All Shook Up

All Shook Up

For other uses, see All Shook Up .
"All Shook Up"

"All Shook Up" single
Single by Elvis Presley
B-side "That's When Your Heartaches Begin"
Released March 22, 1957
Recorded January 12 1957
Genre Rock and roll
Length 1:57
Label RCA
Writer(s) Otis Blackwell and Elvis Presley
Certification (US) RCA 47-6870 (45) 20-6870 (78)
Elvis Presley singles chronology
"Too Much"
(1957) "All Shook Up"

(1957) "(Let Me Be Your) Teddy Bear"
(1957)
"All Shook Up"

Single by Billy Joel
from the album Honeymoon in Vegas soundtrack
B-side "Wear My Ring Around My Neck", "Surrender"
Released 1992
Format CD single
Genre Rock
Writer(s) Otis Blackwell, Elvis Presley
Billy Joel singles chronology
"Shameless"
(1991) "All Shook Up"
(1992) "The River of Dreams"
(1993)
"All Shook Up" is a song recorded by Elvis Presley and published by Elvis Presley Music and composed by Otis Blackwell and Elvis Presley. The single topped the U. S. Pop chart on April 13, 1957, staying there for eight weeks. It also topped the R&B chart for four weeks, becoming Presley's second single to do so, and peaked at #3 on the country chart. It is certified 2X Platinum by the RIAA.
It was ranked #352 on Rolling Stone's list of the 500 Greatest Songs of All Time.
Contents

History

Blackwell wrote the song at the offices of Shalimar Music in 1956 after Al Stanton, one of Shalimar's owners, shaking a bottle of Pepsi at the time, suggested he write a song based around the phrase "all shook up".
According to Peter Guralnick the song has a different origin. In his book "Last Train To Memphis" he wrote that Elvis thought "All Shook Up" was a good phrase for a refrain. For this he received a co-writing credit, his last.
Elvis himself, during an interview on October 28, 1957, said: "I've never even had an idea for a song. Just once, maybe. I went to

bed one night, had quite a dream, and woke up all shook up. I phoned a pal and told him about it. By morning, he had a new song, 'All Shook Up'. "
David Hill was the first to record the song and release it a few weeks before Elvis on Aladdin Records under the name I'm All Shook Up.
Vicki Young recorded a different song with the same title, "(I'm) All Shook Up", on Capitol Records with Big Dave and His Orchestra, written by Bill Bellman and Hal Blaine in 1956.

Presley's Recording

On January 12, 1957, Presley recorded the song at Radio Recorders in Hollywood. Take 10 was selected for release, and in March the song entered Billboard's Top 100 chart at #25. Within three weeks it had knocked Perry Como's "Round and Round" off the top spot, and stayed there for eight consecutive weeks. The song also became Presley's first UK #1 single, remaining there for seven weeks. Sales of the single exceeded 2 million, and the song was named Billboard's Year End number one song for 1957.

Other recordings and performances

The Jeff Beck Group released a rendition of the song on the Beckola album (1969), with Rod Stewart on lead vocals and Ronnie Wood on bass.
The Beatles performed the song during their oldies jams during the Let It Be sessions in 1969.
Suzi Quatro recorded the song for her debut solo album Suzi Quatro in 1973. (The title of this album in Australia is Can the Can). Her recording of the song was released as a single in 1974 and peaked at number 85 on Billboard's Hot 100. Presley invited Quatro to Graceland, commenting that her version was the best since the original. Quatro declined the offer.
Anson Williams performed the song on the Happy Days TV show in the 1970s.
The Gyromatics covered the song in 1984 and can be heard in the film Roadhouse 66.
In 1991, Billy Joel recorded the song for the movie Honeymoon in Vegas, which also featured other Elvis Presley songs by various artists. Joel released the song as a single and it peaked at #92 in the US and #27 in the UK.
It was covered by Paul McCartney on his album Run Devil Run (1999), and by Cliff Richard on Wanted (2001).
It has also been recorded by Ry Cooder.
Tito Sotto, Vic Sotto, and Joey De Leon also used the tune of the

song for their sitcom Iskul Bukol.

Chart positions (Billy Joel version)

Chart (1992)	Peak position
Australian Singles Chart	54
Canadian Singles Chart	28
German Media Control Charts	52
Irish Singles Chart	23
New Zealand Singles Chart	26
UK Singles Chart	27
U. S. Billboard Hot 100	92
U. S. Billboard Hot Adult Contemporary Tracks	15

All Shook Up (musical)

All Shook Up (musical)

All Shook Up

Promotional poster for original Broadway production of All Shook Up
Lyrics various
Book Joe DiPietro
Basis Twelfth Night; Inspired by the music of Elvis Presley
Productions
2005 Broadway

2006 United States tour
All Shook Up is a 2004 American jukebox musical with Elvis Presley music, with a book by Joe DiPietro. The story is based on William Shakespeare's 1602 play Twelfth Night.

Production history

The musical had a developmental staging at the Goodspeed Musicals May 13-June 6, 2004, with most of the Broadway cast, except for Manley Pope in the lead role of Chad. Christopher Ashley directed, with choreography by Jody Moccia. The musical had a tryout in Chicago from December 19, 2004, through January 24, 2005. After the tryout, changes were made to the finale and to add "a more specific instrumental and vocal voice" for Chad.

The musical premiered on Broadway at the Palace Theatre on March 2, 2005 and closed on September 25, 2005 after 213 performances and 33 previews. Directed by Christopher Ashley, with choreography by Ken Roberson, the original Broadway cast included Cheyenne Jackson (Chad), Jenn Gambatese (Natalie Haller/"Ed"), and Jonathan Hadary (Jim Haller).

It has been performed in the USA at regional theatres, colleges and high schools.

Synopsis

Act One

Somewhere in the midwest, within a village that no one knew about, in the 1950s, Chad, a hip-swiveling, guitar-playing roustabout, is being released from prison ("Jailhouse Rock"). The warden doesn't appreciate a guy like Chad riding into town, playing his music and exciting the local women. With a sneer, Chad rides off.

In a nearby dreary little town, Natalie, a young mechanic, is dreaming of love and adventure. She yearns for one true love to take her away, but she doesn't realize that her best friend Dennis has a secret crush on her. Sitting in Sylvia's, the local honky tonk, the whole town sings the blues ("Heartbreak Hotel"). Natalie's widowed father Jim enters and joins in, until they're interrupted by the roar of a motorcycle: it is Chad, the most gorgeous man any of the women in this town have ever seen! Most swoon for him, but one unlucky girl has the displeasure of fainting before him, riding into town ("Roustabout"). Chad is in need of a mechanic and he's introduced to Natalie, who is instantly smitten ("One Night With You") and promises to fix his bike, wanting to hold him in her arms.

Chad asks about any excitement in town, but he's told that excitement is outlawed under the Mayor's strict rules: no tight pants, no public kissing, and no loud music. Chad, incensed, promises to breathe some life into this sad, little town and he touches a broken-down jukebox, and it immediately comes to life ("C'mon Everybody"). As Chad and Natalie go off to fix his bike, Mayor Matilda enters with Earl, the sheriff, and her son, Dean. Matilda scolds the citizens for dancing and singing, then goes off to find the root of this new found evil. As soon as she exits, Dean meets Lorraine, Sylvia's pretty African-American daughter, and the two share a nervous and flirtatious smile. Meanwhile, Natalie is working on Chad's motorcycle. She tells him of her dreams of the open road, and he tells her that she must follow her heart ("Follow That Dream").

After Chad exits, Natalie, in an attempt to look more girly, puts on the only dress she owns—a tattered old one she uses to clean car engines. Dennis runs into Natalie and he is about to tell her how he feels for her, when Chad enters and interrupts. Ignoring Natalie, Chad asks Dennis to become his sidekick and the overjoyed Dennis accepts. Suddenly, the beautiful and glamorous Sandra appears, and Chad is struck down with a case of hardcore love ("One Night With You"--reprise). Sandra is the owner of the local museum, and she bemoans the lack of culture in this depressing little town. Chad tries to smooth-talk her, but she resists ("Teddy Bear/Hound Dog").

Later that day, at Sylvia's Honky Tonk, Jim and Sylvia speak about the strange, lascivious behavior that seems to have befallen the town since Chad's arrival. Natalie enters in her greasy dress, and Lorraine has her change into one of her dresses—it is clean and cute and Natalie looks lovely. She rushes off in pursuit of Chad. Both Sylvia and Jim agree that at a certain point in life, it's better to be alone, when Sandra enters, and Jim instantly falls for her ("One Night With You"--reprise). Too nervous to speak to such a vision of beauty, he rushes out.

Dean enters to tell Lorraine that he thinks she's beautiful. Lorraine, thrilled, begins to teach him to dance ("That's All Right"). But Sylvia interrupts and insists that it's NOT all right for them to be together, and Dean rushes out. Dean meets Matilda at the bus stop, and she tells him that she's sending him back to military school on the next bus. Lorraine enters, and Dean tells her the terrible news: they're about to be separated. Hopelessly in love, Dean and Lorraine decide to run off together ("It's Now Or Never").

Dennis meets Natalie on the street and shows off his new hunting cap, which makes him feel like "one of the guys. " Natalie has a sudden inspiration and she grabs Dennis' hunting cap. Alone in the garage, she dresses like a leather-jacketed male roustabout ("Love Me Tender").

As Chad bemoans Sandra's lack of attraction to him Dennis comes up with an idea. He volunteers to take a Shakespearean sonnet to her. Desperate, Chad agrees. But before Dennis leaves, a leather-jacketed roustabout rides into town ("Blue Suede Shoes"). It is Natalie, dressed as a fellah named Ed. Chad is excited by Ed's coolness and manliness and he asks Ed to be his new sidekick. Heartbroken, Dennis exits. Chad instructs Ed that his first job as his new sidekick is to give the sonnet to Miss Sandra. Jim enters, and Ed grabs the sonnet and rushes off.

Jim tells Chad that he's in love with a woman who doesn't love him back. Chad looks over the slovenly Jim, and tells him that in order to win a girl, Jim must dress and act more like Chad. Chad gives Jim a much-needed lesson in coolness ("Don't Be Cruel"). Ed arrives at the museum and gives Sandra the sonnet. Sandra is so moved by the sonnet that she finds herself drawn to this strange-looking young man ("One Night With You"--reprise). Ed tries to leave, but Sandra is intent on seducing him ("Let Yourself Go").

As the sun goes down, Mayor Matilda is cracking down on the perceived immoral behavior that is now running rampant through the town. She comes upon a couple kissing, and she's stunned to see that it's her precious Dean kissing Lorraine. Dean, for the first time, disobeys his mother and shows her that he can now dance. He and Lorraine run off into the night. Matilda promises to throw Chad in jail for what he has done, and she and Sheriff Earl drive after Dean. Ed tells Chad that in order to avoid jail, he should hide in the abandoned fairgrounds just outside of town. Chad runs off, and Ed runs off after him. Jim, now dressed like Chad, enters and asks Sylvia if she's seen Sandra. Sylvia tells Jim that he's crazy to fall for a woman like that, and Jim admonishes Sylvia for having grown cold and bitter. Jim gives Sylvia a very surprising kiss, and a stunned Sylvia suddenly falls for him. Soon, everyone in town find themselves escaping to the fairgrounds, searching for someone to love ("Can't Help Falling in Love").

Act Two

In the midst of the abandoned fairgrounds, the citizens of the town are restless and randy ("All Shook Up"). Dennis comes upon Natalie, who's still dressed as Ed, and Dennis reveals that he's upset about the way Chad treats her ("It Hurts Me"). But Natalie insists that Chad is the only guy for her.

In an attempt to win Chad, Natalie gets an idea: she convinces Chad to teach her (as Ed) how to seduce a woman ("A Little Less Conversation") but in the process, Ed winds up kissing Chad. Chad is stunned and Ed runs off as Jim enters. Chad reaffirms his machismo ("Power Of My Love") when Jim and Chad suddenly realize they are both in love with the same woman. Sandra enters, lustfully looking for Ed. Jim confesses his love for Sandra, but she doesn't even remember meeting him. As the heartbroken Jim slinks off, Ed enters, and he insists that Sandra leave them alone. Sandra, still hot for Ed, relents and promises to find him later. Left alone, Chad is about to hit Ed, but he realizes that he can't. Ed gives Chad some "alone time", and Chad realizes that he has feelings for his new sidekick ("I Don't Want To").

In another part of the fairgrounds, Mayor Matilda enters, followed, as always, by the silent Sheriff Earl, and she vows to bring the roustabout down ("Devil In Disguise").

A heartbroken Jim wanders about and runs into Sylvia, who is wearing her best Sunday dress. He wonders what she's doing out there this time of night, and she confesses her newfound feelings for him ("There's Always Me"). But Jim can't handle this revelation, and he rushes off.

In another part of the grounds, Dean and Lorraine plan to catch the morning train out of town, but Chad convinces them to stay and fight for their love ("If I Can Dream").

In the center of the fairgrounds, Matilda gathers the townspeople together to form a pious posse to both find her son and arrest Chad. But Chad enters, as does Dean and Lorraine.

In front of everyone Chad confesses his love for Ed, he takes off the hat and reveals to everyone that he is actually Natalie. Chad confesses that it was actually Ed he liked, not Natalie, so he leaves the town. Earl speaks and professes his love for Matilda, Dean and Lorraine are allowed to be together, and Jim realizes its actually Sylvia that he's loved ("Can't Help Falling In Love -- reprise"). Dennis and Sandra share a moment where they both realize a love for Shakespeare, and subsequently, a love for each other. Natalie sings of her falling in love with Chad ("Fools Fall In Love"). The last scene is a triple wedding (Jim and Sylvia, Matilda and Earl, Dennis and Sandra), with flower girl/bridesmaid Lorraine. Chad interrupts the wedding and declares his new found love for Natalie ("Burning Love"). The show ends with Natalie riding off on her motorbike, with Chad on the back.

Characters

NATALIE HALLER (Early 20's): a mechanic.

CHAD: a great-lookin', motorcycling, guitar-playing, leather-jacketed roustabout.

JIM HALLER (mid 40's-50's): Natalie's widowed father.

SYLVIA (mid 40's): the no-nonsense, African-American owner of SYLVIA'S HONKY-TONK.

LORRAINE: Sylvia's 16 year-old daughter.

DENNIS: a young, awkward, aspiring dentist.

MISS SANDRA: the beautiful, intellectual caretaker of the town's museum.

MAYOR MATILDA HYDE (mid 40's-50's): the town's conservative mayor.

DEAN HYDE: Matilda's 16 year-old son. He has grown up at a military boarding school.

SHERIFF EARL (mid 40's-50's): the law in town. A man of not many words.

CHORUS

Song list

Act I
"Jailhouse Rock" - Chad and Prisoners (Music and lyrics by Jerry Leiber and Mike Stoller)
"Heartbreak Hotel" - Henrietta, Dennis, Sylvia, Lorraine, Jim and Barflies (Music and lyrics by Presley, Mae Boren Axton and Tommy Durden)
"Roustabout" - Chad (Music and lyrics by Florence Kaye, Bernie Baum and Bill Giant)
"One Night With You" - Natalie (Music and lyrics by Pearl King and Dave Bartholomew)
"C'mon Everybody" - Chad, Natalie, Dennis, and Company (Music and lyrics by Joy Byers)
"Follow That Dream" - Chad and Natalie (Lyrics by Fred Wise, music

by Ben Weisman)
"Teddy Bear/Hound Dog" - Chad, Miss Sandra, Dennis and Natalie (Music and lyrics by Kal Mann and Bernie Lowe/Leiber and Stoller)
"That's All Right" - Sylvia, Lorraine, Chad, Dennis, Dean and Barflies (Music and lyrics by Arthur Crudup)
"It's Now or Never" - Dean, Lorraine and Company (Music and lyrics by Aaron Schroeder and Wally Gold)
"Love Me Tender" - Natalie and Dennis (Music and Lyrics By Elvis Presley and Vera Matson)
"Blue Suede Shoes" - Ed and Chad (Music and lyrics by Carl Perkins)
"Don't Be Cruel" - Chad and Jim (Music and lyrics by Presley and Otis Blackwell)
"Let Yourself Go" - Miss Sandra and Statues (Music and lyrics by Joy Byers)
"Can't Help Falling In Love" - Company (Music and Lyrics by Hugo Peretti, Luigi Creatore, George David Weiss)
Act II
Entr'acte
"All Shook Up" - Company (Music and lyrics by Presley and Blackwell)
"It Hurts Me" - Dennis and Company (Music and lyrics by Byers and Charlie Daniels)
"A Little Less Conversation" - Ed and Company (Music and lyrics by Mac Davis and Billy Strange)
"The Power of My Love" - Chad, Jim and Miss Sandra (Music and lyrics by Giant, Baum and Kaye)
"I Don't Want To" - Chad (Lyrics by Janice Torre, music by Fred Spielman)
"(You're the) Devil in Disguise" - Mayor Matilda and Ladies Church Council (Music and lyrics by Giant, Baum and Kaye)
"There's Always Me" - Sylvia (Music and lyrics by Don Robertson)
"If I Can Dream" - Chad, Lorraine, Dean and Company (Music and lyrics by W. Earl Brown)
"Can't Help Falling In Love" (Reprise) - Earl, Jim,Sylvia and Matilda
"Fools Fall in Love" - Natalie and Company (Music and Lyrics By Leiber and Stoller)
Burning Love - Company (Music and lyrics by Dennis Linde)
Instrumentation

The original Broadway production had fifteen musicians, including the musical director and associate conductor. The original production was scored for two keyboards, two guitars, electric bass, drums, percussion, four woodwinds, three trumpets, and trombone. The first keyboard part was played by the conductor and the second keyboard part also doubled on organ. The first woodwind part doubled on piccolo, flute, clarinet, and alto sax; the second on flute, clarinet, and alto sax; the third on clarinet and tenor sax; the fourth on bass clarinet and baritone sax. There were also three trumpets where the first trumpet is the lead trumpet. The trumpets also doubled on flugelhorn.

The orchestration that is under the current license is based on the national tour version; there are only twelve musicians. The percussion part is removed, there are now three woodwind parts, and two trumpets. The rest remain the same. This time the first woodwind part doubles on flute and alto sax; the second on clarinet and tenor sax; the third on bass clarinet and baritone sax.

Awards and nominations

2005 Theatre World Award (Cheyenne Jackson) WINNER
2005 Drama Desk Award Outstanding Set Design of a Musical (David Rockwell) (nominee)
Recording

The Original Broadway cast recording was released on May 31, 2005 by BMG Marketing.

Almost in Love

Almost in Love

Almost in Love

Studio album by Elvis Presley
Released November 1970
Recorded 1968-1970
Genre Rock
Label RCA Camden
Elvis Presley chronology
On Stage: February 1970
(1970) Almost in Love
(1970) That's the Way It Is
(1970)
Professional ratings
Review scores

Source Rating
Allmusic

Almost in Love is the 39th album by Elvis Presley, released in 1970 on RCA Camden, a budget-priced subsidiary of the main RCA label. This album consisted mostly of singles dating from the late 1960s that had previously not been released in album format, including 1968's "A Little Less Conversation" (a re-recording of this song by Elvis for his 1968 TV Special would later be remixed by Tom Holkenborg aka Junkie XL and become a hit in 2002) and "Rubberneckin", a 1969 single from the film Change of Habit recorded at American Sound Studio in Memphis during the 1969 recording sessions that had produced From Elvis in Memphis and Elvis Back in Memphis. The song would later be remixed by Oakenfold in 2003. Included as a bonus is "My Little Friend," a leftover again from the same 1969 recording sessions in Memphis. The song "Stay Away, Joe" (the theme from Elvis's 1967 film of the same title) was included in error (it was already released earlier in 1970 on the compilation Let's Be Friends); when RCA-Camden reissued Almost in Love in 1973, it replaced it with a different song, "Stay Away", from the same film. The title track of the album is a song from Presley's 1968 film, Live a Little, Love a Little. The album was re-released by Pickwick Records in 1975 and was issued on compact disc (Sony/BMG A 681610) in 2006. It was certified Gold and Platinum on 1/6/2004 by the RIAA.

Track listing

"Almost in Love" (Luiz Bonfá, Randy Starr) (from Live a Little, Love a Little)
"Long Legged Girl (With the Short Dress On)" (Winfield Scott, J. Leslie McFarland) (from Double Trouble - previously released on the Double Trouble soundtrack)
"Edge of Reality" (Bernie Baum, Bill Giant, Florence Kaye) (from Live a Little, Love a Little)
"My Little Friend" (Shirl Milete)
"A Little Less Conversation" (Mac Davis, Billy Strange) (from Live a Little, Love a Little)
"Rubberneckin'" (Dory Jones, Bunny Warren) (from Change of Habit)
"Clean Up Your Own Backyard" (Mac Davis, Billy Strange) (from The Trouble with Girls)
"U. S. Male" (Jerry Reed Hubbard)
"Charro!" (Mac Davis, Billy Strange) (from the film of the same title)

"Stay Away, Joe" (Ben Weisman, Sid Wayne) (replaced by Stay Away on 1973 re-release and the 2006 compact disc release) (from the film of the same title)

Aloha from Hawaii

Aloha from Hawaii

Aloha from Hawaii via Satellite

Directed by Marty Pasetta
Produced by Marty Pasetta
Starring Elvis Presley
Editing by Stephen McKeown
Studio Pasetta Productions
Distributed by RCA
Release date(s)
Running time 85 minutes
Language English
Budget $2. 5 million

Aloha from Hawaii is a music concert that was headlined by Elvis Presley, and was broadcast live via satellite on January 14, 1973. The concert took place at the Honolulu International Center (HIC) in Honolulu (now known as the Neal S. Blaisdell Center) and aired in over 40 countries across Asia and Europe (who received the telecast the next day, also in primetime). Despite the satellite innovation, the United States did not air the concert until April 4, 1973 (the concert took place the same day as Super Bowl VII). Viewing figures are debatable, with several sources, including Elvis Presley Enterprises, claiming 1 billion. However, some other sources claim that these figures are "an Elvis Myth" promoted by Colonel Tom Parker, and quoted by many biographers since. These sources suggest only several hundred million would have tuned into the broadcast. The show was the most expensive entertainment special at the time, costing $2. 5 million.

Background

On July 8, 1972, inspired by a recent visit made by U. S. President Richard Nixon to China a few months earlier, Presley's manager, Colonel Tom Parker, announced that there would be a worldwide satellite broadcast from Hawaii to allow the whole world the chance to see a Presley concert "since it is impossible for us to play in every major city". Parker initially stated that it would take place in either October or November 1972 but this date was changed to early 1973 after MGM showed concern about it clashing with the release of their documentary film Elvis on Tour. As the show had already been planned prior to this upset, the original shows, now set for November, would still go ahead but without being filmed.

Parker held another press conference on September 4, 1972 in Las Vegas to confirm that the concert, now titled Aloha From Hawaii, would be broadcast on January 14, 1973. The press were told that an audience of 1 billion was expected to tune in to see the "first entertainment special to be broadcast live around the world", although Parker had not taken into account the fact that many countries, including parts of Europe and America, would not see the concert live due to the time of the broadcast. (This was not a true statement for the Our World broadcast was the first live, international, satellite television production, which was broadcasted worldwide on June 25, 1967 which included entertainment artists such as Maria Callas and headlined by The Beatles). Two weeks after the Las Vegas press conference Parker received a letter from Honolulu Advertiser columnist Eddie Sherman. Sherman had read in news accounts that there was to be no charge for admittance to the concerts, instead a donation for charity was required. He suggested to Parker that, as Presley had recorded and was still performing the song I'll Remember You written by Kui Lee, the donations could go to the Kui Lee Cancer Fund that had been set up following the death of the song writer in 1966. Seeing the chance to publicize Presley's charitable nature once again, Parker eagerly agreed.

Producer-director Marty Pasetta had attended one of Presley's concerts at Long Beach in mid-November, and found it to be "boring" and lacking in any physical excitement. He approached Parker with ideas about the broadcast, including a runway that led out from the stage so Presley could get closer to his audience. Parker insisted that the ideas were useless, and that Presley would agree that they were useless. Pasetta, however, decided to approach Presley about the ideas anyway and was pleasantly surprised to find that he would be happy to do whatever Pasetta felt was best for the show. This was another example of the ever-growing rift between Presley and his manager.

Presley performed three shows over November 17 and 18 in

Honolulu, the dates originally planned for the satellite broadcast, and gave a press conference on November 20 to promote the satellite special. He also announced officially that it would now be in aide of the Kui Lee Cancer Fund.

Presley arrived in Hawaii again on January 9, 1973 to begin rehearsals. He had lost twenty-five pounds for the show and was confident after news that his record sales were increasing and Elvis on Tour had been nominated for a Golden Globe. Rehearsals were held at the Hilton Hawaiian Village while the main set was being constructed. Although there were several technical problems, the rehearsals were an overall success.

Broadcast

Presley taped a January 12 rehearsal concert as a fail-safe in case anything went wrong with the satellite during the actual broadcast – however, nothing went wrong during the January 14 broadcast. For both shows, Presley was dressed in a white "American Eagle" jumpsuit designed by Bill Belew. The broadcast was directed by Marty Pasetta, who was then in charge of directing the Oscar ceremonies.

Audience tickets for the January 14 concert and its January 12 pre-broadcast rehearsal show carried no price. Each audience member was asked to pay whatever he or she could afford. The performance and concert merchandise sales raised $75,000 for the Kui Lee Cancer Fund in Hawaii.

Presley performed a vast array of old and recent hits like "Steamroller Blues", "See See Rider", "Early Morning Rain", "Burning Love", "Blue Suede Shoes", "A Big Hunk o' Love", "Suspicious Minds", "Can't Help Falling in Love", the Beatles' "Something", "I'm So Lonesome I Could Cry", "It's Over", "Welcome to my World", "I'll Remember You" and "What Now My Love". After the concert had finished and the audience had left, Presley recorded five songs on stage to be aired during the American airing of the show.

Viewing figures

For many years, biographers and fan sites, including the official website of Elvis Presley, have claimed that up to 1. 5 billion people watched the broadcast live. This claim has been questioned by other sources who point out that, as the broadcast was only seen in around 40 countries, it would have been near impossible for that figure to have been achieved. Alan Hanson, writing for "Elvis History Blog", states that "the world's total population in 1973 was 3. 973 billion. Does it sound reasonable that fully one-third of the planet's people were glued to the tube when Elvis's special aired in 1973? Hardly. " He also makes the claim that the American figures were only "33. 8 percent of households", approximately 70 million, and that many of the other countries watching were much less populated; "If barely a third of the U. S. population tuned in, does it seem reasonable that an equal amount would have done so in places like South Vietnam, where TV broadcasting only began in 1965?". To further debunk the claims of 1 to 1. 5 billion views, Hanson states;

So how was the exaggerated number of 1. 3 billion viewers of the Elvis special reached? If you add together the 1973 populations of the 38 countries the actually did broadcast the Aloha show, the total comes to—you guessed it—about 1. 3 billion. In what was perhaps the greatest snow job of his career, Colonel Parker convinced four decades of Elvis experts and fans that every single living person in 38 countries tuned in to Elvis: Aloha From Hawaii in 1973.

Soundtrack album

Aloha from Hawaii: Via Satellite
The album containing the music from the concert was a blockbuster hit, becoming Presley's first chart-topping album in the US since the soundtrack to Roustabout in 1965. The original release of the album, however, did not include the five post-show performances.

Initially released only in quadraphonic sound, the album was the first quadraphonic album to top the Billboard album chart, and remains the biggest-selling release in the format.

Presley was accompanied by:

Vocalists

J. D. Sumner & the Stamps Quartet (Ed Enoch, Bill Baize, Donnie Sumner, Edward Wideman)
The Sweet Inspirations (Myrna Smith, Sylvia Shemwell, Estelle Brown)

Kathy Westmoreland
His TCB Band

James Burton (lead guitar)
John Wilkinson (rhythm guitar)
Ronnie Tutt (drums)
Jerry Scheff (Fender bass)
Glen Hardin (piano/keyboards)
Charlie Hodge (vocals/acoustic guitar)
Joe Guercio Orchestra

Joe Guercio was Elvis's conductor and musical director and, with a few exceptions, the orchestra consisted of local musicians contracted for this particular engagement. Brass players were Patrick Houston, Thomas Porrello, Gary Grant and Forrest Buchtel (trumpets); Leslie Benedict and William Barton (trombones); Martin Harrell (bass trombone); and David Baptist (French horn). Saxophonists were Gabriel Baltazar, Jr. , Robert Winn, Peter Dovidio, Wayne Dunstan and Mary Taylor, with Baltazar and Taylor also playing flute. Violinist Bertine Corimby, who performed with Elvis at the Las Vegas Hilton, headed the 12-piece string section, the rest of whom were musicians from the Honolulu Symphony Orchestra: Dale Bechtel, Marianne Fleece, Louise Solmssen, Arthur Loventhal, Mervin Whitcomb, Heidi McCole and Carol Shive (violins); Betty Deeg and Diana Mallery (violas); and William Konney and Beverly LeBeck (cellos). Rounding out the orchestra were Frank Strazzeri (Hammond organ) and Dean Appleman (percussion?). Houston, Porrello, Harrell and Strazzeri had toured with Elvis in 1972 and were brought to Hawaii for the show, as were Buchtel and Corimby. Harvey Ragsdale was the Hawaiian contractor who hired local musicians for the orchestra.
DVD releases

In September 2004, "Aloha from Hawaii" (Special Edition) together with "The '68 Comeback Special" was released on DVD. The 2-Disc deluxe package includes the full-length concert broadcast around the world on January 14, as well as the full rehearsal concert given on January 12, and the extended US version shown on April 4. Additionally, the set contains an uncut 17. 5 min. sequence of Elvis arriving in Honolulu and the complete post-concert session. The picture and the sound (in Dolby Digital 5. 1) have been digitally remastered from the original master tapes.

Early in August 2006 the TV special was also released in a single disc version. This edition contains some new material which was not included in the original deluxe release. The new material consists of some TV news footage shot during the arrival, offering an alternate look on the event and portions of two press conferences held for the upcoming live broadcast in September and November 1972. Those film clips with an overall length of about 9 minutes are so-called "Easter Eggs" and can be found by pressing a hidden button in the menu.

A bronze statue of Elvis was unveiled in front of Neal Blaisdell Center Arena in Honolulu. The statue was sponsored by TV Land channel.

Charts and certifications

Chart (2004)	Peak position
Australian Top 40 Music DVDs	1
Austrian Top 10 Music DVDs	7
Belgium (Flanders) Top 10 Music DVDs	2
Belgium (Wallonia) Top 10 Music DVDs	1
Ireland Top 20 DVDs	17
Japanese DVDs Chart	117
Netherlands Top 30 Music DVDs	2
New Zealand Top 10 Music DVDs	6
Norwegian Top 10 DVDs	2
Spanish Top 20 Music DVDs	6
Swedish Top 20 DVDs	1

Chart (2006)	Peak position
Italian Top 20 Music DVDs	14

Region	Certification	Sales/shipments
Australia (ARIA)	2× Platinum	30,000^
Austria (IFPI Austria)	Gold	5,000x
Canada (Music Canada)	3× Platinum	30,000^
France (SNEP)	Platinum	20,000*
United States (RIAA) 2004 release	4× Platinum	400,000^
United States (RIAA) 2006 release	2× Platinum	200,000^

*sales figures based on certification alone
^shipments figures based on certification alone
xunspecified figures based on certification alone

Aloha from Hawaii: Via Satellite

Aloha from Hawaii: Via Satellite

Aloha from Hawaii: Via Satellite

Live album by Elvis Presley
Released	February 4, 1973
Recorded	January 14, 1973
Genre Rock
Length	62:48
Producer	Joan Deary, Marty Pasetta
Elvis Presley chronology
Separate Ways
(1972) Aloha from Hawaii: Via Satellite
(1973) Elvis
(1973)
Alternative cover

Re-issue Cover
Professional ratings
Review scores
Source	Rating
Allmusic
Aloha from Hawaii: Via Satellite is a live concert album by Elvis Presley, released by RCA Records in February 1973 and peaked on the Billboard chart in the Spring of 1973. Despite the satellite innovation, the United States did not air the concert until April 4, 1973. Aloha from Hawaii (which was a worldwide ratings smash) went to number one on the 'Billboard' album chart. The album dominated the charts, reaching #1 in both the pop and country charts in the United States.
Aloha from Hawaii was a two-disc set—only the second such release of Presley's career (the first being 1969's double set From Memphis to Vegas/From Vegas to Memphis, which contained one album each of studio and concert recordings). It was initially released only in quadraphonic sound, becoming the first album in the format to top the Billboard album chart. A stereo version was initially released only through the RCA Record Club, but later replaced the quadraphonic version in record stores.
The album contains all the live performances from the TV special, but omits the five songs Presley recorded after the show and which

were featured on the original broadcast; these would be issued later on the album Mahalo from Elvis.
The album was certified Gold on 2/13/1973, Platinum and 2x Platinum on 5/20/1988, 3x Platinum on 7/15/1999 and 5x Platinum on 8/1/2002 by the R. I. A. A.
This is the last soundtrack album that Presley released during his lifetime (later soundtracks for the TV special Elvis in Concert and the documentary This Is Elvis were released posthumously).
Contents

Track listing

"Introduction: Also Sprach Zarathustra" (Richard Strauss)
"See See Rider" (Traditional)
"Burning Love" (Dennis Linde)
"Something" (George Harrison)
"You Gave Me a Mountain" (Marty Robbins)
"Steamroller Blues" (James Taylor)
"My Way" (Claude François, Jacques Revaux, Paul Anka)
"Love Me" (Jerry Leiber, Mike Stoller)
"Johnny B. Goode" (Chuck Berry)
"It's Over" (Jimmie Rodgers)
"Blue Suede Shoes" (Carl Perkins)
"I'm So Lonesome I Could Cry" (Hank Williams)
"I Can't Stop Loving You" (Don Gibson)
"Hound Dog" (Leiber, Stoller)
"What Now My Love" (Gilbert Bécaud, Carl Sigman)
"Fever" (Eddie Cooley, John Davenport)
"Welcome to My World" (Jim Reeves)
"Suspicious Minds" (Mark James)
"Introductions By Elvis"
"I'll Remember You" (Kui Lee)
"Long Tall Sally/Whole Lotta Shakin' Goin' On" (Otis Blackwell, Sunny David, William Johnson, Richard Penniman, Dub Williams)
"An American Trilogy" (Mickey Newbury)
"A Big Hunk O' Love" (Aaron Schroeder, Sidney Wyche)
"Can't Help Falling in Love" (George Weiss, Hugo Peretti, Luigi Creatore)
The following tracks were recorded by Presley after the concert

and inserted into the broadcast (with the exception of "No More", which remained unheard until 1978's Mahalo From Elvis). They were not included in the original soundtrack album, but they appear on the 1998 CD re-issue.
"Blue Hawaii" (Ralph Rainger, Leo Robin)
"Ku-U-I-Po" (Luigi Creatore, Hugo Peretti, George David Weiss)
"No More" (Don Robertson, Hal Blair)
"Hawaiian Wedding Song" (Al Hoffman, Dick Manning, Charles King)
"Early Morning Rain" (Gordon Lightfoot)

Chart positions

Year	Chart	Position
1973	Billboard Pop Albums	1

Preceded by
The Dark Side of the Moon by Pink Floyd Billboard 200 number-one album
May 5–11, 1973 Succeeded by
Houses of the Holy by Led Zeppelin

Amazing Grace: His Greatest Sacred Performances

Amazing Grace: His Greatest Sacred Performances

Please help
Amazing Grace: His Greatest Sacred Performances

Compilation album by Elvis Presley
Released October 25, 1994
Recorded January 1957-March 1972
Genre Gospel
Length 1:22:17
Label RCA Records
Producer Ernst Mikael Jorgensen
Roger Semon
Paul Williams
Elvis Presley chronology
From Nashville to Memphis: The Essential 60's Masters

(1993) Amazing Grace: His Greatest Sacred Performances
(1994) Command Performances: The Essential 60's Masters II
(1995)
Professional ratings
Review scores
Source Rating
Allmusic
Amazing Grace: His Greatest Sacred Performances is a two-disc compilation of studio master recordings by Elvis Presley released in 1994 on RCA Records, catalogue number 66421-2. It also includes a booklet with session details and an essay by Charles Wolfe. It was certified Gold, Platinum and 2x Platinum on 7/15/1999 by the R. I. A. A.
Contents

Contents

The set comprises recordings of gospel music made by Presley during his career. The contents of all three gospel albums Presley released in his lifetime are included, while other songs had appeared on singles, an extended play single, and other albums. The set also contains five previously unreleased selections, and the two discs present the studio masters in chronological session order. Disc one contains the entirety of his two albums released respectively in 1960 and 1967, His Hand In Mine and How Great Thou Art. The other five tracks contain the four-song EP Peace in the Valley from 1957, incorporated later that year into his original Christmas album, and the 1965 hit single "Crying in the Chapel" which reached #3 on the Billboard Hot 100.
Disc two contains the entirety of his 1972 album He Touched Me, with the five previously unreleased selections derived from a jam session captured on March 31, 1972, during the filming for Elvis on Tour. The songs "You'll Never Walk Alone" and "We Call On Him" were released as two sides of a single in time for Easter in 1968, and "Only Believe" and "Help Me" appeared as b-sides of singles in the 1970s but were excluded from the 1970s box set discs

compiling his complete singles from that decade. The remaining five tracks appeared on Presley albums released during the 1970s, the songs "How Great Thou Art" and "Why Me Lord" being concert recordings.
This set accompanied RCA's mid-1990s compilation reissue program for Elvis Presley, including the five-disc box sets The King of Rock 'n' Roll: The Complete 50s Masters, From Nashville to Memphis: The Essential 60's Masters, Walk a Mile in My Shoes: The Essential 70's Masters, and the two-disc set anthologizing his 1960s soundtrack recordings, Command Performances: The Essential 60's Masters II. These nineteen compact discs contain 507 recordings total, a substantial percentage of Presley's career output.
All selections recorded at Radio Recorders in Hollywood, RCA Studio B in Nashville, Tennessee, the Stax Recording Studio and the Mid-South Coliseum in Memphis, Tennessee. Unknown location for the March 1972 jam session. Original recordings produced by Steve Sholes or Felton Jarvis.

Collective personnel

Elvis Presley – vocals, guitar, piano
The Jordanaires - vocals
The Imperials - vocals
The Sweet Inspirations - vocals
The Nashville Edition - vocals
J. D. Sumner and the Stamps - vocals
Tim Baty - vocals
Charlie Hodge - vocals, guitar
Millie Kirkham - vocals
Sherrill Nielsen - vocals
Donnie Sumner - vocals
Kathy Westmoreland - vocals
Dolores Edgin - backing vocals
Mary Greene - backing vocals
Ginger Holladay - backing vocals
Mary Holladay - backing vocals
Sonja Montgomery - backing vocals
June Page - backing vocals
Susan Pilkington - backing vocals
Temple Riser - backing vocals
Henry Slaughter - backing vocals, keyboards
Boots Randolph - saxophone
Pete Drake - pedal steel guitar

Harold Bradley - electric guitar
James Burton - electric guitar
Johnny Christopher - electric guitar
Hank Garland - electric guitar
Scotty Moore – electric guitar
Chip Young - electric guitar
John Wilkinson - electric guitar
David Briggs - keyboards
Floyd Cramer - piano
Glen D. Hardin - piano
Joe Moscheo - piano
Gordon Stoker - piano
Hoyt Hawkins - organ
Charlie McCoy - organ, bass
Glen Spreen - organ
Duke Bardwell - bass
Bill Black - double bass
Bob Moore - bass
Norbert Putnam - bass
Kenny Buttrey - drums
Jerry Carrigan - drums, percussion
D. J. Fontana - drums
Buddy Harman – drums
Ronnie Tutt - drums

Track listing

Chart positions for LPs from Billboard Top Pop Albums chart; positions for singles from Billboard Pop Singles chart.

Disc one

Track Recorded Original LP Issue Catalogue Release Date Chart Peak Song Title Writer(s) Time
1. 1/12/57 Elvis' Christmas Album LOC 1035 10/15/57 #1 I Believe Ervin Drake, Irvin Graham, Jimmy Shirl, Al Stillman 2:03
2. 1/13/57 Elvis' Christmas Album LOC 1035 10/15/57 #1 (There'll Be) Peace in the Valley (For Me) Thomas A. Dorsey 3:20
3. 1/13/57 Elvis' Christmas Album LOC 1035 10/15/57 #1 Take My Hand, Precious Lord Thomas A. Dorsey 3:19
4. 1/19/57 Elvis' Christmas Album LOC 1035

10/15/57 #1 It Is No Secret (What God Can Do) Stuart Hamblen 3:54
5. 10/30/60 His Hand in Mine LSP 2328 11/10/60
#13 Milky White Way traditional 2:12
6. 10/30/60 His Hand in Mine LSP 2328 11/10/60
#13 His Hand In Mine Mosie Lister 3:15
7. 10/30/60 His Hand in Mine LSP 2328 11/10/60
#13 I Believe in the Man in the Sky Richard Howard 2:11
8. 10/30/60 His Hand in Mine LSP 2328 11/10/60
#13 He Knows Just What I Need Mosie Lister 2:12
9. 10/31/60 His Hand in Mine LSP 2328 11/10/60
#13 Mansion Over the Hilltop Ira Stanphill 2:55
10. 10/31/60 His Hand in Mine LSP 2328 11/10/60
#13 In My Father's House Aileene Hanks 2:03
11. 10/31/60 His Hand in Mine LSP 2328 11/10/60
#13 Joshua Fit the Battle traditional 2:39
12. 10/31/60 His Hand in Mine LSP 2328 11/10/60
#13 Swing Down Sweet Chariottraditional 2:32
13. 10/31/60 His Hand in Mine LSP 2328 11/10/60
#13 I'm Gonna Walk Dem Golden Stairs Cully Holt 1:50
14. 10/31/60 His Hand in Mine LSP 2328 11/10/60
#13 If We Never Meet Again Alfred E. Brumley 1:58
15. 10/31/60 His Hand in Mine LSP 2328 11/10/60
#13 Known Only to Him Stuart Hamblen 2:07
16. 10/31/60 His Hand in Mine LSP 2328 11/10/60
#13 Working on the Building Hoyle Bowles 1:52
17. 10/31/60 47-0643 4/6/65 #3 Crying in the Chapel Artie Glenn 2:24
18. 5/25/66 How Great Thou Art LSP 3758 2/20/67
#18 Run On traditional 2:21
19. 5/25/66 How Great Thou Art LSP 3758 2/20/67
#18 How Great Thou Art Stuart K. Hine 3:00
20. 5/26/66 How Great Thou Art LSP 3758 2/20/67
#18 Stand By Me traditional 2:26
21. 5/26/66 How Great Thou Art LSP 3758 2/20/67
#18 Where No One Stands Alone Mosie Lister 2:42
22. 5/27/66 How Great Thou Art LSP 3758 2/20/67
#18 So High traditional 1:56
23. 5/27/66 How Great Thou Art LSP 3758 2/20/67
#18 Farther Alongtraditional 4:04
24. 5/27/66 How Great Thou Art LSP 3758 2/20/67
#18 By And By traditional 1:49
25. 5/27/66 How Great Thou Art LSP 3758 2/20/67
#18 In the Garden C. Austin Miles 3:11

26. 5/27/66 How Great Thou Art LSP 3758 2/20/67
#18 Somebody Bigger Than You and I Hy Heath, Sonny Burke, Johnny Lange 2:25
27. 5/27/66 How Great Thou Art LSP 3758 2/20/67
#18 Without Him Mylon LeFevre 2:27
28. 5/28/66 How Great Thou Art LSP 3758 2/20/67
#18 If The Lord Wasn't Walking By My Side Henry Slaughter 1:36
29. 5/28/66 How Great Thou Art LSP 3758 2/20/67
#18 Where Could I Go But to the Lord? J. B. Coats 3:36

Disc two

Track Recorded Original LP Issue Catalogue Release Date Chart Peak Song Title Writer(s) Time
1. 9/11/67 47-9600b 3/68 We Call On Him Fred Karger, Sid Wayne, Ben Weisman 2:31
2. 9/11/67 47-9600 3/68 #90 You'll Never Walk Alone Oscar Hammerstein II and Richard Rodgers 2:43
3. 6/8/70 47-9985b 5/25/71 Only Believe Paul Rader 2:47
4. 3/15/71 He Touched Me LSP 4690 4/3/72 #79 Amazing Grace John Newton 3:34
5. 5/15/71 Elvis Now LSP 4671 2/20/72 #43 Miracle of the Rosary Lee Denson 1:50
6. 5/17/71 He Touched Me LSP 4690 4/3/72 #79 Lead Me Guide Me Doris Akers 2:39
7. 5/18/71 74-0651 3/72 He Touched Me William J. Gaither 2:39
8. 5/18/71 He Touched Me LSP 4690 4/3/72 #79 I've Got Confidence Andrae Crouch 2:20
9. 5/18/71 He Touched Me LSP 4690 4/3/72 #79 An Evening Prayer C. Gabriel Battersby and Charles H. Gabriel 1:54
10. 5/19/71 He Touched Me LSP 4690 4/3/72 #79 Seeing Is Believing Red West and Glen Spreen 2:53
11. 5/18/71 He Touched Me LSP 4690 4/3/72 #79 A Thing Called Love Jerry Hubbard 2:23
12. 6/8/71 Elvis Now LSP 4671 2/20/72 #43 Put Your Hand in the Hand Gene MacLellan 3:15
13. 6/8/71 He Touched Me LSP 4690 4/3/72 #79 Reach Out to Jesus Ralph Carmichael 3:14
14. 6/9/71 He Touched Me LSP 4690 4/3/72 #79 He Is My Everything Dallas Frazier 2:39

15. 6/9/71 He Touched Me LSP 4690 4/3/72 #79 There Is No God But God Bill Kenny 2:17
16. 6/9/71 He Touched Me LSP 4690 4/3/72 #79 I, John William J. Gaither 2:15
17. 6/9/71 74-0651b 3/72 Bosom of Abraham W. Johnson, G. McFadden, P. Brooks 1:35
18. 12/12/73 APBO 0280b 5/10/74 Help Me Larry Gatlin 2:27
19. 12/16/73 Good Times CPL1 0475 3/20/74 #90 If That Isn't Love Dottie Rambo 3:39
20. 3/20/74 On Stage In Memphis CPL1 0606 7/7/74 #33 Why Me Lord Kris Kristofferson 2:52
21. 3/20/74 On Stage In Memphis CPL1 0606 7/7/74 #33 How Great Thou Art Stuart K. Hine 3:34
22. 3/31/72 previously unreleased I, John William J. Gaither 2:11
23. 3/31/72 previously unreleased Bosom of Abraham W. Johnson, G. McFadden, P. Brooks 0:53
24. 3/31/72 previously unreleased You Better Run traditional 2:09
25. 3/31/72 previously unreleased Lead Me Guide Me Doris Akers 2:36
26. 3/31/72 previously unreleased Turn Your Eyes Upon Jesus/Nearer My God to Thee Helen Lemmel / Sarah Flower Adams and John Bacchus Dykes 2:52

American Music Award

American Music Award

The American Music Awards is an annual American music awards show, created by Dick Clark in 1973 for ABC when the network's contract to present the Grammy Awards expired. Unlike the Grammys, which are awarded on the basis of votes by members of the entertainment industry, the AMAs are determined by a poll of music buyers.

History and overview

Conception

The AMAs were created by Dick Clark in 1973 to compete with the

Grammy Awards after the move of that year's show to Nashville, Tennessee led to CBS picking up the Grammy telecasts after its first two in 1971 and 1972 were broadcast on ABC. Michael Jackson and Donny Osmond co-hosted the first award show with Rodney Allen Rippy and Ricky Segall in 1974.

Differences between the AMAs and Grammy Awards

While the Grammy Awards are awarded based on votes by members of the entertainment industry, the AMAs are determined by a poll of music buyers. The American Music Awards have nominations based on sales, airplay, activity on social networks, and video viewing and can nominate only the works released between 1 December of the previous year and 1 September of the current year. Before 2010 had nominations based only on sales and airplay and nominated every work, even if old. The Grammys have nominations based on vote of the Academy and only nominate a work from their eligibility period that changes often.

Favorite Artist of the Year

In 1996, the AMAs instituted a new award, Favorite Artist of the Year, which was awarded to Garth Brooks. Brooks left the award on the podium because he didn't believe in the concept of picking an artist of the year. The category was discontinued.

In 2004, the AMAs brought in a new category entitled "T-Mobile Text-In Award", which resembled the Favorite Artist of the Year. The academy chose one artist each from five genres of music (rap, rock, pop, R&B, country) to compete in one category, with the public texting its votes.

Hosts

The first hosts for the first telecast of the AMAs were Helen Reddy, Roger Miller, and Smokey Robinson. Helen Reddy not only hosted the show but also became the first female artist to win an AMA for Favorite Pop/Rock Female artist. For the first decade or so, the AMAs had multiple hosts, each representing a genre of music. For instance, Glen Campbell would host the country portion (Campbell, in fact, has co-hosted the AMAs more times than any other host or co-host), while other artists would co-host to represent his/her genre. In recent years, however, there has been one single host. For the 2008 awards, Jimmy Kimmel hosted for the fourth consecutive year. In 2009, there was no host for the first time in history. Instead, the AMAs followed the Grammys' lead in having various celebrities give introductions.

From its inception in 1973 until 2003, the AMAs have been held in mid- to late-January, but were moved to November beginning in 2003 so as not to further compete with other major awards shows (such as the Golden Globe Awards and the Academy Awards) and allows for ABC to have a well-rated awards show during November sweeps.

klm8ju mnuioki

Artists that won the most in a single year

The record for the most American Music Awards won in a single year is held by Michael Jackson (in 1984) and Whitney Houston (in 1994), each with 8 awards to their credit (including the Award of Merit, with which both artists were honored in the respective years).

Michael Jackson 8 (1984)
Whitney Houston 8 (1994)
Artist of the Decade (special poll)

In 2000 the AMAs held a poll to elect the Artist of the Decade for each previous decade of the Rock & Roll era. The results were:

'50s: Elvis Presley
'60s: The Beatles
'70s: Stevie Wonder
'80s: Michael Jackson
'90s: Garth Brooks
According to some sources, the result of this poll is not counted in the total of AMAs won by these artists.

Ann-Margret

Ann-Margret

Ann-Margret

Ann-Margret in 1966

Born Ann-Margret Olsson
April 28, 1941 (age 71)
Stockholm, Sweden
Occupation Actress, singer, dancer
Years active 1961–present
Spouse Roger Smith
(m. 1967-present)
Website
http://www. ann-margret. com/

Ann-Margret Olsson (born April 28, 1941) is a Swedish-American actress, singer and dancer whose professional name is Ann-Margret. She is best known for her roles in Bye Bye Birdie (1963), Viva Las Vegas (1964), The Cincinnati Kid (1965), Carnal Knowledge (1971), and Tommy (1975). She has won five Golden Globe Awards and been nominated for two Academy Awards, two Grammy Awards, a Screen Actors Guild Award, and six Emmy Awards. In 2010, she won her first Emmy Award for her guest appearance on Law & Order: SVU.

Early life

Ann-Margret was born in Stockholm, the daughter of Anna (née Aronsson) and Gustav Olsson, a native of Örnsköldsvik. While young she moved with her parents to Valsjöbyn, Jämtlands län, which she later described as a small town "of lumberjacks and farmers high up near the Arctic Circle". Her father worked in the United States during his youth and moved there again in 1942, working with the Johnson Electrical Company, while his wife and daughter stayed behind.

Ann-Margret and her mother moved to the United States in November 1946, and her father took her to Radio City Music Hall on the day they arrived. They settled just outside of Chicago in Wilmette, Illinois. She became a naturalized citizen of the United States in 1949 and took her first dance lessons at the Marjorie Young School of Dance, showing natural ability from the start, easily mimicking all the steps. Her parents were supportive and her mother handmade all her costumes. Ann-Margret's mother became a funeral parlor receptionist after her husband suffered a severe injury on his job. While a teenager, Ann-Margret appeared on the Morris B. Sachs Amateur Hour, Don McNeill's Breakfast Club and Ted Mack's Amateur Hour.

Through high school, where she graduated from New Trier High

School in Winnetka, Illinois, she continued to star in theatricals. She attended Northwestern University (1959-1960), where she was a member of the sorority Kappa Alpha Theta but did not graduate. As part of a group known as the "Suttletones," they performed at the Mist, a Chicago nightclub, and went to Las Vegas for a promised club date which fell through after they arrived. They plugged ahead to Los Angeles and, through agent Georgia Lund, secured club dates in Newport Beach and Reno, where Ann-Margret had a chance encounter with Marilyn Monroe, who was on location for The Misfits. Monroe noticed the striking girl in a crowd of onlookers, then chatted privately with her, offering her encouragement.

The group finally arrived at The Dunes in Las Vegas, which also headlined Tony Bennett and Al Hirt at that time. George Burns heard of her performance and she auditioned for his annual holiday show, in which she and Burns did a softshoe routine. Variety proclaimed, "George Burns has a gold mine in Ann-Margret. . . she has a definite style of her own, which can easily guide her to star status. "

Recording career

Ann-Margret began recording for RCA in 1961. Her first RCA recording was "Lost Love" from her debut album And Here She Is: Ann-Margret, produced in Nashville with Chet Atkins on guitar, the Jordanaires (Elvis Presley's backup singers), and the Anita Kerr Singers, with liner notes by mentor George Burns. She had a sexy, throaty singing voice, and RCA attempted to capitalize on the 'female Elvis' comparison by having her record a version of "Heartbreak Hotel" and other songs stylistically similar to Presley's. She scored the minor hit "I Just Don't Understand" (from her second LP), which entered the Billboard Top 40 in the third week of August 1961 and stayed six weeks, peaking at #17. The song was later covered in live performances by The Beatles and was recorded during a live performance at the BBC. Her only charting album was The Beauty and the Beard (1964), on which she was accompanied by trumpeter Al Hirt. She also sang at the Academy Awards presentation in 1962, singing the Oscar-nominated song "Theme from Bachelor in Paradise. " Her contract with RCA ended in 1966. In the late 1970s and early 1980s, she had hits on the dance charts, the most successful being 1979's "Love Rush," which peaked at #8 on the disco/dance charts. In 2001, working with Grammy Award-Winning producer-arranger-musician Art Greenhaw who calls

Ann-Margret his favorite female vocalist, she recorded the critically acclaimed album God Is Love: The Gospel Sessions. The album went on to earn a Grammy Nomination and a Dove Nomination for best album of the year in a gospel category. Her album Ann-Margret's Christmas Carol Collection, also produced and arranged by Art Greenhaw, was recorded in 2004 and continues to be available every year during the holiday season.

Film career

1960–66

In 1961, she filmed a screen test at 20th Century Fox and was signed to a seven-year contract. Ann-Margret made her film debut in a loan-out to United Artists in Pocketful of Miracles, with Bette Davis. It was a remake of the 1933 movie Lady for a Day. Both versions were directed by Frank Capra.

Then came a 1962 remake of Rodgers and Hammerstein's musical State Fair, playing the "bad girl" role of Emily opposite Bobby Darin and Pat Boone. She had tested for the part of Margy, the "good girl," but she seemed too seductive to the studio bosses, who decided on the switch. The two roles mimicked her real-life personality — shy and reserved offstage, but wildly exuberant and sensuous onstage. As she summed up in her autobiography, she would easily transform herself from "Little Miss Lollipop to Sexpot-Banshee" once she stepped on stage and the music began.

Her next starring role, as the all-American teenager Kim from Sweet Apple, Ohio, in Bye Bye Birdie (1963), made her a major star. The premiere at Radio City Music Hall, 16 years after her first visit to the famed theater, was a smash hit: the highest first-week grossing film to date at that venue. Life magazine put her on the cover for the second time and announced that the "torrid dancing almost replaces the central heating in the theater. " She was asked to sing "Baby, Won't You Please Come Home" at President John F. Kennedy's private birthday party at the Waldorf-Astoria, one year after Marilyn Monroe's famous "Happy Birthday. "

Ann-Margret met Elvis Presley on the MGM soundstage when the two filmed Viva Las Vegas (1964). Ann-Margret introduced Presley to David Winters, whom she recommended as a choreographer for their film. Viva Las Vegas was Winters' first feature film choreography job and was his first of four movies with Presley and his first of five films, including Kitten with a Whip (1964), Bus Riley's Back in Town (1965), Made in Paris (1966) and The Swinger (1966), and two TV specials with Ann-Margret. Ann-Margret was Winters's dance student at the time and Winters credits Ann-Margret as being 'that special person who changes your life'. Winters was nominated for the 1970 Emmy Award for 'Outstanding Achievement in Choreography' for his CBS Television Special: "Ann-Margret: From Hollywood with Love" (1969)

In 1963, Ann-Margret guest-starred in a popular episode of the animated TV series The Flintstones, voicing Ann-Margrock, an animated version of herself. She sang the ballad "The Littlest Lamb" as a lullaby and the (literally) rock-ing song, "Ain't Gonna Be a Fool. " Decades later, she recorded the theme song, a modified version of the Viva Las Vegas theme, to the live-action film The Flintstones in Viva Rock Vegas, in character as Ann-Margrock.

While working on the film Once a Thief (1965), she met future husband Roger Smith, who, after his successful run on the private-eye television series 77 Sunset Strip, was performing a live club show at the Hungry i on a bill with Bill Cosby and Don Adams. That meeting began their courtship, which met with resistance from her parents.

Ann-Margret starred in The Cincinnati Kid in 1965 opposite Steve McQueen. She also co-starred along with friend Dean Martin in the spy spoof Murderers' Row (1966). Finally she starred as the lead in The Swinger in 1966 with Tony Franciosa.

Her redhead hair color (she is a "natural brunette") was the idea of Sydney Guilaroff, a hairdresser who changed the hair color of other famous actresses such as Lucille Ball.

She was offered the title role in Cat Ballou (1965), but her manager turned it down without telling her. In March 1966, Ann-Margret and entertainers Chuck Day and Mickey Jones teamed up for a USO tour to entertain U. S. servicemen in remote parts of Vietnam and other parts of Southeast Asia. She still has great affection for the veterans and refers to them as "my gentlemen. " Ann-Margret, Day and Jones reunited in November 2005 for an encore of this tour for veterans and troops at Nellis Air Force Base, Nevada.

1967–79

During a lull in her film career in July 1967, Ann-Margret gave her first live performance in Las Vegas, with her husband Roger Smith (whom she had married in 1967) taking over as her manager after that engagement. Elvis Presley and his entourage came to see her during the show's five-week run and to celebrate backstage. From thereon until his death, Presley sent her a guitar-shaped floral arrangement for each of her Vegas openings. After the first Vegas run ended, she followed up with a CBS television special "The Ann-Margret Show", produced and directed by David Winters on December 1, 1968, with guest-stars Bob Hope, Jack Benny, Danny Thomas, and Carol Burnett. Then she went back to Saigon as part of Hope's Christmas show. A second Columbia Broadcasting System (CBS) television special followed, directed and choreographed by David Winters and produced and distributed by Winters' company Winters-Rosen with Dean Martin and Lucille Ball. In 1970, she returned to films with R. P. M. and C. C. and Company. David Winters and the show were nominated for a Primetime Emmy in Outstanding Choreography.

In 1971, she starred in Mike Nichols' Carnal Knowledge, playing the over-loving girlfriend of a viciously abusive Jack Nicholson and garnering a nomination for the Academy Award for Best Supporting Actress.

On the set of The Train Robbers in Durango, Mexico, in June 1972, she told Nancy Anderson of Copley News Service that she had been on the "grapefruit diet" and had lost almost twenty pounds (134 to 115) eating unsweetened citrus.

On Sunday, September 10, 1972, while performing at Lake Tahoe, Nevada, she fell 22 feet from an elevated platform to the stage and suffered injuries including a broken left arm, cheekbone and jawbone. Husband Roger Smith flew a stolen plane from Burbank, California, to Lake Tahoe in order to get his wife to the surgeons at the medical center at UCLA for treatment. She required meticulous facial reconstructive surgery that required wiring her mouth shut and putting her on a liquid diet. Unable to work for ten weeks, she ultimately returned to the stage almost (some would say miraculously) back to normal.

Throughout the 1970s, Ann-Margret balanced her live musical performances with a string of dramatic film roles that played against her glamorous image. In 1973 she starred with John

Wayne in The Train Robbers. Then came the musical Tommy in 1975, for which she was nominated the Academy Award for Best Actress. In addition, she has been nominated for 10 Golden Globe Awards and has won five, including her Best Actress in a Musical or Comedy for Tommy. She also did a string of successful TV specials, starting with The Ann-Margret Show for NBC / CBS in 1968.

On August 17, 1977, Ann-Margret and Roger Smith traveled to Memphis to attend Elvis Presley's funeral. Three months later, she hosted Memories Of Elvis featuring abridged versions of the Elvis 1968 TV and Aloha from Hawaii specials.

In 1978, she co-starred with Anthony Hopkins in the horror/suspense thriller Magic.

1980–89

In 1982, Ann-Margret co-starred with Walter Matthau and Dinah Manoff in the film version of Neil Simon's play I Ought to Be in Pictures. That same year, she appeared with a six-year-old Angelina Jolie in Lookin' to Get Out, playing Jolie's mother. To round out 1982, she appeared alongside Alan Bates, Glenda Jackson, and Julie Christie in the film adaptation of The Return of the Soldier. She also starred in the TV movies Who Will Love My Children? (1983) and a remake of A Streetcar Named Desire (1984). These performances collectively won her two Golden Globe Awards and two Emmy nominations. She appeared as the wife of Roy Scheider's character in the 1986 crime thriller 52 Pick-Up.

In 1989, an illustration was done of Oprah Winfrey that was on the cover of TV Guide, and although the head was Oprah's, the body was referenced from a 1979 publicity shot of Ann-Margret. The illustration was rendered so tightly in color pencil by freelance artist Chris Notarile that most people thought it was a composite photograph.

1990–2009

In 1992 she co-starred with Robert Duvall and Christian Bale in the Disney musical, Newsies. In 1993, Ann-Margret starred in the hit comedy Grumpy Old Men reuniting with Matthau and Jack Lemmon. Her character returned for Grumpier Old Men (1995), the equally successful sequel which this time co-starred Sophia Loren.

Ann-Margret published an autobiography in 1994 titled Ann-Margret: My Story, in which she publicly acknowledged her battle with and ongoing recovery from alcoholism. In 1995, she was chosen by Empire magazine as one of the 100 Sexiest Stars in film history; she ranked 10th.

She also filmed Any Given Sunday (1999) for director Oliver Stone, portraying the mother of football team owner Cameron Diaz. She filmed a cameo appearance for The Limey but her entire performance was cut from the movie.

She also appeared in several made-for-TV movies and miniseries during this time, including the 1993 adaptation of Alex Haley's Queen with Halle Berry. Ann-Margret's performance in the 1999 television film Life of the Party garnered her Emmy, Golden Globe, and Screen Actors Guild Award nominations.

She made guest appearances on the television shows Touched by an Angel in 2000 and three episodes of Third Watch in 2003. In 2001, she made her first appearance in a stage musical, playing the character of brothel owner Mona Stangley in a new touring production of The Best Little Whorehouse in Texas. The production co-starred Gary Sandy and Ed Dixon . She played Jimmy Fallon's mother in the 2004 comedy Taxi, co-starring Queen Latifah. In 2001, Ann-Margret worked with Art Greenhaw on the album God Is Love: The Gospel Sessions. The critically acclaimed project resulted in her first Grammy Award nomination and first Dove Award nomination for Best Album of the Year in a Gospel category. They teamed up again in 2004 for the album Ann-Margret's Christmas Carol Collection. She performed material from the album at two auditorium church services at Crystal Cathedral in Garden Grove, California, and broadcast worldwide on the program Hour of Power.

In 2006, Ann-Margret had supporting roles in the box-office hits The Break-Up with Jennifer Aniston and Vince Vaughn, and The Santa Clause 3: The Escape Clause with Tim Allen. She also starred in a few independent films, including Memory (2006) with Billy Zane and Dennis Hopper.

2010–present

Ann-Margret guest-starred in an episode of Law & Order: Special

Victims Unit, "Bedtime," which first aired on March 31, 2010. She received her sixth Emmy nomination for her performance. She also appeared in the Lifetime series, Army Wives, in the episode "Guns and Roses" (Season 4, Episode 5), which originally aired May 9, 2010. On August 29, 2010, she won an Emmy Award for Guest Performance by an Actress for her "SVU" performance. It was the first Emmy win of her career, and she received a standing ovation from the Emmy venue audience as she approached the stage to receive her award.

On October 14, 2010, Ann-Margret appeared on CBS' CSI.

Personal life

Ann-Margret was raised into the Lutheran religion. She has been married to Roger Smith since May 8, 1967; he was an actor who later became her manager. Now Smith is semi-retired due to myasthenia gravis.

She rode a 500cc Triumph T100C Tiger motorcycle in The Swinger (1966). She used the same model, fitted with a non-standard electric starter, in her stage show and her TV specials. A keen motorcyclist, she was featured in Triumph Motorcycles' official advertisements in the 1960s. She suffered three broken ribs and a fractured shoulder when she was thrown off a motorcycle she was riding in rural Minnesota in 2000.

Portrayal

In the 2005 CBS miniseries, Elvis, she is portrayed by Rose McGowan, in which her affair with Elvis Presley (played by Jonathan Rhys Meyers) is depicted during the filming of Viva Las Vegas. Kristen Wiig portrayed her in a skit during the May 14, 2011, episode of Saturday Night Live.

Filmography

Movies

TV

Discography

Singles

I Just Don't Understand (1961)
It Do Me So Good (1961)
What Am I Supposed To Do (1962)
Sleep In the Grass (1969)
Love Rush (1979)
Midnight Message (1980)
Everybody Needs Somebody Sometimes (1981)
EPs
And Here She Is. . . Ann-Margret (1961)
Side 1: I Just Don't Understand/I Don't Hurt Anymore
Side 2: Teach Me Tonight/Kansas City
More and More American Hits (compilation) (1962)
Side 2: What Am I Supposed To Do
Albums
And Here She Is. . . Ann-Margret (1961)
On the Way Up (1962)
The Vivacious One (1962)
Bachelor's Paradise (1963)
Beauty and the Beard (1964) (with Al Hirt)
David Merrick Presents Hits from His Broadway Hits (1964) (with David Merrick)
Songs from "The Swinger (And Other Swingin' Songs) (1966)
The Cowboy and the Lady (1969) (with Lee Hazlewood)
Ann-Margret (1979)
God Is Love: The Gospel Sessions (2001)
Ann-Margret's Christmas Carol Collection (2004)
Love Rush (reissue of Ann-Margret) (2007)
Everybody Needs Somebody Sometimes (single, reissue) (2007)
All's Faire In Love (2008)
Soundtracks
State Fair (1962)
Bye Bye Birdie (1963)
The Pleasure Seekers (1965)
Tommy (1975)
Newsies (1992)
Theatre productions

Love Letters, with Burt Reynolds
The Best Little Whorehouse in Texas (2001, touring production)
Honors

Year	Award	Category	Result	For
1962	Grammy Award	Best New Artist	Nominated	
1962	Golden Laurel	Top Female New Personality	Won	

1962 Golden Globe Most Promising Newcomer — Female Won
1963 Golden Laurel Top Female Musical Performance Won State Fair
1963 Golden Laurel Top Female Star Nominated
1964 Golden Laurel Top Female Comedy Performance Won Bye Bye Birdie
1964 Golden Laurel Top Female Star Nominated
1964 Golden Globe Best Motion Picture Actress — Musical/ Comedy Nominated Bye Bye Birdie
1964 Photoplay Award Most Popular Female Star Won
1965 Golden Laurel Musical Performance, Female Won Viva Las Vegas
1966 Golden Laurel Musical Performance, Female Won Made in Paris
1967 Golden Laurel Top Female Star Nominated
1972 Academy Award Best Actress in a Supporting Role Nominated Carnal Knowledge
1972 Golden Globe Best Motion Picture Actress in a Supporting Role Won Carnal Knowledge
1975 Academy Award Best Actress in a Leading Role Nominated Tommy
1975 Golden Globe Best Motion Picture Actress — Musical/ Comedy Won Tommy
1978 Golden Globe Best Motion Picture Actress in a Supporting Role Nominated Joseph Andrews
1979 Saturn Award Best Actress Nominated Magic
1981 Genie Award Best Performance by a Foreign Actress Nominated Middle Age Crazy
1983 Emmy Outstanding Lead Actress in a Limited Series or a Special Nominated Who Will Love My Children?
1983 Golden Apple Award Female Star of the Year Won
1984 Emmy Outstanding Lead Actress in a Limited Series or a Special Nominated A Streetcar Named Desire
1984 Golden Globe Best Performance by an Actress in a Mini-Series or Motion Picture Made for TV Won Who Will Love My Children?
1985 Golden Globe Best Performance by an Actress in a Mini-Series or Motion Picture Made for TV Won A Streetcar Named Desire
1987 Emmy Outstanding Lead Actress in a Mini Series or a Special Nominated The Two Mrs. Grenvilles
1987 Women in Film Crystal Award For outstanding women who, through their endurance and the excellence of their

work, have helped to expand the role of women within the entertainment industry. Recipient
1988 Golden Globe Best Performance by an Actress in a Mini-Series or Motion Picture Made for TVNominated The Two Mrs. Grenvilles
1993 Emmy Outstanding Lead Actress in a Mini Series or a Special Nominated Queen: The Story of an American Family
1994 Golden Globe Best Performance by an Actress in a Supporting Role in a Series, Mini-Series or Motion Picture Made for TV Nominated Queen: The Story of an American Family
1999 Emmy Outstanding Lead Actress in a Miniseries or a Movie Nominated Life of the Party: The Pamela Harriman Story
1999 Golden Globe Best Performance by an Actress in a Mini-Series or Motion Picture Made for TVNominated Life of the Party: The Pamela Harriman Story
1999 SAG Awards Outstanding Performance by a Female Actor in a TV Movie or Miniseries Nominated Life of the Party: The Pamela Harriman Story
2001 Grammy Award Best Southern, Country, or Bluegrass Gospel Album Nominated God is Love: The Gospel Sessions
2002 GMA Dove Award Best Country Album Nominated God is Love: The Gospel Sessions
2005 CineVegas International Film Festival Centennial Award Won
2010 Emmy Outstanding Guest Actress in a Drama Series Won Law & Order: SVU
Notes

^ a b "Religious Affiliation Ann-Margret". Adherents. com. Archived from the original on 12 July 2010. Retrieved 2010-08-04.
"Ann-Margret Biography". FilmReference. com. Retrieved 2010-08-04.
"Ann-Margret biography". movies. Yahoo. com. Yahoo movies. Retrieved 2010-08-04.
Ann-Margret 1994, p. 77.
"I Just Don't Understand, Ann Margret". Billboard. com. Billboard Top 100. 1961-10-02.
Whitburn, Joel (2004). Hot Dance/Disco: 1974–2003. Record Research. p. 21. ISBN 0-89820-156-X.
official records, National Academy of Recording Arts & Sciences; official records, Gospel Music Association; Mesquite (Texas) News, 2001 Volumes; holiday record release data, Select-O-Hits Distribution, 2004-2010
Ann-Margret 1994, p. 91.

Ann-Margret 1994, p. 96.
Ann-Margret 1994, p. 102.
Ann-Margret 1994, p. 104.
David Winters Bio IMDb web site
Ann Margret Bio IMDb web site
"Ann-Margret: From Hollywood With Love" The New York Times
Ann Margret Bio Lyricfreak. com
Ann-Margret Will Entertain Her Troops Again at Aviation Nation. Las Vegas Events. 20 September 2005[dead link]
The Ann Margret Show at IMDb
"From Hollywood with Love" at IMdb
"Company credits for Ann-Margret: From Hollywood with Love" at IMDb
"Awards for Ann-Margret: From Hollywood with Love" at IMDb
Anderson, Nancy (June 4, 1972). "John Wayne A Father Figure On Movie Set in Durango, Mexico". The Joplin Globe (Copley New Service).
Ann-Margret 1994, pp. 236–254.
"Going Too Far With the Winfrey Diet". NYTimes. com (New York Times). 1989-08-30. Retrieved 2010-04-25.
Ann-Margret 1994.
Los Angeles Times, December 20, 2004, Local section
"Exclusive: Ann-Margret to Guest on SVU". TVGuide. com.
"Keck's Exclusives: How CSI Nabbed Ann-Margret". TVGuide. com. Retrieved September 23, 2010.
Past Recipients Crystal Award WIF web site

Arthur Crudup

Arthur Crudup

Arthur Crudup

Arthur Crudup at the College of Commerce, Edinburgh, 1969 (Photo by Phil Wight)
Background information
Birth name Arthur Crudup
Also known as Arthur "Big Boy" Crudup; Arthur William Crudup; Elmer Jones; Percy Lee Crudup
Born August 24, 1905
Forest, Mississippi, United States
Died March 28, 1974 (aged 68)
Northampton County, Virginia, United States

Genres Blues, Delta blues, Rock and roll
Instruments Guitar, vocals
Years active 1939–1974
Labels Bluebird

Arthur "Big Boy" Crudup (August 24, 1905 – March 28, 1974) was an American Delta blues singer, songwriter and guitarist. He is best known outside blues circles for writing songs such as "That's All Right" (1946), "My Baby Left Me" and "So Glad You're Mine", later covered by Elvis Presley and dozens of other artists.

Contents

Career

Arthur Crudup was born in Forest, Mississippi, United States. For a time he lived and worked throughout the South and Midwest as a migrant worker. He and his family returned to Mississippi in 1926. He sang gospel, then began his career as a blues singer around Clarksdale, Mississippi. As a member of the Harmonizing Four, he visited Chicago in 1939. Crudup stayed in Chicago to work as a solo musician, but barely made a living as a street singer. Record producer Lester Melrose allegedly found him while he was living in a packing crate, introduced him to Tampa Red and signed him to a recording contract with RCA Victor's Bluebird label.

He recorded with RCA in the late 1940s and with Ace Records, Checker Records and Trumpet Records in the early 1950s and toured throughout the country, specifically black establishments in the South, with Sonny Boy Williamson II and Elmore James (around 1948). He also recorded under the names Elmer James and Percy Lee Crudup. He was popular in the South with records such as "Mean Old 'Frisco Blues", "Who's Been Foolin' You" and "That's All Right".

Crudup stopped recording in the 1950s, because of further battles over royalties. His last Chicago session was in 1951. His 1952-54 recording sessions for Victor were held at radio station WGST in Atlanta, Georgia. He returned to recording with Fire Records and Delmark Records and touring in 1965. Sometimes labeled as "The Father of Rock and Roll", he accepted this title with some bemusement. Un-gratified due to the loss of royalties, he would refer to his admirer Presley as 'Elvin Preston'. Throughout this time Crudup worked as a laborer to augment the non-existent royalties and the small wages he received as a singer. Crudup returned to Mississippi after a dispute with Melrose over royalties, then went into bootlegging, and later moved to Virginia where he had lived and worked as a musician and laborer. In the early 1970s, two local Virginia activists, Celia Santiago and Margaret Carter, assisted him in an attempt to gain royalties he felt he was due, with little success.

From the mid-1960s, Crudup returned to bootlegging and working as an agricultural laborer, chiefly in Virginia, where he lived with his family including three sons and several of his own siblings. On the Eastern Shore of Virginia, while he lived in relative poverty as a field laborer, he occasionally sang and supplied moonshine to a number of drinking establishments, including one called The Dew-Drop Inn, in Northampton County, for some time prior to his death from complications of heart disease and diabetes. On a 1970 trip to the U. K. , he recorded "Roebuck Man" with local musicians. His last professional engagements were with Bonnie Raitt.

There was some confusion as to his actual date of death because of his use of several names, including those of his siblings. He died of a heart attack in the Nassawadox hospital in Northampton County, Virginia in March 1974.

Crudup was honored with a marker on the Mississippi Blues Trail placed at Forest.

Discography

Mean Ol' Frisco (1962)
Crudup's Mood (1969)
Look On Yonder's Wall (1969)
Roebuck Man (1974)

Arthur Godfrey's Talent Scouts

Arthur Godfrey's Talent Scouts

Country	United States
Languages	English
Starring	Arthur Godfrey

Air dates July 2, 1946 to October 1, 1956
Sponsor(s) Lipton Tea
Arthur Godfrey's Talent Scouts (also known as Talent Scouts) is an American radio and television variety show which ran on CBS from 1946 until 1958. Sponsored by Lipton Tea, it stars Arthur Godfrey, who was also hosting Arthur Godfrey and His Friends at the same time.

Contents

Overview

The concept for the show was that Godfrey had several "talent scouts" who brought their discoveries onto the program to showcase their talents. The winner of each show was determined by a meter that judged the audience's applause. The radio series began July 2, 1946, and was heard on CBS Tuesday evenings at 9pm. The winner on October 1, 1946, was pianist José Melis, who later became a familiar late night television personality as the orchestra leader on Jack Paar's Tonight show.
In the summer of 1947, Arthur Godfrey's Talent Scouts moved to Fridays at 9:30 p. m. After August 1947 it aired on Mondays at 8:30 p. m. The radio show continued until October 1, 1956. With Archie Bleyer leading the orchestra, the show's announcer was George Bryan. The show's opening (to the tune of "Four and Twenty Blackbirds") featured Peggy Marshall and the Holidays singing:
Here comes Arthur Godfrey
Your talent scout emcee
Brought to you by Lipton
Brisk Lipton Tea
You know it's Lipton Tea
If it's B-R-I-S-K
You know it's Arthur Godfrey
When you hear them play . . .
At that point, the music would segue into trombonist Lou McGarity and the orchestra playing Godfrey's familiar theme song, "Seems

Like Old Times," sometimes with Godfrey singing or humming along. Contestants on the show included Pat Boone, The Chordettes, The McGuire Sisters and Carmel Quinn, all of whom went on to perform on Arthur Godfrey and His Friends. Other contestants included Tony Bennett, The Blackwood Brothers, Lenny Bruce, Roy Clark, Rosemary Clooney, Ken Berry, Florian ZaBach, Wally Cox, Vic Damone, The Diamonds, Eddie Fisher, Connie Francis, Don Knotts, Steve Lawrence, Al Martino, Barbara McNair, Marian McPartland, Johnny Nash, Leslie Uggams, Lorraine Donahue (who later appeared on The Voice of Firestone) and Jonathan Winters. Patsy Cline's appearance on the show can be seen on the DVD Patsy Cline: Sweet Dreams Still (2005). Among those who auditioned but were not chosen to appear on the broadcast were Buddy Holly and Elvis Presley.

Television

Arthur Godfrey's Talent Scouts
Also known as Talent Scouts
Genre Variety
Directed by Dave Rich
Robert Stevens
Starring Arthur Godfrey
Country of origin United States
Language(s) English
No. of seasons 10
Production
Camera setup Multi-camera
Running time 22–24 minutes
Production company(s) Columbia Broadcasting System
Distributor Columbia Broadcasting System
Broadcast
Original channel CBS
Picture format Black-and-white
Audio format Monaural
Original run December 6, 1948 – January 1, 1958

On television, Arthur Godfrey's Talent Scouts premiered December 6, 1948. According to the Nielsen ratings, it was the highest rated television show for the 1951–1952 season. It remained a highly popular show through the decade. The show took a great drop in ratings after orchestra bandleader Archie Bleyer left in the 1954–1955 season, but rebounded as the scouts continued to discover more talent. However, by 1957, television audiences began to

prefer adventure shows to variety shows and Godfrey's ratings dropped out of the top 30 Nielsen Chart. The show aired its final episode on January 1, 1958.
On December 24, 1956, the show became the first entertainment program to be videotaped for broadcast, as the then-new technology was used for a time-delayed rebroadcast in the Pacific Time Zone. An Ampex Quadruplex videotape machine recorded the initial live broadcast to the Eastern part of the country, which was replayed three hours later.

Broadcast History

Arthur Godfrey's Talent Scouts aired Monday at 8:30-9:00 PM on CBS its entire run.

Ratings

1950–1951:#8
1951–1952:#1
1952–1953:#2
1953–1954:#3
1954–1955:#18
1955–1956:#16
1956–1957:#12

Barbra Streisand

Barbra Streisand

Barbra Streisand

early career, c. mid 1960s
Background information
Birth name Barbara Joan Streisand
Born April 24, 1942 (age 70)
Brooklyn, New York, U. S.
Genres Broadway, jazz, traditional pop, adult contemporary
Occupations Singer-songwriter, actress, film producer, director
Years active 1957–present
Labels Columbia
Website barbrastreisand. com
Barbra Joan Streisand (born Barbara Joan Streisand /□stra□sænd/;

April 24, 1942) is an American singer, actress, writer, film producer, and director. She has won two Academy Awards, eight Grammy Awards, five Emmy Awards including one Daytime Emmy, a Special Tony Award, an American Film Institute award, a Kennedy Center Honors award, a Peabody Award, and is one of the few entertainers who have won an Oscar, Emmy, Grammy, and Tony Award.

She is one of the most commercially and critically successful entertainers in modern entertainment history, with more than 71. 5 million albums shipped in the United States and 140 million albums sold worldwide. She is the best-selling female artist on the Recording Industry Association of America's (RIAA) Top Selling Artists list, the only female recording artist in the top ten, and the only artist outside of the rock and roll genre. Along with Frank Sinatra, Cher, and Shirley Jones, she shares the distinction of being awarded an acting Oscar and also recording a number-one single on the U. S. Billboard Hot 100 chart.

According to the RIAA, Streisand holds the record for the most top-ten albums of any female recording artist – a total of 31 since 1963. Streisand has the widest span (48 years) between first and latest top-ten albums of any female recording artist. With her 2009 album, Love Is the Answer, she became one of the rare artists to achieve number-one albums in five consecutive decades. According to the RIAA, she has released 51 Gold albums, 30 Platinum albums, and 13 Multi-Platinum albums in the United States.

Early life

Barbara Joan Streisand (see name change) was born on April 24, 1942, in Brooklyn, New York, the daughter of Emanuel and Diana (née Rosen) Streisand. She is the second of two siblings sired by Emanuel (her older brother is Sheldon), who was a respected high school teacher. Fifteen months after Streisand's birth, her father died of a cerebral hemorrhage and the family fell into near-poverty. Streisand first attended the Jewish Orthodox Yeshiva of Brooklyn, giving a solo performance at the age of 7. She later attended Erasmus Hall High School in Brooklyn and joined the Freshman Chorus and Choral Club. Streisand recollects, "I'm so glad I came from Brooklyn--it's down to earth. "

Diana Rosen Streisand remarried Louis Kind in 1949 and gave Streisand a half-sister, the singer Roslyn Kind Kind is 9 years younger than Barbara.

Barbra Streisand became a nightclub singer while in her teens. She wanted to be an actress and appeared in summer stock and in a number of Off-Off-Broadway productions, including Driftwood (1959), with then-unknown Joan Rivers. (In her autobiography, Rivers wrote that she played a lesbian with a crush on Streisand's character, but this was later denied by the play's author.) Driftwood ran for only six weeks. When her boyfriend, Barry Dennen, helped her create a club act — first performed at The Lion, a popular gay nightclub in Manhattan's Greenwich Village in 1960 — she achieved success as a singer. While singing at The Lion for several weeks, she changed her name from Barbara to Barbra. Afterward she appeared at other New York nightclubs, including the Bon Soir and the Blue Angel. One early appearance outside of New York City was at Enrico Banducci's hungry i nightclub in San Francisco. In 1961, Streisand appeared at the Town and Country nightclub in Winnipeg, Manitoba, Canada, but her appearance was cut short; the club owner did not appreciate her singing style. Streisand appeared at Baker's Keyboard Lounge in Detroit in 1961. Streisand's first television appearance was on The Tonight Show, then hosted by Jack Paar, in 1961, singing Harold Arlen's "A Sleepin' Bee". Orson Bean, who substituted for Paar that night, had seen the singer perform at a gay bar and booked her for the telecast. (Her older brother Sheldon paid NBC for a kinescope film so she could use it in 1961 to promote herself. Decades later the film was preserved through digitizing and is available for viewing on a website.) Later in 1961, Streisand became a semi-regular on PM East/PM West, a talk/variety series. PM East was hosted by Mike Wallace and Joyce Davidson. PM West was hosted by Terrence O'Flaherty. Westinghouse Broadcasting, which aired the television show in a select few cities (Boston, New York, Baltimore, Washington DC, Pittsburgh, Cleveland, Chicago and San Francisco), wiped all the videotapes soon after broadcasting them. Audio segments from some episodes, which were saved by Streisand's fans, are part of the compilation CD Just for the Record, which went platinum in 1991. The singer said on 60 Minutes in 1991 that 30 years earlier Mike Wallace had been "mean, very mean" to her on PM East/PM West. He countered that she had been "totally self-absorbed. " (Her response: "You invited me on your show to talk about subjects that interested me, and you dare to call me self-absorbed?") 60 Minutes included the audio of Streisand saying to him in 1961, "I like the fact that you are provoking. But don't provoke me. "

In 1962, after several appearances on PM East/PM West, Streisand first appeared on Broadway, in the small but star-making role of Miss Marmelstein in the musical I Can Get It for You Wholesale. Her first album, The Barbra Streisand Album, won two Grammy Awards in 1963. Following her success in I Can Get It for You Wholesale, Streisand made several appearances on The Tonight Show in 1962 and 1963. Topics covered in her interviews with host Johnny Carson included the empire-waisted dresses that she bought wholesale and her "crazy" reputation at Erasmus Hall High School. As is the case with Mike Wallace, only audio survives from small portions of her telecast conversations with Carson. It was at about this time that Streisand entered into a long and successful professional relationship with Lee Solters and Sheldon Roskin as her publicists with the firm Solters/Roskin (later Solters/Roskin/Friedman).

Streisand returned to Broadway in 1964 with an acclaimed performance as entertainer Fanny Brice in Funny Girl at the Winter Garden Theatre. The show introduced two of her signature songs, "People" and "Don't Rain on My Parade. " Because of the play's overnight success, she appeared on the cover of Time. In 1966, she repeated her success with Funny Girl in London's West End at the Prince of Wales Theatre. From 1965 to 1967 she appeared in her first four solo television specials.

Career

Singing

Streisand has recorded 50 studio albums, almost all with Columbia Records. Her early works in the 1960s (her debut The Barbra Streisand Album, The Second Barbra Streisand Album, The Third Album, My Name Is Barbra, etc.) are considered classic renditions of theater and cabaret standards, including her pensive version of the normally uptempo "Happy Days Are Here Again". She performed this in a duet with Judy Garland on The Judy Garland Show. Garland referred to her on the air as one of the last great belters. They also sang "There's No Business Like Show Business" with Ethel Merman joining them.

Beginning with My Name Is Barbra, her early albums were often medley-filled keepsakes of her television specials. Starting in 1969, she began attempting more contemporary material, but like many talented singers of the day, she found herself out of her element with rock. Her vocal talents prevailed, and she gained newfound success with the pop and ballad-oriented Richard Perry-produced album Stoney End in 1971. The title track, written by Laura Nyro, was a major hit for Streisand.

During the 1970s, she was also highly prominent on the pop charts, with Top 10 recordings such as "The Way We Were" (US No. 1), "Evergreen (Love Theme from A Star Is Born)" (US No. 1), "No More Tears (Enough Is Enough)" (1979, with Donna Summer), which as of 2010 is reportedly still the most commercially successful duet, (US No. 1), "You Don't Bring Me Flowers" (with Neil Diamond) (US No. 1) and "The Main Event" (US No. 3), some of which came from soundtrack recordings of her films. As the 1970s ended, Streisand was named the most successful female singer in the U. S. — only Elvis Presley and The Beatles had sold more albums. In 1980, she released her best-selling effort to date, the Barry Gibb-produced Guilty. The album contained the hits "Woman in Love" (which spent several weeks atop the pop charts in the Fall of 1980), "Guilty", and "What Kind of Fool".

After years of largely ignoring Broadway and traditional pop music in favor of more contemporary material, Streisand returned to her musical-theater roots with 1985's The Broadway Album, which was unexpectedly successful, holding the coveted No. 1 Billboard position for three straight weeks, and being certified quadruple platinum. The album featured tunes by Rodgers & Hammerstein, George Gershwin, Jerome Kern, and Stephen Sondheim, who was persuaded to rework some of his songs especially for this recording. The Broadway Album was met with acclaim, including a Grammy nomination for album of the year and, ultimately, handed Streisand her eighth Grammy as Best Female Vocalist. After releasing the live album One Voice in 1986, Streisand was set to take another musical journey along the Great White Way in 1988. She recorded several cuts for the album under the direction of Rupert Holmes, including "On My Own" (from Les Misérables), a medley of "How Are Things in Glocca Morra?" and "Heather on the Hill" (from Finian's Rainbow and Brigadoon, respectively), "All I Ask of You" (from The Phantom of the Opera), "Warm All Over" (from The Most Happy Fella) and an unusual solo version of "Make Our Garden Grow" (from Candide). Streisand was not happy with the direction of the project and it was ultimately scrapped. Only "Warm All Over" and a reworked, lite FM-friendly version of "All I Ask of You" were ever released, the latter appearing on Streisand's 1988 effort, Till I Loved You. At the beginning of the 1990s, Streisand started focusing on her film directorial efforts and became almost inactive in the recording studio. In 1991, a four-disc box set, Just for the Record, was released. A compilation spanning Streisand's entire career to date, it featured over 70 tracks of live performances, greatest hits, rarities and previously unreleased material.

The following year, Streisand's concert fundraising events helped propel former President Bill Clinton into the spotlight and into office. Streisand later introduced Clinton at his inauguration in 1993. Streisand's music career, however, was largely on hold. A 1992 appearance at an APLA benefit as well as the aforementioned inaugural performance hinted that Streisand was becoming more receptive to the idea of live performances. A tour was suggested, though Streisand would not immediately commit to it, citing her well-known stage fright as well as security concerns. During this time, Streisand finally returned to the recording studio and released Back to Broadway in June 1993. The album was not as universally lauded as its predecessor, but it did debut at No. 1 on the pop charts (a rare feat for an artist of Streisand's age, especially given that it relegated Janet Jackson's Janet to the No. 2 spot). One of the album's highlights was a medley of "I Have A Love" / "One Hand, One Heart", a duet with Johnny Mathis, who Streisand said is one of her favorite singers (this is stated in the CD's liner notes).

In 1993, New York Times music critic Stephen Holden wrote that Streisand "enjoys a cultural status that only one other American entertainer, Frank Sinatra, has achieved in the last half century. " In September 1993, Streisand announced her first public concert appearances in 27 years. What began as a two-night New Year's event at the MGM Grand Hotel in Las Vegas eventually led to a multi-city tour in the summer of 1994. Tickets to the tour were sold out in under one hour. Streisand also appeared on the covers of major magazines in anticipation of what Time magazine named "The Music Event of the Century. " The tour was one of the biggest all-media merchandise parlays in history. Ticket prices ranged from US$50 to US$1,500 – making Streisand the highest-paid concert performer in history. Barbra Streisand: The Concert went on to be the top-grossing concert of the year and earned five Emmy Awards and the Peabody Award, while the taped broadcast on HBO is, to date, the highest-rated concert special in HBO's 30-year history. Following the tour's conclusion, Streisand once again kept a low profile musically, instead focusing her efforts on acting and directing duties as well as a burgeoning romance with actor James Brolin.

In 1997, she finally returned to the recording studio, releasing Higher Ground, a collection of songs of a loosely-inspirational nature which also featured a duet with Céline Dion. The album received generally favorable reviews and, remarkably, once again debuted at No. 1 on the pop charts. Following her marriage to Brolin in 1998, Streisand recorded an album of love songs entitled A Love Like Ours the following year. Reviews were mixed, with many critics carping about the somewhat syrupy sentiments and overly-lush arrangements; however, it did produce a modest hit for Streisand in the country-tinged "If You Ever Leave Me", a duet with Vince Gill.

On New Year's Eve 1999, Streisand returned to the concert stage, with the highest-grossing single concert in Las Vegas history to date. At the end of the millennium, she was the number-one female singer in the U. S. , with at least two No. 1 albums in each decade since she began performing. A two-disc live album of the concert entitled Timeless: Live in Concert was released in 2000. Streisand performed versions of the Timeless concert in Sydney and Melbourne, Australia, in early 2000. In advance of four concerts (two each in Los Angeles and New York) in September 2000, Streisand announced she was retiring from paying public concerts. Her performance of the song "People" was broadcast on the Internet via America Online.

Streisand's most-recent albums have been Christmas Memories (2001), a somewhat somber collection of holiday songs (which felt entirely —albeit unintentionally— appropriate in the early post-9/11 days), and The Movie Album (2003), featuring famous film themes and backed by a large symphony orchestra. Guilty Pleasures (called Guilty Too in the UK), a collaboration with Barry Gibb and a sequel to their Guilty, was released worldwide in 2005.

In February 2006, Streisand recorded the song "Smile" alongside Tony Bennett at Streisand's Malibu home. The song is included on Tony Bennett's 80th birthday album, Duets. In September 2006, the pair filmed a live performance of the song for a special directed by Rob Marshall entitled Tony Bennett: An American Classic. The special aired on NBC November 21, 2006, and was released on DVD the same day. Streisand's duet with Bennett opened the special. In 2006, Streisand announced her intent to tour again, in an effort to raise money and awareness for multiple issues. After four days of rehearsal at the Sovereign Bank Arena in Trenton, New Jersey, the tour began on October 4 at the Wachovia

Center in Philadelphia, continued with a featured stop in Fort Lauderdale, Florida, (this was the concert Streisand chose to film for a TV special), and concluded at Staples Center in Los Angeles on November 20, 2006. Special guests Il Divo were interwoven throughout the show. The show was known as Streisand: The Tour.

Streisand's 20-concert tour set box-office records. At the age of 64, well past the prime of most performers, she grossed $92,457,062 and set house gross records in 14 of the 16 arenas played on the tour. She set the third-place record for her October 9, 2006, show at Madison Square Garden, the first- and second-place records of which are held by her two shows in September 2000. She set the second-place record at the MGM Grand Garden Arena, with her December 31, 1999, show being the house record and the highest-grossing concert of all time. This led many people to openly criticize Streisand for price gouging, as many tickets sold for upwards of $1,000.

A collection of performances culled from different stops on this tour, Live in Concert 2006, debuted at No. 7 on the Billboard 200, making it Streisand's 29th Top 10 album. Billboard. com May 18, 2007. </ref> In the summer of 2007, Streisand gave concerts for the first time in continental Europe. The first concert took place in Zürich (June 18), then Vienna (June 22), Paris (June 26), Berlin (June 30), Stockholm (July 4, canceled), Manchester (July 10) and Celbridge, near Dublin (July 14), followed by three concerts in London (July 18, 22 and 25), the only European city where Streisand had performed before 2007. Tickets for the London dates cost between £100. 00 and £1,500. 00 and for the Ireland date between €118 and €500. The tour included a 58-piece orchestra.

In February 2008, Forbes listed Streisand as the No. 2 earning female musician, between June 2006 and June 2007, with earnings of about $60 million. Although Streisand's range has changed with time and her voice has deepened over the years, her vocal prowess has remained remarkably secure for a singer whose career has endured for nearly half a century. Streisand is a contralto or possibly a mezzo-soprano who has a range consisting of well over two octaves from "low E to a high G and probably a bit more that [sic?] in either direction. " On November 17, 2008, Streisand returned to the studio to begin recording what would be her sixty-third album and it was announced that Diana Krall was producing the album. Streisand is one of the recipients of the 2008 Kennedy Center Honors. On December 7, 2008, she visited the White House as part of the ceremonies.

On April 25, 2009, CBS aired Streisand's latest TV special, Streisand: Live in Concert, highlighting the aforementioned featured stop from her 2006 North American tour, in Fort Lauderdale, Florida. On September 26, 2009, Streisand performed a one-night-only show at the Village Vanguard in New York City's Greenwich Village. This performance was later released on DVD as One Night Only Barbra Streisand and Quartet at The Village Vanguard. On September 29, 2009, Streisand and Columbia Records released her newest studio album, Love is the Answer, produced by Diana Krall. On October 2, 2009, Streisand made her British television performance debut with an interview on Friday Night With Jonathan Ross to promote the album. This album debuted at No. 1 on the Billboard 200 and registered her biggest weekly sales since 1997, making Streisand the only artist in history to achieve No. 1 albums in five different decades.

On February 1, 2010, Streisand joined over 80 other artists in recording a new version of the 1985 charity single "We Are the World". Quincy Jones and Lionel Richie planned to release the new version to mark the 25th anniversary of its original recording. These plans changed, however, in view of the devastating earthquake that hit Haiti on January 12, 2010, and on February 12, the song, now called "We Are the World 25 for Haiti", made its debut as a charity single to support relief aid for the beleaguered island nation.

In 2011, she sang "Somewhere from the Broadway musical West Side Story, with child prodigy Jackie Evancho on Evancho's album Dream With Me.

Streisand was honored as MusiCares Person of the Year on February 11, 2011, two days prior to the 53rd Annual Grammy Awards.

Streisand is one of many singers who use teleprompters during their live performances. Streisand has defended her choice in using teleprompters to display lyrics and, sometimes, banter.

Streisand is a mezzo-soprano.

Acting

Her first film was a reprise of her Broadway hit, Funny Girl (1968), an artistic and commercial success directed by Hollywood veteran William Wyler. Streisand won the 1968 Academy Award for Best Actress for the role, sharing it with Katharine Hepburn (The Lion in Winter), the only time there has been a tie in this Oscar category. Her next two movies were also based on musicals, Jerry Herman's Hello, Dolly!, directed by Gene Kelly (1969), and Alan Jay Lerner's and Burton Lane's On a Clear Day You Can See Forever, directed by Vincente Minnelli (1970), while her fourth film was based on the Broadway play The Owl and the Pussycat (1970).

During the 1970s, Streisand starred in several screwball comedies, including What's Up, Doc? (1972) and The Main Event (1979), both co-starring Ryan O'Neal, and For Pete's Sake (1974) with Michael Sarrazin. One of her most famous roles during this period was in the drama The Way We Were (1973) with Robert Redford, for which she received an Academy Award nomination as Best Actress. She earned her second Academy Award for Best Original Song as composer (together with lyricist Paul Williams) for the song "Evergreen", from A Star Is Born in 1976.

Along with Paul Newman, Sidney Poitier and later Steve McQueen, Streisand formed First Artists Production Company in 1969, so the actors could secure properties and develop movie projects for themselves. Streisand's initial outing with First Artists was Up the Sandbox (1972).

From a period beginning in 1969 and ending in 1980, Streisand appeared in the annual motion picture exhibitors poll of Top 10 Box Office attractions a total of 10 times, often as the only woman on the list. After the commercially disappointing All Night Long in 1981, Streisand's film output decreased considerably. She has acted in only six films since.

Streisand produced a number of her own films, setting up Barwood Films in 1972. For Yentl (1983), she was producer, director, and star, an experience she repeated for The Prince of Tides (1991) and The Mirror Has Two Faces (1996). There was controversy when Yentl received five Academy Award nominations, but none for the major categories of Best Picture, Actress, or Director. The Prince of Tides received even more Oscar nominations, including Best Picture, but the director was not nominated. Streisand also scripted Yentl, something she is not always given credit for. According to New York Times Editorial Page Editor Andrew Rosenthal in an interview (story begins at minute 16) with Allan Wolper, "the one thing that makes Barbra Streisand crazy is when nobody gives her the credit for having written Yentl. "

In 2004, Streisand made a return to film acting, after an eight-year hiatus, in the comedy Meet the Fockers (a sequel to Meet the Parents), playing opposite Dustin Hoffman, Ben Stiller, Blythe Danner and Robert De Niro.

In 2005, Streisand's Barwood Films, Gary Smith, and Sonny Murray purchased the rights to Simon Mawer's book Mendel's Dwarf. In December 2008, she stated that she was considering directing an adaptation of Larry Kramer's play The Normal Heart, a project she has worked on since the mid-1990s In 2009, Andrew Lloyd Webber stated that Streisand was one of several actresses (alongside Meryl Streep and Glenn Close) who were interested in playing the role of Norma Desmond in the film adaptation of Webber's musical version of Sunset Boulevard.

In December 2010, Streisand appeared in Little Fockers, the third film from the Meet the Parents trilogy. She reprised the role of Roz Focker alongside Dustin Hoffman.

On January 4, 2011, the New York Post reported that Streisand was in negotiations to produce, direct, and star in a new film version of Gypsy. In an interview with the New York Post, Arthur Laurents said: "We've talked about it a lot, and she knows what she's doing. She has my approval. " He said that he would not write the screenplay. The following day, the New York Times reported that Arthur Laurents clarified in a telephonic interview that Streisand would not direct the film "but playing Rose is enough to make her happy. " Streisand's spokesperson confirmed that "there have been conversations". After Laurents' subsequent death there was no official word on the status of the film for months, until it was announced on March 13, 2012 that Gypsy was moving forward, with Julian Fellowes writing the screenplay for the project.

On January 28, 2011, The Hollywood Reporter announced that Paramount Pictures has given the road-trip comedy My Mother's Curse the green light to begin shooting, with Streisand and Seth Rogen playing mother and son. Anne Fletcher is slated to direct the project with a script by Dan Fogelman. Lorne Michaels and John Goldwyn will produce it with Evan Goldberg. Executive producers include Streisand, Rogen, Fogelman, and David Ellison, whose

Skydance will co-finance the pic. Shooting began in spring of 2011 and wrapped in July. In August the Internet Movie Database began listing the film with the new title Guilt Trip. This was eventually altered to "The Guilt Trip" The film is set for a Christmas 2012 release (originally it was slated to release in March 2012 and later scheduled for November 2012).

Personal life

Marriages and family

Streisand has been married twice. Her first husband was actor Elliott Gould, to whom she was married from 1963 until 1971. They had one child, Jason Gould, who appeared as her on-screen son in The Prince of Tides. Her second husband is actor James Brolin, whom she married on July 1, 1998. While they have no children together, Brolin has two children from his first marriage, including Academy Award-nominated actor Josh Brolin, and one child from his second marriage. Both of her husbands starred in the 1970s conspiracy sci-fi thriller Capricorn One. Jon Peters' daughters, Caleigh Peters and Skye Peters, are her god-daughters.

Name

Streisand changed her name from Barbara to Barbra because, she said, "I hated the name, but I refused to change it. " Streisand further explained, "Well, I was 18 and I wanted to be unique, but I didn't want to change my name because that was too false. You know, people were saying you could be Joanie Sands, or something like that. [My middle name is Joan.] And I said, 'No, let's see, if I take out the 'a,' it's still 'Barbara,' but it's unique. " A 1967 biography with a concert program said, "the spelling of her first name is an instance of partial rebellion: she was advised to change her last name and retaliated by dropping an "a" from the first instead. "

Politics

Streisand has long been an active supporter of the Democratic Party and many of their causes. Streisand said, "The Democrats have always been the party of working people and minorities. I've always identified with the minorities. "

In 1971, Streisand was one of the celebrities listed on President

Richard Nixon's infamous Enemies List.

Streisand is a supporter of gay rights, and in 2008 helped raise funds in an unsuccessful attempt to defeat Proposition 8 in California.

Philanthropy

Streisand has personally raised $25 million for organizations through her live performances. The Streisand Foundation, established in 1986, has contributed over $16 million through nearly 1,000 grants to "national organizations working on preservation of the environment, voter education, the protection of civil liberties and civil rights, women's issues and nuclear disarmament. "

In 2006, Streisand donated $1 million to the William J. Clinton Foundation in support of former President Bill Clinton's climate change initiative.

In 2008, Streisand gifted $5 million to endow the Barbra Streisand Women's Cardiovascular Research and Education Program at Cedars-Sinai Medical Center's Women's Heart Center. In September that year, Parade magazine included Streisand on their Giving Back Fund's second annual Giving Back 30 survey, "a ranking of the celebrities who have made the largest donations to charity in 2007 according to public records", as the third most generous celebrity. The Giving Back Fund claimed Streisand donated $11 million, which The Streisand Foundation distributed.

At Julien's Auctions in October 2009, Streisand, a long-time collector of art and furniture, sold 526 items with all the proceeds going to her foundation. Items included a costume from Funny Lady and a vintage dental cabinet purchased by the performer at 18 years old. The sale's most valuable lot was a painting by Kees van Dongen. In December 2011 she agreed to sing at a fundraising gala for Israel Defence Forces charities.

Big Mama Thornton

Big Mama Thornton

Big Mama Thornton

Big Mama Thornton circa 1955-1960
Background information
Birth name Willie Mae Thornton
Born December 11, 1926
Origin Ariton, Alabama, United States
Died July 25, 1984 (aged 57)
Los Angeles, California, United States
Genres Rhythm and blues, Texas blues
Occupations Singer, songwriter
Instruments drums, harmonica
Years active 1947–1984
Labels Peacock, Arhoolie, Mercury, Pentagram, Backbeat, Vanguard, Ace Records (UK)
Associated acts Muddy Waters Blues Band, Lightnin' Hopkins, John Lee Hooker

Willie Mae "Big Mama" Thornton (December 11, 1926 – July 25, 1984) was an American rhythm and blues singer and songwriter. She was the first to record the hit song "Hound Dog" in 1952. The song was #1 on the Billboard R&B charts for seven weeks in 1953. The B-side was "They Call Me Big Mama", and the single sold almost two million copies. Three years later, Elvis Presley recorded his version, based on a version performed by Freddie Bell and the Bellboys. In a similar occurrence, she wrote and recorded "Ball 'n' Chain", which became a hit for her. Janis Joplin later recorded "Ball and Chain", and was a huge success in the late 1960s.

Biography

Early life

Thornton was born in Montgomery, Alabama, United States. Her introduction to music started in a Baptist church, where her father was a minister and her mother a church singer. She and her six siblings began to sing at very early ages. Thornton left Montgomery at age 14 in 1941, following her mother's death. She joined Sammy Green's Georgia-based Hot Harlem Revue. Her seven-year tenure with them gave her valuable singing and stage experience, and enabled her[vague] to tour the South. In 1948, she settled in Houston, Texas, where she hoped to further her career as a singer She was also a self-taught drummer and harmonica player, and frequently played each instrument onstage.

Career

Thornton began her recording career in Houston, signing a recording contract with Peacock Records in 1951. While working with another Peacock artist, Johnny Otis, she recorded "Hound Dog", a song that composers Jerry Leiber and Mike Stoller had given her in Los Angeles. The record was produced by Johnny Otis, and went to number one on the R&B chart. Although the record made her a star, she saw little of the profits. She continued to record for Peacock until 1957 and performed with R&B package tours with Junior Parker and Esther Phillips. In 1954, Thornton was one of the eyewitnesses to the accidental self-inflicted handgun death of blues singer Johnny Ace.

Thornton's account was, that Johnny was sitting with girlfriend Olivia on his lap, waving his pistol around, pointing it at Willie Mae. "Don't snap that on me," she told him. Johnny grinned and put the gun to Olivia's head. "Stop that, Johnny, you'll git someone killed," Willie Mae shouted at him. "Nothin' to worry about," Johnny replied, coolly, "ain't but one bullet here and I know exactly where it is. " He turned the gun on himself, put it to his temple and pulled the trigger.

Her career began to fade in the late 1950s and early 1960s. She left Houston and relocated to the San Francisco Bay Area, where she mostly played local blues clubs.

In 1966, Thornton recorded Big Mama Thornton With The Muddy Waters Blues Band, with Muddy Waters (guitar), Sammy Lawhorn (guitar), James Cotton (harmonica), Otis Spann (piano), Luther Johnson (bass guitar), and Francis Clay (drums). Songs included "Everything Gonna Be Alright", "Big Mama's Blues", "I'm Feeling Alright", "Big Mama's Bumble Bee Blues", "Looking The World Over", "Big Mama's Shuffle", and "Since I Fell For You", amongst others.

Her Ball 'n' Chain album in 1968, included other artists: Lightnin' Hopkins and Larry Williams. Big Mama's portion included only the songs "Wade in the Water", "My Love" and "Ball 'n' Chain". Songs by Hopkins included "Money Taker" and "Prison Blues".

One of Thornton's last albums was Jail (1975) for Vanguard Records. It captured her performances during a couple of mid 1970s concerts at two northwestern prisons. She became the talented leader of a blues ensemble that featured sustained jams from George "Harmonica" Smith, as well as guitarists Doug Macleod, B. Huston and Steve Wachsman, drummer Todd Nelson, saxophonist

Bill Potter, bassist Bruce Sieverson, and pianist J. D. Nicholson.

Thornton performed at the Monterey Jazz Festival in 1966 and 1968, and at the San Francisco Blues Festival in 1979. In 1965 she performed with the American Folk Blues Festival package in Europe. While in England that year, she recorded Big Mama Thornton in Europe and followed it up the next year in San Francisco with Big Mama Thornton with the Chicago Blues Band. Both albums came out on the Arhoolie label. Thornton continued to record for Vanguard, Mercury, and other small labels in the 1970s and to work the blues festival circuit until her death in 1984, the same year she was inducted into the Blues Hall of Fame.

During her career, she appeared on stages from New York City's Apollo Theater in 1952 to the Newport Jazz Festival in 1980, and was nominated for the Blues Music Awards six times. In addition to "Ball 'n' Chain" and "They Call Me Big Mama," Thornton wrote twenty other blues songs.

In the 1970s years of heavy drinking began to hurt Thornton's health. She was in a serious auto accident but recovered to perform at the 1973 Newport Jazz Festival with Muddy Waters, B. B. King, and Eddie "Cleanhead" Vinson, a recording of which is called The Blues—A Real Summit Meeting on Buddha Records.

Thornton died of a heart attack in Los Angeles on July 25, 1984, at age 57.

Legacy

In 2007, in the film, Hounddog, singer Jill Scott played Thornton.

Thornton is also the namesake of the Willie Mae Rock Camp for Girls.

Discography

Year	Title	Label
1964	Big Mama Thornton in Europe	Arhoolie
1966	Big Mama Thornton with the Muddy Water Blues Band	Arhoolie
1969	Stronger Than Dirt	Arhoolie
1970	The Way It Is	Mercury
1970	Maybe	Roulette Records

1970 She's Black Backbeat
1973 Saved Backbeat
1975 Jail (Live) Vanguard
1975 Sassy Mama! (Live) Vanguard
1978 Mama's Pride Vanguard

Bill Black

Bill Black

Bill Black
Birth name William Patton Black, Jr.
Born September 17, 1926
Memphis, Tennessee, USA
Died October 21, 1965 (aged 39)
Memphis, Tennessee, USA
Genres Rock and roll
Occupations Bassist
Instruments Kay Maestro M1
Fender Precision Bass
Years active 1954-65
Labels Sun (Presley), Hi, UK Felsted, London (Combo)
Associated acts Elvis Presley
The Blue Moon Boys
Bill Black's Combo
William Patton "Bill" Black, Jr. (September 17, 1926 – October 21, 1965) was an American musician who is noted as one of the pioneers of rockabilly music. Black was the bassist in Elvis Presley's early trio and the leader of Bill Black's Combo.

Early life

Black was born in Memphis, Tennessee, to a motorman for the Memphis Street Railway. He was the oldest of nine children. His father played popular songs on the banjo and fiddle to entertain the family. Black learned to play music at the age of 14 on an instrument made by his father—a cigar box with a board nailed to it and strings attached. At the age of sixteen, Black was performing "honky-tonk" music on acoustic guitar in local bars.

During World War II, Black was stationed with the U. S. Army at Fort Lee in Virginia. While in the Army, he met Evelyn, who played guitar as the member of a musical family. They married in 1946 and returned to Memphis. Black worked at the Firestone plant.

Career

Black began playing the upright bass fiddle. He modeled his "slap bass" technique after one of his idols, Fred Maddox of Maddox Brothers and Rose. Black also developed a "stage clown" persona in the same way that Maddox entertained audiences. Black performed as an exaggerated hillbilly with blacked-out teeth, straw hat and overalls. According to his son, Black said his goal was always to give his audience "a few moments of entertainment and maybe a little bit of humor that'll tickle 'em for a while. "

In 1952, Black began playing club and radio shows with guitarist Scotty Moore. Along with two other guitarists and a fiddler, they performed country music tunes by Hank Williams and Red Foley in Doug Poindexter's band, the Starlight Wranglers. Black and Moore also played in a band with Paul Burlison, Johnny Burnette, Dorsey Burnette on steel guitar, and a drummer.

In 1954, Black and Moore were formed into a trio with Elvis Presley.

The Blue Moon Boys

In July 1954, Sam Phillips of Sun Records asked Black and Moore to play back-up for the as-yet-unknown Elvis Presley. Black played slap bass with guitarist Scotty Moore, while Elvis Presley played rhythm guitar and sang lead. Neither musician was overly impressed with Presley, but they agreed a studio session would be useful to explore his potential.

On July 5, 1954, the trio met at Sun studios to rehearse and record a handful of songs. According to Moore, the first song they recorded was "I Love You Because", but after a few country music songs that weren't impressive they decided to take a break. During the break, Presley began "acting the fool" with Arthur Crudup's "That's All Right (Mama)", a blues song. When the other two musicians joined in, Phillips taped the song. The upbeat sound was original. Black remarked, "Damn. Get that on the radio and they'll run us out of town. "

The next day, the group recorded four more songs, including bluegrass musician Bill Monroe's "Blue Moon of Kentucky", which he had written and recorded as a slow waltz. Sources credit Bill Black with initiating the song, with Presley and Moore joining in. Moore said, "Bill is the one who came up with "Blue Moon of Kentucky. ". . . We're taking a little break and he starts beating on the bass and singing "Blue Moon of Kentucky," mocking Bill Monroe, singing the high falsetto voice. Elvis joins in with him, starts playing and singing along with him. . . " They ended up with a fast version of the song in 4/4 time. After an early take, Phillips can be heard on tape saying: "Fine, man. Hell, that's different—that's a pop song now, just about. "

Phillips took several acetates of the session to DJ Dewey Phillips (no relation) of Memphis radio station WHBQ's Red, Hot And Blue show. From August 18 through December 8, "Blue Moon of Kentucky" was consistently higher on the charts, and then both sides began to chart across the South.

Black and Moore became Presley's back-up group, earning 25% of his takings. Moore and Black left the Starlight Wranglers after the success of "That's All Right", jealousy within the group forcing them to split. Their recordings at Sun were released with the credits as "Elvis Presley, Scotty and Bill". The group was later billed as "Elvis Presley and the Blue Moon Boys".

Over the next 15 months, the trio released five singles, toured across the South, and appeared regularly on the Louisiana Hayride. They had originally auditioned for the Opry in October 1954, but they failed to impress the people in charge, or the audience, and were not invited back.

In 1955, Black went to RCA along with Presley and Moore when Presley's contract was sold to that company. Except for the RCA reissue of "Mystery Train" and "I Forgot to Remember to Forget" ('with Scotty and Bill'), they were no longer credited on record labels.

Black played on early Presley recordings including "Good Rockin' Tonight", "Heartbreak Hotel", "Baby Let's Play House", "Mystery Train", "That's All Right", and "Hound Dog", and eventually became one of the first bass players to use the Fender Precision Bass (bass guitar) in popular music, on "Jailhouse Rock" in the late 1950s.

Black, Moore and drummer D. J. Fontana toured extensively during Presley's early career. Black continued his on-stage "clown" persona and developed comedy routines with Presley. Black's on-stage personality was a sharp contrast to the introverted stage presence of Moore. The balance fit the group's performances.

According to Black's son Louis, Moore said, "Elvis used to just stand up there and not move, and Bill would jump around on the bass. Your daddy would come down through there and get everybody to laughing and loosen them up. " Fontana called Black the mainstay of the band in the early days. "He was a comedian who could warm up a crowd. That was necessary for us because we played for a lot of country crowds that weren't used to people jumping up and down on stage. "

Although both the crowd and Presley enjoyed Black's clowning, Presley's manager Colonel Parker declared that there be no more showing up Elvis. Gordon Stoker told Black, "Hey, man, you've got to cut this out. You're not the star. Elvis is the star. " Black and Moore left Presley on September 21, 1957. Although Black continued to record with Presley until 1958, he and Moore discontinued the band because of poor wages.

Bill Black's Combo

In 1959 Black joined a group of musicians which became Bill Black's Combo. The lineup was Black (bass), Joe Lewis Hall (piano), Reggie Young (guitar), Martin Wills (saxophone), and Jerry Arnold (drums). There were several personnel changes. While Young was in the army, his position was filled by Hank Hankins, Chips Moman and Tommy Cogbill. Ace Cannon replaced Wills on sax. Carl McVoy replaced Hall in the studio, while Bobby Emmons replaced him on tour.

The band released blues instrumental Smokie for Hi Records in December 1959. Smokie, Part 2 became a No. 17 pop hit, and made number one on the "black" music charts. The song made the Top 20 in the Billboard Hot 100 chart. A follow-up release, White Silver Sands (Hi 2021), was a Top 10 hit (#9) and, like its predecessor, topped the R&B charts for four weeks.

Eight of the recordings by Bill Black's Combo placed in the Top 40 between 1959 and 1962. These were "White Silver Sands" (U. S. No. 9), "Josephine" (U. S. No. 18), "Don't Be Cruel" (U. S. No. 11), "Blue Tango" (U. S. No. 16), and "Hearts of Stone" (U. S. No. 20).

Advertised as "Terrific for Dancing" their Saxy Jazz spent a record whole year in the top 100.

The Combo appeared in the 1961 film The Teenage Millionaire and on The Ed Sullivan Show, where they performed a medley of "Don't Be Cruel," "Cherry Pink," and "Hearts of Stone", and were voted Billboard's number one instrumental group of 1961.

Albums with themes included Bill Black's Combo Plays Tunes by Chuck Berry, Bill Black's Combo Goes Big Band, Bill Black's Combo Goes West, and Bill Black's Combo Plays the Blues. The Combo's sound of danceable blues became a popular accompaniment for striptease dancers. Another unique characteristics of the Combo was Reggie Young thwacking on the guitar with a pencil.

Lyn Lou Studio

In 1962, Bill Black opened a recording studio called "Lyn Lou Studio" (named for his son and daughter) on Chelsa Street in Memphis, Tennessee, with Larry Rogers (Studio 19, Nashville) as his engineer and producer. Johnny Black, Bill's brother and also upright bass player, who knew Elvis at Lauderdale Courts before Bill, recalls visiting Bill at the studio and reported that Bill would be totally absorbed mixing and playing back tracks. The studio featured a 1958 Ampex 351 mono tape recorder retired from Sun Studios in 1960, basically just like the one Bill recorded on with Elvis in 1954. Sam Phillips replaced the 2 original Ampex 350's with 2 new Ampex 351's in 1958. Bob Tucker and Larry Rogers purchased Lyn Lou Studios after Bill Black's death in 1965. The studio recorded many Bill Black Combo albums (now billed as "The Best Honky Tonk Band in America" as well as "The band who opened for the Beatles"), and produced number-one country hits for Charly McClain, T. G. Shepard, Billy Swan and others. The house band for these sessions was the Shylo Band, featuring guitarist/songwriter Ronnie Scaife, nephew of Cecil Scaife, famed Sun Studio engineer.

Early in 1963, Black sent from two to five different versions of the Combo to different regions of the country at the same time, while staying off the road himself, wanting to concentrate on his business, family and his health.

Ill health and death

In 1963, Bob Tucker joined the Bill Black Combo as a road manager and guitar/bass player.

Black himself had been ill for the past year and a half and unable to travel. Nonetheless, he insisted that the band continue without him. The Bill Black Combo created musical history in 1964 when they became the opening act for the Beatles (at their request) on their historical 13-city tour of America after their appearance on the Ed Sullivan Show. Black himself was not well enough to make the tour.

After two operations and lengthy hospital stays, Black died of a brain tumor on October 21, 1965, at the age of thirty-nine. Black died during his third operation that doctors had hoped would eradicate the tumor once and for all. Black was buried at Forest Hill Cemetery in Memphis, Tennessee. Presley received criticism for not attending his funeral; however, he believed that his presence would turn the funeral into a media frenzy. He decided instead to visit the family privately after the service to express his condolences. According to Louis Black, Presley said, "If there's anything that y'all need, you just let me know and it's yours. "

Black's widow sold Bob Tucker and Larry Rogers both the right to use the name Bill Black's Combo. The band changed to country when it joined Columbia Records, and won Billboard's Country Instrumental Group of the Year award in 1976.

Legacy

Bill Black's Combo cut more than 20 albums, toured the United States and Europe and won awards as the best instrumental group in America in 1966 and 1967. Bob Tucker worked for the University of Memphis as Professor of Music Business as well as being leader of the Best Honky Tonk Band in America.

Black's main stand-up bass is today owned by ex-Beatle Paul McCartney, who received the instrument as a birthday present from his late wife Linda McCartney in the late 1970s. The bass can be seen in the video clip to McCartney's song "Baby's Request". In the documentary film The World Tonight, McCartney can be seen playing the bass and singing his version of "Heartbreak Hotel". In 1995, he played it on "Real Love", the last "new" Beatles record (one of two in which McCartney, George Harrison and Ringo Starr overdubbed a full arrangement onto a John Lennon home recording from the late 1970s). In 2005, Clay Steakley portrayed

Black in the Elvis Presley biopic miniseries Elvis.

On April 4, 2009, Bill Black was inducted into the Rock and Roll Hall of Fame.

Bill Monroe

Bill Monroe

Bill Monroe

Background information
Birth name William Smith Monroe
Also known as Bill Monroe
Born September 13, 1911
Origin Rosine, Kentucky, USA
Died September 9, 1996 (aged 84)
Genres Bluegrass, Bluegrass gospel
Occupations Bluegrass artist
Instruments Mandolin
Years active 1930s–1996
Members
Country Music Hall of Fame
Nashville Songwriters Hall of Fame
International Bluegrass Music Hall of Honor
Rock and Roll Hall of Fame
Past members
Grand Ole Opry
(1939 – 1996)
The Monroe Brothers
Blue Grass Boys
Notable instruments
Gibson F-5 Mandolin
William Smith Monroe (September 13, 1911 – September 9, 1996) was an American musician who created the style of music known as bluegrass, which takes its name from his band, the "Blue Grass Boys," named for Monroe's home state of Kentucky. Monroe's performing career spanned 60 years as a singer, instrumentalist, composer and bandleader. He is often referred to as The Father of Bluegrass.

Early life

Monroe was born on his family's farm near Rosine, Kentucky, the youngest of eight children of James Buchanan "Buck" and Malissa (Vandiver) Monroe. His mother and her brother, Pendleton "Pen" Vandiver, were both musically talented, and Monroe and his family grew up playing and singing at home. Bill was of Scottish heritage. Because his older brothers Birch and Charlie already played the fiddle and guitar, Bill Monroe was resigned to playing the less desirable mandolin. He recalled that his brothers insisted he should remove four of the mandolin's eight strings so he would not play too loudly.

Monroe's mother died when he was ten, followed by his father six years later. As his brothers and sisters had moved away, after bouncing among uncles and aunts, Monroe settled in with his disabled uncle Pendleton Vandiver, often accompanying him when Vandiver played the fiddle at dances. This experience inspired one of Monroe's most famous compositions, "Uncle Pen," recorded in 1950, and the 1972 album, "Bill Monroe's Uncle Pen. " On that album, Monroe recorded a number of traditional fiddle tunes he had often heard performed by Vandiver. Uncle Pen has been credited with giving Monroe "a repertoire of tunes that sank into Bill's aurally trained memory and a sense of rhythm that seeped into his bones. " Also significant in Monroe's musical life was Arnold Shultz, an influential fiddler and guitarist who introduced Monroe to the blues.

Professional career

In 1929, Monroe moved to Indiana to work at an oil refinery with his brothers Birch, Charlie, and childhood friend and guitarist William "Old Hickory" Hardin. Together with a friend Larry Moore, they formed a musical group, the Monroe Brothers, to play at local dances and house parties. Birch Monroe and Larry Moore soon left the group, and Bill and Charlie carried on as a duo, eventually winning spots performing live on radio stations— first in Indiana and then, sponsored by Texas Crystals, on several radio broadcasts in Iowa, Nebraska, South Carolina and North Carolina 1934 to 1936. RCA Victor signed the Monroe Brothers to a recording contract in 1936. They scored an immediate hit single with the gospel song "What Would You Give In Exchange For Your Soul?" and ultimately recorded 60 tracks for Victor's Bluebird label between 1936 and 1938.

After the Monroe Brothers disbanded in 1938, Bill Monroe formed The Kentuckians in Little Rock, Arkansas, but the group only lasted for three months. Monroe then left Little Rock for Atlanta, Georgia, to form the first edition of the Blue Grass Boys with singer/guitarist Cleo Davis, fiddler Art Wooten, and bassist Amos Garren. Bill had wanted "Old Hickory" to become one of the original members of his "Blue Grass Boys", however William Hardin had to decline. In October 1939, he successfully auditioned for a regular spot on the Grand Ole Opry, impressing Opry founder George D. Hay with his energetic performance of Jimmie Rodgers's "Mule Skinner Blues". Monroe recorded that song, along with seven others, at his first solo recording session for RCA Victor in 1940; by this time, the Blue Grass Boys consisted of singer/guitarist Clyde Moody, fiddler Tommy Magness, and bassist Bill Wesbrooks.

While the fast tempos and instrumental virtuosity characteristic of bluegrass music are apparent even on these early tracks, Monroe was still experimenting with the sound of his group. He seldom sang lead vocals on his Victor recordings, often preferring to contribute high tenor harmonies as he had in the Monroe Brothers. A 1945 session for Columbia Records featured an accordion, soon dropped from the band. Most importantly, while Monroe added banjo player David "'Stringbean" Akeman to the Blue Grass Boys in 1942, Akeman played the instrument in a relatively primitive style and was rarely featured in instrumental solos. Monroe's pre-1946 recordings represent a transitional style between the string-band tradition from which he came and the musical innovation to follow.

The "Original Bluegrass Band" and Monroe's heyday as a star

A key development occurred in Monroe's music with the addition of North Carolina banjo prodigy Earl Scruggs to the Blue Grass Boys in December 1945. Scruggs played the instrument with a distinctive three-finger picking style that immediately caused a sensation among Opry audiences. Scruggs joined a highly accomplished group that included singer/guitarist Lester Flatt, and would soon include fiddler Chubby Wise, and bassist Howard Watts, who often performed under the name "Cedric Rainwater. " In retrospect, this lineup of the Blue Grass Boys has been dubbed the "Original Bluegrass Band," as Monroe's music finally included all the elements that characterize the genre, including breakneck tempos, sophisticated vocal harmony arrangements, and impressive instrumental proficiency demonstrated in solos or "breaks" on the mandolin, banjo, and fiddle. By this point, Monroe had acquired the 1923 Gibson F5 model "Lloyd Loar" mandolin which became his trademark instrument for the remainder of his career.

The 28 songs recorded by this version of the Blue Grass Boys for Columbia Records in 1946 and 1947 soon became classics of the genre, including "Toy Heart," "Blue Grass Breakdown," "Molly and Tenbrooks", "Wicked Path of Sin," "My Rose of Old Kentucky," "Little Cabin Home on the Hill," and Monroe's most famous song, "Blue Moon of Kentucky". The last-named was recorded by Elvis Presley in 1954, appearing as the B-side of his first single for Sun Records. Monroe gave his blessing to Presley's rock-and-roll cover of the song, originally a slow ballad in waltz time, and in fact re-recorded it himself with a faster arrangement after Presley's version became a hit. Several gospel-themed numbers are credited to the "Blue Grass Quartet," which featured four-part vocal arrangements accompanied solely by mandolin and guitar — Monroe's usual practice when performing "sacred" songs.

Both Flatt and Scruggs left Monroe's band in early 1948, soon forming their own group, the Foggy Mountain Boys, which met with notable commercial success in the 1950s and 1960s with such hits as "Foggy Mountain Breakdown", "Cabin on the Hill," and "The Ballad of Jed Clampett". In 1949, after signing with Decca Records, Monroe quickly regrouped, entering the "golden age" of his career with what many consider the classic "high lonesome" version of the Blue Grass Boys, featuring the lead vocals and rhythm guitar of Jimmy Martin, the banjo of Rudy Lyle (replacing Don Reno), and fiddlers such as Merle "Red" Taylor, Charlie Cline, Bobby Hicks and Vassar Clements. This band recorded a number of bluegrass classics, including "My Little Georgia Rose," "On and On," "Memories of Mother and Dad," and "Uncle Pen," as well as instrumentals such as "Roanoke", "Big Mon", "Stoney Lonesone", "Get Up John" and the mandolin feature "Raw Hide. " Carter Stanley joined the Blue Grass Boys as guitarist for a short time in 1951 during a period when the Stanley Brothers had temporarily disbanded.

On January 16, 1953 Monroe was critically injured in a two-car wreck. He and "Bluegrass Boys" bass player, Bessie Lee Mauldin, were returning home from a fox hunt north of Nashville. On highway 31-W, near White House, their car was struck by a drunken driver. Monroe, who had suffered injuries to his back, left arm and nose, was rushed to General Hospital in Nashville. It took him almost four months to recover and resume touring. In the meantime Charlie

Cline and Jimmy Martin kept the band together.

By the late 1950s, however, Monroe's commercial fortunes had begun to slip. The rise of rock-and-roll and the development of the "Nashville sound" in mainstream country music both represented threats to the viability of bluegrass. While still a mainstay on the Grand Ole Opry, Monroe found diminishing success on the singles charts, and struggled to keep his band together in the face of declining demand for live performances.

The folk revival

Monroe's fortunes began to improve during the "folk revival" of the early 1960s. Many college students and other young people were beginning to discover Monroe, associating his style more with traditional folk music than with the country-and-western genre with which it had previously been identified. The word "bluegrass" first appeared around this time to describe the sound of Monroe and similar artists such as Flatt and Scruggs, the Stanley Brothers, Reno and Smiley, Jim and Jesse, and the Osborne Brothers. While Flatt and Scruggs immediately recognized the potential for a lucrative new audience in cities and on college campuses in the North, Monroe was slower to respond. Under the influence of Ralph Rinzler, a young musician and folklorist from New Jersey who briefly became Monroe's manager in 1963, Monroe gradually expanded his geographic reach beyond the traditional southern country music circuit. Rinzler was also responsible for a lengthy profile and interview in the influential folk music magazine Sing Out! that first publicly referred to Monroe as the "father" of bluegrass. Accordingly, at the first bluegrass festival organized by Carlton Haney at Roanoke, Virginia in 1965, Bill Monroe was the central figure.

The growing national popularity of Monroe's music during the 1960s was also apparent in the increasingly diverse background of musicians recruited into his band. Non-southerners who served as Blue Grass Boys during this period included banjo player Bill Keith and singer/guitarist Peter Rowan from Massachusetts, fiddler Gene Lowinger from New York, banjo player Lamar Grier from Maryland, banjo player Steve Arkin from New York, and singer/guitarist Roland White and fiddler Richard Greene from California.

Later years

Even after the folk revival faded in the mid-1960s, it left a loyal audience for bluegrass music. Bluegrass festivals became common, with fans often traveling long distances to see a number of different acts over several days of performances.

In 1967 Monroe himself founded an annual bluegrass festival at Bean Blossom in southern Indiana, a park he had purchased in 1951, which routinely attracted a crowd of thousands; a double LP from the festival featuring Monroe, Jimmy Martin, Lester Flatt, and Jim and Jesse was released in 1973. The annual Bill Monroe Bean Blossom Bluegrass Festival is now the world's oldest continuously running annual bluegrass festival.

Monroe's compositions during his later period were largely instrumentals, including "Jerusalem Ridge", "Old Dangerfield"(stylized as Old Daingerfield), and "My Last Days on Earth"; he settled into a new role as a musical patriarch who continued to influence younger generations of musicians. Monroe recorded two albums of duets in the 1980s; the first featured collaborations with country stars such as Emmylou Harris, Waylon Jennings, and the Oak Ridge Boys, while the second paired him with other prominent bluegrass musicians. A 1989 live album celebrated his 50th year on the Grand Ole Opry. Monroe also kept a hectic touring schedule. On April 7, 1990, Monroe performed for Farm Aid IV in Indianapolis, Indiana along with Willie Nelson, John Mellencamp, Neil Young and with many other artists.

Death

Monroe suffered a stroke in April 1996, effectively ending his touring and playing career. He died on September 9, 1996, only four days before his 85th birthday.

Awards and legacy

Bill Monroe was made an honorary Kentucky colonel in 1966. He was inducted into the Country Music Hall of Fame in 1970, the Nashville Songwriters Hall of Fame in 1971, and the Rock and Roll Hall of Fame (as an "early influence") in 1997. Jimmie Rodgers, Bob Wills, Hank Williams Sr. , and Johnny Cash are the only other performers honored in all three. As the "father of bluegrass," he was also an inaugural inductee into the International Bluegrass Music Hall of Honor in 1991. In 1993, he received the Grammy Lifetime Achievement Award, and he was awarded the National Medal of

Arts in 1995. His well-known song "Blue Moon of Kentucky" has been covered not only by bluegrass but also rock and country artists, most notably Elvis Presley, Paul McCartney, and Patsy Cline. In 2003, CMT had Bill Monroe ranked No. 16 on CMT 40 Greatest Men of Country Music. Artists that claimed to be influenced by or to be playing the bluegrass genre were often bullied by Bill Monroe. He always considered himself the father and caretaker of bluegrass. He would often say of new bands that did not perform to his standards, "That ain't no part of nothin'. " Even those who question the scope of bluegrass refer to Monroe as a "musical giant" and recognize that "there would be no bluegrass without Bill Monroe. "

Artists influenced by Monroe

More than 150 musicians played in the Blue Grass Boys over the nearly 60 years of Monroe's performing career. Monroe tended to recruit promising young musicians who served an apprenticeship with him before becoming accomplished artists in their own right. Some of Monroe's band members who went on to greater prominence include singer/guitarists Clyde Moody, Lester Flatt, Jack Cook, Mac Wiseman, Jimmy Martin, Carter Stanley, Del McCoury, Peter Rowan, Roland White, Roland Dunn and Doug Green; banjo players Earl Scruggs, Don Reno, Sonny Osborne, and Bill Keith; and fiddlers Tommy Magness, Chubby Wise, Vassar Clements, Byron Berline, Kenny Baker, Bobby Hicks, Gordon Terry, and Glen Duncan. Monroe also regularly performed with flat-picking guitar virtuoso Doc Watson.

Modern bluegrass singer and mandolin player Ricky Skaggs was influenced by Monroe. Skaggs was only six years old when he first got to perform on stage with Monroe and his band. He stated, "I think Bill Monroe's importance to American music is as important as someone like Robert Johnson was to blues, or Louis Armstrong. He was so influential: I think he's probably the only musician that had a whole style of music named after his band".

Pseudonyms used by Monroe as a composer

Joe Ahr; Rupert Jones; Wilbur Jones; Albert Price; James B. Smith; James W. Smith

Discography

Bill Monroe discography

Billboard 200

Billboard 200

The Billboard 200 is a ranking of the 200 highest-selling music albums and EPs in the United States, published weekly by Billboard magazine. It is frequently used to convey the popularity of an artist or groups of artists. Often, a recording act will be remembered by its "number ones", those of their albums that outsold all others during at least one week.

The chart is based solely on sales (both at retail and digitally) of albums in the United States. The sales tracking week begins on Monday and ends on Sunday. A new chart is published the following Thursday with an issue date of the Saturday of the following week.

Example:
Monday January 1 – sales tracking week begins
Sunday January 7 – sales tracking week ends
Thursday January 11 – new chart published, with issue date of Saturday January 20.
Normally new products are released to the American market on Tuesdays. Digital downloads are included in Billboard 200 tabulation, as long as the entire album is purchased as a whole. Albums that are not licensed for retail sale in the United States (yet purchased in the U. S. as imports) are not eligible to chart. A long-standing policy which made titles that are sold exclusively by specific retail outlets (such as Wal-Mart and Starbucks) ineligible for charting, was reversed on November 7, 2007, and took effect in the issue dated November 17.

The current number-one album (as of the issue dated September 29, 2012) on the Billboard 200 is Away from the World by Dave Matthews Band.

History

Billboard began an album chart in 1945. Initially only five positions long, the album chart was not published on a weekly basis, sometimes three to seven weeks passing before it was updated. A biweekly (though with a few gaps), 15-position Best-Selling Popular

Albums chart appeared in 1955. With the explosion of rock and roll music, Billboard premiered a weekly Best-Selling Popular Albums chart on March 24, 1956. The position count varied anywhere from 10 to 30 albums. The first number-one album on the new weekly list was Belafonte by Harry Belafonte. The chart was renamed to Best-Selling Pop Albums later in 1956, and then to Best-Selling Pop LPs in 1957.

Beginning on May 25, 1959, Billboard split the ranking into two charts Best-Selling Stereophonic LPs for stereo albums (30 positions) and Best-Selling Monophonic LPs for mono albums (50 positions). These were renamed to Stereo Action Charts (30 positions) and Mono Action Charts (40 positions) in 1960. In January 1961, they became Action Albums—Stereophonic (15 positions) and Action Albums—Monophonic (25 positions). Three months later, they became Top LPs—Stereo (50 positions) and Top LPs—Monaural (150 positions).

On August 17, 1963 the stereo and mono charts were combined into a 150-position chart called Top LPs. On April 1, 1967, the chart was expanded to 175 positions, then finally to 200 positions on May 13, 1967. In 1972 the album chart's title was changed to Top LPs & Tapes; in 1984 it was retitled Top 200 Albums; in 1985 it was retitled again to Top Pop Albums; in 1991 it became The Billboard 200 Top Albums; and it was given its current title of The Billboard 200 on March 14, 1992.

Catalog albums

In 1960, Billboard began concurrently publishing album charts which ranked sales of older or mid-priced titles. These Essential Inventory charts were divided by stereo and mono albums, and featured titles that had already appeared on the main stereo and mono album charts. Mono albums were moved to the Essential Inventory—Mono chart (25 positions) after spending 40 weeks on the Mono Action Chart, and stereo albums were moved to the Essential Inventory—Stereo chart (20 positions) after 20 weeks on the Stereo Action Chart.

In January 1961, the Action Charts became Action Albums—Monophonic (24 positions), and Action Albums—Stereophonic (15 positions). Albums appeared on either chart for up to nine weeks, then were moved to an Essential Inventory list of approximately 200 titles, with no numerical ranking. This list continued to be published until the consolidated Top LPs chart debuted in 1963.

In 1982, Billboard began publishing a Midline Albums chart which ranked older or mid-priced titles. The chart held 50 positions and was published on a bi-weekly (and later tri-weekly) basis.

On May 25, 1991 Billboard premiered the Top Pop Catalog Albums chart. The criteria for this chart were albums that were more than 18 months old and had fallen below position 100 on the Billboard 200. An album needed not have charted on the Billboard 200 at all to qualify for catalog status.

Starting with the issue dated December 5, 2009, however, the catalog limitations which removed albums over 18 months old, that have dropped below position 100 and have no currently-running single, from the Billboard 200 was lifted, turning the chart into an all-inclusive list of the 200 highest-selling albums in the country (essentially changing Top Comprehensive Albums into the Billboard 200). A new chart that keeps the previous criteria for the Billboard 200 (dubbed Top Current Albums) was also introduced in the same issue.

Holiday albums

Billboard has adjusted its policies for Christmas and holiday albums several times. The albums were eligible for the main album charts until 1963, when a Christmas Albums list was created. Albums appearing here were not listed on the Top LPs chart. In 1974 this rule was reverted and holiday albums again appeared within the main list.

In 1983 the Christmas Albums chart was resurrected, but a title's appearance here did not disqualify it from appearing on the Top Pop Albums chart. In 1994 the chart was retitled Top Holiday Albums. As of 2009 the chart holds 50 positions and is run for several weeks during the end-of-calendar-year holiday season. Its current policy allows holiday albums to concurrently chart on the Top Holiday Albums list and the Billboard 200.

Nielsen SoundScan

Since May 25, 1991, the Billboard 200's positions have been derived from Nielsen SoundScan sales data, as of 2008 contributed by approximately 14,000 music sellers. Because these numbers are supplied by a subset of sellers rather than record labels, it is common for these numbers to be substantially lower than those reported by the Recording Industry Association of America when Gold, Platinum and Diamond album awards are announced (RIAA awards reflect wholesale shipments, not retail sales).

Year-end charts

Billboard's "chart year" runs from the first week of December to the final week in November. This altered calendar allows for Billboard to calculate year-end charts and release them in time for its final print issue on the last week of December. Prior to Nielsen SoundScan, year-end charts were calculated by an inverse-point system based solely on an album's performance on the Billboard 200 (for example, an album would be given one point for a week spent at position 200, two points for a week spent at position 199... up to 200 points for each week spent at number one). Other factors including the total weeks on the chart and at its peak position were calculated into an album's year-end total.

After Billboard began obtaining sales information from Nielsen SoundScan, the year-end charts are now calculated by a very straightforward cumulative total of yearlong sales. This gives a more accurate picture of any given year's best-selling albums, as a title that hypothetically spent nine weeks at number one in March could possibly have sold fewer copies than one spending six weeks at number three in January. Interestingly, albums at the peak of their popularity at the time of the November/December chart-year cutoff many times end up ranked lower than one would expect on a year-end tally, yet are ranked on the following year's chart as well, as their cumulative points are split between the two chart-years.

Uses

The Billboard 200 can be helpful to radio stations as an indication of the types of music listeners are interested in hearing. Retailers can also find it useful as a way to determine which recordings should be given the most prominent display in a store. Other outlets, such as airline music services, also employ the Billboard charts to determine their programming.

Limitations

The chart omits unit sales for listed albums and total recorded sales, making it impossible to determine, for example, if the number one album this week sold as well as the number one from the same period in the prior year. It is also impossible to determine the relative success of albums on a single chart; there is no indication of whether the number one album sold thousands more copies than number 50, or only dozens more. All music genres are combined, but there are separate Billboard charts for individual market segments. The complete sales data broken down by location is made available, but only in the form of separate SoundScan subscriptions.

Artist milestones

Most top-ten albums

The Rolling Stones (36)
Frank Sinatra (33)
The Beatles (30)
Barbra Streisand (30)
Elvis Presley (27)
Most number-one albums

The Beatles (19)
Jay-Z (12)
Elvis Presley (10) (tie)
Bruce Springsteen (10) (tie)
The Rolling Stones (9) (tie)
Barbra Streisand (9) (tie)
Most consecutive number-one albums

The Beatles (8)
Eminem (6) (tie)
Dave Matthews Band (6) (tie)
DMX (5) (tie)
Elton John (5) (tie)
Madonna (5) (tie)
U2 (5) (tie)
Wings (5) (tie)
Most consecutive studio albums to debut at number-one

Dave Matthews Band (6)
Metallica (5) (tie)
Eminem (5) (tie)

Madonna (5) (tie)
U2 (5) (tie)
Most cumulative weeks at number one

The Beatles (132)
Elvis Presley (67)
Michael Jackson (51) (tie)
Garth Brooks (51) (tie)
Whitney Houston (46) (tie)
The Kingston Trio (46) (tie)
Album milestones

Most weeks at number one

(54 weeks) West Side Story – Soundtrack (1962–63)
(37 weeks) Thriller – Michael Jackson (1983–84)
(31 weeks) Rumours – Fleetwood Mac (1977–78)
(31 weeks) South Pacific – Soundtrack (1958–59)
(31 weeks) Calypso – Harry Belafonte (1956–57)
(24 weeks) 21 – Adele (2011–12)
(24 weeks) Purple Rain – Prince and the Revolution/Soundtrack (1984–85)
(24 weeks) Saturday Night Fever: The Original Movie Sound Track – Bee Gees/Soundtrack (1978)
(21 weeks) Please Hammer, Don't Hurt 'Em – MC Hammer (1990)
(20 weeks) The Bodyguard: Original Soundtrack Album – Whitney Houston/Soundtrack (1992–93)
(20 weeks) Blue Hawaii – Elvis Presley/Soundtrack (1961–62)
Most weeks on the chart

Note that totals are for the main albums chart only, catalog chart totals are not factored in.
(814 weeks) The Dark Side of the Moon – Pink Floyd
(490 weeks) Johnny's Greatest Hits – Johnny Mathis
(480 weeks) My Fair Lady – Original Cast
(331 weeks) Highlights from the Phantom of the Opera – Original Cast
(308 weeks) Tapestry – Carole King
(305 weeks) Oklahoma! – Soundtrack
(295 weeks) Heavenly - Johnny Mathis
(284 weeks) Metallica – Metallica
(282 weeks) MCMXC a. D. – Enigma
(277 weeks) The King and I – Soundtrack
Biggest jumps to number-one

(176-1) Life After Death – The Notorious B. I. G. (April 12, 1997)
(173-1) Vitalogy – Pearl Jam (December 24, 1994)
(156-1) In Rainbows – Radiohead (January 19, 2008)
(137-1) Ghetto D – Master P (September 20, 1997)
(122-1) More of the Monkees – The Monkees (February 11, 1967)
(112-1) MP da Last Don – Master P (June 20, 1998)
(98-1) Beatles '65 – The Beatles (January 9, 1965)
(61-1) Help! – The Beatles (September 11, 1965)
(60-1) Rubber Soul – The Beatles (January 8, 1966)
(53-1) Ballad of the Green Berets – Barry Sadler (March 12, 1966)
Biggest drops from number-one

(1-37) Light Grenades – Incubus (December 23, 2006)
(1-26) Mission Bell — Amos Lee (February 19, 2011)
(1-25) Showroom of Compassion — Cake (February 5, 2011)
(1-24) Christmas – Michael Bublé (January 14, 2012)
(1-24) Blue Slide Park - Mac Miller (December 3, 2011)
(1-21) The Golden Age of Grotesque – Marilyn Manson (June 7, 2003)
(1-19) The Circle – Bon Jovi (December 5, 2009)
(1-18) The Inspiration – Young Jeezy (January 6, 2007)
(1-16) The Fragile – Nine Inch Nails (October 16, 1999)
(1-15) Greatest Hits – The Notorious B. I. G. (March 31, 2007)
Additional milestones

The first number one album of the SoundScan era (1991 to present) is Time, Love & Tenderness by Michael Bolton.
The only album to attain the pole position before and after the May 25, 1991 introduction of SoundScan is R. E. M. 's album Out of Time.
The first album to debut at number one was Captain Fantastic and the Brown Dirt Cowboy by Elton John. John repeated the same feat with the album Rock of the Westies – the second album to debut at number one – making John the first artist to have two consecutive studio albums debut at number one. Whitney Houston's second album Whitney was the first album by a female artist to debut at number one.
In the early 1960s, Bob Newhart had the accomplishment of having the number one and number two albums simultaneously on the Billboard 200, with The Button-Down Mind and The Button-Down Mind Strikes Back! This feat was equaled by The Beatles multiple times. They did this twice in 1964 with Meet The Beatles! and Introducing. . . The Beatles, and then with A Hard Day's Night and Something New, followed in 1969 with the album The Beatles

(commonly known as The White Album) and the soundtrack for the film Yellow Submarine. In 1991, Guns N' Roses held the top two with Use Your Illusion I and Use Your Illusion II, and in 2004, Nelly's Suit and Sweat.

As a musician, Paul McCartney has the most #1 albums, with 26. This includes 19 albums from his work with The Beatles (referenced earlier in this article), 2 solo albums, and 5 albums as a part of his 1970s group Wings. John Lennon is in second place with 22, including 19 albums with The Beatles, 2 solo albums, and 1 album credited to him and his wife Yoko Ono.

McCartney also has the most top 10 albums, with 48. This includes 30 with The Beatles (referenced earlier in this article), 9 albums with the group Wings, 1 album credited to him and his first wife Linda McCartney, and 8 solo albums.

As of 2008, Pink Floyd's The Dark Side of the Moon has been on the charts for over 1,630 weeks, or approximately thirty-one years. Consecutively, the album spent a record 773 weeks on the Billboard 200. The other weeks were spent on the Top Pop Catalog Albums chart. Its closest rival is Bob Marley's Legend, checking in at over 975 weeks (Billboard 200 and Top Pop Catalog Albums combined).

Tapestry by Carole King holds the record for the longest time for an album by a female solo artist to remain on the Billboard 200, with nearly six years. King also holds the record for most consecutive weeks at #1 on the Billboard 200 for any one album by a female solo artist with 15 weeks, also by Tapestry.

Forever Your Girl by Paula Abdul spent 64 consecutive weeks on the Billboard 200 before hitting number one, making it the longest time for an album to reach the number one spot, while the soundtrack to O Brother, Where Art Thou took 63 weeks to reach number one in 2001 making it the longest run since Nielsen SoundScan began tracking sales.

At one point in early 1980s, all nine studio albums released to that date by Led Zeppelin were on the Billboard 200 chart, and is the most studio albums by a single artist to chart at the same time.

The only EPs to reach number one on the chart are Alice in Chains's Jar of Flies in 1994, Linkin Park and Jay-Z's collaboration EP, Collision Course in 2004, the cast of the television series Glee with Glee: The Music, The Power of Madonna and Glee: The Music, Journey to Regionals in 2010, and Bad Meets Evil's Hell: The Sequel.

The Monkees are only band to have had four number one albums in the same year. Elvis Presley, The Kingston Trio, The Beatles, and the cast of the television series Glee had three different albums hit number one in the same year. Nine artists have had two different albums hit number one in the same year: The Kingston Trio in 1959, Led Zeppelin, DMX, Jay-Z, Garth Brooks, 2Pac, System of a Down, Eminem and Susan Boyle.

The Kingston Trio is the only artist to have four albums simultaneously in the Top Ten, which occurred for five consecutive weeks in November and December 1959.

The only artist in history to have his first five studio albums debut at number one is DMX.

The only artists to have five consecutive studio albums debut at number one are Dave Matthews Band, Jay-Z, DMX and Metallica.

In 2001, Britney Spears became the first female artist in the chart's history to have her first three albums debut at number one. She broke this record two years later with a fourth number one debut. With the number one debut of her Circus album in 2008, Spears also became the youngest female artist in history to have five number one albums. She later beat the record when her 7th studio album, Femme Fatale debuted at number one on April, 2011.

The first UK solo artist to debut at number one with a debut album is Leona Lewis on April 26, 2008 with the album Spirit. The first UK group to debut at number one with a debut album is One Direction on March 31, 2012 with the album Up All Night.

Oldest male to debut at # 1: Tony Bennett on October 8, 2011 (85 years, 66 days old) with the album Duets II. He was born August 3, 1926.

Oldest female to debut at # 1: Barbra Streisand on October 17, 2009 (67 years, 176 days old) with the album Love Is the Answer. She was born April 24, 1942.

The issue dated July 11, 2009 was the first time any catalog album outsold the number-one album on the Billboard 200. Three of Michael Jackson's albums (Number Ones, The Essential Michael Jackson and Thriller) claimed positions 1-3 respectively on Top Pop Catalog Albums and Top Comprehensive Albums in the week following Jackson's death.

With 24 weeks at #1 for her album 21, Adele holds the record for the longest time for a solo album by a female to remain at the top of the Billboard 200. This run was concurrent with her three number one singles on the Hot 100. During this run, Adele also appeared on 4 of the top 5 albums: in addition to her own two top five albums, her songs were included on the 2012 Grammy Nominees album and the Now That's What I Call Music! 41 album.

Adele's album 21 was in the top 10 for 78 weeks, finally dropping to #12 on the chart dated September 8, 2012. This is the most weeks in the top 10 for an album by a woman, and the third most overall, after Bruce Springsteen's Born in the U. S. A. 84-week and The

Sound of Music soundtrack's 109-week runs.
There have been 16 albums released on an independent label to reach #1 on the Billboard 200.
Only seventeen artists have topped the Billboard 200 without having had any single appear in the Hot 100: Van Cliburn, Bob Newhart, Judy Garland (who had hit singles which predated the Hot 100), Frank Fontaine, Blind Faith, N. W. A. , Pantera, Makaveli (alter ego of 2Pac), Bob Carlisle, Slipknot, Vampire Weekend, Arcade Fire, The Decemberists, and Amos Lee.

Billboard Hot 100

Billboard Hot 100

The Billboard Hot 100 is the United States music industry standard singles popularity chart issued weekly by Billboard magazine. Chart rankings are based on radio play and sales; the tracking-week for sales begins on Monday and ends on Sunday, while the radio play tracking-week runs from Wednesday to Tuesday. A new chart is compiled and officially released to the public by Billboard on Thursday. Each chart is dated with the "week-ending" date of the Saturday two weeks after. Example:

Monday, January 1 – sales tracking-week begins
Wednesday, January 3 – airplay tracking-week begins
Sunday, January 7 – sales tracking-week ends
Tuesday, January 9 – airplay tracking-week ends
Thursday, January 11 – new chart released, with issue date of Saturday, January 20.
The first number one song of the Hot 100 was "Poor Little Fool" by Ricky Nelson on August 4, 1958. As of the issue for the week ending September 29, 2012, the Hot 100 has had 1,019 different number-one hits. Its current number-one is "One More Night" by Maroon 5.

History

What has always been known as the Hot 100 had existed for nearly fifteen years as numerous charts, tracking and ranking the most popular singles of the day in several areas. During the 1940s and 1950s, popular singles were ranked in three significant charts:

Best Sellers In Stores—ranked the biggest selling singles in retail stores, as reported by merchants surveyed throughout the country

(20 to 50 positions).
Most Played By Jockeys—ranked the most played songs on United States radio stations, as reported by radio disc jockeys and radio stations (20 to 25 positions).
Most Played In Jukeboxes—ranked the most played songs in jukeboxes across the United States (20 positions). This was one of the main outlets of measuring song popularity with the younger generation of music listeners, as many radio stations resisted adding rock 'n roll music to their playlists for many years.
Although officially all three charts had equal "weight" in terms of their importance, many chart historians refer to the Best Sellers In Stores chart when referencing a song's performance prior to the creation of the Hot 100. Billboard eventually created a fourth singles popularity chart that combined all aspects of a single's performance (sales, airplay and jukebox activity), based on a point system that typically gave sales (purchases) more weight than radio airplay. On the week ending November 12, 1955, Billboard published The Top 100 for the first time. The Best Sellers In Stores, Most Played By Jockeys and Most Played In Jukeboxes charts continued to be published concurrently with the new Top 100 chart.

On June 17, 1957, Billboard discontinued the Most Played In Jukeboxes chart, as the popularity of jukeboxes waned and radio stations incorporated more and more rock-oriented music into their playlists. The week ending July 28, 1958 was the final publication of the Most Played By Jockeys and Top 100 charts, both of which had Perez Prado's instrumental version of "Patricia" ascending to the top.

On August 4, 1958, Billboard premiered one main all-genre singles chart: the Hot 100. Although similar to the Top 100, the first Hot 100 chart reset all songs' "weeks on chart" status to "1". The Hot 100 quickly became the industry standard and Billboard discontinued the Best Sellers In Stores chart on October 13, 1958.

The Billboard Hot 100 is still the standard by which a song's popularity is measured in the United States. The Hot 100 is ranked by radio airplay audience impressions as measured by Nielsen BDS, sales data compiled by Nielsen Soundscan (both at retail and digitally) and streaming activity provided by online music sources.

There are several component charts that contribute to the overall calculation of the Hot 100. The most significant ones are shown below.

Hot 100 Airplay—(per Billboard) approximately 1,000 stations, "composed of adult contemporary, R&B, hip-hop, country, rock, gospel, Latin and Christian formats, digitally monitored twenty-four hours a day, seven days a week. Charts are ranked by number of gross audience impressions, computed by cross-referencing exact times of radio airplay with Arbitron listener data. "
Hot Singles Sales—(per Billboard) "the top selling singles compiled from a national sample of retail store, mass merchant and internet sales reports collected, compiled, and provided by Nielsen SoundScan. "
The chart is released weekly and measures sales of physical commercial singles. With the decline in sales of physical singles in the US, songs that become number one on this chart often do not even chart on the Hot 100. Elton John has the record for most physical singles sold in a week, with 3. 4 million copies of "Candle in the Wind 1997/Something about the Way You Look Tonight" sold the week of October 11, 1997.
Hot Digital Songs—Digital sales are tracked by Nielsen SoundScan and are included as part of a title's sales points.
On-Demand Songs — A collaboration between Billboard, Nielsen SoundScan and National Association of Recording Merchandisers which measures every on-demand play request and plays from unlimited listener-controlled radio channels.
Hot 100 policy changes

The methods and policies by which this data is obtained and compiled have changed many times throughout the chart's history.

As the advent of a singles music chart spawned chart historians and chart-watchers and greatly affected pop culture and produced countless bits of trivia, the main purpose of the Hot 100 is to aid those within the music industry – to reflect the popularity of the "product" (the singles, the albums, etc.) and to track the trends of the buying public. Billboard has (many times) changed its methodology and policies to give the most precise and accurate reflection of what is popular. A very basic example of this would be the ratio given to sales and airplay. During the Hot 100's early history, singles were the leading way by which people bought music. At times when singles sales were robust, more weight was given to a song's retail points than to its radio airplay.

As the decades passed, the recording industry concentrated more on album sales than singles sales. Musicians eventually expressed their creative output in the form of full-length albums rather than singles, and by the 1990s many record companies stopped releasing singles altogether (see Album Cuts, below). Eventually a song's airplay points were weighted more so than its sales. Billboard has adjusted the sales/airplay ratio many times to more accurately reflect the true popularity of songs.

Double-sided singles

Billboard has also changed its Hot 100 policy regarding "two-sided singles" several times. The pre-Hot 100 chart "Best Sellers in Stores" listed popular A- and-B-sides together, with the side that was played most often (based on its other charts) listed first. One of the most notable of these, but far from the only one, was Elvis Presley's "Don't Be Cruel" / "Hound Dog. " During the Presley single's chart run, top billing was switched back and forth between the two sides several times. But on the concurrent "Most Played in Juke Boxes," "Most Played by Jockeys" and the "Top 100," the two songs were listed separately, as was true of all songs. With the initiation of the Hot 100 in 1958, A- and-B-sides charted separately, as they had on the former Top 100.

Starting with the Hot 100 chart for the week ending November 29, 1969, this rule was altered; if both sides received significant airplay, they were listed together. This started to become a moot point by 1972, as most major record labels solidified a trend they had started in the 1960s by putting the same song on both sides of the singles it serviced to radio.

More complex issues began to arise as the typical A-and-B-side format of singles gave way to 12 inch singles and maxi-singles, many of which contained more than one B-side. Further problems arose when, in several cases, a B-side would eventually overtake the A-side in popularity, thus prompting record labels to release a new single, featuring the former B-side as the A-side, along with a "new" B-side.

The inclusion of album cuts on the Hot 100 put the double-sided hit issues to rest permanently.

Album cuts

As many Hot 100 chart policies have been modified over the years, one rule always remained constant: songs were not eligible to enter the Hot 100 unless they were available to purchase as a single. However, on December 5, 1998 the Hot 100 changed from being a "singles" chart to a "songs" chart. During the 1990s, a growing trend in the music industry was to promote songs to radio without ever releasing them as singles. It was claimed by major record labels that singles were cannibalizing album sales, so they were slowly phased out. During this period, accusations began to fly of chart manipulation as labels would hold off on releasing a single until airplay was at its absolute peak, thus prompting a top ten or, in some cases, a number one debut. In many cases, a label would delete a single from its catalog after only one week, thus allowing the song to enter the Hot 100, make a high debut and then slowly decline in position as the one-time production of the retail single sold out.

It was during this period that several popular mainstream hits never charted on the Hot 100, or charted well after their airplay had declined. During the period that they were not released as singles the songs were not eligible to chart. Many of these songs dominated the Hot 100 Airplay chart for extended periods of time:

1995 The Rembrandts – "I'll Be There For You" (number one for eight weeks)
1996 No Doubt – "Don't Speak" (number one for 16 weeks)
1997 Sugar Ray featuring Super Cat – "Fly" (number one for six weeks)
1997 Will Smith – "Men in Black" (number one for four weeks)
1997 The Cardigans – "Lovefool" (number two for eight weeks)
1998 Natalie Imbruglia – "Torn" (number one for 11 weeks)
1998 Goo Goo Dolls – "Iris" (number one for 18 weeks)
As debate and conflicts occurred more and more often, Billboard finally answered the requests of music industry artists and insiders by including airplay-only singles (or "album cuts") in the Hot 100.

EPs

Extended play (EP) releases were listed by Billboard on the Hot 100 and in pre-Hot 100 charts (Top 100) until the mid-to-late 1960s. With the growing popularity of albums, it was decided to move EPs (which typically contain four to six tracks) from the Hot 100 to the Billboard 200, where they are included to this day.

Paid digital downloads

Since February 12, 2005, the Billboard Hot 100 tracks paid digital downloads from such internet services as iTunes, Napster, Musicmatch, and Rhapsody. With paid digital downloads added to the airplay/sales formula of the Hot 100, many songs benefited on the charts from the change. Billboard initially started tracking downloads in 2003 with the Hot Digital Tracks chart. However, these downloads did not count towards the Hot 100 and that chart (as opposed to Hot Digital Songs) counted each version of a song separately (the chart still exists today along with Hot Digital Songs). This is the first major overhaul of the Hot 100's chart formula since December 1998.

The change in formula has shaken up the chart considerably, with some songs debuting on the chart strictly with robust online sales and others making drastic leaps. In recent years, several songs have been able to achieve 80-to-90 position jumps in a single week as their digital components were made available at online music stores. Since 2006, the all-time record for the biggest single-week upward movement was broken nine times.

In the issue dated August 11, 2007, Billboard began incorporating weekly data from Streaming media and On-demand services into the Hot 100. The first two major companies to provide their statistics to Nielsen BDS on a weekly basis are AOL Music and Yahoo! Music, with more to follow in the future. On March 24, 2012, Billboard premiered its On-Demand Songs chart, and its data was newly incorporated into the equation that compiles the Hot 100.

Remixes

Billboard has also answered the call of music industry insiders[who?] who raised an issue regarding song remixes. A growing trend in the early first decade of the 21st century was to issue a song as a "remix" that was so drastically different in structure and lyrical content from its original version that it was essentially a whole new song. Under normal circumstances, airplay points from a song's album version, "radio" mix and/or dance music remix, etc. were all combined and factored into the song's performance on the Hot 100, as the structure, lyrics and melody remained intact. Criticisms began when songs were being completely re-recorded to the point that they no longer resembled the original recording. The first such example of this scenario is Jennifer Lopez' "I'm Real".

Originally entering the Hot 100 in its album version, a "remix" was issued in the midst of its chart run that featured rapper Ja Rule. This new version proved to be far more popular than the album version and the track was propelled to number one.

To address this issue, Billboard now separates airplay points from a song's original version and its remix, if the remix is determined to be a "new song". Since administering this new chart rule, several songs have charted twice, normally credited as "Part 1" and "Part 2". The remix rule is still in place.

Recurrents

Billboard, in an effort to allow the chart to remain as current as possible and to give proper representation to new and developing artists and tracks, has (since 1991) removed titles that have reached certain criteria regarding its current rank and number of weeks on the chart. Recurrent criteria have been modified several times and currently (as of 2010), a song is permanently moved to "recurrent status" if it has spent 20 weeks on the Hot 100 and fallen below position number 50. Exceptions are made to re-releases and sudden resurgence in popularity of tracks that have taken a very long time to gain mainstream success. These rare cases are handled on a case-by-case basis and ultimately determined by Billboard's chart managers and staff.

The most notable exception to the recurrent entry policy applies to holiday-themed releases, which are commonly reissued year after year in anticipation of Christmas purchasing. After its initial chart run, a holiday entry cannot re-enter the Hot 100 in subsequent years.

Year-end charts

Billboard's "chart year" runs from the first week of December to the final week in November. This altered calendar allows for Billboard to calculate year-end charts and release them in time for its final print issue on the last week of December. Prior to Nielsen SoundScan, year-end singles charts were calculated by an inverse-point system based solely on a song's performance on the Hot 100 (for example, a song would be given one point for a week spent at position 100, two points for a week spent at position ninety-nine and so forth, up to 100 points for each week spent at number one). Other factors including the total weeks a song spent on the chart and at its peak position were calculated into its year-end total.

After Billboard began obtaining sales and airplay information from Nielsen SoundScan, the year-end charts are now calculated by a very straightforward cumulative total of yearlong sales and airplay points. This gives a more accurate picture of any given year's most popular tracks, as a song that hypothetically spent nine weeks at number one in March could possibly have earned fewer cumulative points than a song that spent six weeks at number three in January. Songs at the peak of their popularity at the time of the November/December chart-year cutoff many times end up ranked on the following year's chart as well, as their cumulative points are split between the two chart-years, but often are ranked lower than they would have been had the peak occurred in a single year.

Limitations

The limitations of the Hot 100 have become more pronounced over time. Since the Hot 100 was based on singles sales, as singles have themselves become a less common form of song release, the Hot 100's data represented a narrowing segment of sales until the December 1998 change in the ranking formula.

Few music historians believe that the Hot 100 has been a perfectly accurate gauge of the most popular songs for each week or year. For example, during the 1950s and 1960s, payola and other problems skewed the numbers in largely undetectable ways.

Further, the history of popular music shows nearly as many remarkable failures to chart as it does impressive charting histories. Certain artists (such as Pink Floyd and Led Zeppelin) had tremendous album sales while being oblivious to the weekly singles charts. Business changes in the industry also affect artists' statistical "records. " Single releases were more frequent and steady, and were expected to have much shorter shelf lives in earlier decades, making direct historical comparisons somewhat specious. Of the sixteen singles to top the Billboard chart for more than ten weeks since 1955, just one was released before 1992. During the first forty years of the rock era, no song had ever debuted at number one; since a 1995 change in methodology, nineteen songs have.

Strategizing also plays a role. Numerous artists have taken deliberate steps to maximize their chart positions by such tactics as timing a single's debut to face the weakest possible competition, or massively discounting the price of singles to the point where each individual sale represented a financial loss. Meanwhile, other artists would deliberately withhold even their most marketable songs in order to boost album sales. Particularly in the 1990s, many of the most heavily played MTV and radio hits were unavailable for separate purchase. Because of such countervailing strategies, it cannot be said that a Hot 100 chart necessarily lists the country's 100 most popular or successful songs. Strategies like these were the main reason behind the December 1998 change in the charts.

Some critics have argued that an overemphasis on a limited number of singles has distorted record industry development efforts, and there are nearly as many critics of the Hot 100 as there are supporters. Certain of these criticisms, however, are becoming less and less germane as digital downloads have revitalized the concept of "singles sales. "

The Billboard charts have endured as the only widely-circulated published report on songs that have been popular across the United States over the last half-century. Competing publications such as Cash Box, Record World, Radio & Records and most recently Mediabase have offered alternate charts, which sometimes differed widely.

Use in media

The Hot 100 served for many years as the data source for the weekly radio countdown show American Top 40. This relationship ended on November 30, 1991, as American Top 40 started using the airplay-only side of the Hot 100 (then called Top 40 Radio Monitor). The ongoing splintering of Top 40 radio in the early 1990s led stations to lean into specific formats, meaning that practically no station would play the wide array of genres that typically composed each weekly Hot 100 chart.

Similar charts

A new chart, the Pop 100, was created by Billboard in February 2005 to answer criticism that the Hot 100 was biased in favor of rhythmic songs, as throughout most of its existence, the Hot 100 was seen predominantly as a pop chart. It was discontinued in June 2009 due to the charts becoming increasingly similar.

The Canadian Hot 100 was launched June 16, 2007. Like the Hot

100 chart, it uses sales and airplay tracking compiled by Nielsen SoundScan and BDS.

The Japan Hot 100 was launched in the issue dated May 31, 2008, using the same methodologies as the Hot 100 charts for the U. S. and Canada, utilizing sales and airplay data from SoundScan Japan and radio tracking service Plantech.

Blue Christmas

Blue Christmas

For other uses, see Blue Christmas .
"Blue Christmas"

Single by Elvis Presley
from the album Elvis' Christmas Album
B-side "Wooden Heart" (447-0720)
"Santa Claus Is Back in Town" (447-0647)
Released November 9, 1964 (447-0720)
November 26, 1965 (447-0647)
Format 7-inch
Recorded September 5, 1957
Genre Christmas, Pop, Rock and roll
Length 2:07
Label RCA Victor 447-0720
RCA Victor 447-0647
Writer(s) Billy Hayes, Jay W. Johnson
Elvis Presley singles chronology
"Ain't That Loving You Baby"
(1964) "Blue Christmas"
(1964) "Do the Clam"
(1965)
Elvis' Christmas Album track listing
12 tracks
"Blue Christmas"
Single by The Beach Boys
from the album The Beach Boys' Christmas Album
A-side "The Man with All the Toys"
Released November 9, 1964
Format 7-inch
Recorded June 24, 1964 - June 28, 1964

Genre Christmas, Pop, Rock
Length 4:41 (for both songs)
Label Capitol Records
Writer(s) Billy Hayes, Jay W. Johnson
Producer Brian Wilson
The Beach Boys singles chronology
"Dance, Dance, Dance"
(1964) "The Man with All the Toys"
(1964) "Do You Wanna Dance?"
(1965)

"Blue Christmas" is a Christmas song written by Billy Hayes and Jay W. Johnson. Its tale of unrequited love during the holidays and is a longstanding staple of Christmas music, especially in the country genre.

Contents

Initial recordings and major versions

The song was first recorded by Doye O'Dell in 1948, and was popularized the following year in three separate recordings: one by country artist Ernest Tubb; one by bandleader Hugo Winterhalter and his orchestra; and one by bandleader Russ Morgan and his orchestra (the latter featuring lead vocals by Morgan and backing vocals by singers credited as the Morganaires). Tubb's version spent the first week of January 1950 at # 1 on Billboard magazine's Most-Played Juke Box (Country & Western) Records chart, while Winterhalter's version peaked at # 9 on Billboard's Records Most Played by Disk Jockeys chart and Morgan's version reached # 11 on Billboard's Best-Selling Pop Singles chart.

Elvis Presley cemented the status of "Blue Christmas" as a rock-and-roll holiday classic by deleting one verse from Tubb's version and recording the remainder on his 1957 LP Elvis' Christmas Album. Presley's version is notable musicologically as well as culturally in that its backing vocalists (especially in the soprano line) replace many major and just minor thirds with neutral and septimal minor thirds, respectively. In addition to contributing to the overall tone of the song, the resulting "blue notes" constitute a musical play

on words that provides an "inside joke" or "Easter egg" to trained ears. Presley's original 1957 version was released as a commercially-available single for the first time in 1964.
American rock band The Beach Boys recorded a version featuring Brian Wilson on lead vocals, releasing it on November 16, 1964, in two separate formats simultaneously: a) the B-side of the "The Man with All the Toys" single and b) a track on The Beach Boys' Christmas Album. The Beach Boys' version reached #3 on the U. S. Christmas charts but did not chart in the U. K.

Cover versions

Following the success of Presley's version, the song has been recorded by a host of rock and country artists, as well as some working in other genres, with over 65 recorded versions:
A version by The Browns peaked at #97 on the Billboard Hot 100 singles chart in December 1960.

Use in film and television

The song was featured in the children's Christmas special The Year Without a Santa Claus.
In 2009, Elvis' version was used in a TV commercial for Verizon Wireless.

Blue Christmas (Elvis Presley album)

Blue Christmas (Elvis Presley album)

Blue Christmas
Compilation album by Elvis Presley
Released 1992
Genre Christmas
Length 17:04
Producer Felton Jarvis, Steve Sholes
Blue Christmas is a 1992 Christmas compilation album with songs sung by Elvis Presley.

Track listing

All songs arranged and sung by Elvis Presley except where noted.
O Come, All Ye Faithful - 2:47
The First Noel - 2:08
Winter Wonderland - 2:17 (Arranged by Richard B. Smith and Felix Bernard)
Silver Bells - 2:27 (Arranged by Ray Evans and Jay Livingston)
Blue Christmas - 2:05 (Arranged by Billy Hayes and Jay Johnson)
Silent Night - 2:23 (Arranged by Leon Young and Franz Gruber)
White Christmas - 2:23 (Arranged by Irving Berlin)
I'll Be Home For Christmas - 1:54 (Arranged by Walter Kent and Ken Gannon)
v t e
Elvis Presley

Blue Hawaii

Blue Hawaii

Blue Hawaii

Directed by Norman Taurog
Michael D. Moore (assistant)
Produced by Hal B. Wallis
Paul Nathan (associate)
Written by Allan Weiss (story)
Hal Kanter (screenwriter)
Starring Elvis Presley
Joan Blackman
Angela Lansbury
Music by Joseph J. Lilley
Cinematography Charles Lang, Jr.
Editing by Terry O. Morse
Studio Hal Wallis Productions
Distributed by Paramount Pictures
Release date(s) November 22, 1961(USA),
December 8, 1963 (Turkey),
March 1962-January 1964 (Europe)
Running time 102 minutes
Language English
Blue Hawaii is a 1961 musical film set in the state of Hawaii and starring Elvis Presley. The screenplay by Hal Kanter was nominated by the Writers Guild of America in 1962 in the category of Best Written American Musical. The movie opened at no. 2 in box office

receipts for that week and despite mixed reviews from critics, finished as the 10th top-grossing movie of 1961 and 14th for 1962 on the Variety national box office survey, earning $5 million. The film won a fourth place prize Laurel Award in the category of Top Musical of 1961.

Plot

Chadwick Gates (Presley) has just gotten out of the Army, and is happy to be back in Hawaii with his surfboard, his beach buddies, and his girlfriend. His mother wants him to go to work at the Great Southern Hawaiian Fruit Company, but Chad is reluctant, so Chad goes to work as a tour guide at his girlfriend's agency.

Primary cast

Elvis Presley as Chad (Chadwick) Gates
Joan Blackman as Maile Duval
Angela Lansbury as Sarah Lee Gates
Nancy Walters as Abigail Prentice
Roland Winters as Fred Gates
John Archer as Jack Kelman
Howard McNear as Mr. Chapman
Steve Brodie as Tucker Garvey
Iris Adrian as Enid Garvey
Hilo Hattie as Waihila
Jenny Maxwell as Ellie Corbett
Pamela Austin as Selena "Sandy" Emerson (as Pamela Kirk)
Darlene Tompkins as Patsy Simon
Christian Kay as Beverly Martin
Lani Kai as Carl Tanami
Jose De Vega as Ernie Gordon
Frank Atienza as Ito O'Hara
Tiki Hanalei as Ping Pong
Production notes

Blue Hawaii was the first of three Elvis films to be shot in Hawaii, followed by Girls! Girls! Girls! in 1962 and Paradise, Hawaiian Style in 1965. Producer Hal B. Wallis was keen to put Presley into a film that showed how the army affected a man. Actress Juliet Prowse, who had starred with Presley in GI Blues, was approached to be his love interest again. However, after her demands were put forward, Paramount decided to drop her as a possible candidate for the role, choosing Joan Blackman instead. Presley was apparently so pale before shooting that Wallis personally recommended a brand of tanning lamp to darken his skin. The film was announced in the fall of 1960 as Hawaii Beach Boy. At the time, film producer Walter Mirisch had a similar titled film in production, "Hawaii", and he was upset that Wallis had chosen such a similar name.

Presley arrived in Hawaii on March 18, 1961, to prepare for a charity concert that he was performing on March 25 to raise funds for the Arizona Memorial at Pearl Harbour. He arrived at the recording studio on March 21 to start the recording of the film's soundtrack. Three weeks later location filming had finished, including scenes at Waikiki Beach, Diamond Head, Mount Tantalus, and Hanauma Bay, a volcanic crater that is open to the sea, near the bedroom community of Hawaii-Kai, a few miles away from Waikiki. Following location filming, the crew returned to the Paramount lot to finish other scenes for the film. Presley would relax during filming by giving karate demonstrations with his friend and employee, Red West, which resulted in Presley's fingers becoming bruised and swollen. Wallis warned the female stars of the film to avoid parties hosted by Presley because they were turning up for shooting looking tired.

It could be argued that this film set the tone for Presley's future film career — pretty locations, gorgeous girls, dull plots, and mediocre songs. Almost all of these musical-comedy films performed well, whereas more "serious" films, such as Flaming Star, Wild in the Country and Charro!, did poorly at the box office. Blue Hawaii, on the other hand, was one of Elvis' most successful films, opening at #2 at the box office when released on November 22, 1961.

Producer Hal Wallis would use the box office returns from Blue Hawaii to finance an upcoming Wallis film, 1964's Becket, starring Richard Burton and Peter O'Toole.

Presley was 26 at the time this film was released, and a not yet 36-year-old Angela Lansbury played his character's mother. Lansbury would later comment that her appearance here was one of the worst in her career.

Much of the film was shot on location at the Coco Palms Resort on the east coast of Kauai. The resort has been abandoned since Hurricane Iniki in 1992.

Although it is mentioned in the film that Chad's parents live in Kahala, one of the most expensive and exclusive areas of Honolulu in 1961, the view from their "lanai" (porch or terrace) shows Diamond Head as it appears from Waikiki and downtown Honolulu. In actuality, Kahala is located on the other side of Diamond Head from Waikiki.

There were several scenes filmed in and around the famous Waikiki Beach, including the opening driving scenes, as well as the office scene across the street from the "International Market. " The scenes where Chad's clients stayed in a hotel and where he picked up his tour group - as well as the beach he spent time with his girlfriend - were all filmed on the property that is now known as the Hilton Hawaiian Village on Waikiki Beach.

Soundtrack

Blue Hawaii (album)
Presley's remake of the title song introduced it to an audience too young to remember Bing Crosby's original hit version.

The Blue Hawaii soundtrack album was on the Billboard Pop Albums chart for 79 weeks, where it spent 20 weeks at #1. It has been certified by the RIAA for sales of three million copies in the U. S.

The Blue Hawaii soundtrack album was nominated for a Grammy Award in 1961 in the category of Best Sound Track Album Or Recording Of Original Cast From A Motion Picture Or Television.

Blue Hawaii (album)

Blue Hawaii

Soundtrack album by Elvis Presley
Released October 1, 1961
Recorded 1961
Genre Rock and roll, hawaiian music
Length 32:02
Label RCA Victor
Producer Steve Sholes
Elvis Presley chronology
Something for Everybody
(1961) Blue Hawaii

(1961) Pot Luck
(1962)
Professional ratings
Review scores

Source	Rating
Allmusic	

Blue Hawaii is the fourteenth album by Elvis Presley, released on RCA Victor Records in mono and stereo, LPM/LSP 2426, in October 1961 - the exact date of October 1 is disputed. It is a soundtrack for Presley's film of the same name. Recording sessions took place at Radio Recorders in Hollywood on March 21, 22, and 23, 1961. It spent 20 weeks at the #1 slot and 39 weeks in the Top 10 on the US Top Pop Albums chart. It was certified Gold on 12/21/1961, Platinum and 2x Platinum on 3/27/1992 and 3x Platinum on 7/30/2002 by the RIAA. On the US Top Pop Albums chart Blue Hawaii is the #2 most successful album of the 1960s, second only to West Side Story.

Contents

Content

RCA and the Colonel had initially planned a schedule of one soundtrack and one popular music release per year for Presley, in addition to the requisite four singles . To coincide with the location of the film, touches of Hawaiian music were included, from instrumentation to the traditional song "Aloha Oe. " The title song was taken from a similar film Waikiki Wedding starring Bing Crosby in 1937, and "Hawaiian Wedding Song" dates from a 1926 operetta. The songs "Can't Help Falling In Love" and "Rock-A-Hula Baby" were pulled off the album for two sides of a single released the following month. The A-side "Can't Help Falling In Love," which would become the standard closer for an Elvis Presley concert in the 1970s, went to #2 on the Billboard Hot 100, while the b-side charted independently at #23.
The Blue Hawaii soundtrack was nominated for a Grammy Award

in 1961 in the category of Best Sound Track Album Or Recording Of Original Cast From A Motion Picture Or Television.
The success of this soundtrack and its predecessor G. I. Blues, both of which sold in much greater quantity than Presley's two regular releases of the time, Elvis Is Back! and Something for Everybody, set the pace for the rest of the decade. The Colonel and Presley would focus on Elvis' film career, "normal" albums taking a back seat with only six during the 1960s against sixteen full-length soundtrack albums among 27 movies and the comeback special. Five songs from this album appear on the 1995 compendium of soundtrack recordings: the two sides of the single, "Blue Hawaii," "Hawaiian Wedding Song," and "Beach Boy Blues. "
On April 29, 1997, RCA released a remastered and expanded version for compact disc with eight bonus tracks. All had been recorded during the sessions for the original album, and all were unreleased except for "Steppin' Out of Line" which appeared on Pot Luck with Elvis.

Personnel

Elvis Presley - vocals
The Surfers - Background Vocals
The Jordanaires - Background Vocals
Boots Randolph - Saxophone
George Field - Harmonica
Fred Tavares, Bernie Lewis - Ukulele
Tiny Timbrell - Rhythm Archtop guitar
Hank Garland, Scotty Moore - Lead Electric Guitar
Alvino Rey - Pedal Steel Guitar
Floyd Cramer, Dudley Brooks - Piano
Bob Moore - Bass
D. J. Fontana, Bernie Mattinson, Hal Blaine - Drums

Track listing

Side one

Track Recorded Song Title Writer(s) Time
1. 3/22/61 Blue Hawaii Leo Robin and Ralph Rainger
2:36
2. 3/22/61 Almost Always True Ben Weisman and Fred
Wise 2:25
3. 3/21/61 Aloha 'Oe Queen Lydia Lili'uokalani 1:53

4. 3/21/61 No More Don Robertson, Hal Blair and Sebastián Iradier 2:22
5. 3/23/61 Can't Help Falling in Love George David Weiss, Hugo Peretti, Luigi Creatore 3:01
6. 3/23/61 Rock-A-Hula Baby Ben Weisman, Fred Wise, Dolores Fuller 1:59
7. 3/22/61 Moonlight Swim Ben Weisman and Sylvia Dee 2:20

Side two

Track Recorded Song Title Writer(s) Time
1. 3/21/61 Ku-U-I-Po George David Weiss, Hugo Peretti, Luigi Creatore 2:23
2. 3/22/61 Ito Eats Sid Tepper and Roy C. Bennett 1:23
3. 3/21/61 Slicin' Sand Sid Tepper and Roy C. Bennett 1:36
4. 3/21/61 Hawaiian Sunset Sid Tepper and Roy C. Bennett 2:32
5. 3/23/61 Beach Boy Blues Sid Tepper and Roy C. Bennett 2:03
6. 3/22/61 Island Of Love Sid Tepper and Roy C. Bennett 2:41
7. 3/22/61 Hawaiian Wedding Song Al Hoffman, Charles King, Dick Manning 2:48

1997 reissue bonus tracks

Chart positions for albums from Billboard 200
Track Recorded Album Title Catalogue Release date Chart peak Song title Writer(s) Time
1. 3/22/61 Pot Luck with Elvis LSP 2523 6/5/62 #4 Steppin' Out of Line Ben Weisman, Fred Wise, Dolores Fuller 1:53
2. 3/23/61 previously unreleased Can't Help Falling in Love (alternate take) George David Weiss, Hugo Peretti, Luigi Creatore 1:54
3. 3/21/61 previously unreleased Slicin' Sand (alternate take) Sid Tepper and Roy C. Bennett 1:45
4. 3/21/61 previously unreleased No More (alternate take) Don Robertson and Hal Blair 2:35
5. 3/23/61 previously unreleased Rock-A-Hula Baby (alternate take) Ben Weisman, Fred Wise, Dolores Fuller 2:15
6. 3/23/61 previously unreleased Beach Boy Blues (alternate take) Sid Tepper and Roy C. Bennett 1:58

7. 3/22/61 previously unreleased Steppin' Out of Line
(alternate take) Ben Weisman, Fred Wise, Dolores Fuller 1:54
8. 3/22/61 previously unreleased Blue Hawaii
(alternate take) Leo Robin and Ralph Rainger 2:40

Chart positions

Year Chart Position
1961 Billboard Pop Albums (Billboard 200) (mono and stereo)
1
1962 UK Albums Chart
Billboard Pop Albums (Billboard 200) (mono and stereo)
Preceded by
Judy at Carnegie Hall by Judy Garland Billboard 200 number-one album (mono)
December 11, 1961 - May 4, 1962 Succeeded by
West Side Story (soundtrack)
by Leonard Bernstein and Stephen Sondheim
Preceded by
Stereo 35/MM by Enoch Light & the Light Brigade Billboard 200 number-one album (stereo)
December 11, 1961 - January 12, 1962 Succeeded by
Holiday Sing Along with Mitch by Mitch Miller
Preceded by
Another Black and White Minstrel Show by George Mitchell Minstrels
The Young Ones by Cliff Richard & The Shadows UK Albums Chart number-one album
6 January 1962 - 13 January 1962
24 February 1962 - 23 June 1962 Succeeded by
The Young Ones by Cliff Richard & The Shadows
West Side Story (soundtrack) by Leonard Bernstein and Steven Sondheim

Blue Moon of Kentucky

Blue Moon of Kentucky

"Blue Moon of Kentucky" is a waltz written in 1946 by bluegrass musician Bill Monroe and recorded by his band, The Blue Grass Boys. The song has since been recorded by many artists, including Elvis Presley.

"Blue Moon of Kentucky" is the official bluegrass song of Kentucky. In 2002, Monroe's version was one of 50 recordings chosen that year by the Library of Congress to be added to the National Recording Registry. In 2003, CMT ranked "Blue Moon of Kentucky" #11 on its 100 Greatest Songs in Country Music.

Bill Monroe

Bill Monroe wrote the song in 1946, recording it for Columbia Records on September 16. It was released in early 1947. At the time, the Bluegrass Boys included vocalist and guitarist Lester Flatt and banjoist Earl Scruggs, who would later form their own bluegrass band, the Foggy Mountain Boys. Both Flatt and Scruggs performed on the recording, although Bill Monroe supplied the vocals on this song.

The song, described as a "bluegrass waltz", had become a nationwide hit by 1947 and also became enormously popular with other bluegrass, country, and early rockabilly acts. Although the song was revered by the Grand Ole' Opry and others, Carl Perkins played an uptempo version of this song in his early live performances.

In 1954, The Stanley Brothers recorded a version of the song using Presley's 4/4 arrangement with bluegrass instrumentation, neatly bridging the stylistic gap between Monroe's and Presley's approaches. Bill Monroe subsequently rerecorded and performed the song using a mixture of the two styles, starting the song in its original 3/4 arrangement, then launching into an uptempo 4/4 rendition.

Elvis Presley

The search for another song to release along with "That's All Right" at Sun Records in July 1954 led to "Blue Moon of Kentucky" via Bill Black. "We all of us knew we needed something," according to Scotty Moore, and things seemed hopeless after a while. "Bill is the one who came up with "Blue Moon of Kentucky. ". . . We're taking a little break and he starts beating on the bass and singing "Blue Moon of Kentucky," mocking Bill Monroe, singing the high falsetto voice. Elvis joins in with him, starts playing and singing along with him," as did Moore himself. Presley, Moore, and Black, with the encouragement of Sam Phillips, transformed Monroe's slow waltz (3/4 time) into an upbeat, blues-flavored tune in 4/4 time.

After an early rendition of the song, Sun Records owner Sam Phillips exclaimed, "BOY, that's fine, that's fine. That's a POP song now!. " As with all of the Presley records issued by Sun, the artists were listed as "ELVIS PRESLEY SCOTTY and BILL".

The same night that Dewey Phillips first played the flip side of this first release of Presley's music on WHBQ ("That's All Right"), Sleepy Eye John at WHHM loosed "Blue Moon of Kentucky". Bob Neal of WMPS played the record too. The pop jockeys, entranced by something new, began slipping "That's All Right" and "Blue Moon of Kentucky" in among the more "easy listening" pop of Teresa Brewer, Nat Cole and Tony Bennett.

With Presley's version of Monroe's song consistently rated higher, both sides began to chart across the South. Billboard has the song listed only in Memphis, and as #6 with That's All Right at #7 on October 9 in the C&W Territorial Best Sellers. By October 23, "Blue Moon" was in the top 10 in Memphis, Nashville, and New Orleans, with "That's All Right" absent from the listings.

Fellow Sun Records artist Charlie Feathers has often claimed that he came up with the arrangement of the song used by Presley.

The song was later used for the 2005 TV miniseries Elvis in a scene.

Other recordings

Numerous artists have recorded the song, including John Fogerty, Elvis Presley, Patsy Cline, Ronnie Hawkins, Rory Gallagher, Jerry Lee Lewis, LeAnn Rimes, Paul McCartney, Boxcar Willie, Ray Charles, Jerry Reed, Jimmy Martin, Brian Setzer, Patrick Wall and Raul Seixas. The song was also performed in 1980 by Levon Helm (The Band) for the movie "Coal Miner's Daughter".

In 1995, the remaining Beatles - Paul McCartney, George Harrison, and Ringo Starr - performed an impromptu 4/4 version of the song that was eventually released on the Bonus DVD of The Beatles Anthology video release. McCartney had earlier performed and released the song in 1991 as part of his appearance on MTV Unplugged.

On the late '80s/early '90s time travelling sci-fi show, Quantum Leap, Sam Beckett performed "Blue Moon of Kentucky" after

Leaping in as Elvis Presley in the "Memphis Melody" episode. John Candy and Steve Martin sing the song in the 1987 film Planes, Trains and Automobiles. In the King of the Hill episode "The Bluegrass Is Always Greener", first aired in 2002, Jeff Boomhauer performed the song, with Vince Gill providing the singing voice.

Blue Suede Shoes

Blue Suede Shoes

"Blue Suede Shoes"

Single by Elvis Presley
from the album Elvis Presley
B-side "Tutti Frutti"
Released September 8, 1956
Format 7" single
Recorded January 30, 1956
Genre Rock and roll
Length 1:58
Label RCA Records, RCA 47-6636
Writer(s) Carl Perkins
Producer Steve Sholes
Elvis Presley singles chronology
"Blue Suede Shoes" is a rock and roll standard written and first recorded by Carl Perkins in 1955 and is considered one of the first rockabilly (rock and roll) records and incorporated elements of blues, country and pop music of the time. The song was notably covered by Elvis Presley and Buddy Holly.

Origin

Johnny Cash planted the seed for the song in the fall of 1955, while Perkins, Cash, Elvis Presley, and other Louisiana Hayride acts toured throughout the South. Cash told Perkins of a black airman whom he had met when serving in the military in Germany. He had referred to his military regulation air shoes as "blue suede shoes. " Cash suggested that Carl write a song about the shoes. Carl replied, "I don't know anything about shoes. How can I write a song about shoes?"

When Perkins played a dance on December 4, 1955, he noticed a couple dancing near the stage. Between songs, Carl heard a stern, forceful voice say, "Uh-uh, don't step on my suedes!" Carl looked down and noted that the boy was wearing blue suede shoes and one had a scuff mark. Good gracious, a pretty little thing like that and all he can think about is his blue suede shoes, thought Carl.

That night Perkins began working on a song based on the incident. His first thought was to frame it with a nursery rhyme. He considered, and quickly discarded "Little Jack Horner. . . " and "See a spider going up the wall. . . ", then settled on "One for the money. . . " Leaving his bed and working with his Les Paul guitar, he started with an A chord. After playing five chords while singing "Well, it's one for the money. . . Two for the show. . . Three to get ready. . . Now go, man, go!" he broke into a boogie rhythm. He quickly grabbed a brown paper potato sack and wrote the song down, writing the title out as "Blue Swade"; "S-W-A-D-E — I couldn't even spell it right," he later said. According to Perkins, "On December 17, 1955, I wrote 'Blue Suede Shoes'. I recorded it on December 19. " Producer Sam Phillips suggested that Perkins's line "go cat go" be changed to "go man go", but it didn't.

Success of Perkins' Sun Records release

The Sun recording of "Blue Suede Shoes" was released on January 1, 1956, as Sun 234. Two copies of the song on 78 rpm records were sent to Perkins, but arrived broken. Carl soon discovered that the song was available in the newer 7" microgrooved 45 rpm format and was disappointed that he didn't have a copy in the older, more substantial 78 rpm format.

In both Jackson, where Perkins lived, and in Memphis, radio stations were playing the flip side of the record, "Honey Don't. " In Cleveland, Ohio, however, disc jockey Bill Randle was featuring "Blue Suede Shoes" prominently on his nightly show, and before January was over, the Cleveland distributor of the record asked Phillips for an additional 25,000 copies of the record.

"Shoes" became the side of choice throughout the South and Southwest. On February 11 it was the No. 2 single on Memphis charts, was number one the next week, and remained there for the next 3 months. Perkins made four appearances on the Big D Jamboree on radio station KRLD (AM) in Dallas where he played the song every Saturday night, and was booked on a string of one nighters in the Southwest. The Jamboree emanated from the Dallas

Sportatorium with about four thousand seats, and it sold out for each of Perkins' performances. Music shops in Dallas ordered a huge number of records, and at one point the record was selling at a rate of 20,000 copies per day.

A Song Hits review of the song, published February 18, stated that "Perkins has come up with some wax here that has hit the national retail chart in almost record time. Interestingly enough, the disk has a measure of appeal for pop and r. &b. customers. "

On March 17, Perkins became the first country artist to reach the number three spot on the rhythm & blues charts. That night, Perkins and his band first performed "Blue Suede Shoes" on television on ABC-TV's Ozark Jubilee (coincidentally, Presley was on Stage Show on CBS-TV that same night, singing the song for a second time).

Perkins was booked to next appear on The Perry Como Show on NBC-TV on March 24, but on March 22 he and his band members had a serious automobile accident on the way to New York City, resulting in the death of a truck driver and the hospitalization of both Perkins and his brother. While Perkins recuperated from the accident, "Blue Suede Shoes" rose to number one on most pop, R&B, and country regional charts. It also held the number two position on the Billboard Hot 100 and country charts. Presley's "Heartbreak Hotel" held the number one position on the pop and country charts, while "Shoes" did better than "Heartbreak" on the R&B charts.

By mid-April, more than one million copies of "Shoes" had been sold, earning Perkins a Gold Record. "Blue Suede Shoes" was the first million selling country song to cross over to both rhythm and blues and pop charts.

Sam Phillips retained the rights to the song, although it was represented by the New York house of Hill and Range as part of the agreement when Phillips sold Presley's contract. Perkins would acquire the rights to "Shoes," along with all of his Sun Records songs, in 1977.

Presley's RCA cover

Recording cover versions of songs was standard practice during the 1940s and 1950s, and "Blue Suede Shoes" was one of the first tunes RCA wanted their new performer, Elvis Presley, to record.

"Heartbreak Hotel" and "Shoes" rose on the charts at roughly the same time. RCA, with its superior distribution and radio contacts, knew it could probably steal a hit record from Phillips and Perkins. For his part, when Presley, who knew both Perkins and Phillips from his days at Sun Records, gave in to pressure from RCA, he requested that they hold back his version from release as a single. The Elvis version features two guitar solos by Scotty Moore, along with Bill Black on bass, and D. J. Fontana on drums.

According to Scotty Moore, when the song was recorded, "We just went in there and started playing, just winged it. Just followed however Elvis felt. " According to reports confirmed by Sam Phillips, RCA producer Steve Sholes agreed not to release Presley's version of the song as a single while Carl's release was hot.

Presley performed the song on national television three times in 1956. The first was February 11 on Stage Show. He performed it again on his third Stage Show appearance on March 17, then again on the Milton Berle Show on April 3. On July 1, Steve Allen introduced Elvis on The Steve Allen Show, and Presley, appearing in formal evening wear, stated "I think that I have on something tonight that's not quite right for evening wear. " Allen asked, "What's that, Elvis?" "Blue suede shoes" was the answer, as he lifted his left foot to show the audience. Presley mentioned blue suede shoes a second time on this show: in a song during the "Range Roundup" comedy skit with Steve Allen, Andy Griffith, and Imogene Coca, he delivers the line, "I'm a warnin' you galoots, don't step on my blue suede shoes. "

Moore has said that Presley recorded the song to help out Perkins after his accident. "Elvis wasn't really thinking at that time that it was going to make money for Carl; he was doing it as more of a tribute type thing. Of course Carl was glad he did. It really helped as his record started going down. "

"Blue Suede Shoes" was the first song on the groundbreaking album Elvis Presley, which was released in March. RCA released two other records with "Blue Suede Shoes" the same month: one an Extended Play with four songs, RCA EPA 747, and a 2x extended play version with eight songs, RCA EPB 1254.

RCA released the Presley version as a single on September 8. This single reached No. 20, whereas the Perkins version had topped the chart.

In 1960, Presley re-recorded "Blue Suede Shoes" for the soundtrack of the film G. I. Blues. While Elvis' character's group "The Three Blazes" plays a ballad at a Frankfurt night club ("Doin' The Best I Can" by Doc Pomus & Mort Shuman), a bored GI plays "Blue Suede Shoes" by Elvis Presley on the jukebox, remarking that he wants "to hear an original". When another soldier tries to unplug the jukebox, the entire place erupts into a fight. This studio re-recording marked one of only a few occasions in Presley's career in which he agreed to re-record a previously issued song.

In 1999, Presley's version was certified Gold by the RIAA.

Eddie Cochran version

Rockabilly artist Eddie Cochran recorded his version in May or June 1956. It was first released in 1962.

Other 1956 recordings

"Blue Suede Shoes" was recorded and released many times in 1956. February releases were by Delbert Barker and the Gateway All Stars on the Gateway and Big Hits labels, Thumper Jones (George Jones), Hank Smith, and Buzz Williams. RCA Victor released a Pee Wee King version on March 3 of that same year, the same date as a Capitol release by Bob Rubian. These releases were followed closely by the March 10 releases of a Boyd Bennett version on King and the Columbia release of a Sid King version. Decca, too, released a version by Roy Hall, and the Dot label then released a recording by Jim Lowe. The song was also recorded in 1956 by Loren Becker with the Light Brigade on Waldorf Music Hall Records and Bob Harris and the John Weston Orchestra on Sapphire. By April there were also recorded versions of by Lawrence Welk (Coral), Sam Taylor (MGM), and Jerry Mercer (Mercury).

The Boyd Bennett and his Rockets version was also issued by Parlophone (R4167 MSP 6233) in the UK.

"Blue Suede Shoes" was one of many songs that were included in the mashup novelty record "The Flying Saucer" that was a No. 3 hit in 1956. It was referenced in the record as "Shoes" by Pa Gherkins.

Legacy

"Blue Suede Shoes" is often referred to in other songs including Chuck Berry's "Roll Over Beethoven" with "I'm giving you the warning, don't you step on my blue suede shoes. "

"Blue Suede Shoes" was chosen as one of the Rock and Roll Hall of Fame's 500 Songs that Shaped Rock and Roll. In 1986 Perkins' version was inducted in the Grammy Hall of Fame, and was included by the National Recording Preservation Board in the Library of Congress National Recording Registry in 2006. The board selects songs on an annual basis that are "culturally, historically, or aesthetically significant. "

In 2004, Perkins' version was ranked No. 95 on Rolling Stone's list of "The 500 Greatest Songs of All Time. " It is his only song on that list. Presley's recording of the song was also on the list at No. 423.

In 1999, National Public Radio included "Blue Suede Shoes" in the "NPR 100," in which NPR's music editors sought to compile the 100 most important American musical works of the 20th century.

The Grateful Dead's hit "U. S. Blues" features the line "Red and white, blue suede shoes, I'm Uncle Sam, how do you do?"

The song is referenced in the Beastie Boys song "Johnny Ryall" from their album Paul's Boutique. The title character, a homeless man, "claims that he wrote the Blue Suede Shoes".

It is also referenced with "maybe some blue suede shoes" in The Lowest of the Low's 1991 song "Henry Needs a New Pair of Shoes" about a homeless man trying to survive "these cold gray days. "

Additionally, the song is referenced in Marc Cohn's signature track, "Walking in Memphis," which begins, "Put on my blue suede shoes, and I boarded the plane. "

The song appears in the TV miniseries Elvis, where Jonathan Rhys Meyers, portraying Presley, performs the song on stage at the Chicago International Auditorium, in his famous gold lamé suit.

"Blue Suede Shoes" is the opening number of the Broadway musical Million Dollar Quartet, which opened in New York in April, 2010.

A similar version of the song, with different lyrics, is performed by

Susan Cabot twice in the movie Carnival Rock (1957) (at approx. 0:30 and 1:03) under the name Ou-Shoo-Bla-D.

Selected list of recorded versions

The song is a rock and roll standard and has been performed and recorded by many artists, including:

Carl Perkins, US No. 1 (3 weeks), Billboard Country & Western Chart, No. 2 (4 weeks), Billboard Juke Box chart, No. 3 Best Seller chart, No. 4 Top 100 chart, No. 5 Jockey chart, No. 2, R&B Chart; Cashbox pop singles chart, No. 2, 1956; UK, No. 10
Elvis Presley, US, No. 20, Billboard Best Seller chart, No. 24 Top 100 chart, No. 24 Jockey chart; UK, No. 9, 1956
Bill Haley and His Comets, 1960, Warner Bros. album
Buddy Holly as recorded on the Buddy Holly Story compilation and the 1964 LP Buddy Holly Showcase.
The Dave Clark Five, 1965, Weekend in London; 1970, No. 7, UK singles chart, as part of medley "Good Old Rock 'n' Roll"
The Beatles, 1969, Anthology 3
Cat Mother & the All Night Newsboys, No. 21, Billboard, 1969, as part of medley "Good Old Rock 'n' Roll" produced by Jimi Hendrix
Mountain, Woodstock, 1969
Plastic Ono Band, with John Lennon, Eric Clapton, 1969, Live Peace in Toronto
Ten Years After, Woodstock, 1969, as part of medley
Albert King, 1970, Blues for Elvis – King Does the King's Things
Black Sabbath on the Black Mass EP, 1970
Jerry Lee Lewis, 1973, The London Rock and Roll Show
Johnny Rivers, US No. 38, 1973
Jimi Hendrix, Midnight Lightning, Hendrix in the West, Loose Ends, 1975
Johnny Cash, 1976, in concert
Paul McCartney, Eric Clapton, Robbie Robertson, Paul Shaffer, Rock and Roll Hall of Fame, 1999
Dion, 2008 Heroes: Giants of Early Guitar Rock album
Bruce Springsteen, live in concert
Grateful Dead, sound check
Pat Boone
Merle Haggard
Conway Twitty
Mary J. Blige
Brian Setzer

The Toy Dolls
Helloween, 1991, "Kids of the Century" single
Hasil Adkins, a previously unreleased version that was included on the 1990 Norton album, Peanut Butter Rock and Roll.
Notes

Rockabilly Legends by Jerry Naylor and Steve Halliday p. 131
Go, Cat, Go! by Carl Perkins and David McGee 1996 p. 129 Hyperion Press ISBN 0-7868-6073-1
Go, Cat, Go! by Carl Perkins and David McGee 1996 p. 130 Hyperion Press ISBN 0-7868-6073-1
Rockabilly Legends by Jerry Naylor and Steve Halliday p. 131; also on DVD
The Top Beats the Bottom: Carl Perkins and his Music. The Atlantic. December 1970. page 100.
^ a b Go, Cat, Go! by Carl Perkins and David McGee 1996 pp. 152,153 Hyperion Press ISBN 0-7868-6073-1
Go, Cat, Go! by Carl Perkins and David McGee 1996 p. 157 Hyperion Press ISBN 0-7868-6073-1
"Big D Jamboree". Rockabillyhall. com. Retrieved 2011-04-21.
Go, Cat, Go! by Carl Perkins and David McGee 1996 pp. 154 Hyperion Press ISBN 0-7868-6073-1
Go, Cat, Go! by Carl Perkins and David McGee 1996 p. 158 Hyperion Press ISBN 0-7868-6073-1
Rockabilly Legends by Jerry Naylor page 137 ISBN 978-1-4234-2042-2
Go, Cat, Go! by Carl Perkins and David McGee 1996 p. 163 Hyperion Press ISBN 0-7868-6073-1
Go, Cat, Go! by Carl Perkins and David McGee 1996 p. 187 Hyperion Press ISBN 0-7868-6073-1
The Atlantic. December 1970. page 102
NPR story on Blue Suede Shoes
Go, Cat, Go! by Carl Perkins and David McGee 1996 pp. 188, 344 Hyperion Press ISBN 0-7868-6073-1
The Blue Moon Boys - The Story of Elvis Presley's Band. Ken Burke and Dan Griffin. 2006. Chicago Review Press. pages 87,88. ISBN 1-55652-614-8
"Go, Cat, Go! by Carl Perkins and David McGee 1996 pp. 162, 163 Hyperion Press ISBN 0-7868-6073-1
"Elvis' Television Appearances 1956–1973". Kki. pl. Retrieved 2011-04-21.
Elvis Volume 1 Home Video Syndications, Ltd 1990
The Blue Moon Boys - The Story of Elvis Presley's Band. Ken Burke and Dan Griffin. 2006. Chicago Review Press. page 88. ISBN

1-55652-614-8
"Elvis Discography 1956". Sergent. com. au. Retrieved 2011-04-21.
^ a b "Search Results for BLUE SUEDE SHOES". Rockin' Country Style.
"Songwriters Doc Pomus and Mort Shuman - Elvis Articles, By: Elvis Australia". Elvis. com. au. Retrieved 2011-04-21.
G. I. Blues DVD
"American certifications – Elvis Presley – Blue Suede Shoes". Recording Industry Association of America.
"Eddie Cochran 1957 Sessions on www. eddiecochran. info". Eddiecochran. info. Retrieved 2012-01-04.
LIBERTY LRP 3220 - 5 January 1962. Long Play - "Never To Be Forgotten" http://www. eddiecochran. info/Discography/USA/III. htm
Carl Perkin's Smash! (sic) Billboard April 14, 1956. page 36.
"RCS Label Shot for Gateway (Ohio) 1162". rcs-discography. com. Retrieved April 21, 2011.
"Jones, George (RCS Artist Discography)". rcs-discography. com. Retrieved 21 April 2011.
"RCS Label Shot for Dixie (mail) (Ill.) 502". rcs-discography. com. Retrieved April 21, 2011.
Ted Barron (2007-07-26). "Boogie Woogie Flu: Who Are The Mystery Guests?". Boogiewoogieflu. blogspot. com. Retrieved 2011-04-21.
"Barker, Delbert (RCS Artist Discography)". rcs-discography. com. Retrieved April 21, 2011.
"RCS Label Shot for Big 4 Hits (Ohio) 185". rcs-discography. com. Retrieved April 21, 2011.
"King, Pee Wee (RCS Artist Discography)". rcs-discography. com. Retrieved April 21, 2011.
"RCS Label Shot for RCA Victor (N. J.) 6450". rcs-discography. com. Retrieved April 21, 2011.
"Roubian, Bob (RCS Artist Discography)". rcs-discography. com. Retrieved April 21, 2011.
"RCS Label Shot for Capitol (Calif.) 3373". rcs-discography. com. Retrieved April 21, 2011.
"RCS Label Shot for King (Ohio) 4903". rcs-discography. com. Retrieved April 21, 2011.
"King, Sid (RCS Artist Discography)". rcs-discography. com. Retrieved April 21, 2011.
"RCS Label Shot for Columbia (N. Y.) 21505". rcs-discography. com. Retrieved April 21, 2011.
"Hall, Roy (RCS Artist Discography)". rcs-discography. com. Retrieved April 21, 2011.
"RCS Label Shot for Decca (N. Y.) 29880". rcs-discography. com. Retrieved April 21, 2011.

"Lowe, Jim (RCS Artist Discography)". rcs-discography. com. Retrieved April 21, 2011.
"RCS Label Shot for Dot (Calif.) 15456". rcs-discography. com. Retrieved April 21, 2011.
Always "The Man" : Sam Taylor
Billboard April 7, 1956. page 21 http://books. google. com/books?id=ZB8EAAAAMBAJ&pg=PA20&dq=%22lindy+hop%22&as_pt=MAGAZINES&cd=8#v=onepage&q=%22lindy%20hop%22&f=false
http://www. globaldogproductions. info/p/parlophone-uk4000. html 78 & 45 Discography for Parlophone Records UK - 4000 series 3. 2012
2006 National Recording Registry choices
"The RS 500 Greatest Songs of All Time". RollingStone. com. Retrieved 2007-06-02.
"Grateful Dead Movie - U. S. Blues".
MDQ Merchandising LLC (2010). "Song List" and "Performing Credits". In Million Dollar Quartet (p. 5) CD booklet. New York City: Avatar Studios; and Chicago: Chicago Recording Company.
Zielinski, Peter James (April 12, 2010). "Photo Coverage: Million Dollar Quartet Opens on Broadway".
Cashbox Best Selling Singles.
External links

NPR story on Blue Suede Shoes
Carl Perkins performs the song in a 1956 TV appearance
Excerpt form Ballet San Jose's Blue Suede Shoes Ballet
Template:Carl Perkins

Blues

Blues

Blues is the name given to both a musical form and a music genre that originated in African-American communities of primarily the "Deep South" of the United States around the end of the 19th century from spirituals, work songs, field hollers, shouts and chants, and rhymed simple narrative ballads. The blues form, ubiquitous in jazz, rhythm and blues, and rock and roll is characterized by specific chord progressions, of which the twelve-bar blues chord progression is the most common. The blue notes that, for expressive purposes are sung or played flattened or gradually bent (minor 3rd to major 3rd) in relation to the pitch of the major scale, are also an important part of the sound.

The blues genre is based on the blues form but possesses other characteristics such as specific lyrics, bass lines and instruments. Blues can be subdivided into several subgenres ranging from country to urban blues that were more or less popular during different periods of the 20th century. Best known are the Delta, Piedmont, Jump and Chicago blues styles. World War II marked the transition from acoustic to electric blues and the progressive opening of blues music to a wider audience, especially white listeners. In the 1960s and 1970s, a hybrid form called blues-rock evolved.

The term "the blues" refers to the "blue devils", meaning melancholy and sadness; an early use of the term in this sense is found in George Colman's one-act farce Blue Devils (1798). Though the use of the phrase in African-American music may be older, it has been attested to since 1912, when Hart Wand's "Dallas Blues" became the first copyrighted blues composition. In lyrics the phrase is often used to describe a depressed mood.

Form

The blues form is a cyclic musical form in which a repeating progression of chords mirrors the call and response scheme commonly found in African and African-American music. During the first decades of the 20th century blues music was not clearly defined in terms of a particular chord progression. With the popularity of early performers, such as Bessie Smith, use of the twelve-bar blues spread across the music industry during the 1920s and 30s. Other chord progressions, such as 8-bar forms, are still considered blues; examples include "How Long Blues", "Trouble in Mind", and Big Bill Broonzy's "Key to the Highway". There are also 16-bar blues, as in Ray Charles's instrumental "Sweet 16 Bars" and in Herbie Hancock's "Watermelon Man". Idiosyncratic numbers of bars are also encountered occasionally, as with the 9-bar progression in "Sitting on Top of the World" by Walter Vinson.

Chords played over a 12-bar scheme: Chords for a blues in C:

I	I or IV	I	I7
IV	IV	I	I7
V	V or IV	I	I or V
C	C or F	C	C7
F	F	C	C7
G	G or F	C	C or G

The basic 12-bar lyric framework of a blues composition is reflected by a standard harmonic progression of 12 bars in a 4/4 time signature. The blues chords associated to a twelve-bar blues are typically a set of three different chords played over a 12-bar scheme. They are labeled by Roman numbers referring to the degrees of the progression. For instance, for a blues in the key of C, C is the tonic chord (I) and F is the subdominant (IV).

The last chord is the dominant (V) turnaround, marking the transition to the beginning of the next progression. The lyrics generally end on the last beat of the tenth bar or the first beat of the 11th bar, and the final two bars are given to the instrumentalist as a break; the harmony of this two-bar break, the turnaround, can be extremely complex, sometimes consisting of single notes that defy analysis in terms of chords.

Much of the time, some or all of these chords are played in the harmonic seventh (7th) form. The use of the harmonic seventh interval is characteristic of blues and is popularly called the "blues seven". Blues seven chords add to the harmonic chord a note with a frequency in a 7:4 ratio to the fundamental note. At a 7:4 ratio, it is not close to any interval on the conventional Western diatonic scale. For convenience or by necessity it is often approximated by a minor seventh interval or a dominant seventh chord.

In melody, blues is distinguished by the use of the flattened third, fifth and seventh of the associated major scale. These specialized notes are called the blue or bent notes. These scale tones may replace the natural scale tones, or they may be added to the scale, as in the case of the minor blues scale, in which the flattened third replaces the natural third, the flattened seventh replaces the natural seventh and the flattened fifth is added between the natural fourth and natural fifth. While the 12-bar harmonic progression had been intermittently used for centuries, the revolutionary aspect of blues was the frequent use of the flattened third, flattened seventh, and even flattened fifth in the melody, together with crushing—playing directly adjacent notes at the same time (i. e. , minor second)—and sliding, similar to using grace notes. The blue notes allow for key moments of expression during the cadences, melodies, and embellishments of the blues.

Blues shuffles or walking bass reinforce the trance-like rhythm and call-and-response, and they form a repetitive effect called a groove. Characteristic of the blues since its Afro-American origins, the shuffles played a central role in swing music. The simplest shuffles, which were the clearest signature of the R&B wave that started in the mid 1940s, were a three-note riff on the bass strings of the guitar. When this riff was played over the bass and the drums, the groove "feel" was created. Shuffle rhythm is often vocalized as "dow, da dow, da dow, da" or "dump, da dump, da dump, da": it consists of uneven, or "swung," eighth notes. On a guitar this may be played as a simple steady bass or it may add to that stepwise quarter note motion from the fifth to the sixth of the chord and back. An example is provided by the following guitar tablature for the first four bars of a blues progression in E:

```
E7        A7        E7        E7
E |---------------|---------------|---------------|---------------|
B |---------------|---------------|---------------|---------------|
G |---------------|---------------|---------------|---------------|
D |---------------|2—2-4—2-5—2-4—2-|---------------|---------------|
A |2—2-4-2-5-2-4—2-|0—0-0—0-0—0-0—2-|2—2-4—2-5—2-4—2-
|2—2-4—2-5—2-4—2-|
E |0—0-0—0-0—0-0—2-|---------------|0—0-0—0-0—0-0—2-|0—0-
0—0-0—0-0—2-|
```

Lyrics

The lyrics of early traditional blues verses probably often consisted of a single line repeated four times; it was only in the first decades of the 20th century that the most common current structure became standard: the so-called AAB pattern, consisting of a line sung over the four first bars, its repetition over the next four, and then a longer concluding line over the last bars. Two of the first published blues songs, "Dallas Blues" (1912) and "Saint Louis Blues" (1914), were 12-bar blues featuring the AAB structure. W. C. Handy wrote that he adopted this convention to avoid the monotony of lines repeated three times.

The lines are often sung following a pattern closer to a rhythmic talk than to a melody. Early blues frequently took the form of a loose narrative. The singer voiced his or her "personal woes in a world of harsh reality: a lost love, the cruelty of police officers, oppression at the hands of white folk, [and] hard times. " This melancholy has led to the suggestion of an Igbo origin for blues because of the reputation the Igbo had throughout plantations in the Americas for their melancholic music and outlook to life when they were enslaved.

The lyrics often relate troubles experienced within African American society. For instance Blind Lemon Jefferson's "Rising High Water Blues" (1927) tells about the Great Mississippi Flood of 1927:

"Backwater rising, Southern peoples can't make no time
I said, backwater rising, Southern peoples can't make no time
And I can't get no hearing from that Memphis girl of mine. "
However, although the blues gained an association with misery and oppression, the lyrics could also be humorous and raunchy as well:

"Rebecca, Rebecca, get your big legs off of me,
Rebecca, Rebecca, get your big legs off of me,
It may be sending you baby, but it's worrying the hell out of me. "
From Big Joe Turner's "Rebecca", a compilation of traditional blues lyrics
Hokum blues celebrated both comedic lyrical content and a boisterous, farcical performance style. Tampa Red's classic "Tight Like That" (1928) is a sly wordplay with the double meaning of being "tight" with someone coupled with a more salacious physical familiarity. Explicit contents led to blues sometimes being called dirty blues. Lyrical content of music became slightly simpler in post war-blues which focused almost exclusively on relationship woes or sexual worries. Many lyrical themes that frequently appeared in pre-war blues such as economic depression, farming, devils, gambling, magic, floods and dry periods were less common in post-war blues.

Author Ed Morales has claimed that Yoruba mythology played a part in early blues, citing Robert Johnson's "Cross Road Blues" as a "thinly veiled reference to Eleggua, the orisha in charge of the crossroads". However, the Christian influence was far more obvious. Many seminal blues artists such as Charley Patton or Skip James had several religious songs or spirituals in their repertoires. Reverend Gary Davis and Blind Willie Johnson are examples of artists often categorized as blues musicians for their music, although their lyrics clearly belong to the spirituals.

History

Origins

Origins of the blues

The origin of the term of was most likely derived from mysticism involving blue indigo, which was used by many West African cultures in death and mourning ceremonies where all the mourner's garments would have been dyed blue to indicate suffering. This mystical association towards the indigo plant, grown in many southern US slave plantations, combined with the West African slaves who sang of their suffering as they worked on the cotton that the indigo dyed eventually resulted in these expressed songs being known as "the Blues".

The first publication of blues sheet music was Hart Wand's "Dallas Blues" in 1912; W. C. Handy's "The Memphis Blues" followed in the same year. The first recording by an African American singer was Mamie Smith's 1920 rendition of Perry Bradford's "Crazy Blues". But the origins of the blues date back to some decades earlier, probably around 1890. They are very poorly documented, due in part to racial discrimination within American society, including academic circles, and to the low literacy rate of the rural African American community at the time.

Chroniclers began to report about blues music in Southern Texas and Deep South at the dawn of the 20th century. In particular, Charles Peabody mentioned the appearance of blues music at Clarksdale, Mississippi and Gate Thomas reported very similar songs in southern Texas around 1901–1902. These observations coincide more or less with the remembrance of Jelly Roll Morton, who declared having heard blues for the first time in New Orleans in 1902; Ma Rainey, who remembered her first blues experience the same year in Missouri; and W. C. Handy, who first heard the blues in Tutwiler, Mississippi in 1903. The first extensive research in the field was performed by Howard W. Odum, who published a large anthology of folk songs in the counties of Lafayette, Mississippi and Newton, Georgia between 1905 and 1908. The first non-commercial recordings of blues music, termed "proto-blues" by Paul Oliver, were made by Odum at the very beginning of the 20th century for research purposes. They are now utterly lost.

Other recordings that are still available were made in 1924 by Lawrence Gellert. Later, several recordings were made by Robert W. Gordon, who became head of the Archive of American Folk Songs of the Library of Congress. Gordon's successor at the Library was John Lomax. In the 1930s, together with his son Alan, Lomax made a large number of non-commercial blues recordings that testify to the huge variety of proto-blues styles, such as field hollers and ring shouts. A record of blues music as it existed before the

1920s is also given by the recordings of artists such as Lead Belly or Henry Thomas who both performed archaic blues music. All these sources show the existence of many different structures distinct from the twelve-, eight-, or sixteen-bar.

The social and economic reasons for the appearance of the blues are not fully known. The first appearance of the blues is often dated after the Emancipation Act of 1863, between 1870 and 1900, a period that coincides with Emancipation and, later, the development of juke joints as places where Blacks went to listen to music, dance, or gamble after a hard day's work. This period corresponds to the transition from slavery to sharecropping, small-scale agricultural production, and the expansion of railroads in the southern United States. Several scholars characterize the early 1900s development of blues music as a move from group performances to a more individualized style. They argue that the development of the blues is associated with the newly acquired freedom of the enslaved people.

According to Lawrence Levine, "there was a direct relationship between the national ideological emphasis upon the individual, the popularity of Booker T. Washington's teachings, and the rise of the blues. " Levine states that "psychologically, socially, and economically, African-Americans were being acculturated in a way that would have been impossible during slavery, and it is hardly surprising that their secular music reflected this as much as their religious music did. "

There are few characteristics common to all blues music, because the genre took its shape from the idiosyncrasies of individual performances. However, there are some characteristics that were present long before the creation of the modern blues. Call-and-response shouts were an early form of blues-like music; they were a "functional expression . . . style without accompaniment or harmony and unbounded by the formality of any particular musical structure. " A form of this pre-blues was heard in slave ring shouts and field hollers, expanded into "simple solo songs laden with emotional content".

Blues has evolved from the unaccompanied vocal music and oral traditions of slaves imported from West Africa and rural blacks into a wide variety of styles and subgenres, with regional variations across the United States. Though blues, as it is now known, can be seen as a musical style based on both European harmonic structure and the African call-and-response tradition, transformed into an interplay of voice and guitar, the blues form itself bears no resemblance to the melodic styles of the West African griots, and the influences are faint and tenuous.

In particular, no specific African musical form can be identified as the single direct ancestor of the blues. However many blues elements, such as the call-and-response format and the use of blue notes, can be traced back to the music of Africa. That blue notes pre-date their use in blues and have an African origin is attested by English composer Samuel Coleridge-Taylor's "A Negro Love Song", from his The African Suite for Piano composed in 1898, which contains blue third and seventh notes.

The Diddley bow (a homemade one-stringed instrument found in parts of the American South in the early twentieth century) and the banjo are African-derived instruments that may have helped in the transfer of African performance techniques into the early blues instrumental vocabulary. The banjo seems to be directly imported from western African music. It is similar to the musical instrument that griots and other Africans such as the Igbo played (called halam or akonting by African peoples such as the Wolof, Fula and Mandinka). However, in the 1920s, when country blues began to be recorded, the use of the banjo in blues music was quite marginal and limited to individuals such as Papa Charlie Jackson and later Gus Cannon.

Blues music also adopted elements from the "Ethiopian airs", minstrel shows and Negro spirituals, including instrumental and harmonic accompaniment. The style also was closely related to ragtime, which developed at about the same time, though the blues better preserved "the original melodic patterns of African music".

The musical forms and styles that are now considered the "blues" as well as modern "country music" arose in the same regions during the 19th century in the southern United States. Recorded blues and country can be found from as far back as the 1920s, when the popular record industry developed and created marketing categories called "race music" and "hillbilly music" to sell music by blacks for blacks and by whites for whites, respectively. At the time, there was no clear musical division between "blues" and "country," except for the ethnicity of the performer, and even that was sometimes documented incorrectly by record companies.

Though musicologists can now attempt to define "the blues" narrowly in terms of certain chord structures and lyric strategies thought to have originated in West Africa, audiences originally heard the music in a far more general way: it was simply the music of the rural south, notably the Mississippi Delta. Black and white musicians shared the same repertoire and thought of themselves as "songsters" rather than "blues musicians. " The notion of blues as a separate genre arose during the black migration from the countryside to urban areas in the 1920s and the simultaneous development of the recording industry. "Blues" became a code word for a record designed to sell to black listeners.

The origins of the blues are closely related to the religious music of the Afro-American community, the spirituals. The origins of spirituals go back much further than the blues, usually dating back to the middle of the 18th century, when the slaves were Christianized and began to sing and play Christian hymns, in particular those of Isaac Watts, which were very popular. Before the blues gained its formal definition in terms of chord progressions, it was defined as the secular counterpart of the spirituals. It was the low-down music played by the rural Blacks.

Depending on the religious community a musician belonged to, it was more or less considered as a sin to play this low-down music: blues was the devil's music. Musicians were therefore segregated into two categories: gospel and blues singers, guitar preachers and songsters. However, at the time rural Black music began to get recorded in the 1920s, both categories of musicians used very similar techniques: call-and-response patterns, blue notes, and slide guitars. Gospel music was nevertheless using musical forms that were compatible with Christian hymns and therefore less marked by the blues form than its secular counterpart.

Pre-war blues

The American sheet music publishing industry produced a great deal of ragtime music. By 1912, the sheet music industry had published three popular blues-like compositions, precipitating the Tin Pan Alley adoption of blues elements: "Baby Seals' Blues" by "Baby" F. Seals (arranged by Artie Matthews), "Dallas Blues" by Hart Wand and "The Memphis Blues" by W. C. Handy.

Handy was a formally trained musician, composer and arranger who helped to popularize the blues by transcribing and orchestrating blues in an almost symphonic style, with bands and singers. He became a popular and prolific composer, and billed himself as the "Father of the Blues"; however, his compositions can be described as a fusion of blues with ragtime and jazz, a merger facilitated using the Cuban habanera rhythm that had long been a part of ragtime; Handy's signature work was the "Saint Louis Blues".

In the 1920s, the blues became a major element of African American and American popular music, reaching white audiences via Handy's arrangements and the classic female blues performers. The blues evolved from informal performances in bars to entertainment in theaters. Blues performances were organized by the Theater Owners Bookers Association in nightclubs such as the Cotton Club and juke joints such as the bars along Beale Street in Memphis. Several record companies, such as the American Record Corporation, Okeh Records, and Paramount Records, began to record African American music.

As the recording industry grew, country blues performers like Bo Carter, Jimmie Rodgers (country singer), Blind Lemon Jefferson, Lonnie Johnson, Tampa Red and Blind Blake became more popular in the African American community. Kentucky-born Sylvester Weaver was in 1923 the first to record the slide guitar style, in which a guitar is fretted with a knife blade or the sawed-off neck of a bottle. The slide guitar became an important part of the Delta blues. The first blues recordings from the 1920s are categorized as a traditional, rural country blues and a more polished 'city' or urban blues.

Country blues performers often improvised, either without accompaniment or with only a banjo or guitar. Regional styles of country blues varied widely in the early 20th century. The (Mississippi) Delta blues was a rootsy sparse style with passionate vocals accompanied by slide guitar. The little-recorded Robert Johnson combined elements of urban and rural blues. In addition to Robert Johnson, influential performers of this style included his predecessors Charley Patton and Son House. Singers such as Blind Willie McTell and Blind Boy Fuller performed in the southeastern "delicate and lyrical" Piedmont blues tradition, which used an elaborate ragtime-based fingerpicking guitar technique. Georgia also had an early slide tradition, with Curley Weaver, Tampa Red, "Barbecue Bob" Hicks and James "Kokomo" Arnold as representatives of this style.

The lively Memphis blues style, which developed in the 1920s and 1930s near Memphis, Tennessee, was influenced by jug bands such as the Memphis Jug Band or the Gus Cannon's Jug Stompers. Performers such as Frank Stokes, Sleepy John Estes, Robert Wilkins, Joe McCoy, Casey Bill Weldon and Memphis Minnie used a variety of unusual instruments such as washboard, fiddle, kazoo or mandolin. Memphis Minnie was famous for her virtuoso guitar style. Pianist Memphis Slim began his career in Memphis, but his distinct style was smoother and had some swing elements. Many blues musicians based in Memphis moved to Chicago in the late 1930s or early 1940s and became part of the urban blues movement, which blended country music and electric blues.

City or urban blues styles were more codified and elaborate as a performer was no longer within their local, immediate community and had to adapt to a larger, more varied audience's aesthetic. Classic female urban and vaudeville blues singers were popular in the 1920s, among them Mamie Smith, Gertrude "Ma" Rainey, Bessie Smith, and Victoria Spivey. Mamie Smith, more a vaudeville performer than a blues artist, was the first African-American to record a blues in 1920; her second record, "Crazy Blues", sold 75,000 copies in its first month.

Ma Rainey, the "Mother of Blues", and Bessie Smith each "[sang] around center tones, perhaps in order to project her voice more easily to the back of a room. " Smith would ". . . sing a song in an unusual key, and her artistry in bending and stretching notes with her beautiful, powerful contralto to accommodate her own interpretation was unsurpassed. " Urban male performers included popular black musicians of the era, such Tampa Red, Big Bill Broonzy and Leroy Carr. An important label of this era was the chicagoean Bluebird label. Before WWII, Tampa Red was sometimes referred to as "the Guitar Wizard". Carr accompanied himself on the piano with Scrapper Blackwell on guitar, a format that continued well into the 50s with people such as Charles Brown, and even Nat "King" Cole.

Boogie-woogie was another important style of 1930s and early 1940s urban blues. While the style is often associated with solo piano, boogie-woogie was also used to accompany singers and, as a solo part, in bands and small combos. Boogie-Woogie style was characterized by a regular bass figure, an ostinato or riff and shifts of level in the left hand, elaborating each chord and trills and decorations in the right hand. Boogie-woogie was pioneered by the Chicago-based Jimmy Yancey and the Boogie-Woogie Trio (Albert Ammons, Pete Johnson and Meade Lux Lewis). Chicago boogie-woogie performers included Clarence "Pine Top" Smith and Earl Hines, who "linked the propulsive left-hand rhythms of the ragtime pianists with melodic figures similar to those of Armstrong's trumpet in the right hand. " The smooth Louisiana style of Professor Longhair and, more recently, Dr. John blends classic rhythm and blues with blues styles.

Another development in this period was big band blues. The "territory bands" operating out of Kansas City, the Bennie Moten orchestra, Jay McShann, and the Count Basie Orchestra were also concentrating on the blues, with 12-bar blues instrumentals such as Basie's "One O'Clock Jump" and "Jumpin' at the Woodside" and boisterous "blues shouting" by Jimmy Rushing on songs such as "Going to Chicago" and "Sent for You Yesterday". A well-known big band blues tune is Glenn Miller's "In the Mood". In the 1940s, the jump blues style developed. Jump blues grew up from the boogie woogie wave and was strongly influenced by big band music. It uses saxophone or other brass instruments and the guitar in the rhythm section to create a jazzy, up-tempo sound with declamatory vocals. Jump blues tunes by Louis Jordan and Big Joe Turner, based in Kansas City, Missouri, influenced the development of later styles such as rock and roll and rhythm and blues. Dallas-born T-Bone Walker, who is often associated with the California blues style, performed a successful transition from the early urban blues à la Lonnie Johnson and Leroy Carr to the jump blues style and dominated the blues-jazz scene at Los Angeles during the 1940s.

1950s

The transition from country to urban blues, that began in the 1920s, had always been driven by the successive waves of economic crisis and booms and the associated move of the rural Blacks to urban areas, the Great Migration. The long boom in the aftermath of World War II induced a massive migration of the African American population, the Second Great Migration, which was accompanied by a significant increase of the real income of the urban Blacks. The new migrants constituted a new market for the music industry. The name race record disappeared and was succeeded by Rhythm and Blues. This rapidly evolving market was mirrored by the Billboard Rhythm and Blues Chart. This marketing strategy reinforced trends within urban blues music such as the progressive electrification of the instruments, their amplification and the generalization of the blues beat, the blues shuffle, that became ubiquitous in R&B. This commercial stream had important consequences for blues music which, together with Jazz and Gospel music, became a component of the R&B wave.

After World War II and in the 1950s, new styles of electric blues music became popular in cities such as Chicago, Memphis, Detroit and St. Louis. Electric blues used electric guitars, double bass (slowly replaced by bass guitar), drums, and harmonica played through a microphone and a PA system or a guitar amplifier. Chicago became a center for electric blues from 1948 on, when Muddy Waters recorded his first success: "I Can't Be Satisfied". Chicago blues is influenced to a large extent by the Mississippi blues style, because many performers had migrated from the Mississippi region.

Howlin' Wolf, Muddy Waters, Willie Dixon, and Jimmy Reed were all born in Mississippi and moved to Chicago during the Great Migration. Their style is characterized by the use of electric guitar, sometimes slide guitar, harmonica, and a rhythm section of bass and drums. J. T. Brown who played in Elmore James's bands, or J. B. Lenoir's also used saxophones, but these were used more as "backing" or rhythmic support than as solo instruments.

Little Walter and Sonny Boy Williamson (Rice Miller) are well known harmonica (called "harp" by blues musicians) players of the early Chicago blues scene. Other harp players such as Big Walter Horton were also influential. Muddy Waters and Elmore James were known for their innovative use of slide electric guitar. Howlin' Wolf and Muddy Waters were known for their deep, "gravelly" voices.

Bassist and composer Willie Dixon played a major role on the Chicago blues scene. He composed and wrote many standard blues songs of the period, such as "Hoochie Coochie Man", "I Just Want to Make Love to You" (both penned for Muddy Waters) and, "Wang Dang Doodle" and "Back Door Man" for Howlin' Wolf. Most artists of the Chicago blues style recorded for the Chicago-based Chess Records and Checker Records labels. Smaller blues labels of this era included Vee-Jay Records and J. O. B. Records. During the early 1950s, the dominating Chicago labels were challenged by Sam Phillips' Sun Records company in Memphis, which recorded B. B. King and Howlin' Wolf before he moved to Chicago in 1960. After Phillips discovered Elvis Presley in 1954, the Sun label turned to the rapidly expanding white audience and started recording mostly rock 'n' roll.

In the 1950s, blues had a huge influence on mainstream American popular music. While popular musicians like Bo Diddley and Chuck Berry, both recording for Chess, were influenced by the Chicago blues, their enthusiastic playing styles departed from the melancholy aspects of blues. Chicago blues also influenced Louisiana's zydeco music, with Clifton Chenier using blues accents. Zydeco musicians used electric solo guitar and cajun arrangements of blues standards.

Overseas, in England, electric blues took root there during a much acclaimed Muddy Waters tour. Waters, unsuspecting of his audience's tendency towards skiffle, an acoustic, softer brand of blues, turned up his amp and started to play his Chicago brand of electric blues. Although the audience was largely jolted by the performance, the performance influenced local musicians such as Alexis Korner and Cyril Davies to emulate this louder style, inspiring the British invasion of the Rolling Stones and the Yardbirds.

In the late 1950s, a new blues style emerged on Chicago's West Side pioneered by Magic Sam, Buddy Guy and Otis Rush on Cobra Records. The 'West Side Sound' had strong rhythmic support from a rhythm guitar, bass guitar and drums and as pefected by Guy, Freddie King, Magic Slim and Luther Allison was dominated by amplified electric lead guitar.

Other blues artists, such as John Lee Hooker had influences not directly related to the Chicago style. John Lee Hooker's blues is more "personal", based on Hooker's deep rough voice accompanied by a single electric guitar. Though not directly influenced by boogie woogie, his "groovy" style is sometimes called "guitar boogie". His first hit, "Boogie Chillen", reached #1 on the R&B charts in 1949.

By the late 1950s, the swamp blues genre developed near Baton Rouge, with performers such as Lightnin' Slim, Slim Harpo, Sam Myers and Jerry McCain around the producer J. D. "Jay" Miller and the Excello label. Strongly influenced by Jimmy Reed, Swamp blues has a slower pace and a simpler use of the harmonica than the Chicago blues style performers such as Little Walter or Muddy Waters. Songs from this genre include "Scratch my Back", "She's Tough" and "I'm a King Bee". Alan Lomax's recordings of Mississippi Fred McDowell would eventually bring him wider attention on both the blues and folk circuit, with McDowell's droning style influencing North Mississippi hill country blues musicians.

1960s and 1970s

By the beginning of the 1960s, genres influenced by African American music such as rock and roll and soul were part of mainstream popular music. White performers had brought African-American music to new audiences, both within the US and abroad. However, the blues wave that brought artists such as Muddy Waters to the foreground had stopped. Bluesmen such as Big Bill Broonzy and Willie Dixon started looking for new markets in Europe. Dick Waterman and the blues festivals he organized in Europe played a major role in propagating blues music abroad. In the UK, bands emulated US blues legends, and UK blues-rock-based bands had an influential role throughout the 1960s.

Blues performers such as John Lee Hooker and Muddy Waters continued to perform to enthusiastic audiences, inspiring new artists steeped in traditional blues, such as New York–born Taj Mahal. John Lee Hooker blended his blues style with rock elements and playing with younger white musicians, creating a musical style that can be heard on the 1971 album Endless Boogie. B. B. King's virtuoso guitar technique earned him the eponymous title "king of the blues".

In contrast to the Chicago style, King's band used strong brass support from a saxophone, trumpet, and trombone, instead of using slide guitar or harp. Tennessee-born Bobby "Blue" Bland, like B. B. King, also straddled the blues and R&B genres. During this period, Freddie King and Albert King often played with rock and soul musicians (Eric Clapton, Booker T & the MGs) and had a major influence on those styles of music.

The music of the Civil Rights and Free Speech movements in the US prompted a resurgence of interest in American roots music and early African American music. As well as Jimmi Bass Music festivals such as the Newport Folk Festival brought traditional blues to a new audience, which helped to revive interest in prewar acoustic blues and performers such as Son House, Mississippi John Hurt, Skip James, and Reverend Gary Davis. Many compilations of classic prewar blues were republished by the Yazoo Records. J. B. Lenoir from the Chicago blues movement in the 1950s recorded several LPs using acoustic guitar, sometimes accompanied by Willie Dixon on the acoustic bass or drums. His songs, originally distributed in Europe only, commented on political issues such as racism or Vietnam War issues, which was unusual for this period. His Alabama Blues recording had a song that stated:

I never will go back to Alabama, that is not the place for me (2x)
You know they killed my sister and my brother,
and the whole world let them peoples go down there free

White audiences' interest in the blues during the 1960s increased due to the Chicago-based Paul Butterfield Blues Band and the British blues movement. The style of British blues developed in the UK, when bands such as The Animals, Fleetwood Mac, John Mayall & the Bluesbreakers, The Rolling Stones, The Yardbirds, and Cream and Irish musician Rory Gallagher performed classic blues songs from the Delta or Chicago blues traditions. Many of Led Zeppelin's earlier hits were renditions of traditional blues songs.

The British and blues musicians of the early 1960s inspired a number of American blues rock fusion performers, including Canned Heat, the early Jefferson Airplane, Janis Joplin, Johnny Winter, The J. Geils Band, Ry Cooder, and The Allman Brothers Band. One blues rock performer, Jimi Hendrix, was a rarity in his field at the time: a black man who played psychedelic rock. Hendrix was a skilled guitarist, and a pioneer in the innovative use of distortion and feedback in his music. Through these artists and others, blues music influenced the development of rock music.

Santana, which was originally called the Carlos Santana Blues Band, also experimented with Latin-influenced blues and blues-rock music around this time. At the end of the 1950s appeared the very bluesy Tulsa Sound merging rock'n'roll, jazz and country influences. This particular music style started to be broadly popularized within the 1970s by J. J. Cale and the cover versions performed by Eric Clapton of "After Midnight" and "Cocaine".

In the early 1970s, The Texas rock-blues style emerged, which used guitars in both solo and rhythm roles. In contrast with the West Side blues, the Texas style is strongly influenced by the British rock-blues movement. Major artists of the Texas style are Johnny Winter, Stevie Ray Vaughan, The Fabulous Thunderbirds, and ZZ Top. These artists all began their musical journey in the 1970s, but they did not achieve major international success until the next decade.

1980s to the 2000s

Since at least the 1980s, there has been a resurgence of interest in the blues among a certain part of the African-American population, particularly around Jackson, Mississippi and other deep South regions. Often termed "soul blues" or "Southern soul", the music at the heart of this movement was given new life by the unexpected success of two particular recordings on the Jackson-based Malaco label: Z. Z. Hill's Down Home Blues (1982) and Little Milton's The Blues is Alright (1984). Contemporary African-American performers who work this vein of the blues include Bobby Rush, Denise LaSalle, Sir Charles Jones, Bettye LaVette, Marvin Sease, Peggy Scott-Adams, Mel Waiters, Clarence Carter, Dr. "Feelgood" Potts, O. B. Buchana, Ms. Jody, Shirley Brown, and dozens of others.

During the 1980s, blues also continued in both traditional and new forms. In 1986, the album Strong Persuader revealed Robert Cray as a major blues artist. The first Stevie Ray Vaughan recording, Texas Flood, was released in 1983, and the Texas-based guitarist exploded onto the international stage. 1989 saw a revival of John Lee Hooker's popularity with the album The Healer. Eric Clapton, known for his performances with the Blues Breakers and Cream, made a comeback in the 1990s with his album Unplugged, in which he played some standard blues numbers on acoustic guitar. However, beginning in the 1990s, digital multitrack recording and other technological advances and new marketing strategies that include video clip production have increased costs, and challenge the spontaneity and improvisation that are an important component of blues music.

In the 1980s and 1990s, blues publications such as Living Blues and Blues Revue began to be distributed, major cities began forming blues societies, outdoor blues festivals became more common, and more nightclubs and venues for blues emerged.

In the 1990s, largely ignored hill country blues gained minor recognition in both blues and alternative rock music circles with North Mississippi artists R. L. Burnside and Junior Kimbrough. Blues performers explored a range of musical genres, as can be seen, for example, from the broad array of nominees of the yearly Blues Music Awards, previously named W. C. Handy Awards or of the Grammy Awards for Best Contemporary and Traditional Blues Album. The Bilboard Blues Album chart monitors and therefore provides an overview over the current blues production. Contemporary blues music is nurtured by several blues labels such as: Alligator Records, Ruf Records, Severn Records, Chess Records (MCA), Delmark Records, NorthernBlues Music, Fat Possum Records and Vanguard Records (Artemis Records). Some labels are famous for their rediscovering and remastering of blues rarities such as Arhoolie Records, Smithsonian Folkways Recordings (heir of Folkways Records) and Yazoo Records (Shanachie Records).

Musical impact

Blues musical styles, forms (12-bar blues), melodies, and the blues scale have influenced many other genres of music, such as rock and roll, jazz, and popular music. Prominent jazz, folk or rock performers, such as Louis Armstrong, Duke Ellington, Miles Davis, and Bob Dylan have performed significant blues recordings. The blues scale is often used in popular songs like Harold Arlen's "Blues in the Night", blues ballads like "Since I Fell for You" and "Please Send Me Someone to Love", and even in orchestral works such as George Gershwin's "Rhapsody in Blue" and "Concerto in F". Gershwin's second "Prelude" for solo piano is an interesting example of a classical blues, maintaining the form with academic strictness. The blues scale is ubiquitous in modern popular music and informs many modal frames, especially the ladder of thirds used in rock music (for example, in "A Hard Day's Night"). Blues forms are used in the theme to the televised Batman, teen idol Fabian's hit, "Turn Me Loose", country music star Jimmie Rodgers' music, and guitarist/vocalist Tracy Chapman's hit "Give Me One Reason".

R&B music can be traced back to spirituals and blues. Musically, spirituals were a descendant of New England choral traditions, and in particular of Isaac Watts's hymns, mixed with African rhythms and call-and-response forms. Spirituals or religious chants in the African-American community are much better documented than the "low-down" blues. Spiritual singing developed because African-American communities could gather for mass or worship gatherings, which were called camp meetings.

Early country bluesmen such as Skip James, Charley Patton, Georgia Tom Dorsey played country and urban blues and had influences from spiritual singing. Dorsey helped to popularize Gospel music. Gospel music developed in the 1930s, with the Golden Gate Quartet. In the 1950s, soul music by Sam Cooke, Ray Charles and James Brown used gospel and blues music elements. In the 1960s and 1970s, gospel and blues were these merged in soul blues music. Funk music of the 1970s was influenced by soul; funk can be seen as an antecedent of hip-hop and contemporary R&B.

Before World War II, the boundaries between blues and jazz were less clear. Usually jazz had harmonic structures stemming from brass bands, whereas blues had blues forms such as the 12-bar blues. However, the jump blues of the 1940s mixed both styles. After WWII, blues had a substantial influence on jazz. Bebop classics, such as Charlie Parker's "Now's the Time", used the blues form with the pentatonic scale and blue notes. Bebop marked a major shift in the role of jazz, from a popular style of music for dancing, to a "high-art," less-accessible, cerebral "musician's music". The audience for both blues and jazz split, and the border between blues and jazz became more defined.

The blues' 12-bar structure and the blues scale was a major influence on rock and roll music. Rock and roll has been called "blues with a backbeat"; Carl Perkins called rockabilly "blues with a country beat". Rockabillies were also said to be 12-bar blues played with a bluegrass beat. "Hound Dog", with its unmodified 12-bar structure (in both harmony and lyrics) and a melody centered on flatted third of the tonic (and flatted seventh of the subdominant), is a blues song transformed into a rock and roll song. Jerry Lee Lewis's style of rock and roll was heavily influenced by the blues and its derivative boogie woogie. His style of music was not exactly rockabilly but it has been often called real rock and roll (this is a label he shares with several African American rock and roll performers).

Early country music was infused with the blues. Jimmie Rodgers, Moon Mullican, Bob Wills, Bill Monroe and Hank Williams have all described themselves as blues singers and their music has a blues feel that is different to the country pop of Eddy Arnold. A lot of the 1970s-era "outlaw" country music by Willie Nelson and Waylon Jennings also borrowed from the blues. When Jerry Lee Lewis returned to country after the decline of 1950s style rock and roll, he sang his country with a blues feel and often included blues standards on his albums.

Many early rock and roll songs are based on blues: "That's All Right Mama", "Johnny B. Goode", "Blue Suede Shoes", "Whole Lotta Shakin' Goin On", "Shake, Rattle, and Roll", and "Long Tall Sally". The early African American rock musicians retained the sexual themes and innuendos of blues music: "Got a gal named Sue, knows just what to do" ("Tutti Frutti", Little Richard) or "See the girl with the red dress on, She can do the Birdland all night long" ("What'd I Say", Ray Charles). The 12-bar blues structure can be found even in novelty pop songs, such as Bob Dylan's "Obviously Five Believers" and Esther and Abi Ofarim's "Cinderella Rockefella".

In popular culture

Like jazz, rock and roll, heavy metal music, hip hop music, reggae, country music, and pop music, blues has been accused of being the "devil's music" and of inciting violence and other poor behavior. In the early 20th century, the blues was considered disreputable, especially as white audiences began listening to the blues during the 1920s. In the early twentieth century, W. C. Handy was the first to popularize blues-influenced music among non-black Americans.

During the blues revival of the 1960s and '70s, acoustic blues artist Taj Mahal and legendary Texas bluesman Lightnin' Hopkins wrote and performed music that figured prominently in the popularly and critically acclaimed film Sounder (1972). The film earned Mahal a Grammy nomination for Best Original Score Written for a Motion Picture and a BAFTA nomination. Almost 30 years later, Mahal wrote blues for, and performed a banjo composition, claw-hammer style, in the 2001 movie release Songcatcher, which focused on the story of the preservation of the roots music of Appalachia.

Perhaps the most visible example of the blues style of music in the late 20th century came in 1980, when Dan Aykroyd and John Belushi released the film The Blues Brothers. The film drew many of the biggest living influencers of the Rhythm and blues genre together, such as Ray Charles, James Brown, Cab Calloway, Aretha Franklin, and John Lee Hooker. The band formed also began a successful tour under the Blues Brothers marquee. 1998 brought a sequel, Blues Brothers 2000 that, while not holding as great a critical and financial success, featured a much larger number of blues artists, such as B. B. King, Bo Diddley, Erykah Badu, Eric Clapton, Steve Winwood, Charlie Musselwhite, Blues Traveller, Jimmie Vaughan, Jeff Baxter.

In 2003, Martin Scorsese made significant efforts to promote the blues to a larger audience. He asked several famous directors such as Clint Eastwood and Wim Wenders to participate in a series of documentary films for PBS called The Blues. He also participated in the rendition of compilations of major blues artists in a series of high-quality CDs. Blues guitarist and vocalist Keb' Mo' performed his blues rendition of "America, the Beautiful" in 2006 to close out the final season of the television series The West Wing.

Bo Diddley

Bo Diddley

Bo Diddley

Background information
Birth name Ellas Otha Bates
Also known as Ellas McDaniel
Born December 30, 1928
McComb, Mississippi, United States
Died June 2, 2008 (aged 79)
Archer, Florida, United States
Genres Chicago blues, rhythm and blues, rock and roll, blues
Occupations Singer-songwriter, musician
Instruments Vocals, guitar, electric guitar, violin, synthesizer, keyboards, piano, organ, percussion, drums
Years active 1943–2008
Labels Checker, Chess, BoKay Productions, RCA, MF Productions, Triple X, Atlantic
Website BoDiddley. com
Notable instruments
Gretsch G6138
Ellas Otha Bates (December 30, 1928 – June 2, 2008), known by his stage name Bo Diddley, was an American rhythm and blues vocalist, guitarist, songwriter (usually as Ellas McDaniel), and rock and roll pioneer. He was also known as The Originator because of his key role in the transition from the blues to rock, influencing a host of acts, including Buddy Holly, Jimi Hendrix, The Rolling Stones,

The Velvet Underground, The Who, The Yardbirds, Eric Clapton, Elvis Presley, The Beatles, and George Michael, among others. He introduced more insistent, driving rhythms and a hard-edged electric guitar sound on a wide-ranging catalog of songs, along with African rhythms and a signature beat (a simple, five-accent rhythm) that remains a cornerstone of rock and pop. Accordingly, he was inducted into the Rock and Roll Hall of Fame and received Lifetime Achievement Awards from the Rhythm and Blues Foundation and a Grammy Award from the National Academy of Recording Arts and Sciences. He was known in particular for his technical innovations, including his trademark rectangular guitar.

History

Early life and career

Born in McComb, Mississippi, as Ellas Otha Bates, he was adopted and raised by his mother's cousin, Gussie McDaniel, whose surname he assumed, becoming Ellas McDaniel. In 1934, the McDaniel family moved to the largely black South Side area of Chicago, where the young man dropped the name Otha and became known as Ellas McDaniel, until his musical ambitions demanded that he take on a more catchy identity. In Chicago, he was an active member of his local Ebenezer Baptist Church, where he studied the trombone and the violin, becoming proficient enough on the latter for the musical director to invite him to join the orchestra, with which he performed until the age of 18. He was more impressed, however, by the pulsating, rhythmic music he heard at a local Pentecostal Church, as well as an interest in the guitar.

Inspired by a concert where he saw John Lee Hooker perform, he supplemented his work as a carpenter and mechanic with a developing career playing on street corners with friends, including Jerome Green (c. 1934–1973), in a band called The Hipsters (later The Langley Avenue Jive Cats). During the summer of 1943–44, he played for tips at the Maxwell Street market in a band with Earl Hooker. By 1951 he was playing on the street with backing from Roosevelt Jackson (on washtub bass) and Jody Williams (whom he had taught to play the guitar). Williams later played lead guitar on "Who Do You Love?" (1956). In 1951 he landed a regular spot at the 708 Club on Chicago's South Side, with a repertoire influenced by Louis Jordan, John Lee Hooker, and Muddy Waters.

In late 1954, he teamed up with harmonica player Billy Boy Arnold, drummer Clifton James, and bass player Roosevelt Jackson, and recorded demos of "I'm A Man" and "Bo Diddley". They re-recorded the songs at Chess Studios with a backing ensemble comprising Otis Spann (piano), Lester Davenport (harmonica), Frank Kirkland (drums), and Jerome Green (maracas). The record was released in March 1955, and the A-side, "Bo Diddley", became a #1 R&B hit.

Stage Name

McDaniel adopted the stage name Bo Diddley The origin of the name is somewhat unclear, as several differing stories and claims exist. Diddley claims that his peers gave him the nickname, which he first suspected to be an insult. Bo Diddley himself said that the name first belonged to a singer his adoptive mother was familiar with, while harmonicist Billy Boy Arnold once said in an interview that it was originally the name of a local comedian that Leonard Chess borrowed for the song title and artist name for Bo Diddley's first single, and guitar craftsman Ed Roman reported that another (unspecified) source says it was his nickname as a Golden Gloves boxer.

A "diddley bow" is a typically homemade American string instrument of African origin, probably developed from instruments found on the coast of west Africa.

The American slang phrase bo diddly meaning "absolutely nothing" goes back possibly to the early 20th century or earlier. Diddly is a truncation of diddly-squat, retaining the same meaning of "nothing" and bo is an intensifier.

Success in the 1950s and 1960s

On November 20, 1955, he appeared on The Ed Sullivan Show, a popular television variety show, where he infuriated the host. "I did two songs and he got mad," Bo Diddley later recalled. "Ed Sullivan said that I was one of the first colored boys to ever double-cross him. Said that I wouldn't last six months". The show had requested that he sing the Merle Travis-penned Tennessee Ernie Ford hit "Sixteen Tons", but when he appeared on stage, he sang "Bo Diddley" instead. This substitution resulted in his being banned from further appearances.

The request came about because Sullivan's people heard Diddley casually singing "Sixteen Tons" in the dressing room. Diddley's accounts of the event were inconsistent.

Diddley was an excellent story teller whose stories varied from time to time, however, Diddley contended to friends and family that he was not trying to double-cross Sullivan and attributed the "misunderstanding" to the fact that; when he saw "Bo Diddley" on a cue card, he was under the impression he was to perform two songs, "Bo Diddley" and "Sixteen Tons".

Chess included Diddley's recording of "Sixteen Tons" on the album Bo Diddley Is a Gunslinger, which was originally released in 1960.

He continued to have hits through the rest of the 1950s and even the 1960s, including "Pretty Thing" (1956), "Say Man" (1959), and "You Can't Judge a Book by the Cover" (1962). He released a string of albums whose titles, including Bo Diddley Is a Gunslinger and Have Guitar, Will Travel, bolstered his self-invented legend. Between 1958 and 1963, Checker Records released 11 full-length albums by Bo Diddley. Although he broke through as a crossover artist with white audiences (appearing at the Alan Freed concerts, for example), he rarely tailored his compositions to teenage concerns. The album title Surfing with Bo Diddley was a boast about his influence on surf guitarists.

In 1963, he starred in a UK concert tour with the Everly Brothers and Little Richard. The Rolling Stones, still barely known outside London at that time, appeared as a supporting act on the same bill.

In addition to the many songs recorded by him, in 1956 he co-wrote, with Jody Williams, the pioneering pop song "Love Is Strange", a hit for Mickey & Sylvia in 1957.

Bo Diddley was one of the first American male musicians to include women in his band, including "The Duchess" Norma-Jean Wofford, Peggy Jones (aka "Lady Bo"), Cornelia Redmond (aka Cookie), and Debby Hastings, who led his band for the final 25 years of his performing career. After moving from his home in Chicago to Washington, D. C. , he set up one of the first home recording studios where he not only recorded the album Bo Diddley Is a Gunslinger but he recorded his valet, Marvin Gaye. The Diddley-penned, "Wyatt Earp" was a single released on Okeh Records, since the Chess brothers did not want to release the record. Also during this time, Moonglows founder Harvey Fuqua who sang background on many of Diddley's home studio recordings was introduced to Gaye, and asked him to join the Moonglows. When Fuqua went to Motown, Gaye followed.

Later years

Over the decades, Bo Diddley's venues ranged from intimate clubs to stadiums. On March 25, 1972, he played with The Grateful Dead at the Academy of Music in New York City. The Grateful Dead released part of this concert as Volume 30 of the band's Dick's Picks concert album series. Also in the early 1970s, the soundtrack for the ground-breaking animated film Fritz The Cat contained his song "Bo Diddley", in which a crow idly finger-pops along to the track.

Bo Diddley spent many years in New Mexico, living in Los Lunas, New Mexico from 1971 to 1978 while continuing his musical career. He served for two and a half years as Deputy Sheriff in the Valencia County Citizens' Patrol; during that time he personally purchased and donated three highway patrol pursuit cars. In the late 1970s, Diddley left Los Lunas and moved to Hawthorne, Florida where he lived on a large estate in a custom made log-cabin home, which he helped to build. For the remainder of his life he spent time between Albuquerque, New Mexico and Florida, living the last 13 years of his life in Archer, Florida, a small farming town near Gainesville.

He appeared as an opening act for The Clash in their 1979 US tour; in Legends of Guitar (filmed live in Spain, 1991) with B. B. King, Les Paul, Albert Collins, George Benson, among others, and joined The Rolling Stones as a guest on their 1994 concert broadcast of Voodoo Lounge, performing "Who Do You Love?" with the band. Sheryl Crow and Robert Cray also appeared on the pay-per-view special.

Illness

On May 13, 2007, Bo Diddley was admitted to intensive care in Creighton University Medical Center in Omaha, Nebraska, following a stroke after a concert in Council Bluffs, Iowa on May 12. Starting the show, he had complained that he did not feel well. He referred to smoke from the wildfires that were ravaging South

Georgia and blowing south to the area near his home in Archer, Florida. Nonetheless, he delivered an energetic performance to an enthusiastic crowd. The next day, as Bo Diddley was heading back home, he seemed dazed and confused at the airport. His manager, Margo Lewis, called 911 and airport security and Bo was immediately taken by ambulance to Creighton University Medical Center and admitted to the Intensive-care unit, where he stayed for several days. After numerous tests, it was confirmed that Bo Diddley had suffered a stroke. He had a history of hypertension and diabetes, and the stroke affected the left side of his brain, causing receptive and expressive aphasia (speech impairment). The stroke was followed by a heart attack, suffered in Gainesville, Florida, on August 28, 2007.

While recovering from the stroke and heart attack, Diddley came back to his home town of McComb, Mississippi, in early November 2007 for the unveiling of a plaque devoted to him on the National Blues Trail stating that he was "acclaimed as a founder of rock and roll. " He was not supposed to perform, but as he listened to the music of local musician Jesse Robinson who sang a song written for this occasion, Robinson sensed that he wanted to perform and handed him a microphone. That was the first and last time that Bo Diddley performed publicly after suffering a stroke.

Death

Bo Diddley died on June 2, 2008 of heart failure at his home in Archer, Florida. Garry Mitchell, a grandson of Diddley and one of more than 35 family members at the musician's home when he died at 1:45 a. m. EDT (05:45 GMT), said his death was not unexpected. "There was a gospel song that was sung (at his bedside) and (when it was done) he said 'wow' with a thumbs up," Mitchell told Reuters, when asked to describe the scene at Diddley's deathbed. "The song was 'Walk Around Heaven' and in his last words he said 'I'm going to heaven. '"

His funeral, a four-hour "homegoing" service, took place on June 7, 2008, at Showers of Blessings Church in Gainesville, Florida and kept in tune with the vibrant spirit of Bo Diddley's life and career. The many in attendance chanted "Hey Bo Diddley" as a gospel band played the legend's music. A number of notable musicians sent flowers, including: George Thorogood, Tom Petty, and Jerry Lee Lewis. Little Richard, who had been asking his audiences to pray for Bo Diddley throughout his illness, had to fulfill concert commitments in Westbury and New York City the weekend of the funeral. He took time to remember Bo Diddley, his friend of a half-century, performing his namesake tune in his honor.

After the funeral service, a tribute concert was held at the Martin Luther King Center, also in Gainesville, and featured performances by his son and daughter, Anthony McDaniel and Evelyn Kelly, long-time background vocalist Gloria Jolivet, co-producer Scott "Skyntyte" Free, Diddley's touring band, The Debby Hastings Band, and guest artist Eric Burdon.

In the days following his death, tributes were paid to him by then-President George W. Bush, the United States House of Representatives, and an uncounted number of musicians and performers, including Eric Burdon, Elvis Costello, Ronnie Hawkins, Mick Jagger, B. B. King, Tom Petty, Robert Plant, Bonnie Raitt, George Thorogood, Robert Randolph and the Family Band, the Black Lips and Ronnie Wood. He was posthumously awarded a Doctor of Fine Arts degree by the University of Florida for his influence on American popular music and in its "People in America" radio series about influential people in American history, the Voice of America radio service paid tribute to him, describing how "his influence was so widespread that it is hard to imagine what rock and roll would have sounded like without him. " Mick Jagger stated that "he was a wonderful, original musician who was an enormous force in music and was a big influence on The Rolling Stones. He was very generous to us in our early years and we learned a lot from him. " Jagger also praised the late star as a one of a kind musician, adding, "We will never see his like again. As his bass player Debby Hastings said: he was the rock that the roll was built on. "

The documentary film Cheat You Fair: The Story of Maxwell Street by director Phil Ranstrom features Bo Diddley's last on-camera interview.

In November 2009 the guitar used by Diddley in his last-ever stage performance sold for $60,000 at auction.

Bit acting parts

His pawnbroker character's offering Louis Winthorpe III "fifty bucks" created one of more quoted scenes in 1983's Trading Places.

In the late 1980s, he teamed with Bo Jackson in Nike's famous "Bo Knows" commercials, saying his one line: "Bo, you don't know Diddley!" He would later reprise his role along with Jackson in a spoof of the commercial on Sesame Street.

In 1998, Bo appeared alongside legendary guitarists B. B. King, Eric Clapton, and Jeff "Skunk" Baxter as members of the Louisiana Gator Boys in the film Blues Brothers 2000.

In 2003, Bo was cast as himself in an episode of According to Jim, titled "Bo Diddley".

Music Videos

In 1982, Bo was featured in the music video, Bad To The Bone by George Thorogood and the Destroyers as a pool shark. Bo also had small Part in an Episode of Disney TV Show "So Weird" (1999-2001) playing a Shopkeeper.

Accolades

Bo Diddley achieved numerous accolades in recognition of his significant role as one of the founding fathers of rock and roll.

1986: inducted into the Washington Area Music Association's Hall of Fame.
1987: inducted the Rock and Roll Hall of Fame and the Rockabilly Hall of Fame.
1990: Lifetime Achievement Award from Guitar Player magazine.
1998: Lifetime Achievement Awards from the Rhythm and Blues Foundation and the National Academy of Recording Arts and Sciences.
1999: His 1955 recording of his song "Bo Diddley" inducted into the Grammy Hall of Fame as a recording of lasting qualitative or historical significance.
2000: Inducted into the Mississippi Musicians Hall of Fame and into the North Florida Music Association's Hall of Fame.
2002: Pioneer in Entertainment Award from the National Association of Black Owned Broadcasters
2002: Bo Diddley was honored as one of the first BMI Icons at the 50th annual BMI Pop Awards. He was presented the award along with BMI affiliates Chuck Berry and Little Richard.
2008: Although confirmed before his death in June 2008, an honorary degree was posthumously conferred upon Diddley by the

University of Florida in August 2008.
2009: Florida's Secretary of State announces Bo's induction into the Florida Artists Hall of Fame (induction to occur during Florida Heritage Month, March 2010).
2010: Bo Diddley was inducted into the Hit Parade Hall of Fame.
In 2003, U. S. Representative John Conyers paid tribute to Bo Diddley in the United States House of Representatives describing him as "one of the true pioneers of rock and roll, who has influenced generations".

In 2004, Mickey and Sylvia's 1956 recording of his song "Love Is Strange" was inducted into the Grammy Hall of Fame as a recording of qualitative or historical significance, and he was inducted into the Blues Foundation's Blues Hall of Fame. In 2004, Rolling Stone ranked him #20 on their list of the 100 Greatest Artists of All Time.

In 2005, Bo Diddley celebrated his 50th anniversary in music with successful tours of Australia and Europe, and with coast-to-coast shows across North America. He performed his song "Bo Diddley" with Eric Clapton, Robbie Robertson, and longtime bassist and musical director Debby Hastings at the Rock and Roll Hall of Fame's 20th annual induction ceremony and in the UK, Uncut magazine included his 1957 debut album "Bo Diddley" in its listing of the '100 Music, Movie & TV Moments That Have Changed The World'.

In 2006, Bo Diddley participated as the headliner of a grassroots organized fundraiser concert, to benefit the town of Ocean Springs, Mississippi, which had been devastated by Hurricane Katrina. The "Florida Keys for Katrina Relief" had originally been set for October 23, 2005, when Hurricane Wilma barreled through the Florida Keys on October 24, causing flooding and economic mayhem. In January 2006, the Florida Keys had recovered enough to host the fundraising concert to benefit the more hard-hit community of Ocean Springs. When asked about the fundraiser Bo Diddley stated, "This is the United States of America. We believe in helping one another. ". In an interview with Holger Petersen, on Saturday Night Blues on CBC Radio in the fall of 2006 Bo Diddley commented about the racism that existed in the music industry establishment during the early part of his career that saw him deprived of his royalties from the most successful part of his career.

Bo Diddley performed a number of shows around the country in 2005 and 2006 with the fellow Rock and Roll Hall of Famer Johnnie

Johnson Band, featuring Johnson on keyboards, Richard Hunt on drums, and Gus Thornton on bass. But from 1985 until he died, his touring band consisted of Debby Hastings (bass/musical director), Frank Daley or Nunzio Signore (guitar), Tom Major, Dave Johnson, Yoshi Shimada or Sandy Gennaro (drums), and his personal manager, Margo Lewis (keyboards).

The Bo Diddley beat

Bo Diddley was well known for the Bo Diddley beat, which is essentially the clave rhythm, and one of the most common bell patterns found in sub-Saharan African music traditions. Bo Diddley has given different accounts of the riff's origins. Sublette asserts: "In the context of the time, and especially those maracas [heard on the record], 'Bo Diddley' has to be understood as a Latin-tinged record. A rejected cut recorded at the same session was titled only 'Rhumba' on the track sheets. " The Bo Diddley beat is similar to "hambone", a style used by street performers who play out the beat by slapping and patting their arms, legs, chest, and cheeks while chanting rhymes. Somewhat resembling "shave and a haircut, two bits" rhythm, Diddley came across it while trying to play Gene Autry's "(I've Got Spurs That) Jingle, Jangle, Jingle". Three years before Bo's "Bo Diddley", a song similar syncopation "Hambone", was cut by Red Saunders' Orchestra with The Hambone Kids. In 1944, "Rum and Coca Cola", containing the Bo Diddley beat, was recorded by The Andrews Sisters and later Buddy Holly's "Not Fade Away" (1957) and Them's "Mystic Eyes" (1965) used the beat. In its simplest form, the Bo Diddley beat can be counted out as either an on-bar, or a two-bar phrase.

Other songs employing the Bo Diddley beat include "(Marie's the Name) His Latest Flame" (1961) by Elvis Presley, "I Want Candy" by The Strangeloves, "1969" (1969) by The Stooges, "Panic in Detroit" (1973) by David Bowie, "Mr. Brownstone" (1987) by Guns N' Roses, "Faith (1987) by George Michael, "Desire" (1988) by U2, "Boa-Diddley" (1990) by Phillip Boa and the Voodooclub, "Movin' on Up" (1991) by Primal Scream, "Woodcutter's Son" (1995) by Paul Weller, and "Screwdriver" (1999) by The White Stripes. Other examples include "Magic Bus" by The Who, "Rudie Can't Fail" by The Clash, "Get Me to the World on Time" by The Electric Prunes, and "Party at the Leper Colony" by "Weird Al" Yankovic. Some of the more subtle uses of the Biddley beat include "Hateful" (1979) by The Clash and "How Soon Is Now?" (1985) by The Smiths.

Here is the count as a one-bar phrase: One e and ah, two e and ah, three e and ah, four e and ah. The bolded counts are the clave rhythm.

Many songs (for example, "Hey Bo Diddley" and "Who Do You Love?") often have no chord changes; that is, the musicians play the same chord throughout the piece, so that the rhythms create the excitement, rather than having the excitement generated by harmonic tension and release. In his other recordings, Bo Diddley used a variety of rhythms, from straight back beat to pop ballad style to doo-wop, frequently with maracas by Jerome Green.

Also an influential guitar player, he developed many special effects and other innovations in tone and attack. Bo Diddley's trademark instrument was the rectangular-bodied Gretsch nicknamed "The Twang Machine" (referred to as "cigar-box shaped" by music promoter Dick Clark). Although he had other odd-shaped guitars custom-made for him by other manufacturers throughout the years, most notably the "Cadillac" design made by Tom Holmes (who also made guitars for ZZ Top's Billy Gibbons, among others), Diddley fashioned the square guitar himself around 1958 and wielded it in thousands of concerts over the years. In a 2005 interview on JJJ radio in Australia, Bo implied that the design sprang from an embarrassing moment. During an early gig, while jumping around on stage with a Gibson L5 guitar, he landed awkwardly hurting his groin. He then went about designing a smaller, less restrictive guitar that allowed him to keep jumping around on stage while still playing his guitar. He also played the violin, which is featured on his mournful instrumental "The Clock Strikes Twelve", a twelve-bar blues.

He often created lyrics as witty and humorous adaptations of folk music themes. The song "Bo Diddley" was based on the African American clapping rhyme "Hambone" (which in turn was based on the lullaby "Hush Little Baby"). Likewise, "Hey Bo Diddley" is based on the song "Old MacDonald". The rap-style boasting of "Who Do You Love", a wordplay on hoodoo, used many striking lyrics from the African-American tradition of toasts and boasts. His "Say Man" and "Say Man, Back Again," both of which were later cited as progenerators of hip-hop music, share a strong connection to the insult game known as "the dozens". For example: "You got the nerve to call somebody ugly, why you so ugly the stork that brought you into the world ought to be arrested".

I used to get mad about people recording my things; now I got a new thing going. . . . I don't get mad about them recording my material because they keep me alive.

Notable cover versions

Bo Diddley's songs have frequently been covered by other artists.

Captain Beefheart covered "Diddy Wah Diddy" in 1966. The Blues Band and Tom Petty have played the song in concert.

Buddy Holly's rendition of "Bo Diddley" (recorded in 1957) was a posthumous top-10 hit in the UK, peaking at No. 7 in the summer of 1963.

The Rolling Stones covered several Bo Diddley numbers in concert and in early BBC Radio broadcasts. In 1964 they released "I Need You Baby (Mona)" on the UK version of their first album (the US version featured their cover of the Diddley-inspired Buddy Holly song "Not Fade Away").

The Kinks covered "Cadillac" on their debut album in 1964.

The Pretty Things covered "Road Runner", "She's Fine, She's Mine" and "Mama, Keep Your Big Mouth Shut" on their debut album in 1965, where "Road Runner" was featured as the opening track.

"Road Runner" has also been covered by Humble Pie, The Zombies, The Animals, The Who and Aerosmith.

The Animals and Bob Seger have both covered "The Story of Bo Diddley".

Long John Baldry covered Bo Diddley's song "You Can't Judge a Book" on his 1972 album Everything Stops for Tea.

The Yardbirds, The Who, Dr. Feelgood, Tom Petty, The Remains and the Dutch group Q65 covered "I'm a Man".

The Grateful Dead, The Woolies, George Thorogood, Dion, Townes Van Zandt, Ronnie Hawkins, The Jesus and Mary Chain and Juicy Lucy covered "Who Do You Love", which was also a concert favorite of The Doors.

The Grateful Dead Did a set with him (March 25, 1972) Dick's Picks, Volume Thirty; Hey Bo Diddley>I'm A Man>I've Seen Them All >Mona

Quicksilver Messenger Service covered both "Who Do You Love" and "Mona".

Creedence Clearwater Revival and Eric Clapton have both covered "Before You Accuse Me".

The New York Dolls and The Lurkers have both recorded their own versions of the song "Pills".

Dr. Feelgood led off their second album, Malpractice (1975), with a

cover of "I Can Tell. "
The Clash recorded "Mona" during the London Calling sessions.
Ex-Velvet Underground drummer Maureen Tucker counts Diddley as one of her chief influences and covered "Bo Diddley" on her 1989 solo album, Life in Exile After Abdication.
Chris Isaak covered "Diddley Daddy" on his third album, Heart Shaped World (1989).
Craig McLachlan, an Australian soap opera star, reached Number 2 in the UK singles charts in 1990 with a version of "Mona" that inserted the chord change Buddy Holly used in the Diddley-inspired "Not Fade Away"
Black Strobe covered "I'm a Man" on their Album Burn Your Own Church (2007).
Tom Petty has played "I Need You Baby (Mona)" in concert, and performed it with Diddley himself in 1999.
Historic marker and other dedications

Bo Diddley was honored by the Mississippi Blues Commission with a Mississippi Blues Trail historic marker placed in McComb, his birthplace, in recognition of his enormous contribution to the development of the blues in Mississippi.

On June 5, 2009 the city of Gainesville, Florida, officially renamed and dedicated its downtown plaza the Bo Diddley Community Plaza. The plaza was the site of many benefit concerts at which Bo Diddley performed during his lifetime to raise awareness about the plight of the homeless in Alachua County, and to raise money for local charities, including the Red Cross.

The Obamas' dog, Bo, is also said to be named after him.

The Mario characters known as Boos were originally called "Boo Diddleys" in Super Mario Bros. 3 as a reference to Bo Diddley, though this was long before Bo Diddley died.

Peter Cook & Dudley Moore did a sketch in which Moore played a character called "(the famous coloured singer) Bo Dudley" in reference to Diddley. Moore's vocal performance during the sketch, however, was a parody of James Brown's "Papa's Got A Brand New Bag".

Scottish alternative rock band The Jesus and Mary Chain have frequently cited Bo Diddley as an influence. This is most notable via the song 'Bo Diddley Is Jesus', a b-side to their 1987 UK Top Ten hit

April Skies, the 12-inch version of which also included a cover of Bo Diddley's Who Do You Love?.

Discography

Bo Diddley discography
Books

George R. White, Living Legend, Sanctuary Publishing Ltd, 1995.
Laurent Arsicaud, Bo Diddley, Je suis un homme, Camion Blanc editions, 2012.

Bob Dylan

Bob Dylan

Bob Dylan

Dylan onstage at Azkena Rock Festival, Vitoria-Gasteiz, Spain, June 26, 2010
Background information
Birth name Robert Allen Zimmerman
Also known as Elston Gunnn, Blind Boy Grunt, Bob Landy, Robert Milkwood Thomas, Tedham Porterhouse, Lucky/Boo Wilbury, Jack Frost, Sergei Petrov
Born May 24, 1941 (age 71)
Duluth, Minnesota, U. S.
Origin Hibbing, Minnesota, U. S.
Genres Rock, folk, folk rock, blues, blues rock, country, rock and roll, gospel, country rock
Occupations Musician, singer-songwriter, producer, visual artist, poet, writer, director, screenwriter
Instruments Vocals, harmonica, guitar, keyboards
Years active 1961–present
Labels Columbia, Asylum
Associated acts Joan Baez, The Band, Johnny Cash, Grateful Dead, Mark Knopfler, Tom Petty and the Heartbreakers, Traveling Wilburys
Website bobdylan. com
Bob Dylan (/□d□l□n/; born Robert Allen Zimmerman; May 24, 1941) is an American singer-songwriter, musician, and artist. He has been an influential figure in popular music and culture for over five decades. Much of his most celebrated work dates from the 1960s

when he was an informal chronicler and a seemingly reluctant figurehead of social unrest. A number of Dylan's early songs, such as "Blowin' in the Wind" and "The Times They Are a-Changin'", became anthems for the US civil rights and anti-war movements. Leaving his initial base in the culture of folk music behind, Dylan's six-minute single "Like a Rolling Stone" has been described as radically altering the parameters of popular music in 1965. His recordings employing electric instruments attracted denunciation and criticism from others in the folk movement.

Dylan's lyrics incorporated a variety of political, social, philosophical, and literary influences. They defied existing pop music conventions and appealed hugely to the then burgeoning counterculture. Initially inspired by the songs of Woody Guthrie, Robert Johnson, and Hank Williams, and the music and performance styles of Buddy Holly, Little Richard and Elvis Presley, Dylan has both amplified and personalized musical genres. His recording career, spanning fifty years, has explored numerous distinct traditions in American song—from folk, blues and country to gospel, rock and roll, and rockabilly to English, Scottish, and Irish folk music, embracing even jazz and swing.

Dylan performs with guitar, keyboards, and harmonica. Backed by a changing line-up of musicians, he has toured steadily since the late 1980s on what has been dubbed the Never Ending Tour. His accomplishments as a recording artist and performer have been central to his career, but his greatest contribution is generally considered to be his songwriting.

Since 1994, Dylan has published three books of drawings and paintings, and his work has been exhibited in major art galleries. As a songwriter and musician, Dylan has received numerous awards over the years including Grammy, Golden Globe, and Academy Awards; he has been inducted into the Rock and Roll Hall of Fame, Nashville Songwriters Hall of Fame, and Songwriters Hall of Fame. The Pulitzer Prize jury in 2008 awarded him a special citation for "his profound impact on popular music and American culture, marked by lyrical compositions of extraordinary poetic power. " In May 2012, Dylan received the Presidential Medal of Freedom from President Barack Obama.

Life and career

Origins and musical beginnings

Bob Dylan was born "Robert Allen Zimmerman" (Hebrew name □□□□□ □□□□□ □□ □□□□□ [Shabtai Zisel ben Avraham]) in St. Mary's Hospital on May 24, 1941, in Duluth, Minnesota, and raised in Hibbing, Minnesota, on the Mesabi Iron Range west of Lake Superior. His paternal grandparents, Zigman and Anna Zimmerman, emigrated from Odessa in the Russian Empire (now Ukraine) to the United States following the anti-Semitic pogroms of 1905. His maternal grandparents, Benjamin and Lybba Edelstein, were Lithuanian Jews who arrived in the United States in 1902. In his autobiography Chronicles: Volume One, Dylan writes that his paternal grandmother's maiden name was Kirghiz and her family originated from Ka□ızman in Turkey.

Dylan's parents, Abram Zimmerman and Beatrice "Beatty" Stone, were part of the area's small but close-knit Jewish community. Robert Zimmerman lived in Duluth until age six, when his father was stricken with polio and the family returned to his mother's home town, Hibbing, where Zimmerman spent the rest of his childhood. Robert Zimmerman spent much of his youth listening to the radio—first to blues and country stations broadcasting from Shreveport, Louisiana and, later, to early rock and roll. He formed several bands while he attended Hibbing High School. The Shadow Blasters was short-lived, but his next, The Golden Chords, lasted longer and played covers of Little Richard rock and roll and other popular songs. Their performance of Danny and the Juniors' "Rock and Roll Is Here to Stay" at their high school talent show was so loud that the principal cut the microphone off. In 1959, his high school yearbook carried, beneath his photo, the caption: "Robert Zimmerman: to join 'Little Richard'. " The same year, using the name Elston Gunnn [sic], he performed two dates with Bobby Vee, playing piano and providing handclaps.

Zimmerman moved to Minneapolis in September 1959 and enrolled at the University of Minnesota, where his early focus on rock and roll gave way to an interest in American folk music. In 1985, Dylan explained the attraction that folk music had exerted on him:

The thing about rock'n'roll is that for me anyway it wasn't enough . . . There were great catch-phrases and driving pulse rhythms . . . but the songs weren't serious or didn't reflect life in a realistic way. I knew that when I got into folk music, it was more of a serious type of thing. The songs are filled with more despair, more sadness, more triumph, more faith in the supernatural, much deeper feelings.

He soon began to perform at the Ten O'Clock Scholar, a coffeehouse a few blocks from campus, and became actively involved in the local Dinkytown folk music circuit.

During his Dinkytown days, Zimmerman began introducing himself as "Bob Dylan". In his autobiography, Dylan acknowledged that he had been influenced by the poetry of Dylan Thomas. [a 1] Explaining his change of name in a 2004 interview, Dylan remarked: "You're born, you know, the wrong names, wrong parents. I mean, that happens. You call yourself what you want to call yourself. This is the land of the free. "

1960s

Relocation to New York and record deal

Dylan dropped out of college at the end of his freshman year. In January 1961, he traveled to New York City, hoping to perform there and visit his musical idol Woody Guthrie, who was seriously ill with Huntington's Disease in Greystone Park Psychiatric Hospital. Guthrie had been a revelation to Dylan and was the biggest influence on his early performances. Describing Guthrie's impact on him, Dylan later wrote: "The songs themselves had the infinite sweep of humanity in them . . . [He] was the true voice of the American spirit. I said to myself I was going to be Guthrie's greatest disciple. " As well as visiting Guthrie in the hospital, Dylan befriended Guthrie's acolyte Ramblin' Jack Elliott. Much of Guthrie's repertoire was actually channeled through Elliott, and Dylan paid tribute to Elliott in Chronicles (2004).

From February 1961, Dylan played at various clubs around Greenwich Village. He befriended and picked up material from many folk singers in the Village scene, including Dave Van Ronk, Fred Neil, Odetta, the New Lost City Ramblers, and Irish musicians Tommy Makem and the Clancy Brothers. In September, Dylan gained some public recognition when Robert Shelton wrote a positive review in The New York Times of a show at Gerde's Folk City. The same month Dylan played harmonica on folk singer Carolyn Hester's eponymous third album, which brought his talents to the attention of the album's producer, John Hammond. Hammond signed Dylan to Columbia Records in October. The performances on his first Columbia album, Bob Dylan (1962), consisted of familiar folk, blues and gospel material combined with two original compositions. The album made little impact, selling only 5,000 copies in its first year, just enough to break even. Within Columbia Records, some referred to the singer as "Hammond's Folly" and suggested dropping his contract. Hammond defended Dylan vigorously. In March 1962, Dylan contributed harmonica and back-up vocals to the album Three Kings and the Queen, accompanying Victoria Spivey and Big Joe Williams on a recording for Spivey Records. While working for Columbia, Dylan also recorded several songs under the pseudonym Blind Boy Grunt, for Broadside Magazine, a folk music magazine and record label. Dylan used the pseudonym Bob Landy to record as a piano player on the 1964 anthology album, The Blues Project, issued by Elektra Records. Under the pseudonym Tedham Porterhouse, Dylan contributed harmonica to Ramblin' Jack Elliott's 1964 album Jack Elliott.

Dylan made two important career moves in August 1962. He legally changed his name to Bob Dylan, and signed a management contract with Albert Grossman. Grossman remained Dylan's manager until 1970, and was notable both for his sometimes confrontational personality, and for the fiercely protective loyalty he displayed towards his principal client. Dylan subsequently said of Grossman, "He was kind of like a Colonel Tom Parker figure . . . you could smell him coming. " Tensions between Grossman and John Hammond led to Hammond being replaced as the producer of Dylan's second album by the young African American jazz producer Tom Wilson.

From December 1962 to January 1963, Dylan made his first trip to the United Kingdom. He had been invited by TV director Philip Saville to appear in a drama, The Madhouse on Castle Street, which Saville was directing for BBC Television. At the end of the play, Dylan performed "Blowin' in the Wind", one of the first major public performances of the song. The film recording of The Madhouse on Castle Street was destroyed by the BBC in 1968. While in London, Dylan performed at several London folk clubs, including Les Cousins, and Bunjies. He also learned new songs from several UK performers, including Martin Carthy.

By the time Dylan's second album, The Freewheelin' Bob Dylan, was released in May 1963, he had begun to make his name as both a singer and a songwriter. Many of the songs on this album were labeled protest songs, inspired partly by Guthrie and influenced by Pete Seeger's passion for topical songs. "Oxford Town", for example, was a sardonic account of James Meredith's ordeal as the first black student to risk enrollment at the University of Mississippi.

His most famous song at this time, "Blowin' in the Wind", partially derived its melody from the traditional slave song "No More Auction Block", while its lyrics questioned the social and political status quo. The song was widely recorded and became an international hit for Peter, Paul and Mary, setting a precedent for many other artists who had hits with Dylan's songs. "A Hard Rain's a-Gonna Fall" was based on the tune of the folk ballad "Lord Randall". With its veiled references to nuclear apocalypse, it gained even more resonance when the Cuban missile crisis developed only a few weeks after Dylan began performing it. Like "Blowin' in the Wind", "A Hard Rain's a-Gonna Fall" marked an important new direction in modern songwriting, blending a stream-of-consciousness, imagist lyrical attack with a traditional folk form.

While Dylan's topical songs solidified his early reputation, Freewheelin' also included a mixture of love songs and jokey, surreal talking blues. Humor was a large part of Dylan's persona, and the range of material on the album impressed many listeners, including The Beatles. George Harrison said, "We just played it, just wore it out. The content of the song lyrics and just the attitude—it was incredibly original and wonderful. "

The rough edge of Dylan's singing was unsettling to some early listeners but an attraction to others. Describing the impact that Dylan had on her and her husband, Joyce Carol Oates wrote: "When we first heard this raw, very young, and seemingly untrained voice, frankly nasal, as if sandpaper could sing, the effect was dramatic and electrifying. " Many of his most famous early songs first reached the public through more immediately palatable versions by other performers, such as Joan Baez, who became Dylan's advocate, as well as his lover. Baez was influential in bringing Dylan to national and international prominence by recording several of his early songs and inviting him onstage during her own concerts.

Others who recorded and had hits with Dylan's songs in the early and mid-1960s included The Byrds; Sonny and Cher; The Hollies; Peter, Paul and Mary; The Association; Manfred Mann; and The Turtles. Most attempted to impart a pop feel and rhythm to the songs, while Dylan and Baez performed them mostly as sparse folk pieces. The cover versions became so ubiquitous that CBS started to promote him with the tag "Nobody Sings Dylan Like Dylan. "

"Mixed Up Confusion", recorded during the Freewheelin' sessions with a backing band, was released as a single and then quickly withdrawn. In contrast to the mostly solo acoustic performances on the album, the single showed a willingness to experiment with a rockabilly sound. Cameron Crowe described it as "a fascinating look at a folk artist with his mind wandering towards Elvis Presley and Sun Records. "

Protest and Another Side

In May 1963, Dylan's political profile was raised when he walked out of The Ed Sullivan Show. During rehearsals, Dylan had been informed by CBS Television's "head of program practices" that the song he was planning to perform, "Talkin' John Birch Paranoid Blues", was potentially libelous to the John Birch Society. Rather than comply with the censorship, Dylan refused to appear on the program.

By this time, Dylan and Baez were both prominent in the civil rights movement, singing together at the March on Washington on August 28, 1963. Dylan's third album, The Times They Are a Changin', reflected a more politicized and cynical Dylan. The songs often took as their subject matter contemporary, real life stories, with "Only A Pawn In Their Game" addressing the murder of civil rights worker Medgar Evers; and the Brechtian "The Lonesome Death of Hattie Carroll" the death of black hotel barmaid Hattie Carroll, at the hands of young white socialite William Zantzinger. On a more general theme, "Ballad of Hollis Brown" and "North Country Blues" address the despair engendered by the breakdown of farming and mining communities. This political material was accompanied by two personal love songs, "Boots of Spanish Leather" and "One Too Many Mornings".

By the end of 1963, Dylan felt both manipulated and constrained by the folk and protest movements. These tensions were publicly displayed when, accepting the "Tom Paine Award" from the National Emergency Civil Liberties Committee shortly after the assassination of John F. Kennedy, an intoxicated Dylan brashly questioned the role of the committee, characterized the members as old and balding, and claimed to see something of himself (and of every man) in Kennedy's alleged assassin, Lee Harvey Oswald.

Another Side of Bob Dylan, recorded on a single June evening in 1964, had a lighter mood than its predecessor. The surreal, humorous Dylan reemerged on "I Shall Be Free No. 10" and "Motorpsycho Nightmare". "Spanish Harlem Incident" and "To Ramona" are romantic and passionate love songs, while "Black Crow Blues" and "I Don't Believe You (She Acts Like We Never Have Met)" suggest the rock and roll soon to dominate Dylan's music. "It Ain't Me Babe", on the surface a song about spurned love, has been described as a rejection of the role his reputation had thrust at him. His newest direction was signaled by two lengthy songs: the impressionistic "Chimes of Freedom", which sets elements of social commentary against a denser metaphorical landscape in a style later characterized by Allen Ginsberg as "chains of flashing images," and "My Back Pages", which attacks the simplistic and arch seriousness of his own earlier topical songs and seems to predict the backlash he was about to encounter from his former champions as he took a new direction.

In the latter half of 1964 and 1965, Dylan's appearance and musical style changed rapidly, as he made his move from leading contemporary songwriter of the folk scene to folk-rock pop-music star. His scruffy jeans and work shirts were replaced by a Carnaby Street wardrobe, sunglasses day or night, and pointy "Beatle boots". A London reporter wrote: "Hair that would set the teeth of a comb on edge. A loud shirt that would dim the neon lights of Leicester Square. He looks like an undernourished cockatoo. " Dylan also began to spar in increasingly surreal ways with his interviewers. Appearing on the Les Crane TV show and asked about a movie he was planning to make, he told Crane it would be a cowboy horror movie. Asked if he played the cowboy, Dylan replied, "No, I play my mother. "

Going electric

Electric Dylan controversy

Dylan's April 1965 album Bringing It All Back Home was yet another stylistic leap, featuring his first recordings made with electric instruments. The first single, "Subterranean Homesick Blues", owed much to Chuck Berry's "Too Much Monkey Business"; its free association lyrics have been described as both harkening back to the manic energy of Beat poetry and as a forerunner of rap and hip-hop. The song was provided with an early music video which opened D. A. Pennebaker's cinéma vérité presentation of Dylan's 1965 tour of England, Dont Look Back. Instead of miming to the recording, Dylan illustrated the lyrics by throwing cue cards containing key words from the song on the ground. Pennebaker has said the sequence was Dylan's idea, and it has been widely imitated in both music videos and advertisements.

The second side of Bringing It All Back Home consisted of four long songs on which Dylan accompanied himself on acoustic guitar and harmonica. "Mr. Tambourine Man" quickly became one of Dylan's best known songs when The Byrds recorded an electric version that reached number one in both the U. S. and the U. K. charts. "It's All Over Now Baby Blue" and "It's Alright Ma (I'm Only Bleeding)" were acclaimed as two of Dylan's most important compositions.

In the summer of 1965, as the headliner at the Newport Folk Festival, Dylan performed his first electric set since his high school days with a pickup group drawn mostly from the Paul Butterfield Blues Band, featuring Mike Bloomfield (guitar), Sam Lay (drums) and Jerome Arnold (bass), plus Al Kooper (organ) and Barry Goldberg (piano). Dylan had appeared at Newport in 1963 and 1964, but in 1965 Dylan, met with a mix of cheering and booing, left the stage after only three songs. One version of the legend has it that the boos were from the outraged folk fans whom Dylan had alienated by appearing, unexpectedly, with an electric guitar. Murray Lerner, who filmed the performance, said: "I absolutely think that they were booing Dylan going electric. " An alternative account claims audience members were merely upset by poor sound quality and a surprisingly short set. This account is supported by Kooper and one of the directors of the festival, who reports his audio recording of the concert proves that the only boos were in reaction to the emcee's announcement that there was only enough time for a short set.

Nevertheless, Dylan's 1965 Newport performance provoked a hostile response from the folk music establishment. In the September issue of Sing Out!, singer Ewan MacColl wrote: "Our traditional songs and ballads are the creations of extraordinarily talented artists working inside disciplines formulated over time. . . 'But what of Bobby Dylan?' scream the outraged teenagers. . . Only a completely non-critical audience, nourished on the watery pap of pop music, could have fallen for such tenth-rate drivel. " On July 29, just four days after his controversial performance at

Newport, Dylan was back in the studio in New York, recording "Positively 4th Street". The lyrics teemed with images of vengeance and paranoia, and it was widely interpreted as Dylan's put-down of former friends from the folk community—friends he had known in the clubs along West 4th Street.

Highway 61 Revisited and Blonde on Blonde

In July 1965, Dylan released the single "Like a Rolling Stone", which peaked at No. 2 in the U. S. and at No. 4 in the UK charts. At over six minutes, the song has been widely credited with altering attitudes about what a pop single could convey. Bruce Springsteen, in his speech during Dylan's inauguration into the Rock and Roll Hall of Fame said that on first hearing the single, "that snare shot sounded like somebody'd kicked open the door to your mind". In 2004, and again in 2011, Rolling Stone magazine listed it as number one on its list of "The 500 Greatest Songs of All Time". The song also opened Dylan's next album, Highway 61 Revisited, titled after the road that led from Dylan's Minnesota to the musical hotbed of New Orleans. The songs were in the same vein as the hit single, flavored by Mike Bloomfield's blues guitar and Al Kooper's organ riffs. "Desolation Row", backed by acoustic guitar and understated bass, offers the sole exception, with Dylan making surreal allusions to a variety of figures in Western culture during this epic song, described by Andy Gill as "an 11-minute epic of entropy, which takes the form of a Fellini-esque parade of grotesques and oddities featuring a huge cast of celebrated characters, some historical (Einstein, Nero), some biblical (Noah, Cain and Abel), some fictional (Ophelia, Romeo, Cinderella), some literary (T. S. Eliot and Ezra Pound), and some who fit into none of the above categories, notably Dr. Filth and his dubious nurse. "

In support of the record, Dylan was booked for two U. S. concerts and set about assembling a band. Mike Bloomfield was unwilling to leave the Butterfield Band, so Dylan mixed Al Kooper and Harvey Brooks from his studio crew with Robbie Robertson and Levon Helm, best known at the time for being part of Ronnie Hawkins's backing band The Hawks (later to become The Band). On August 28 at Forest Hills Tennis Stadium, the group was heckled by an audience still annoyed by Dylan's electric sound. The band's reception on September 3 at the Hollywood Bowl was more favorable.

While Dylan and the Hawks met increasingly receptive audiences on tour, their studio efforts floundered. Producer Bob Johnston persuaded Dylan to record in Nashville in February 1966, and surrounded him with a cadre of top-notch session men. At Dylan's insistence, Robertson and Kooper came down from New York City to play on the sessions. The Nashville sessions produced the double-album Blonde on Blonde (1966), featuring what Dylan later called "that thin wild mercury sound". Al Kooper described the album as "taking two cultures and smashing them together with a huge explosion": the musical world of Nashville and the world of the "quintessential New York hipster" Bob Dylan.

On November 22, 1965, Dylan secretly married 25-year-old former model Sara Lownds. Some of Dylan's friends (including Ramblin' Jack Elliott) claim that, in conversation immediately after the event, Dylan denied that he was married. Journalist Nora Ephron first made the news public in the New York Post in February 1966 with the headline "Hush! Bob Dylan is wed. "

Dylan undertook a world tour of Australia and Europe in the spring of 1966. Each show was split into two parts. Dylan performed solo during the first half, accompanying himself on acoustic guitar and harmonica. In the second half, backed by the Hawks, he played high voltage electric music. This contrast provoked many fans, who jeered and slow handclapped. The tour culminated in a famously raucous confrontation between Dylan and his audience at the Manchester Free Trade Hall in England on May 17, 1966. An official recording of this concert was finally released in 1998: The Bootleg Series Vol. 4: Bob Dylan Live 1966. At the climax of the evening, a member of the audience, angered by Dylan's electric backing, shouted: "Judas!" to which Dylan responded, "I don't believe you . . . You're a liar!" Dylan turned to his band and said, "Play it fucking loud!" as they launched into the final song of the night—"Like a Rolling Stone. "

During his 1966 tour, Dylan was frequently described as exhausted and acting "as if on a death trip". D. A. Pennebaker, the film maker accompanying the tour, described Dylan as "taking a lot of amphetamine and who-knows-what-else. " In a 1969 interview with Jann Wenner, Dylan said, "I was on the road for almost five years. It wore me down. I was on drugs, a lot of things. . . just to keep going, you know?" In 2011, BBC Radio 4 reported that, in an interview which Robert Shelton had taped in 1966, Dylan claimed that he had kicked a heroin habit in New York City: "I got very, very strung out for a while. . . I had about a $25-a-day habit and I kicked it. " Some journalists questioned the validity of this confession, pointing out that Dylan had "been telling journalists wild lies about his past since the earliest days of his career. "

Motorcycle accident and reclusion

After his European tour, Dylan returned to New York, but the pressures on him increased. ABC Television had paid an advance for a TV show they could screen. His publisher, Macmillan, was demanding a finished manuscript of the poem/novel Tarantula. Manager Albert Grossman had already scheduled an extensive concert tour for that summer and fall.

On July 29, 1966, Dylan crashed his 500cc Triumph Tiger 100 motorcycle on a road near his home in Woodstock, New York, throwing him to the ground. Though the extent of his injuries were never fully disclosed, Dylan said that he broke several vertebrae in his neck. Mystery still surrounds the circumstances of the accident since no ambulance was called to the scene and Dylan was not hospitalized. Dylan's biographers have written that the crash offered Dylan the much-needed chance to escape from the pressures that had built up around him. Dylan confirmed this interpretation of the crash when he stated in his autobiography, "I had been in a motorcycle accident and I'd been hurt, but I recovered. Truth was that I wanted to get out of the rat race. " In the wake of his accident, Dylan withdrew from the public and, apart from a few select appearances, did not tour again for almost eight years.

Once Dylan was well enough to resume creative work, he began editing film footage of his 1966 tour for Eat the Document, a rarely exhibited follow-up to Dont Look Back. A rough-cut was shown to ABC Television and was promptly rejected as incomprehensible to a mainstream audience. In 1967 he began recording music with the Hawks at his home and in the basement of the Hawks' nearby house, called "Big Pink". These songs, initially compiled as demos for other artists to record, provided hit singles for Julie Driscoll ("This Wheel's on Fire"), The Byrds ("You Ain't Goin' Nowhere", "Nothing Was Delivered"), and Manfred Mann ("Mighty Quinn"). Columbia belatedly released selections from them in 1975 as The Basement Tapes. Over the years, more and more of the songs recorded by Dylan and his band in 1967 appeared on various bootleg recordings, culminating in a five-CD bootleg set titled The Genuine Basement Tapes, containing 107 songs and alternate takes. In the coming months, the Hawks recorded the album Music from Big Pink using songs they first worked on in their basement in Woodstock, and renamed themselves The Band, thus beginning a long and successful recording and performing career of their own.

In October and November 1967, Dylan returned to Nashville. Back in the recording studio after a 19-month break, he was accompanied only by Charlie McCoy on bass, Kenny Buttrey on drums, and Pete Drake on steel guitar. The result was John Wesley Harding, a quiet, contemplative record of shorter songs, set in a landscape that drew on both the American West and the Bible. The sparse structure and instrumentation, coupled with lyrics that took the Judeo-Christian tradition seriously, marked a departure not only from Dylan's own work but from the escalating psychedelic fervor of the 1960s musical culture. It included "All Along the Watchtower", with lyrics derived from the Book of Isaiah (21:5–9). The song was later recorded by Jimi Hendrix, whose version Dylan later acknowledged as definitive. Woody Guthrie died on October 3, 1967, and Dylan made his first live appearance in twenty months at a Guthrie memorial concert held at Carnegie Hall on January 20, 1968, where he was backed by The Band.

Dylan's next release, Nashville Skyline (1969), was virtually a mainstream country record featuring instrumental backing by Nashville musicians, a mellow-voiced Dylan, a duet with Johnny Cash, and the hit single "Lay Lady Lay. " Variety magazine wrote, "Dylan is definitely doing something that can be called singing. Somehow he has managed to add an octave to his range. " Dylan and Cash also recorded a series of duets, but only their recording of Dylan's "Girl from the North Country" was used on the album.

In May 1969, Dylan appeared on the first episode of Johnny Cash's new television show, duetting with Cash on "Girl from the North Country", "I Threw It All Away" and "Living the Blues". Dylan next travelled to England to top the bill at the Isle of Wight rock festival on August 31, 1969, after rejecting overtures to appear at the Woodstock Festival far closer to his home.

1970s

In the early 1970s, critics charged that Dylan's output was of varied and unpredictable quality. Rolling Stone magazine writer Greil Marcus notoriously asked "What is this shit?" on first listening to Self Portrait, released in June 1970. In general, Self Portrait, a double LP including few original songs, was poorly received. In October

1970, Dylan released New Morning, which some considered a return to form. In November 1968, Dylan had co-written "I'd Have You Anytime" with George Harrison; Harrison recorded both "I'd Have You Anytime" and Dylan's "If Not for You" for his 1970 solo triple album All Things Must Pass. Dylan's surprise appearance at Harrison's 1971 Concert for Bangladesh attracted much media coverage, reflecting that Dylan's live appearances had become rare.

Between March 16 and 19, 1971, Dylan reserved three days at Blue Rock Studios, a small studio in New York's Greenwich Village. These sessions resulted in one single, "Watching the River Flow", and a new recording of "When I Paint My Masterpiece". On November 4, 1971 Dylan recorded "George Jackson", which he released a week later. For many, the single was a surprising return to protest material, mourning the killing of Black Panther George Jackson in San Quentin Prison that summer. Dylan contributed piano and harmony vocals to Steve Goodman's album, Somebody Else's Troubles, under the pseudonym Robert Milkwood Thomas in September 1972.

In 1972, Dylan signed onto Sam Peckinpah's film Pat Garrett and Billy the Kid, providing songs and backing music for the movie, and playing the role of "Alias", a member of Billy's gang with some historical basis. Despite the film's failure at the box office, the song "Knockin' on Heaven's Door" has proven its durability as one of Dylan's most extensively covered songs.

Return to touring

Dylan began 1973 by signing with a new record label, David Geffen's Asylum Records, when his contract with Columbia Records expired. On his next album, Planet Waves, he used The Band as backing group, while rehearsing for a major tour. The album included two versions of "Forever Young", which became one of his most popular songs. As one critic described it, the song projected "something hymnal and heartfelt that spoke of the father in Dylan", and Dylan himself commented: "I wrote it thinking about one of my boys and not wanting to be too sentimental. " Biographer Howard Sounes noted that Jakob Dylan believed the song was about him.

Columbia Records simultaneously released Dylan, a haphazard collection of studio outtakes (almost exclusively cover songs), which was widely interpreted as a churlish response to Dylan's signing with a rival record label. In January 1974, Dylan returned to live touring after a break of seven years; backed by The Band, he embarked on a high-profile, coast-to-coast North American tour, playing 40 concerts. A live double album of the tour, Before the Flood, was released on Asylum Records. Soon, Columbia Records sent word that they "will spare nothing to bring Dylan back into the fold". Dylan had second thoughts about Asylum, apparently miffed that while there had been millions of unfulfilled ticket requests for the 1974 tour, Geffen had managed to sell only 700,000 copies of Planet Waves. Dylan returned to Columbia Records, which subsequently reissued his two Asylum albums on their imprint.

After the tour, Dylan and his wife became publicly estranged. He filled a small red notebook with songs about relationships and ruptures, and quickly recorded a new album entitled Blood on the Tracks in September 1974. Dylan delayed the album's release, however, and re-recorded half of the songs at Sound 80 Studios in Minneapolis with production assistance from his brother David Zimmerman.

Released in early 1975, Blood on the Tracks received mixed reviews. In the NME, Nick Kent described "the accompaniments [as] often so trashy they sound like mere practice takes. " In Rolling Stone, reviewer Jon Landau wrote that "the record has been made with typical shoddiness. " However, over the years critics have come to see it as one of Dylan's greatest achievements, perhaps the only serious rival to his mid-1960s trilogy of albums. In Salon. com, Bill Wyman wrote: "Blood on the Tracks is his only flawless album and his best produced; the songs, each of them, are constructed in disciplined fashion. It is his kindest album and most dismayed, and seems in hindsight to have achieved a sublime balance between the logorrhea-plagued excesses of his mid-1960s output and the self-consciously simple compositions of his post-accident years. " Novelist Rick Moody called it "the truest, most honest account of a love affair from tip to stern ever put down on magnetic tape. "

That summer Dylan wrote a lengthy ballad championing the cause of boxer Rubin "Hurricane" Carter, who had been imprisoned for a triple murder committed in Paterson, New Jersey, in 1966. After visiting Carter in jail, Dylan wrote "Hurricane", presenting the case for Carter's innocence. Despite its 8:32 minute length, the song was released as a single, peaking at No. 33 on the U. S. Billboard Chart, and performed at every 1975 date of Dylan's next tour, the Rolling Thunder Revue, named after the Shoshone medicine man, shaman, teacher, and activist Rolling Thunder. The tour was a varied evening of entertainment featuring about one hundred performers and supporters drawn from the resurgent Greenwich Village folk scene, including T-Bone Burnett, Ramblin' Jack Elliott, Joni Mitchell, David Mansfield, Roger McGuinn, Mick Ronson, Joan Baez, and violinist Scarlet Rivera, whom Dylan discovered while she was walking down the street, her violin case hanging on her back. Allen Ginsberg accompanied the troupe, staging scenes for the film Dylan was simultaneously shooting. Sam Shepard was initially hired to write the film's screenplay, but ended up accompanying the tour as informal chronicler.

Running through late 1975 and again through early 1976, the tour encompassed the release of the album Desire, with many of Dylan's new songs featuring an almost travelogue-like narrative style, showing the influence of his new collaborator, playwright Jacques Levy. The spring 1976 half of the tour was documented by a TV concert special, Hard Rain, and the LP Hard Rain; no concert album from the better-received and better-known opening half of the tour was released until 2002's Live 1975.

The fall 1975 tour with the Revue also provided the backdrop to Dylan's nearly four-hour film Renaldo and Clara, a sprawling and improvised narrative, mixed with concert footage and reminiscences. Released in 1978, the movie received generally poor, sometimes scathing, reviews and had a very brief theatrical run. Later in that year, Dylan allowed a two-hour edit, dominated by the concert performances, to be more widely released.

In November 1976, Dylan appeared at The Band's "farewell" concert, along with other guests including Joni Mitchell, Muddy Waters, Van Morrison and Neil Young. Martin Scorsese's acclaimed cinematic chronicle of this show, The Last Waltz, was released in 1978 and included about half of Dylan's set. In 1976, Dylan also wrote and duetted on the song "Sign Language" for Eric Clapton's No Reason To Cry.

In 1978, Dylan embarked on a year-long world tour, performing 114 shows in Japan, the Far East, Europe and the US, to a total audience of two million people. For the tour, Dylan assembled an eight piece band, and was also accompanied by three backing singers. Concerts in Tokyo in February and March were recorded and released as the live double album, Bob Dylan At Budokan.

Reviews were mixed. Robert Christgau awarded the album a C+ rating, giving the album a derisory review, while Janet Maslin defended it in Rolling Stone, writing: "These latest live versions of his old songs have the effect of liberating Bob Dylan from the originals. " When Dylan brought the tour to the US in September 1978, he was dismayed the press described the look and sound of the show as a 'Las Vegas Tour'. The 1978 tour grossed more than $20 million, and Dylan acknowledged to the Los Angeles Times that he had some debts to pay off because "I had a couple of bad years. I put a lot of money into the movie, built a big house . . . and it costs a lot to get divorced in California. "

In April and May 1978, Dylan took the same large band and backing vocalists into Rundown Studios, a rehearsal space Dylan had rented in Santa Monica, California, to record an album of new material: Street-Legal. It was described by Michael Gray as, "after Blood On The Tracks, arguably Dylan's best record of the 1970s: a crucial album documenting a crucial period in Dylan's own life". However, it suffered from poor sound recording and mixing (attributed to Dylan's studio practices), muddying the instrumental detail until a remastered CD release in 1999 restored some of the songs' strengths.

Born-again period

In the late 1970s, Dylan became a born-again Christian and released two albums of Christian gospel music. Slow Train Coming (1979) featured the guitar accompaniment of Mark Knopfler (of Dire Straits) and was produced by veteran R&B producer, Jerry Wexler. Wexler recalled that when Dylan had tried to evangelize him during the recording, he replied: "Bob, you're dealing with a sixty-two-year old Jewish atheist. Let's just make an album. " The album won Dylan a Grammy Award as "Best Male Vocalist" for the song "Gotta Serve Somebody". The second evangelical album, Saved (1980), received mixed reviews, and was described by Dylan critic Michael Gray as "the nearest thing to a follow-up album Dylan has ever made, Slow Train Coming II and inferior. " When touring from the fall of 1979 through the spring of 1980, Dylan would not play any of his older, secular works, and he delivered declarations of his faith from the stage, such as:

Years ago they . . . said I was a prophet. I used to say, "No I'm not a prophet" they say "Yes you are, you're a prophet. " I said, "No it's not me. " They used to say "You sure are a prophet. " They used to convince me I was a prophet. Now I come out and say Jesus Christ is the answer. They say, "Bob Dylan's no prophet. " They just can't handle it.

Dylan's embrace of born-again Christianity was unpopular with some of his fans and fellow musicians. Shortly before his murder, John Lennon recorded "Serve Yourself" in response to Dylan's "Gotta Serve Somebody". By 1981, Stephen Holden wrote in the New York Times that "neither age (he's now 40) nor his much-publicized conversion to born-again Christianity has altered his essentially iconoclastic temperament. "

1980s

In the fall of 1980 Dylan briefly resumed touring for a series of concerts billed as "A Musical Retrospective", where he restored several of his popular 1960s songs to the repertoire. Shot of Love, recorded the next spring, featured Dylan's first secular compositions in more than two years, mixed with explicitly Christian songs; the song "Every Grain of Sand" reminded some critics of William Blake's verses.

In the 1980s the reception of Dylan's recorded work varied, from the well-regarded Infidels in 1983 to the panned Down in the Groove in 1988. Critics such as Michael Gray condemned Dylan's 1980s albums both for showing an extraordinary carelessness in the studio and for failing to release his best songs. For example, the Infidels recording sessions, which again employed Mark Knopfler on lead guitar and also as the album's producer, resulted in several notable songs which Dylan left off the album. Most well regarded of these were "Blind Willie McTell", a tribute to the dead blues musician and an evocation of African American history, "Foot of Pride" and "Lord Protect My Child". These three songs were later released on The Bootleg Series Volumes 1–3 (Rare & Unreleased) 1961–1991.

Between July 1984 and March 1985, Dylan recorded his next studio album, Empire Burlesque. Arthur Baker, who had remixed hits for Bruce Springsteen and Cyndi Lauper, was asked to engineer and mix the album. Baker has said he felt he was hired to make Dylan's album sound "a little bit more contemporary".

Dylan sang on USA for Africa's famine relief fundraising single "We Are the World". On July 13, 1985, he appeared at the climax at the Live Aid concert at JFK Stadium, Philadelphia. Backed by Keith Richards and Ronnie Wood, Dylan performed a ragged version of "Hollis Brown", his ballad of rural poverty, and then said to the worldwide audience exceeding one billion people: "I hope that some of the money . . . maybe they can just take a little bit of it, maybe . . . one or two million, maybe . . . and use it to pay the mortgages on some of the farms and, the farmers here, owe to the banks. " His remarks were widely criticized as inappropriate, but they did inspire Willie Nelson to organize a series of events, Farm Aid, to benefit debt-ridden American farmers.

In April 1986, Dylan made a brief foray into the world of rap music when he added vocals to the opening verse of "Street Rock", a song featured on Kurtis Blow's album Kingdom Blow. Dylan's next studio album, Knocked Out Loaded, was released in July 1986 and contained three cover songs (by Little Junior Parker, Kris Kristofferson and the traditional gospel hymn "Precious Memories"), plus three collaborations with other writers (Tom Petty, Sam Shepard and Carole Bayer Sager), and two solo compositions by Dylan. One reviewer commented that "the record follows too many detours to be consistently compelling, and some of those detours wind down roads that are indisputably dead ends. By 1986, such uneven records weren't entirely unexpected by Dylan, but that didn't make them any less frustrating. " It was the first Dylan album since Freewheelin' (1963) to fail to make the Top 50. Since then, some critics have called the 11-minute epic that Dylan co-wrote with Sam Shepard, 'Brownsville Girl', a work of genius.

In 1986 and 1987, Dylan toured extensively with Tom Petty and the Heartbreakers, sharing vocals with Petty on several songs each night. Dylan also toured with The Grateful Dead in 1987, resulting in a live album Dylan & The Dead. This album received some very negative reviews: Allmusic said, "Quite possibly the worst album by either Bob Dylan or the Grateful Dead. " After performing with these musical permutations, Dylan initiated what came to be called The Never Ending Tour on June 7, 1988, performing with a tight back-up band featuring guitarist G. E. Smith. Dylan would continue to tour with a small, constantly evolving band for the next 20 years.

In 1987, Dylan starred in Richard Marquand's movie Hearts of Fire, in which he played Billy Parker, a washed-up-rock-star-turned-chicken farmer whose teenage lover (Fiona) leaves him for a jaded

English synth-pop sensation (played by Rupert Everett). Dylan also contributed two original songs to the soundtrack—"Night After Night", and "I Had a Dream About You, Baby", as well as a cover of John Hiatt's "The Usual". The film was a critical and commercial flop. Dylan was inducted into the Rock and Roll Hall of Fame in January 1988, with Bruce Springsteen's introductory speech declaring, "Bob freed your mind the way Elvis freed your body. He showed us that just because music was innately physical did not mean that it was anti-intellectual.

When Dylan released the album Down in the Groove in May 1988, it was even more unsuccessful in its sales than his previous studio album. Michael Gray wrote: "The very title undercuts any idea that inspired work may lie within. Here was a further devaluing of the notion of a new Bob Dylan album as something significant. " The critical and commercial disappointment of that album was swiftly followed by the success of the Traveling Wilburys. Dylan co-founded the band with George Harrison, Jeff Lynne, Roy Orbison, and Tom Petty, and in the fall of 1988 their multi-platinum Traveling Wilburys Vol. 1 reached number three on the US album chart, featuring songs that were described as Dylan's most accessible compositions in years. Despite Orbison's death in December 1988, the remaining four recorded a second album in May 1990, which they released with the unexpected title Traveling Wilburys Vol. 3.

Dylan finished the decade on a critical high note with Oh Mercy produced by Daniel Lanois. Dylan critic Michael Gray wrote that the album was: "Attentively written, vocally distinctive, musically warm, and uncompromisingly professional, this cohesive whole is the nearest thing to a great Bob Dylan album in the 1980s. " The track "Most of the Time", a lost love composition, was later prominently featured in the film High Fidelity, while "What Was It You Wanted?" has been interpreted both as a catechism and a wry comment on the expectations of critics and fans. The religious imagery of "Ring Them Bells" struck some critics as a re-affirmation of faith.

1990s

Dylan's 1990s began with Under the Red Sky (1990), an about-face from the serious Oh Mercy. The album contained several apparently simple songs, including "Under the Red Sky" and "Wiggle Wiggle". The album was dedicated to "Gabby Goo Goo"; this was later explained as a nickname for the daughter of Dylan and Carolyn Dennis, Desiree Gabrielle Dennis-Dylan, who was four at that time. Sidemen on the album included George Harrison, Slash from Guns N' Roses, David Crosby, Bruce Hornsby, Stevie Ray Vaughan, and Elton John. Despite the stellar line-up, the record received bad reviews and sold poorly.

In 1991, Dylan was honored by the recording industry with a Grammy Lifetime Achievement Award from American actor Jack Nicholson. The event coincided with the start of the Gulf War against Saddam Hussein, and Dylan performed his song "Masters of War". Dylan then made a short speech that startled some of the audience.

The next few years saw Dylan returning to his roots with two albums covering old folk and blues numbers: Good as I Been to You (1992) and World Gone Wrong (1993), featuring interpretations and acoustic guitar work. Many critics and fans commented on the quiet beauty of the song "Lone Pilgrim", penned by a 19th century teacher and sung by Dylan with a haunting reverence. In November 1994 Dylan recorded two live shows for MTV Unplugged. He claimed his wish to perform a set of traditional songs for the show was overruled by Sony executives who insisted on a greatest hits package. The album produced from it, MTV Unplugged, included "John Brown", an unreleased 1963 song detailing the ravages of both war and jingoism.

With a collection of songs reportedly written while snowed-in on his Minnesota ranch, Dylan booked recording time with Daniel Lanois at Miami's Criteria Studios in January 1997. The subsequent recording sessions were, by some accounts, fraught with musical tension. Late that spring, before the album's release, Dylan was hospitalized with a life-threatening heart infection, pericarditis, brought on by histoplasmosis. His scheduled European tour was cancelled, but Dylan made a speedy recovery and left the hospital saying, "I really thought I'd be seeing Elvis soon. " He was back on the road by midsummer, and in early fall performed before Pope John Paul II at the World Eucharistic Conference in Bologna, Italy. The Pope treated the audience of 200,000 people to a homily based on Dylan's lyric "Blowin' in the Wind".

September saw the release of the new Lanois-produced album, Time Out of Mind. With its bitter assessment of love and morbid ruminations, Dylan's first collection of original songs in seven years was highly acclaimed. One critic wrote: "the songs themselves are uniformly powerful, adding up to Dylan's best overall collection in years. " This collection of complex songs won him his first solo "Album of the Year" Grammy Award.

In December 1997, U. S. President Bill Clinton presented Dylan with a Kennedy Center Honor in the East Room of the White House, paying this tribute: "He probably had more impact on people of my generation than any other creative artist. His voice and lyrics haven't always been easy on the ear, but throughout his career Bob Dylan has never aimed to please. He's disturbed the peace and discomforted the powerful. "

2000s

Dylan commenced the new millennium by winning his first Oscar; his song "Things Have Changed", penned for the film Wonder Boys, won an Academy Award in March 2001. The Oscar (by some reports a facsimile) tours with him, presiding over shows perched atop an amplifier.

"Love and Theft" was released on September 11, 2001. Recorded with his touring band, Dylan produced the album himself under the pseudonym Jack Frost. The album was critically well received and earned nominations for several Grammy awards. Critics noted that Dylan was widening his musical palette to include rockabilly, Western swing, jazz, and even lounge ballads. "Love and Theft" generated controversy when The Wall Street Journal pointed out similarities between the album's lyrics and Japanese author Junichi Saga's book Confessions of a Yakuza.

In 2003, Dylan revisited the evangelical songs from his "born again" period and participated in the CD project Gotta Serve Somebody: The Gospel Songs of Bob Dylan. That year also saw the release of the film Masked & Anonymous, which Dylan co-wrote with director Larry Charles under the alias Sergei Petrov. Dylan played the central character in the film, Jack Fate, alongside a cast which included Jeff Bridges, Penélope Cruz and John Goodman. The film polarised critics: many dismissed it as an "incoherent mess"; a few treated it as a serious work of art.

In October 2004, Dylan published the first part of his autobiography, Chronicles: Volume One. The book confounded expectations. Dylan devoted three chapters to his first year in New York City in 1961–1962, virtually ignoring the mid-1960s when his fame was at its height. He also devoted chapters to the albums New Morning (1970) and Oh Mercy (1989). The book reached number two on The New York Times' Hardcover Non-Fiction best seller list in December 2004 and was nominated for a National Book Award.

No Direction Home, Martin Scorsese's acclaimed film biography of Dylan, was first broadcast on September 26–27, 2005, on BBC Two in the UK and PBS in the US. The documentary focuses on the period from Dylan's arrival in New York in 1961 to his motorcycle crash in 1966, featuring interviews with Suze Rotolo, Liam Clancy, Joan Baez, Allen Ginsberg, Pete Seeger, Mavis Staples, and Dylan himself. The film received a Peabody Award in April 2006 and a Columbia-duPont Award in January 2007. The accompanying soundtrack featured unreleased songs from Dylan's early career.

Dylan earned yet another distinction in a 2007 study of US legal opinions and briefs that found his lyrics were quoted by judges and lawyers more than those of any other songwriter, 186 times versus 74 by The Beatles, who were second. Among those quoting Dylan were US Supreme Court Chief Justice John Roberts and Justice Antonin Scalia, both conservatives. The most widely cited lines included "you don't need a weatherman to know which way the wind blows" from "Subterranean Homesick Blues" and "when you ain't got nothing, you got nothing to lose" from "Like a Rolling Stone".

Modern Times (2006–08)

May 3, 2006, was the premiere of Dylan's radio presenting career, hosting a weekly radio program, Theme Time Radio Hour, for XM Satellite Radio, with song selections revolving around a chosen theme. Dylan played classic and obscure records from the 1930s to the present day, including contemporary artists as diverse as Blur, Prince, L. L. Cool J and The Streets. The show was praised by fans and critics as "great radio," as Dylan told stories and made eclectic references with his sardonic humor, while achieving a thematic beauty with his musical choices. In April 2009, Dylan broadcast the 100th show in his radio series; the theme was "Goodbye" and the final record played was Woody Guthrie's "So Long, It's Been Good To Know Yuh". This has led to speculation that Dylan's radio series may have ended.

On August 29, 2006, Dylan released his Modern Times album. Despite some coarsening of Dylan's voice (a critic for The Guardian characterised his singing on the album as "a catarrhal death rattle") most reviewers praised the album, and many described it as the final installment of a successful trilogy, embracing Time Out of Mind and "Love and Theft". Modern Times entered the U. S. charts at number one, making it Dylan's first album to reach that position since 1976's Desire. The New York Times published an article exploring similarities between some of Dylan's lyrics in Modern Times and the work of the Civil War poet Henry Timrod.

Nominated for three Grammy Awards, Modern Times won Best Contemporary Folk/Americana Album and Bob Dylan also won Best Solo Rock Vocal Performance for "Someday Baby". Modern Times was named Album of the Year, 2006, by Rolling Stone magazine, and by Uncut in the UK. On the same day that Modern Times was released the iTunes Music Store released Bob Dylan: The Collection, a digital box set containing all of his albums (773 tracks in total), along with 42 rare and unreleased tracks.

In August 2007, the award-winning film biography of Dylan I'm Not There, written and directed by Todd Haynes, was released—bearing the tagline "inspired by the music and many lives of Bob Dylan". The movie uses six distinct characters to represent different aspects of Dylan's life, played by Christian Bale, Cate Blanchett, Marcus Carl Franklin, Richard Gere, Heath Ledger and Ben Whishaw. Dylan's previously unreleased 1967 recording from which the film takes its name was released for the first time on the film's original soundtrack; all other tracks are covers of Dylan songs, specially recorded for the movie by a diverse range of artists, including Eddie Vedder, Mason Jennings, Stephen Malkmus, Jeff Tweedy, Karen O, Willie Nelson, Cat Power, Richie Havens, and Tom Verlaine.

On October 1, 2007, Columbia Records released the triple CD retrospective album Dylan, anthologising his entire career under the Dylan 07 logo. As part of this campaign, Mark Ronson produced a re-mix of Dylan's 1966 tune "Most Likely You Go Your Way (And I'll Go Mine)", which was released as a maxi-single. This was the first time Dylan had sanctioned a re-mix of one of his classic recordings.

The sophistication of the Dylan 07 marketing campaign was a reminder that Dylan's commercial profile had risen considerably since the 1990s. This first became evidenced in 2004, when Dylan appeared in a TV advertisement for Victoria's Secret lingerie. Three years later, in October 2007, he participated in a multi-media campaign for the 2008 Cadillac Escalade. Then, in 2009, he gave the highest profile endorsement of his career, appearing with rapper will. i. am in a Pepsi ad that debuted during the telecast of Super Bowl XLIII. The ad, broadcast to a record audience of 98 million viewers, opened with Dylan singing the first verse of "Forever Young" followed by will. i. am doing a hip hop version of the song's third and final verse.

In October 2008, Columbia released Volume 8 of Dylan's Bootleg Series, Tell Tale Signs: Rare And Unreleased 1989–2006 as both a two-CD set and a three-CD version with a 150-page hardcover book. The set contains live performances and outtakes from selected studio albums from Oh Mercy to Modern Times, as well as soundtrack contributions and collaborations with David Bromberg and Ralph Stanley. The pricing of the album—the two-CD set went on sale for $18. 99 and the three-CD version for $129. 99—led to complaints about "rip-off packaging" from some fans and commentators. The release was widely acclaimed by critics. The abundance of alternative takes and unreleased material suggested to Uncut's reviewer: "Tell Tale Signs is awash with evidence of (Dylan's) staggering mercuriality, his evident determination even in the studio to repeat himself as little as possible. "

Together Through Life, Christmas in the Heart (2009)

Bob Dylan released his album Together Through Life on April 28, 2009. In a conversation with music journalist Bill Flanagan, published on Dylan's website, Dylan explained that the genesis of the record was when French film director Olivier Dahan asked him to supply a song for his new road movie, My Own Love Song; initially only intending to record a single track, "Life Is Hard," "the record sort of took its own direction". Nine of the ten songs on the album are credited as co-written by Bob Dylan and Robert Hunter.

The album received largely favorable reviews, although several critics described it as a minor addition to Dylan's canon of work. Andy Gill wrote in The Independent that the record "features Dylan in fairly relaxed, spontaneous mood, content to grab such grooves and sentiments as flit momentarily across his radar. So while it may not contain too many landmark tracks, it's one of the most naturally enjoyable albums you'll hear all year. "

In its first week of release, the album reached number one in the Billboard 200 chart in the U. S. , making Bob Dylan (67 years of age) the oldest artist to ever debut at number one on that chart. It also reached number one on the UK album chart, 39 years after Dylan's previous UK album chart topper New Morning. This meant that Dylan currently holds the record for the longest gap between solo number one albums in the UK chart.

On October 13, 2009, Dylan released a Christmas album, Christmas in the Heart, comprising such Christmas standards as "Little Drummer Boy", "Winter Wonderland" and "Here Comes Santa Claus". Dylan's royalties from the sale of this album will benefit the charities Feeding America in the USA, Crisis in the UK, and the World Food Programme.

The album received generally favorable reviews. The New Yorker commented that Dylan had welded a pre-rock musical sound to "some of his croakiest vocals in a while", and speculated that Dylan's intentions might be ironic: "Dylan has a long and highly publicized history with Christianity; to claim there's not a wink in the childish optimism of 'Here Comes Santa Claus' or 'Winter Wonderland' is to ignore a half-century of biting satire. " In USA Today, Edna Gundersen pointed out that Dylan was "revisiting yuletide styles popularized by Nat King Cole, Mel Tormé, and the Ray Conniff Singers. " Gundersen concluded that Dylan "couldn't sound more sentimental or sincere".

In an interview published in The Big Issue, journalist Bill Flanagan asked Dylan why he had performed the songs in a straightforward style, and Dylan responded: "There wasn't any other way to play it. These songs are part of my life, just like folk songs. You have to play them straight too. "

2010s

On October 18, 2010, Dylan released Volume 9 of his Bootleg Series, The Witmark Demos. This comprised 47 demo recordings of songs taped between 1962 and 1964 for Dylan's earliest music publishers: Leeds Music in 1962, and Witmark Music from 1962 to 1964. One reviewer described the set as "a kind of alternate early history of Dylan's songwriting process, 'writing five new songs before breakfast,' as he once famously quipped". The critical aggregator website Metacritic awarded the album a Metascore of 86, indicating "universal acclaim". In the same week, Sony Legacy released Bob Dylan: The Original Mono Recordings, a box set which for the first time presented Dylan's eight earliest albums, from Bob Dylan (1962) to John Wesley Harding (1967), in their original mono mix in the CD format. The CDs were housed in miniature facsimiles of the original album covers, replete with original liner notes. The set was accompanied by a booklet which featured an essay by music critic Greil Marcus.

On April 12, 2011, Legacy Recordings released Bob Dylan in Concert – Brandeis University 1963 . The recording was taped at Brandeis University on May 10, 1963, two weeks prior to the release of The Freewheelin' Bob Dylan. The tape had been discovered in the archive of music writer Ralph J. Gleason, and had previously been available as a limited edition supplement to The Bootleg Series Vol. 9. The recording carries liner notes by Dylan scholar Michael Gray, who writes: "(The) Dylan performance it captured, from way back when Kennedy was President and the Beatles hadn't yet reached America, wasn't even on fans' radar. . . . It reveals him not at any Big Moment but giving a performance like his folk club sets of the period. . . This is the last live performance we have of Bob Dylan before he becomes a star. "

The extent to which his work was studied at an academic level was demonstrated on Dylan's 70th birthday on May 24, 2011, when three universities organized symposia on his work. The University of Mainz, the University of Vienna, and the University of Bristol invited literary critics and cultural historians from Europe and the US to give papers on aspects of Dylan's work. Other events, including tribute bands, intellectual debates and simple singalongs, took place around the world, as reported in The Guardian: "From Moscow to Madrid, Norway to Northampton and Malaysia to his home state of Minnesota, self-confessed 'Bobcats' will gather today to celebrate the 70th birthday of a giant of popular music. "

On October 4, 2011, Dylan's label, Egyptian Records, released an album of previously unheard Hank Williams songs, The Lost Notebooks of Hank Williams. Dylan had helped to curate this project, in which songs unfinished when Williams died in 1953 were completed and recorded by a variety of artists, including Dylan himself, his son Jakob Dylan, Levon Helm, Norah Jones, Jack White, and others.

On December 10, 2011, to mark International Human Rights Day, Amnesty International announced they would release a

4-CD set, Chimes of Freedom: Songs of Bob Dylan Honoring 50 Years of Amnesty International, to mark the 50th anniversary of the international human rights organization in January 2012. The album contains 76 newly recorded cover versions of songs by Dylan, contributed by more than 80 artists. Included on the album are "Don't Think Twice, It's All Right" performed by both Kesha and the Kronos Quartet, Pete Townshend performing "Corrina Corrina", Sinéad O'Connor performing "Property of Jesus", and Lucinda Williams performing "Tryin' to Get to Heaven". The 4-CD set of Chimes of Freedom entered the Nielsen SoundScan chart at No. 11, and at No. 39, as it was also released in a 2-CD version by Starbucks.

On May 29, 2012, President Obama awarded Dylan a Presidential Medal of Freedom in the White House. At the ceremony, Obama praised Dylan's voice for its "unique gravelly power that redefined not just what music sounded like but the message it carried and how it made people feel".

On September 11, 2012, Dylan released his 35th studio album, Tempest. The album features a tribute to John Lennon, "Roll On John", and the title track is a 14 minute song about the sinking of the Titanic. In a preview of the album, Neil McCormick reported in The Daily Telegraph that "popular music's greatest troubadour is still as brilliant and bewildering as ever". McCormick added he "was blown away with the mad energy of the album. At 71-years-old Dylan is still striking out into strange new places rather than revisiting his past. "

Reviewing Tempest for Rolling Stone, Will Hermes gave the album five out of five stars, writing: "Lyrically, Dylan is at the top of his game, joking around, dropping wordplay and allegories that evade pat readings and quoting other folks' words like a freestyle rapper on fire. " Hermes called Tempest "one of [Dylan's] weirdest albums ever", and opined, "It may also be the single darkest record in Dylan's catalog. " In The Guardian, Alexis Petridis deprecated attaching such hyperbole to the album, noting that "the music is the same stew of beautifully played blues, rockabilly, folk and country as every Dylan album for the last 12 years: styles you might call pre-rock or, perhaps more pertinently, pre-him. " Petridis argued that: "Bob Dylan, it seems, is determined to see out his days playing pop music from the era before Bob Dylan changed pop music for good, as if he'd rather forget that he ever did so. " The critical aggregator website Metacritic awarded the album a score of 83 out of 100, indicating "universal acclaim".

Never Ending Tour

Never Ending Tour

The Never Ending Tour commenced on June 7, 1988, and Dylan has played roughly 100 dates a year for the entirety of the 1990s and the 2000s (decade)—a heavier schedule than most performers who started out in the 1960s. By the end of 2010, Dylan and his band had played more than 2,300 shows, anchored by long-time bassist Tony Garnier, multi-instrumentalist Donnie Herron and guitarist Charlie Sexton. To the dismay of some of his audience, Dylan's performances remain unpredictable as he alters his arrangements and changes his vocal approach night after night. Critical opinion about Dylan's shows remains divided. Critics such as Richard Williams and Andy Gill have argued that Dylan has found a successful way to present his rich legacy of material. Others have criticised his onstage vocal style for mangling and spitting out "the greatest lyrics ever written so that they are effectively unrecognisable", and a perceived indifference towards his audience.

Dylan's performances in China in April 2011 generated controversy. Some criticised him for not making any explicit comment on the political situation in China, and for, allegedly, allowing the Chinese authorities to censor his set-list. Others defended Dylan's performances, arguing that such criticism represented a misunderstanding of Dylan's art, and that no evidence for the censorship of Dylan's set-list existed. Dylan responded to these allegations of censorship by posting a statement on his website: "As far as censorship goes, the Chinese government had asked for the names of the songs that I would be playing. There's no logical answer to that, so we sent them the set lists from the previous 3 months. If there were any songs, verses or lines censored, nobody ever told me about it and we played all the songs that we intended to play. "

Dylan's 2012 tour commenced in Rio de Janeiro on April 15, and included performances in Brazil, Argentina, Chile, Costa Rica, and Mexico. In the summer, Dylan visited Europe, returning to Kent, England, on June 30, to perform at the Hop Farm Festival. Dylan surprised fans by accompanying himself on grand piano for half the numbers of his 16 song set. He appeared as a headliner at the 46th Montreux Jazz Festival in Switzerland on July 8, 2012.

Dylan began his fall 2012 tour of North America in Lloydminster, Alberta, on August 10. The tour will end in Brooklyn, New York, on November 21.

Artist

Over a decade after Random House had published Drawn Blank (1994), a book of Dylan's drawings, an exhibit of his art, The Drawn Blank Series, opened in October 2007 at the Kunstsammlungen in Chemnitz, Germany. This first public exhibition of Dylan's paintings showcased more than 200 watercolors and gouaches made earlier in 2007 from the original drawings. The exhibition coincided with the publication of the book Bob Dylan: The Drawn Blank Series, which includes 170 reproductions from the series. From September 2010 until April 2011, the National Gallery of Denmark exhibited 40 large-scale acrylic paintings by Dylan, The Brazil Series.

In July 2011, a leading contemporary art gallery, Gagosian Gallery, announced their representation of Dylan's paintings. An exhibition of Dylan's art, The Asia Series, opened at the Gagosian Madison Avenue Gallery on September 20, displaying Dylan's paintings of scenes in China and the Far East. The New York Times reported that "some fans and Dylanologists have raised questions about whether some of these paintings are based on the singer's own experiences and observations, or on photographs that are widely available and were not taken by Mr. Dylan. " The Times pointed to close resemblances between Dylan's paintings and six historic photos of Japan and China which had been posted on the Flickr website. Dylan's paintings also appeared to be based on photographs taken by Dmitri Kessel, Henri Cartier-Bresson, and Jacob Aue Sobol. The Magnum photo agency confirmed that Dylan had licensed the reproduction rights of these photographs.

Discography

Bob Dylan discography
The discography lists 35 studio albums (below), 58 singles, 13 live albums, 9 albums comprising The Bootleg Series, and 14 compilation albums. It also includes three home videos, a bibliography, and a filmography.

Awards

List of awards received by Bob Dylan

Dylan has won many awards throughout his career including 11 Grammy Awards, one Academy Award and one Golden Globe Award; He has been inducted into the Rock and Roll Hall of Fame, Nashville Songwriters Hall of Fame, and Songwriters Hall of Fame. In May 2012, Dylan was one out of thirteen honorees to receive the Presidential Medal of Freedom.

Personal life

Family

Dylan married Sara Lownds on November 22, 1965. Their first child, Jesse Byron Dylan, was born on January 6, 1966, and they had three more children: Anna Lea (born July 11, 1967), Samuel Isaac Abraham (born July 30, 1968), and Jakob Luke (born December 9, 1969). Dylan also adopted Sara's daughter from a prior marriage, Maria Lownds (later Dylan, born October 21, 1961). Bob and Sara Dylan were divorced on June 29, 1977. Maria married musician Peter Himmelman in 1988. In the 1990s, Dylan's son Jakob became well known as the lead singer of the band The Wallflowers. Jesse Dylan is a film director and a successful businessman.

In June 1986, Dylan married his longtime backup singer Carolyn Dennis (often professionally known as Carol Dennis). Their daughter, Desiree Gabrielle Dennis-Dylan, was born on January 31, 1986. The couple divorced in October 1992. Their marriage and child remained a closely guarded secret until the publication of Howard Sounes' Dylan biography, Down the Highway: The Life Of Bob Dylan in 2001. Dylan now lives in Malibu, California, when not on the road. In total, Bob Dylan has six children (five biological and one adopted) and eleven grandchildren as of 2011.

Religious beliefs

Growing up in Hibbing, Minnesota, Dylan and his family were part of the area's small but close-knit Jewish community, and in May 1954 Dylan had his Bar Mitzvah. Around the time of his 30th birthday, in 1971, Dylan visited Israel, and also met Rabbi Meir Kahane, founder of the New York-based Jewish Defense League. Time magazine quoted Dylan saying about Kahane, "He's a really sincere guy. He's really put it all together. " Subsequently, Dylan downplayed the extent of his contact with Kahane.

For a period during the late 1970s and early 1980s, Dylan was a public convert to Christianity. From January to April 1979, he participated in Bible study classes at the Vineyard School of Discipleship in Reseda, California. Pastor Kenn Gulliksen has recalled: "Larry Myers and Paul Emond went over to Bob's house and ministered to him. He responded by saying, 'Yes he did in fact want Christ in his life. ' And he prayed that day and received the Lord. "

By 1984, Dylan was distancing himself from the "born-again" label. He told Kurt Loder of Rolling Stone magazine: "I've never said I'm born again. That's just a media term. I don't think I've been an agnostic. I've always thought there's a superior power, that this is not the real world and that there's a world to come. " In response to Loder's asking whether he belonged to any Church or synagogue, Dylan laughingly replied, "Not really. Uh, the Church of the Poison Mind. " In 1997 he told David Gates of Newsweek:

" Here's the thing with me and the religious thing. This is the flat-out truth: I find the religiosity and philosophy in the music. I don't find it anywhere else. Songs like "Let Me Rest on a Peaceful Mountain" or "I Saw the Light"—that's my religion. I don't adhere to rabbis, preachers, evangelists, all of that. I've learned more from the songs than I've learned from any of this kind of entity. The songs are my lexicon. I believe the songs. "

In an interview published in The New York Times on September 28, 1997, journalist Jon Pareles reported that "Dylan says he now subscribes to no organized religion. "

Dylan has been a supporter of the Chabad Lubavitch movement in the last 20 years, and has privately participated in Jewish religious events, including the bar mitzvahs of his sons and attending Hadar Hatorah, a Chabad Lubavitch yeshiva. In September 1989 and September 1991, Dylan appeared on the Chabad telethon. Dylan reportedly visits Chabad synagogues; on September 22, 2007 (Yom Kippur), he attended Congregation Beth Tefillah, in Atlanta, Georgia, where he was called to the Torah for the sixth aliyah.

Dylan has continued to perform songs from his gospel albums in concert, occasionally covering traditional religious songs. He has also made passing references to his religious faith—such as in a 2004 interview with 60 Minutes, when he told Ed Bradley that "the only person you have to think twice about lying to is either yourself or to God. " He also explained his constant touring schedule as part of a bargain he made a long time ago with the "chief commander—in this earth and in the world we can't see. "

In a 2009 interview with Bill Flanagan promoting his Christmas LP, Christmas in the Heart, Flanagan commented on the "heroic performance" Dylan gave of "O Little Town of Bethlehem" and that Dylan "delivered the song like a true believer". Dylan replied: "Well, I am a true believer. "

Legacy

Bob Dylan is one of the most influential figures of the 20th century, musically and culturally. Dylan was included in the Time 100: The Most Important People of the Century where he was called "master poet, caustic social critic and intrepid, guiding spirit of the counterculture generation". President Barack Obama said of Dylan in 2012, "There is not a bigger giant in the history of American music. " Biographer Howard Sounes placed him among the most exalted company when he said, "There are giant figures in art who are sublimely good—Mozart, Picasso, Frank Lloyd Wright, Shakespeare, Dickens. Dylan ranks alongside these artists. " Rolling Stone magazine ranked Dylan at Number Two in their 2011 list of "100 Greatest Artists" of all time. In their 2008 assessment of the "100 Greatest Singers", Rolling Stone ranked Dylan at #7.

Initially modeling his writing style on the songs of Woody Guthrie, and lessons learned from the blues of Robert Johnson, Dylan added increasingly sophisticated lyrical techniques to the folk music of the early 1960s, infusing it "with the intellectualism of classic literature and poetry". Paul Simon suggested that Dylan's early compositions virtually took over the folk genre: "[Dylan's] early songs were very rich . . . with strong melodies. 'Blowin' in the Wind' has a really strong melody. He so enlarged himself through the folk background that he incorporated it for a while. He defined the genre for a while. "

When Dylan made his move from acoustic music to a rock backing, the mix became more complex. For many critics, Dylan's greatest achievement was the cultural synthesis exemplified by his mid-1960s trilogy of albums—Bringing It All Back Home, Highway 61 Revisited and Blonde on Blonde. In Mike Marqusee's words: "Between late 1964 and the summer of 1966, Dylan created a body of work that remains unique. Drawing on folk, blues, country,

R&B, rock'n'roll, gospel, British beat, symbolist, modernist and Beat poetry, surrealism and Dada, advertising jargon and social commentary, Fellini and Mad magazine, he forged a coherent and original artistic voice and vision. The beauty of these albums retains the power to shock and console. "

One legacy of Dylan's verbal sophistication was the increasing attention paid by literary critics to his lyrics. Professor Christopher Ricks published a 500-page analysis of Dylan's work, placing him in the context of Eliot, Keats and Tennyson, and claiming that Dylan was a poet worthy of the same close analysis. Former British poet laureate, Sir Andrew Motion, argued that Dylan's lyrics should be studied in schools. Since 1996, academics have lobbied the Swedish Academy to award Dylan the Nobel Prize in Literature.

Dylan's voice was, in some ways, as startling as his lyrics. New York Times critic Robert Shelton described Dylan's early vocal style as "a rusty voice suggesting Guthrie's old performances, etched in gravel like Dave Van Ronk's. " David Bowie, in his tribute, "Song for Bob Dylan", described Dylan's singing as "a voice like sand and glue". Dylan's voice continued to develop as he began to work with rock'n'roll backing bands; critic Michael Gray described the sound of Dylan's vocal on his hit single, "Like a Rolling Stone", as "at once young and jeeringly cynical". As Dylan's voice aged during the 1980s, for some critics, it became more expressive. Christophe Lebold writes in the journal Oral Tradition, "Dylan's more recent broken voice enables him to present a world view at the sonic surface of the songs—this voice carries us across the landscape of a broken, fallen world. The anatomy of a broken world in "Everything is Broken" (on the album Oh Mercy) is but an example of how the thematic concern with all things broken is grounded in a concrete sonic reality. "

Dylan's influence has been felt in several musical genres. As Edna Gundersen stated in USA Today: "Dylan's musical DNA has informed nearly every simple twist of pop since 1962. " Many musicians have testified to Dylan's influence, such as Joe Strummer, who praised Dylan as having "laid down the template for lyric, tune, seriousness, spirituality, depth of rock music. " Other major musicians to have acknowledged Dylan's importance include John Lennon, Paul McCartney, Pete Townshend, Neil Young, Bruce Springsteen, David Bowie, Bryan Ferry, Nick Cave, Patti Smith, Syd Barrett, Cat Stevens,Joni Mitchell, and Tom Waits. More directly, both The Byrds and The Band, two 1960s contemporary groups with some measure of influence on popular music themselves, largely owed their initial success to Dylan: the Byrds with their hit of "Mr. Tambourine Man" and subsequent album; and The Band for their association with him on tour in 1966, on retreat in Woodstock, and on their debut album featuring three previously unreleased Dylan songs.

Some critics have dissented from the view of Dylan as a visionary figure in popular music. In his book Awopbopaloobop Alopbamboom, Nik Cohn objected: "I can't take the vision of Dylan as seer, as teenage messiah, as everything else he's been worshipped as. The way I see him, he's a minor talent with a major gift for self-hype. " Similarly, Australian critic Jack Marx credited Dylan with changing the persona of the rock star: "What cannot be disputed is that Dylan invented the arrogant, faux-cerebral posturing that has been the dominant style in rock since, with everyone from Mick Jagger to Eminem educating themselves from the Dylan handbook. " Joni Mitchell described Dylan as a "plagiarist" and his voice as "fake" in a 2010 interview in the Los Angeles Times, in response to a suggestion that she and Dylan were similar since they had both changed their birthnames. Mitchell's comment led to discussions of Dylan's use of other people's material, both supporting and criticizing Dylan.

If Bob Dylan's legacy in the 1960s was seen as bringing intellectual ambition to popular music, now that he has passed the age of 70, he has been described as a figure who has greatly expanded the folk culture from which he initially emerged. As J. Hoberman wrote in The Village Voice, "Elvis might never have been born, but someone else would surely have brought the world rock 'n' roll. No such logic accounts for Bob Dylan. No iron law of history demanded that a would-be Elvis from Hibbing, Minnesota, would swerve through the Greenwich Village folk revival to become the world's first and greatest rock 'n' roll beatnik bard and then—having achieved fame and adoration beyond reckoning—vanish into a folk tradition of his own making. "

Notes

According to Dylan biographer Robert Shelton, the singer first confided his change of name to his high school girlfriend Echo Helstrom in 1958, informing her he had found a "great name, Bob Dillon". Shelton surmises the name Dillon had two sources: Marshal Matt Dillon was the hero of the popular TV western Gunsmoke;

Dillon was also the name of one of Hibbing's principal families. When writing his biography in the mid 1960s, Dylan told Shelton: "Straighten out in your book that I did not take my name from Dylan Thomas. Dylan Thomas's poetry is for people that aren't really satisfied in their bed, for people who dig masculine romance. " At the University of Minnesota, the singer told a few friends that Dillon was his mother's maiden name, which was untrue. The singer later told reporters that he had an uncle named Dillon. Shelton adds that only when he reached New York in 1961 did the singer begin to spell his name 'Dylan', by which time he was acquainted with the life and work of Dylan Thomas. Shelton, No Direction Home, 2011, pp. 44–45.

Boots Randolph

Boots Randolph

Boots Randolph

Randolph performing live March 2000.
Background information
Birth name Homer Louis Randolph III
Also known as "Boots"
Born June 3, 1927
Paducah, Kentucky, United States
Died July 3, 2007 (aged 80)
Nashville, Tennessee, United States
Occupations Saxophonist
Instruments saxophone
Labels RCA, Capitol, Monument
Associated acts Elvis Presley, Chet Atkins, many others
Website Official website

Homer Louis "Boots" Randolph III (June 3, 1927 – July 3, 2007) was an American musician best known for his 1963 saxophone hit, "Yakety Sax" (Benny Hill's signature tune). Randolph was a major part of the "Nashville Sound" for most of his professional career.
Contents

Biography

Randolph was born in Paducah, Kentucky and raised in Cadiz, Kentucky, attending high school in Evansville, Indiana.

At the end of World War II, Boots Randolph played saxophone, trombone, and vibraphone in the United States Army Band. After his service in the Army, he played with Dink Welch's Kopy Kats in Decatur, Illinois from 1948-1954. He briefly resided in Louisville, Kentucky before returning to Decatur to start his own group. He left Decatur in 1957.

During his more than forty year career, Randolph performed in hundreds of venues alongside many artists in pop, rock, jazz, and country music. He played on many recording sessions with Elvis Presley and also performed on soundtracks for a number of Presley's motion pictures, one popular song being "Return to Sender".

Mr. Randolph recorded for Monument Records in Nashville and played on Roy Orbison's 1963 hit, "Mean Woman Blues. " He was also featured on "Little Queenie" by REO Speedwagon, "Java" by Al Hirt, "Turn On Your Lovelight" by Jerry Lee Lewis, and "Rockin' Around the Christmas Tree" by Brenda Lee. Early in his career, he often billed himself as Randy Randolph.

As a solo recording artist, Randolph placed four singles in the Top-100 between 1963 and 1967. The most successful of these was "Yakety Sax" which reached #35 in 1963 and stayed on the charts for 9 weeks. Boots was also successful on Billboard Magazine's album charts, having fourteen entries between 1963 and 1972. "Boots With Strings" from 1967 reached #36 and stayed on the chart for nearly two years.

In 1977, Randolph opened a successful club of his own in Nashville's "Printer's Alley. " He also frequently appeared on the television program Hee Haw, and was a member of the Million Dollar Band.

On July 3, 2007, Randolph died at Skyline Medical Center in Nashville, Tennessee, after suffering a brain hemorrhage. He was 80 years old.

His final solo studio album A Whole New Ballgame was released June 12, 2007.

Bossa Nova Baby

Bossa Nova Baby

"Bossa Nova Baby"

Single by Elvis Presley
B-side "Witchcraft"
Released October 1963
Format 7", 45rpm
Recorded May 27, 1963
Genre Pop, rock n' roll
Label RCA Records
Writer(s) Jerry Leiber, Mike Stoller
Elvis Presley singles chronology
"(You're The) Devil in Disguise"
(1963) "Bossa Nova Baby"
(1963) "Crying in the Chapel"
(1965)
"Bossa Nova Baby" is a song written by Jerry Leiber and Mike Stoller and recorded on May 27, 1963, in RCA Studio B, in Nashville, Tennessee by Elvis Presley as part of the soundtrack of the 1963 motion picture Fun in Acapulco.
The song reached number eight on the Billboard Hot 100 pop chart and number twenty on the Billboard R&B Singles chart in 1963.
It was first recorded and released by Tippie and the Clovers in 1962.

Sources

^ Elvis Discography - 1963
^ Billboard Chart Statistics - Top 20 pop Singles
^ Billboard Top 20 R&B Singles
^ Elvis Presley Original Versions of Songs He Sang http://davidneale.eu/elvis/originals/list2. html#S1155

v t e
Elvis Presley
This 1960s single-related article.

Burning Love

Burning Love

"Burning Love"

Single by Elvis Presley

from the album Burning Love and Hits from His Movies, Volume 2
Released August 1, 1972
Format Vinyl record (7" 45 RPM)
Recorded RCA Studios,
Hollywood, California,
March 28, 1972
Master Take #6
Genre Rock
Length 3:23
Label RCA
Writer(s) Dennis Linde
Producer Felton Jarvis
Elvis Presley singles chronology
"Burning Love" is a song written by Dennis Linde, first recorded by Arthur Alexander, who included it on his self-titled 1972 album, and made famous by Elvis Presley, who took it to #2 in the United States in 1972. It was Presley's final top ten pop hit in the U. S.

Elvis version

Presley's version was released as a single on August 1, 1972, with the B-side "It's a Matter of Time", and it reached the Top 40 on the country charts, peaking at #36. Elvis had recorded it at RCA's Hollywood studios on March 28, 1972. The electric guitar opening and riffs were overdubbed and played by Dennis Linde himself.

For the weeks of October 21 and 28, 1972, "Burning Love" rose to #2 on the Billboard Hot 100, being kept from #1 by Chuck Berry's novelty song "My Ding-a-Ling. " However, it reached #1 on Cashbox's Top 40 Charts for the week of November 11, which gave him 20 US #1 hits. The song was Elvis's 40th and last Top Ten hit on the US charts. It was also one of the last real rock songs in the last years of his life; from 1972 to 1977 the majority of his songs were ballads, and many of those placed on Billboard's Hot Country Singles chart. "Burning Love" was one of the few exceptions, along with "Promised Land" in 1974.

Reportedly, Presley did not care for the song, and did not feel comfortable performing it. Nonetheless, he performed it in at least two high-profile productions: the concert film Elvis on Tour (during which he had to use a lyric sheet as the song was still new to him), and the later Aloha from Hawaii concert.

The song was also released on an album titled Burning Love and

Hits from his Movies: Volume 2 on November 1, 1972. Despite this album's subtitle, none of the movie songs on it were ever hits. The only actual hit on the album was the title song, "Burning Love".

Other versions

Travis Tritt recorded the song for Honeymoon in Vegas soundtrack in 1992.
Melissa Etheridge covered the song in 1994 for the televised Elvis Tribute hosted by John Stamos. It was released on the album "It's Now or Never: The Tribute to Elvis".
Bruce Springsteen used the song in his concert line-ups in the late 90's and 2000's.
Wynonna Judd recorded her version for the Lilo and Stitch soundtrack in 2002.
The 69 Eyes recorded a more upbeat version for their 1992 album Bump 'n' Grind
The Residents covered the song in 1989; it appears on their album The King & Eye.
Uses

"Burning Love" was used as a wake-up song on the space shuttle mission STS-123.
Was recorded for the 1979 film, Elvis The Movie, starring Kurt Russell and Ronnie McDowell as the singing voice of Elvis. The song was not released for a soundtrack.
The song was frequently used by comedian Conan O'Brien to warm up his audience prior to taping his talk show Late Night with Conan O'Brien, with the host singing the lyrics with musical accompaniment by the house band.
A remix of the original was used for the Cirque du Soleil show Viva Elvis and found on its soundtrack. During the live show, it is played during a montage of Elvis's best love scenes on the rear-projection screen, while the band has a spotlight. This remix puts more emphasis on drums and guitars, with a sound like The Who.
Velveeta used the song for a commercial changing the lyrics to "Hunka Hunka Meltin' Love".
The song was used during the Miss Universe 2012 swimsuit competition, where Ximena Navarrete from México won the title of most beautiful woman in the Universe.

CBS

CBS

CBS Broadcasting Inc. (CBS) is a major US commercial broadcasting television network, which started as a radio network, and continues to operate a radio network and a portfolio of large market television and radio stations. The name is derived from the initials of the network's former name, Columbia Broadcasting System. It is the second largest broadcaster in the world behind the BBC. The network is sometimes referred to as the "Eye Network" in reference to the shape of the company's logo. It has also been called the "Tiffany Network," which alludes to the perceived high quality of CBS programming during the tenure of its founder William S. Paley. It can also refer to some of CBS's first demonstrations of color television, which were held in a former Tiffany & Co. building in New York City in 1950.

The network has its origins in United Independent Broadcasters Inc. , a collection of 16 radio stations that was bought by William S. Paley in 1928 and renamed the Columbia Broadcasting System. Under Paley's guidance, CBS would first become one of the largest radio networks in the United States and then one of the big three American broadcast television networks. In 1974, CBS dropped its full name and became known simply as CBS, Inc. The Westinghouse Electric Corporation acquired the network in 1995 and eventually adopted the name of the company it had bought to become CBS Corporation. In 2000, CBS came under the control of Viacom, which coincidentally had begun as a spin-off of CBS in 1971. In late 2005, Viacom split itself and reestablished CBS Corporation with the CBS television network at its core. CBS Corporation is controlled by Sumner Redstone through National Amusements, its parent.

History

Radio years

The origins of CBS date back to January 27, 1927, with the creation of the "United Independent Broadcasters" network in Chicago by New York talent-agent Arthur Judson. The fledgling network soon needed additional investors though, and the Columbia Phonograph Company, manufacturers of Columbia Records, rescued it in April 1927; as a result, the network was renamed "Columbia Phonographic Broadcasting System. " Columbia Phonographic went on the air on September 18, 1927, with a presentation by the Howard Barlow Orchestra from flagship station

WOR in Newark, New Jersey, and fifteen affiliates.

Operational costs were steep, particularly the payments to AT&T for use of its land lines, and by the end of 1927, Columbia Phonograph wanted out. In early 1928, Judson sold the network to brothers Isaac and Leon Levy, owners of the network's Philadelphia affiliate WCAU, and their partner Jerome Louchenheim. None of the three was interested in assuming day-to-day management of the network, so they installed wealthy 26-year-old William S. Paley, son of a Philadelphia cigar family and in-law of the Levys, as president. With the record company out of the picture, Paley quickly streamlined the corporate name to "Columbia Broadcasting System. " He believed in the power of radio advertising since his family's "La Palina" cigars had doubled their sales after young William convinced his elders to advertise on radio. By September 1928, Paley bought out the Louchenheim share of CBS and became its majority owner with 51% of the business.

Turnaround: Paley's first year

During Louchenheim's brief regime, Columbia paid $410,000 to A. H. Grebe's Atlantic Broadcasting Company for a small Brooklyn station, WABC, which would become the network's flagship station. WABC was quickly upgraded, and the signal relocated to a stronger frequency, 860 kHz. The physical plant was relocated also—to Steinway Hall on West 57th Street in Manhattan. It was where much of CBS's programming originated. Other owned-and-operated stations were KNX Los Angeles, KCBS San Francisco (originally KQW), WBBM Chicago, WCAU Philadelphia, WJSV Washington, D. C. (later WTOP, which moved to the FM dial in 2005; the AM facility today is WFED, also a secondary CBS affiliate), KMOX St. Louis, and WCCO Minneapolis. These remain the core affiliates of the CBS Radio Network today, with WCBS still the flagship, and all except WTOP and WFED (both Hubbard Broadcasting properties) owned by CBS Radio. By the turn of 1929, the network could boast to sponsors of having 47 affiliates.

Paley moved right away to put his network on a firmer financial footing. In the fall of 1928, he entered into talks with Adolph Zukor of Paramount Pictures who planned to move into radio in response to RCA's forays into motion pictures with the advent of talkies. The deal came to fruition in September 1929: Paramount got 49 percent of CBS in return for a block of its stock worth $3,800,000 at the time. The agreement specified that Paramount would buy that same stock back by March 1, 1932 for a flat $5,000,000, provided CBS had earned $2,000,000 during 1931 and 1932. For a brief time there was talk that the network might be renamed "Paramount Radio," but it only lasted a month—the 1929 stock market crash sent all stock value tumbling. It galvanized Paley and his troops, though: they "had no alternative but to turn the network around and earn the $2,000,000 in two years. . . . This is the atmosphere in which the CBS of today was born. " The near-bankrupt movie studio sold its CBS shares back to CBS in 1932; Paramount was in trouble, CBS was not.

In the first year of Paley's watch, CBS's gross earnings more than tripled, going from $1,400,000 to $4,700,000.

Much of the increase was a result of Paley's second upgrade to the CBS business plan—improved affiliate relations. There were two types of program at the time: sponsored and sustaining, i. e. , unsponsored. Rival NBC paid affiliates for every sponsored show they carried and charged them for every sustaining show they ran. It was onerous for small and medium stations, and resulted in both unhappy affiliates and limited carriage of sustaining programs. Paley had a different idea, designed to get CBS programs emanating from as many radio sets as possible: he would give the sustaining programs away for free, provided the station would run every sponsored show, and accept CBS's check for doing so. CBS soon had more affiliates than either NBC Red or NBC Blue.

Paley was a man who valued style and taste, and in 1929, once he had his affiliates happy and his company's creditworthiness on the mend, he relocated his concern to sleek, new 485 Madison Avenue, the "heart of the advertising community, right where Paley wanted his company to be" and where CBS would stay until its move to Black Rock in 1965. When his new landlords expressed skepticism about the network and its fly-by-night reputation, Paley overcame their qualms by purchasing a lease for $1,500,000.

1930s: CBS takes on the Red and the Blue

Since NBC was the broadcast arm of radio set manufacturer RCA, its chief David Sarnoff approached his decisions as both a broadcaster and as a hardware executive; NBC's affiliates had the latest RCA equipment, and were often the best-established stations, or were on "clear channel" frequencies. Yet Sarnoff's affiliates were mistrustful of him. Paley had no such split loyalties: his—and his affiliates'—success rose and fell with the quality of CBS programming.

Paley had an innate, pitch-perfect, sense of entertainment, "a gift of the gods, an ear totally pure," wrote David Halberstam. "[H]e knew what was good and would sell, what was bad and would sell, and what was good and would not sell, and he never confused one with another. " As the 1930s loomed, Paley set about building the CBS talent stable. The network became the home of many popular musical and comedy stars, among them Jack Benny, ("Your Canada Dry Humorist"), Al Jolson, George Burns & Gracie Allen, and Kate Smith, whom Paley personally selected for his family's La Palina Hour because she was not the type of woman to provoke jealousy in American wives. When, on a mid-ocean voyage, Paley heard a phonograph record of a young unknown crooner, he rushed to the ship's radio room and "cabled" New York to sign Bing Crosby immediately to a contract for a daily radio show.

While the CBS prime-time lineup featured music, comedy and variety shows, the daytime schedule was a direct conduit into American homes—and into the hearts and minds of American women; for many, it was the bulk of their adult human contact during the course of the day. CBS time salesmen recognized early on that this intimate connection could be a bonanza for advertisers of female-interest products. Starting in 1930, astrologer Evangeline Adams would consult the heavens on behalf of listeners who sent in their birthdays, a description of their problems—and a box-top from sponsor Forhan's toothpaste. The low-key murmuring of smooth-voiced Tony Wons, backed by a tender violin, "made him a soul mate to millions of women" on behalf of the R. J. Reynolds tobacco company, whose cellophane-wrapped Camel cigarettes were "as fresh as the dew that dawn spills on a field of clover. " The most popular radio-friend of all was M. Sayle Taylor, The Voice Of Experience, though his name was never uttered on air. Women mailed descriptions of the most intimate of relationship problems to The Voice in the tens of thousands per week; sponsors Musterole ointment and Haley's M–O laxative enjoyed sales increases of several hundred percent in just the first month on The Voice Of Experience.

As the decade progressed, a new genre joined the daytime lineup: serial dramas—soap operas, so named for the products that sponsored them, by way of the ad agencies that actually produced them. Although the form, usually in quarter-hour episodes, proliferated widely in the middle and late 1930s, they all had the same basic premise: that characters "fell into two categories: 1) those in trouble and 2) those who helped people in trouble. The helping-hand figures were usually older. " At CBS, Just Plain Bill brought human insight and Anacin pain reliever into households; Your Family and Mine came courtesy of Sealtest Dairy products; Bachelor's Children first hawked Old Dutch Cleanser, then Wonder Bread; Aunt Jenny's Real Life Stories was sponsored by Spry Vegetable Shortening. Our Gal Sunday (Anacin again), The Romance of Helen Trent (Angélus cosmetics), Big Sister (Rinso laundry soap) and many others filled the daytime ether.

Thanks to its daytime and primetime schedules, CBS prospered in the 1930s. In 1935, gross sales were $19,300,000, yielding a profit of $2,270,000. By 1937, the network took in $28,700,000 and had 114 affiliates, almost all of which cleared 100% of network-fed programming, thus keeping ratings, and revenue, high. In 1938, CBS even acquired the American Record Corporation, parent of its onetime investor Columbia Records.

In 1938, NBC and CBS each opened studios in Hollywood to attract movieland's top talent to their networks – NBC at Radio City on Sunset and Vine, CBS two blocks away at Columbia Square.

CBS launches an independent news division

The extraordinary potential of radio news showed itself in 1930, when CBS suddenly found itself with a live telephone connection to a prisoner called "The Deacon" who described, from the inside and in real time, a riot and conflagration at the Ohio State Penitentiary; for CBS, it was "a shocking journalistic coup. " Yet as late as 1934, there was still no regularly scheduled newscast on network radio: "Most sponsors did not want network news programming; those that did were inclined to expect veto rights over it. " There had been a longstanding wariness between radio and the newspapers as well; the papers had rightly concluded that the upstart radio business would compete with them on two counts—advertising dollars and news coverage. By 1933, they fought back, many no longer publishing radio schedules for readers' convenience, or allowing "their" news to be read on the air for radio's profit. Radio, in turn, pushed back when urban department stores, newspapers' largest advertisers and themselves owners of many radio stations, threatened to withhold their ads from print. A short-lived attempted truce in 1933 even saw the papers proposing that radio be forbidden from running news before 9:30 am, and then only after 9:00 pm—and that no news story could air until it was twelve hours old.

It was in this climate that Paley set out to "enhance the prestige of CBS, to make it seem in the public mind the more advanced, dignified and socially aware network. " He did it through sustaining programming like the New York Philharmonic, the thoughtful drama of Norman Corwin—and an in-house news division to gather and present news, free of fickle suppliers like newspapers and wire services. In the fall of 1934, CBS launched its independent news division, shaped in its first years by Paley's vice-president, former The New York Times man Ed Klauber, and news director Paul White. Since there was no blueprint or precedent for real-time news coverage, early efforts of the new division used the short-wave link-up CBS had been using for five years to bring live feeds of European events to its American air.

A key early hire was Edward R. Murrow in 1935; his first corporate title was Director of Talks. He was mentored in microphone technique by Robert Trout, the lone full-timer of the News Division, and quickly found himself in a growing rivalry with boss White. Murrow was glad to "leave the hothouse atmosphere of the New York office behind" when he was dispatched to London as CBS's European Director in 1937, a time when the growing Hitler menace underscored the need for a robust European Bureau. Halberstam described Murrow in London as "the right man in the right place in the right era. " Murrow began assembling the staff of broadcast journalists—including William L. Shirer, Charles Collingwood and Eric Sevareid—who would become known as "Murrow's Boys. " They were "in [Murrow's] own image, sartorially impeccable, literate, often liberal, and prima donnas all. " They covered history in the making, and sometimes made it themselves: on March 12, 1938, Hitler boldly annexed nearby Austria and Murrow and Boys quickly assembled coverage with Shirer in London, Edgar Ansel Mowrer in Paris, Pierre Huss in Berlin, Frank Gervasi in Rome and Trout in New York. The News Round-Up format was born and is still ubiquitous today in broadcast news.

Murrow's nightly reports from the rooftops during the dark days of the London Blitz galvanized American listeners: even before Pearl Harbor, the conflict became "the story of the survival of Western civilization, the most heroic of all possible wars and stories. He was indeed reporting on the survival of the English-speaking peoples. " With his "manly, tormented voice," Murrow contained and mastered the panic and danger he felt, thereby communicating it all the more effectively to his audience. Using his trademark self-reference "This reporter," he did not so much report news as interpret it, combining simplicity of expression with subtlety of nuance. Murrow himself said he tried "to describe things in terms that make sense to the truck driver without insulting the intelligence of the professor. " When he returned home for a visit late in 1941, Paley threw an "extraordinarily elaborate reception" for him at the Waldorf-Astoria. Of course, its goal was more than just honoring CBS's latest "star"—it was an announcement to the world that Mr. Paley's network was finally more than just a pipeline carrying other people's programming: it was now a cultural force in its own right.

Once the war was over and Murrow returned for good, it was as "a superstar with prestige and freedom and respect within his profession and within his company. " He possessed enormous capital within that company, and as the unknown form of television news loomed large, he would spend it freely, first in radio news, then in television, taking on Senator Joseph McCarthy first, then eventually William S. Paley himself, and with a foe that formidable, even the vast Murrow account would soon run dry.

Panic: The War of the Worlds radio broadcast

On October 30, 1938, CBS gained a taste of infamy when Orson Welles and the The Mercury Theatre on the Air broadcast a radio adaptation of H. G. Wells's The War of the Worlds. Its unique format, a contemporary version of the story in the form of faux news broadcasts, had many CBS listeners panicked into believing invaders from Mars were actually devastating Grover's Mill, New Jersey, despite three disclaimers during the broadcast that it was a work of fiction. The flood of publicity after the broadcast had two effects: an FCC ban on faux news bulletins within dramatic programming, and sponsorship for The Mercury Theatre on the Air—the former sustaining program became The Campbell Playhouse to sell soup. Welles, for his part, summarized the episode as "the Mercury Theater's own radio version of dressing up in a sheet and jumping out of a bush and saying 'Boo!'"

CBS recruits Edmund A. Chester

Before the onset of World War II, CBS recruited Edmund A. Chester from his position as Bureau Chief for Latin America at Associated Press to serve as Director of Latin American Relations and Director of Short Wave Broadcasts for the CBS radio network (1940). In this capacity, Mr. Chester coordinated the development of the Network of the Americas (La Cadena de las Americas) with the Department of State, the Office for Inter-American Affairs (as chaired by Nelson Rockefeller) and Voice of America. This network provided vital news and cultural programming throughout South America and Central America during the crucial World War II era and fostered diplomatic relations between the United States of America and the less developed nations of the continent. It featured such popular radio broadcasts as Viva América which showcased leading musical talent from both North and South America accompanied by the CBS Pan American Orchestra under the musical direction of Alfredo Antonini. The post war era also marked the beginning of CBS's dominance in the field of radio as well.

1940s: Zenith of network radio

As 1939 wound down, Bill Paley announced that 1940 would "be the greatest year in the history of radio in the United States. " He was right—times ten: the decade of the 1940s would indeed be the apogee of network radio by every gauge. Nearly 100% of 1939's advertisers renewed their contracts for 1940; manufacturers of farm tractors made radios standard equipment on their machines. Wartime rationing of paper limited the size of newspapers—and hence advertisers—and when papers turned them away, they migrated to radio sponsorship. A 1942 act of Congress made advertising expenses a tax benefit and that sent even automobile and tire manufacturers—who had no products to sell since they had been converted to war production—scurrying to sponsor symphony orchestras and serious drama on radio. In 1940, only one-third of radio programs were sponsored, while two-thirds were sustaining; by mid-decade, the statistics had swapped—now two out of three shows had cash-paying sponsors and only one-third were sustaining.

The CBS of the 1940s was vastly different from that of the early days; many of the old guard veterans had died, retired or moved on. No change was greater than that in Paley himself: he had become difficult to work for, and had "gradually shifted from leader to despot. " He spent much of his time seeking social connections and in cultural pursuits; his "hope was that CBS could somehow learn to run itself. " His brief to an interior designer remodeling his townhouse included a requirement for closets that would accommodate three hundred suits, one hundred shirts and had special racks for a hundred neckties.

As Paley grew more remote, he installed a series of buffer executives who sequentially assumed more and more power at CBS: first Ed Klauber, then Paul Kesten, and finally Frank Stanton. Second only to Paley as the author of CBS's style and ambitions in its first half-century, Stanton was "a magnificent mandarin who functioned as company superintendent, spokesman, and image-maker. " He had come to the network in 1933 after sending copies of his PhD thesis "A Critique Of Present Methods and a New Plan for Studying Radio Listening Behavior" to CBS top brass and they responded with a job. He scored an early hit with his study "Memory for Advertising Copy Presented Visually vs. Orally" which CBS salesmen used to great effect bringing in new sponsors. In 1946 Paley named Stanton President of CBS and promoted himself to Chairman. Stanton's colorful, but impeccable, wardrobe—slate-blue pinstripe suit, ecru shirt, robin's egg blue necktie with splashes of saffron—made him, in the mind of one sardonic CBS vice-president, "the greatest argument we have for color television. "

Despite the influx of advertisers and their cash, or perhaps because of them, the 1940s were not without bumps for the radio networks. The biggest challenge came in the form of the FCC's chain broadcasting investigation—the "monopoly probe," as it was often called. Though started in 1938, it only gathered steam in 1940 under new-broom chairman James L. Fly. By the time the smoke had cleared in 1943, NBC found itself shorn of its Blue network, which became ABC. CBS was also hit, though not as severely: Paley's brilliant 1928 affiliate contract which had given CBS first claim on local stations' air during sponsored time—the network option—came under attack as being restrictive to local programming. The final compromise permitted the network option for three out of four hours during certain dayparts, but the new regulations had virtually no practical effect, since most all stations accepted the network feed, especially the sponsored hours that earned them money. Fly's panel also forbade networks from owning artists' representation bureaus, so CBS sold its bureau to Music Corporation of America and it became Management Corporation of America.

On the air, the war had an impact on most every show. Variety shows wove patriotism through their comedy and music segments; dramas and soaps had characters join the service and go off to fight. Even before hostilities commenced in Europe, one of the most played songs on radio was Irving Berlin's "God Bless America," popularized by CBS's own Kate Smith. Although an Office of Censorship sprang up within days of Pearl Harbor, censorship would be totally voluntary. A few shows submitted scripts for review; most did not. The guidelines that the Office did issue banned weather reports, including announcement of sports rainouts, news about troop, ship or plane movements, war production and live man-on-the-street interviews. The ban on ad-libbing caused quizzes, game shows and amateur hours to wither for the duration.

Surprising was "the granite permanence" of the shows at the top of the ratings. The vaudevillians and musicians who were huge after the war were the same stars who had been huge in the 30s: Benny, Crosby, Burns and Allen, Edgar Bergen all had been on the radio almost as long as there had been network radio. A notable exception to this was relative newcomer Arthur Godfrey who, as late as 1942, was still doing a local morning show in Washington, D. C. Godfrey, who had been a cemetery-lot salesman and a cab driver, pioneered the style of talking directly to the listener as an individual, with a singular "you" rather than phrases like "Now, folks. . . " or "Yes, friends. . . . " His combined shows contributed as much as 12% of all CBS revenues; by 1948, he was pulling down a half-million dollars a year.

In 1947, Paley, still the undisputed "head talent scout" of CBS, led a much-publicized "talent raid" on NBC. One day, while Freeman Gosden and Charles Correll were hard at work at NBC writing their venerable Amos and Andy show, a knock came on the door; it was Paley himself, with an astonishing offer: "Whatever you are getting now I will give you twice as much. " Capturing NBC's cornerstone show was coup enough, but Paley repeated in 1948 with longtime NBCers Edgar Bergen and Charlie McCarthy and Red Skelton, as well as former CBS defectors Jack Benny, radio's top-rated comedian, and Burns and Allen. Paley achieved this rout with a legal agreement reminiscent of his 1928 contract that caused some NBC station affiliates to jump ship and join CBS: CBS would buy the stars' names as a property, in exchange for a large lump sum and a salary. The plan relied on the vastly different tax rates between income and capital gains, so not only would the stars enjoy more than twice their income after taxes, but CBS would preclude any NBC counterattack because CBS owned the performers' names. As a result of this sortie, Paley got in 1949 something he had sought for twenty years: CBS finally beat NBC in the ratings.

But it wasn't just to one-up rival Sarnoff that Paley led his talent raid; he, and all of radio, had their eye on the coming force that threw a shadow over radio throughout the 1940s—television.

1950s: Prime time radio gives way to television

In the spring of 1940, CBS staff engineer Peter Goldmark devised a system for color television that CBS management hoped would leapfrog the network over NBC and its existing black-and-white RCA system. The CBS system "gave brilliant and stable colors," while NBC's was "crude and unstable but 'compatible. '" Ultimately, the FCC rejected the CBS system because it was incompatible with RCA's; that, and the fact that CBS had moved to secure many UHF, not VHF, TV licenses, left CBS flatfooted in the early television age. In 1946, only 6,000 TV sets were in operation, all in greater New York; by 1949, the number was 3,000,000, and by 1951, 12,000,000. Sixty-four American cities had TV stations, though most of them only had one.

Radio continued to be the backbone of the company, at least in the early 1950s, but it was "a strange, twilight period. " NBC's venerable Fred Allen saw his ratings plummet when he was pitted against upstart ABC's game show Stop The Music!; within weeks, he was dropped by longtime sponsor Ford Motor Company and was shortly gone from the scene. Radio powerhouse Bob Hope's ratings plunged from 23. 8 in 1949 to 5. 4 in 1953. By 1952, "death seemed imminent for network radio" in its familiar form; most telling of all, the big sponsors were eager for the switch.

Gradually, as the television network took shape, radio stars began to migrate to the new medium. Many programs ran on both media while making the transition. The radio soap opera The Guiding Light moved to television in 1952 and ran another fifty-seven years; Burns & Allen, back "home" from NBC, made the move in 1950; Lucille Ball a year later; Our Miss Brooks in 1952 (though it continued simultaneously on radio for its full television life). The high-rated Jack Benny Program ended its radio run in 1955, and Edgar Bergen's Sunday-night show went off the air in 1957. When CBS announced in 1956 that its radio operations had lost money, while the television network had made money, it was clear where the future lay. When the soap opera Ma Perkins went off the air November 25, 1960 only eight, relatively minor series remained. Prime time radio ended on September 30, 1962, when Yours Truly, Johnny Dollar and Suspense aired for the final time.

CBS's radio programming after 1972

The retirement of Arthur Godfrey in April 1972 marked the end of the longform program on CBS radio; programming thereafter consisted of hourly news summaries and news features, known in the 1970s as Dimension, and commentaries, including the Spectrum series that evolved into the "Point/Counterpoint" feature on the television network's 60 Minutes and First Line Report, a news and analysis feature delivered by CBS correspondents. The network also continued to offer traditional radio programming through its nightly CBS Radio Mystery Theater, the lone holdout of old-style programming, from 1974 through 1982. The CBS Radio Network continues to this day, offering hourly newscasts, including its centerpiece CBS World News Roundup in the morning and evening, weekend sister program CBS News Weekend Roundup, the news-related feature segment The Osgood File, What's In the News, a one-minute summary of one story, and various other segments such as commentary from Seattle radio personality Dave Ross, tip segments from various other sources, and technology coverage from CBS Interactive property CNET.

It is the last of the original Big Four radio networks still owned and operated by its founding company; ABC Radio was sold to Citadel Broadcasting in 2007 (and is now a part of Cumulus Media) while Mutual and NBC Radio were acquired by Westwood One in the 1980s (Westwood One and CBS were under common ownership from 1993 to 2007; the former would be acquired outright by Dial Global in October 2011).

Television years: expansion and growth

CBS's first television broadcasts were experimental, often only for one hour a day, and reaching a limited area in and around New York City (over station W2XAB channel 2, later called WCBW and finally WCBS-TV). To catch up with rival RCA, CBS bought Hytron Laboratories in 1939, and immediately moved into set production and television broadcasting. Though there were many competing patents and systems, RCA dictated the content of the FCC's technical standards, and grabbed the spotlight from CBS, DuMont and others by introducing television to the general public at the 1939 New York World's Fair. The FCC began licensing commercial television stations on July 1, 1941; the first license went to RCA and NBC's WNBT (now WNBC); the second license, issued that same day, was to WCBW, (now WCBS). CBS-Hytron offered a practical color system in 1941, but it was not compatible with the black-and-white standards set down by RCA. In time, and after considerable dithering, the FCC rejected CBS's technology in favor of that by RCA.

During the World War II years, commercial television broadcasting was reduced dramatically. Toward the end of the war, commercial television began to ramp up again, with an increased level of programming evident in the 1945–1947 period on the three New York television stations which operated in those years (the local stations of NBC, CBS and DuMont) But as RCA and DuMont raced to establish networks and offer upgraded programming, CBS lagged, advocating an industry-wide shift and restart to UHF for their incompatible (with black and white) color system. Only in 1950, when NBC was dominant in television and black and white transmission was widespread, did CBS begin to buy or build their own stations (outside of New York) in Los Angeles, Chicago and other major cities. Up to that point, CBS programming was seen on such stations as KTTV Channel 11 in Los Angeles, which CBS—as a bit of insurance and to guarantee program clearance in Los Angeles—quickly purchased a 50% interest in, partnering with the Los Angeles Times newspaper. CBS then sold their interest in KTTV (which today is the West Coast flagship of the Fox network) and purchased outright Los Angeles pioneer station KTSL (Channel 2) in 1950, renaming it KNXT (after CBS's existing Los Angeles radio property, KNX), later to become KCBS-TV. The "talent raid" on NBC of the mid-forties had brought over established radio stars; they now became stars of CBS television as well. One reluctant CBS star refused to bring her radio show, "My Favorite Husband," to television unless the network would re-cast the show with her real-life husband in the lead. Paley and network president Frank Stanton had so little faith in the future of Lucille Ball's series, re-dubbed I Love Lucy, that they granted her wish and allowed the husband, Desi Arnaz, to take financial control of the production. This was the making of the Ball-Arnaz Desilu empire, and became the template for series production to this day.

In the late 1940s, CBS offered the first live television coverage of the proceedings of the United Nations General Assembly (1949). This journalistic tour-de-force was under the direction of Edmund A. Chester, who was appointed to the post of Director for News, Special Events and Sports at CBS Television in 1948.

As television came to the forefront of American entertainment and information, CBS dominated television as it once had radio. In 1953, the CBS television network would make its first profit, and would maintain dominance on television between the years 1955 and 1976 as well By the late 1950s, the network often controlled seven or eight of the slots on the "top ten" ratings list with well-respected shows like Route 66. This success would continue for many years, with CBS bumped from first place only by the rise of ABC in the mid-1970s. Perhaps because of its status as the top-rated network, during the late 1960s and early 1970s CBS felt freer to gamble with controversial properties like the Smothers Brothers Comedy Hour and All in the Family and its many spinoffs during this period.

One of CBS's most popular shows at that time was M*A*S*H, a dramedy based on the hit Robert Altman film. It ran from 1972–1983, and was set, like the film, during the Korean War in a Mobile Army Surgical Hospital. The final episode aired on February 28, 1983 and was 2½ hours long. It was viewed by nearly 106 million Americans (77% of viewership that night) which established it as the most watched episode in United States television history, a record which stood until the broadcast of Super Bowl XLIV in 2010, also on CBS.

Color telecasts (1953–1965)

Although CBS-TV was the first with a working color television system, they lost out to RCA in 1953, due in part because the CBS color system was incompatible with existing black-and-white sets. Although RCA, then-parent company of NBC, made its color system available to CBS, the network was not interested in boosting RCA's profits and televised only a few specials in color for the rest of the decade. The specials included the Ford Star Jubilee programs (which included the first telecast ever of MGM's 1939 film classic The Wizard of Oz). Other specials were also shown: the 1957 telecast of Rodgers and Hammerstein's Cinderella, Cole Porter's musical version of Aladdin, and Playhouse 90's only color broadcast, the 1958 production of The Nutcracker, featuring choreography by George Balanchine. This telecast was based on the famous production staged annually since 1954 in New

York, and performed by the New York City Ballet. CBS would later show two other versions of the ballet, a semi-forgotten one-hour German-American version hosted by Eddie Albert ,shown annually for three years beginning in 1965, and the well-loved Baryshnikov production from 1977 to 1981. (This production later moved to PBS.)

Beginning in 1959, The Wizard of Oz, now telecast by CBS as a family special in its own right (after the cancellation of Ford Star Jubilee), became an annual tradition on color TV. However, it was the success of NBC's 1955 telecast of the musical Peter Pan, starring Mary Martin, the most watched television special of its time, that inspired CBS to telecast The Wizard of Oz, Cinderella and Aladdin.

1960–1967

From 1960 to 1965, CBS-TV limited its color transmissions to only a few specials such as The Wizard of Oz, and only then if the sponsor would pay for it. Red Skelton was the first CBS host to telecast his weekly programs in color, using a converted movie studio, in the early 1960s; he tried unsuccessfully to persuade the network to use his facility for other programs, then was forced to sell it. Color was being pushed hard by rival NBC. Even ABC had several color programs, beginning in the fall of 1962, but those were limited because of the network's financial and technical situations. One famous CBS-TV special made during this era was the Charles Collingwood-hosted tour of the White House with First Lady Jackie Kennedy. It was, however, shown in black-and-white. Beginning in 1963, at least one CBS show, The Lucy Show, began filming in color at its star and producer Lucille Ball's insistence; she realized that color episodes would command more money when they were eventually sold into syndication, but even it was broadcast in black and white through the end of the 1964–65 season. This would all change by the mid-1960s, when market pressure forced CBS-TV to add color programs to the regular schedule for the 1965–66 season and complete the changeover during the 1966–67 season. By the fall of 1967, nearly all of CBS's TV programs were in color, as were NBC's and ABC's. A notable exception was The Twentieth Century, which consisted mostly of newsreel archival footage, though even this program used at least some color footage by the late 1960s.

In 1965, CBS telecast a new color version of Rodgers and Hammerstein's Cinderella. This version, starring Lesley Ann Warren and Stuart Damon in the roles formerly played by Julie Andrews and Jon Cypher, was shot on videotape rather than being telecast live, and would become an annual tradition for the next nine years.

In 1967, NBC outbid CBS for the rights to the annual telecast of The Wizard of Oz and the film moved to NBC. However, the network quickly realized their mistake in allowing what was then one of its prime ratings winners to be acquired by another network, and by 1976, the film was back on CBS, where it remained through the end of 1997. CBS showed it twice in 1991, in March and again the night before Thanksgiving. Thereafter, it was shown the night before Thanksgiving.

1971–86: The "Rural purge" and success in the 1970s

Rural purge

By the end of the 1960s, CBS was broadcasting virtually all of its schedule in color, but many of its shows (including The Beverly Hillbillies, Mayberry R. F. D. , Petticoat Junction, Hee Haw and Green Acres) were appealing more to older and more rural audiences and less to the young, urban and more affluent audiences that advertisers sought to target. Fred Silverman (who would later head ABC, then NBC) made the decision to cancel most of those otherwise hit shows by mid-1971 in what became colloquially referred to as the "Rural Purge," with Green Acres star Pat Buttram remarking that the network cancelled "anything with a tree in it. "

While the "rural" shows got the axe, new hits, like The Mary Tyler Moore Show, All in the Family, M*A*S*H, The Bob Newhart Show, Cannon, Barnaby Jones, Kojak and The Sonny & Cher Comedy Hour took their place and kept CBS at the top of the ratings through the early '70s. The majority of these hits were overseen by then East Coast vice president Alan Wagner. Also, 60 Minutes moved to 7 pm ET on Sundays in 1976 and became an unexpected hit.

Silverman also first developed his strategy of spinning new shows off an established hit while at CBS, with Rhoda and Phyllis spun from The Mary Tyler Moore Show, Maude and The Jeffersons spun from All in the Family and Good Times from Maude.

After Silverman's departure, CBS dropped behind ABC in the 1976–77 season, but still rated strongly, based on its earlier hits and some new ones: One Day at a Time, Alice, Lou Grant, WKRP in Cincinnati, The Dukes of Hazzard (suspiciously "rural") and, the biggest hit of the early '80s, Dallas.

By 1982, ABC had run out of steam, NBC was in dire straits with many failed programming efforts greenlighted by Silverman during his 1978 to 1981 tenure there, and CBS once more nosed ahead, courtesy of Dallas (and its spin-off Knots Landing), Falcon Crest, Magnum, P. I. , Simon & Simon and 60 Minutes. CBS also broadcast the popular NCAA Men's Division I Basketball Tournament every March beginning in 1982 (taking over for NBC). There were a few new hits – Kate & Allie, Newhart, Cagney & Lacey, Scarecrow and Mrs. King, Murder, She Wrote – but the resurgence was short-lived. CBS had gone deeply into debt as a result of the failed effort by Ted Turner to take control over CBS. The battle was headed by CBS chairman Thomas Wyman. CBS sold its St. Louis station KMOX-TV and allowed the purchase of a large portion of its shares (under 25 percent) by Loew's Inc. chairman Lawrence Tisch. Consequently, collaboration between Paley and Tisch led to the slow dismissal of Wyman, Tisch becoming chief operating officer, and Paley returning as chairman.

1986–2002: Tiffany Network in distress

In 1984, The Cosby Show and Miami Vice debuted on NBC and grabbed high ratings immediately, bringing that network back to first place by the 1985–1986 season along with other huge hits Family Ties, The Golden Girls, L. A. Law, and 227. ABC had in turn also rebounded with hits like Dynasty, Who's the Boss?, Hotel, and Growing Pains. By the 1988–1989 season, CBS had fallen to third place behind both ABC and NBC, and had some major rebuilding to do.

Ironically, some of the groundwork had been laid as the network fell in the ratings, with hits Simon & Simon, Falcon Crest, Murder, She Wrote, Kate & Allie and Newhart still on the schedule from the most recent resurgence, and future hits Designing Women, Murphy Brown, Jake and the Fatman, and 48 Hours having recently debuted. Plus, CBS was still getting decent ratings from 60 Minutes, Dallas and Knots Landing. But the ratings for Dallas were a far cry from what they were in the early 1980s. During the early 1990s, the network would bolster its sports lineup by adding Major League Baseball telecasts and the Winter Olympics.

Under network president Jeff Sagansky, the network was able to get strong ratings from new shows Diagnosis: Murder, Touched by an Angel, Dr. Quinn, Medicine Woman, Walker, Texas Ranger, and a resurgent Jake and the Fatman during this period, and CBS was able to reclaim the first place crown briefly, in the 1992–1993 season, though its demographics skewed older than ABC, NBC or even Fox, with its relatively limited presence at that time. In 1993, the network made a breakthrough in establishing a successful late night talk show franchise to compete with NBC's The Tonight Show when it signed David Letterman away from NBC after the Late Night host was passed over as Johnny Carson's successor on Tonight in favor of Jay Leno. However, CBS' would soon suffer a major blow in a move that would change American television forever.

In 1993, the fledgling Fox network outbid CBS for the rights to air the National Football League, resulting in several stations switching to Fox. The loss of the NFL, along with an ill-fated effort to court younger viewers, led to a drop in CBS' ratings. The network also dropped its MLB coverage (after losing approximately US$500 million over a four year span) in 1993 and NBC, which already aired the Summer Olympics, took over coverage of the Winter Olympics beginning with the 2002 Games.

Still, CBS was able to produce some hits, such as Cosby, The Nanny, and Everybody Loves Raymond, and would regain the NFL (taking over the American Football Conference package from NBC) in 1998.

2002–present: Return to top spot, rivalry with Fox

Another turning point for CBS came in the summer of 2000 when it debuted the summer reality shows Survivor, and Big Brother which became surprise summer hits for the network. In January 2001, CBS debuted the second season of the show after its airing of the Super Bowl and scheduled it Thursdays at 8 pm ET, and moved the police procedural CSI (which had debuted that fall Fridays at 9 pm ET) to Thursdays at 9 pm ET and was both able to chip away at and eventually beat NBC's Thursday night lineup, and attract younger viewers to the network.

CBS has had additional successes with police procedurals Cold Case, Without a Trace, Criminal Minds, NCIS, The Mentalist, and Person of Interest, along with CSI spinoffs CSI: Miami and CSI: NY, and sitcoms Everybody Loves Raymond, The King of Queens, Mike & Molly, Two and a Half Men, How I Met Your Mother, The Big Bang Theory, The New Adventures of Old Christine, and 2 Broke Girls.

During the 2007–08 season, Fox ranked as the top-rated network, primarily due to its reliance on American Idol. However, according to Nielsen, CBS has ended up as the top-rated network every season since then. The two tend to nearly equal one another in the 18–34, 18–49, and 25–54 demographics, although Fox typically wins these by the narrowest of margins.

For the 2011–12 season, CBS finished in first place in total viewers but second place in the 18–49 demo.

Conglomerate

During the 1960s, CBS began an effort to diversify, and looked for suitable investments. In 1965, it acquired electric guitar maker Fender from Leo Fender, who agreed to sell his company due to health problems. The purchase also included that of Rhodes electric pianos, which had already been acquired by Fender. This and other acquisitions led to a restructuring of the corporation into various operating groups and divisions; the quality of the products coming out of these acquired companies was extremely lower, hence the term "pre-CBS" (meaning higher, sought after quality) and "CBS" (mass produced lower quality).

In other diversification attempts, CBS would buy (and later sell) sports teams (especially the New York Yankees baseball club), book and magazine publishers (Fawcett Publications including Woman's Day, and Holt, Rinehart and Winston), map-makers, toy manufacturers (Gabriel Toys, Child Guidance, Wonder Products), and other properties.

As William Paley aged, he tried to find the one person who could follow in his footsteps. However, numerous successors-in-waiting came and went. By the mid-1980s, the investor Laurence Tisch had begun to acquire substantial holdings in CBS. Eventually he gained Paley's confidence, and with his support took control of CBS in 1986.

Tisch's sole interest was turning profits. When CBS faltered, under-performing units were given the axe. Among the first properties to go was the Columbia Records group, which had been part of the company since 1938. Tisch also shut down in 1986 the CBS Technology Center in Stamford, which had started in New York City in the 1930s as CBS Laboratories and evolved to be the company's technology Research and development unit.

Columbia Records

Columbia Records
Columbia Records was a record label owned by CBS since 1938. In 1962, CBS launched CBS Records International to market Columbia recordings outside North America, where the Columbia name was controlled by others. In 1966, CBS Records was made a separate subsidiary of Columbia Broadcasting System, Inc. CBS sold the CBS Records Group to the Japanese conglomerate Sony in 1988 initiating the Japanese buying spree of US companies (MCA, Pebble Beach Co. , Rockefeller Center, Empire State Building, et al.) that continued into the 1990s. The record label company was re-christened Sony Music Entertainment in 1991, as Sony had a short term license on the CBS name.

Sony purchased from EMI its rights to the Columbia Records name outside the US, Canada, Spain and Japan. Sony now uses Columbia Records as a label name in all countries except Japan, where Sony Records remains their flagship label. Sony acquired the Spanish rights when Sony Music merged with Bertelsmann subsidiary BMG in 2004 as Sony BMG, co-owned by Sony and Bertelsmann. Sony bought out BMG's share in 2008.

CBS Corporation formed a new CBS Records in 2006.

Publishing

CBS entered the publishing business in 1967 by acquiring Holt, Rinehart & Winston, who published trade books, textbooks, and the magazine Field & Stream. The next year, CBS added the medical publisher Saunders to Holt, Rinehart & Winston. In 1971, CBS acquired Bond/Parkhurst, the publisher of Road & Track and Cycle World.

CBS greatly expanded its magazine business by purchasing Fawcett Publications in 1974, bringing in such magazines as Woman's Day. It acquired the majority of the Ziff Davis publications in 1984.

CBS sold its book publishing businesses in 1985. The educational publishing division, which retained the name Holt, Rinehart & Winston, was sold to Harcourt Brace Jovanovich; the trade book division, renamed Henry Holt and Company, was sold to the West German publisher Holtzbrinck.

CBS exited the magazine business by selling the unit to its executive Peter Diamandis. Diamandis sold the magazines to Hachette Filipacchi Médias in 1988, forming Hachette Filipacchi Media U. S.

CBS Musical Instruments division

Forming the CBS Musical Instruments division, the company also acquired Fender (1965–1983), Electro-Music Inc. (Leslie speakers) (1965–1980), Rogers Drums (1966–1983), Steinway pianos (1972-), Gemeinhardt flutes, Lyon & Healy harps (in the late 1970s), Rodgers (institutional) organs, and Gulbransen home organs. The last musical purchase was the 1981 acquisition of the assets of then-bankrupt ARP Instruments, developer of electronic synthesizers.

Between 1965 and 1985 the quality of Fender guitars and amplifiers declined significantly. Encouraged by outraged Fender fans, CBS Musical Instruments division executives executed a leveraged buyout in 1985 and created FMIC, the Fender Musical Instrument Corporation. At the same time, CBS divested itself of Rodgers, along with Steinway and Gemeinhardt, all of which were purchased by Steinway Musical Properties. The other musical instruments properties were also liquidated.

Film production

CBS Films
CBS made a brief, unsuccessful move into film production in the late 1960s, creating Cinema Center Films. This profit-free unit was shut down in 1972; today the distribution rights to the Cinema Center library rest with Paramount Pictures for home video (via CBS Home Entertainment) and theatrical release, and with CBS Paramount Television for TV distribution (most other ancillary rights remain with CBS). It released such films as The Reivers (1969), starring Steve McQueen, and the musical Scrooge (1970), starring Albert Finney.

Yet ten years later, in 1982, CBS took another try at Hollywood, in a joint venture with Columbia Pictures and HBO called TriStar Pictures. Despite releasing such box office successes as The Natural, Places in the Heart, and Rambo: First Blood Part II, CBS felt the studio was not making a profit and in 1985, sold its stake in TriStar to The Coca-

Cola Company, Columbia Pictures' owner at the time.

In 2007, CBS Corp. announced its desire to get back into the feature film business slowly launching CBS Films and hiring key executives in the Spring of 2008 to startup the new venture. The name CBS Films was actually used once before in 1953 when the name was briefly used for CBS's distributor of off-network and first-run syndicated programming to local TV stations in the United States and abroad.

Home video

CBS entered into the home video market, when joined with MGM to form MGM/CBS Home Video in 1978, but the joint venture was broken by 1982. CBS joined another studio: 20th Century Fox, to form CBS/Fox Video. CBS's duty was to release some of the movies by TriStar Pictures under the CBS/Fox Video label.

Gabriel Toys

CBS entered the video game market briefly, through its acquisition of Gabriel Toys (renamed CBS Toys), publishing several arcade adaptations and original titles under the name "CBS Electronics," for the Atari 2600, and other consoles and computers, also producing one of the first karaoke recording/players. CBS Electronics also distributed all Coleco-related video game products in Canada, including the ColecoVision. CBS later sold Gabriel Toys to View-Master, which eventually ended up as part of Mattel.

Venture to the UK

On September 14, 2009, it was revealed that the international arm of CBS, CBS Studios International, struck a joint venture deal with Chellomedia to launch six CBS-branded channels in the UK during 2009. The new channels would replace Zone Romantica, Zone Thriller, Zone Horror and Zone Reality, plus timeshift services Zone Horror +1 and Zone Reality +1. On October 1, 2009, it was announced that CBS Reality[disambiguation needed], CBS Reality +1, CBS Drama and CBS Action would launch on November 16, 2009 replacing Zone Reality, Zone Reality +1, Zone Romantica and Zone Thriller respectively. On April 5, 2010, Zone Horror and Zone Horror +1 were rebranded as Horror Channel and Horror Channel +1.

New owners

By the early 1990s profits had fallen as a result of competition from cable companies and from video rentals, and in consequence of the high cost of programming. About 20 former CBS affiliates switched to the rapidly rising Fox Television Network in the mid 1990s, while many television markets across the United States (e. g. KDFX in Palm Springs, California and KECY in Yuma, Arizona reportedly the first to do so in August 1994) lost their CBS affiliate for awhile. CBS ratings were acceptable, but the network struggled with an image of stodginess. Laurence Tisch lost interest and sought a new buyer.

Westinghouse Electric Corporation

In 1995, Westinghouse Electric Corporation acquired CBS for $5. 4 billion. As one of the major broadcasting group owners of commercial radio and television stations (as Group W) since 1920, Westinghouse sought to transition from a station operator into a major media company with its purchase of CBS.

Westinghouse's acquisition of CBS had the effect of suddenly turning the combined company's all-news radio stations in New York (WCBS and WINS) and Los Angeles (KNX and KFWB) from bitter rivals to sister stations. While KFWB switched from all-news to news-talk in 2009, WINS and WCBS remain all-news stations, with WINS (which pioneered the all-news format in 1965) concentrating its news on the five core New York City boroughs and WCBS, with its much more powerful signal, covering the surrounding tri-state metro area.

In 1997, Westinghouse acquired Infinity Broadcasting Corporation, owner of more than 150 radio stations, for $4. 9-billion. Also that year, Westinghouse began the CBS Cable division by acquiring two existing cable channels (Gaylord's The Nashville Network (now Spike TV) and Country Music Television) and starting a new one (CBS Eye on People, which was later sold to Discovery Communications).

Following the Infinity purchase, operation and sales responsibilities for the CBS Radio Network was handed to Infinity, which turned management over to Westwood One, a company Infinity managed. WWO is a major radio program syndicator that had previously purchased the Mutual Broadcasting System, NBC's radio networks and the rights to use the "NBC Radio Networks" name. For a time, CBS Radio, NBC Radio Networks and CNN's radio news services were all under the WWO umbrella.

As of 2008, Westwood One continues to distribute CBS radio programming, but as a self-managed company that put itself up for sale and found a buyer for a significant amount of its stock.

CBS also owned CBS Telenoticias, a Spanish-language news network.

In that same year of 1997, Westinghouse changed its name to CBS Corporation, and corporate headquarters were moved from Pittsburgh to New York. And to underline the change in emphasis, all non-entertainment assets were put up for sale. Another 90 radio stations were added to Infinity's portfolio in 1998 with the acquisition of American Radio Systems Corporation for $2. 6 billion.

In 1999, CBS paid $2. 5 billion to acquire King World Productions, a television syndication company whose programs include The Oprah Winfrey Show, Jeopardy! and Wheel of Fortune. By the end of 1999, all pre-CBS elements of Westinghouse's industrial past (beyond retaining rights to the name for brand licensing purposes) were gone.

Viacom

By the 1990s, CBS had become a broadcasting giant, but in 1999 entertainment conglomerate Viacom -- a company that ironically was created by CBS in 1952 as CBS Films, Inc. to syndicate old CBS series and was spun off and renamed Viacom in 1971—announced it was taking over its former parent in a deal valued at $37 billion. Following completion of this effort in 2000, Viacom was ranked as the second-largest entertainment company in the world.

Coincidentally, Viacom had bought Paramount, which as mentioned earlier once invested in CBS, in 1994.

CBS Corporation and CBS Studios

Having assembled all the elements of a communications empire, Viacom found that the promised synergy was not there, and at the end of 2005 it split itself in two. CBS became the center of a new company, CBS Corporation, which included the broadcasting elements, Paramount Television's production operations (currently named CBS Television Studios), UPN (which later merged with Time Warner's The WB into The CW), Viacom Outdoor advertising (renamed CBS Outdoor), Showtime, Simon & Schuster, and Paramount Parks, which the company sold in May 2006. It is the legal successor to the old Viacom.

The second company, keeping the Viacom name, kept Paramount Pictures, assorted MTV Networks, BET, and (until May 2007) Famous Music, which was sold to Sony/ATV Music Publishing.

As a result of the aforementioned Viacom/CBS corporate split, as well as other acquisitions over recent years, CBS (under the moniker CBS Studios) owns a massive film and television library spanning nine decades; these include not only acquired material from Viacom and CBS in-house productions and network programs, but also programs aired originally on competing networks. Shows and other material in this library include I Love Lucy, The Twilight Zone, The Honeymooners, Hawaii Five-O (both the original and current remake), Gunsmoke, The Fugitive, The Love Boat, Little House on the Prairie (US TV rights only), Star Trek, The Brady Bunch, Cheers, Becker, Family Ties, Mork & Mindy, Happy Days, The Young Indiana Jones Chronicles, Evening Shade, Duckman, CSI: Crime Scene Investigation and its spin-offs, the CBS theatrical library (My Fair Lady, Scrooge, etc.), and the entire Terrytoons library from 1921 forward, among others.

Both CBS Corporation and the new Viacom are still owned by Sumner Redstone's company, National Amusements. As such, Paramount Home Entertainment continues to handle DVD distribution for the CBS library.

Coverage and availability

ACNielsen estimated in 2003 that CBS can be seen in 96. 98% of all American households, reaching 103,421,270 homes in the United States. CBS has 204 VHF and UHF affiliated stations in the U. S. and U. S. possessions. CBS is also carried on cable television across Canada, via its affiliates, as well as in Bermuda, via local affiliate ZBM-TV.

Logos and slogans

CBS unveiled its Eye Device logo on October 20, 1951. Before that, from the 1940s through 1951, CBS Television used an oval spotlight on the block letters C-B-S. The Eye device was conceived by William Golden based on a Pennsylvania Dutch hex sign as well as a Shaker drawing. (While commonly attributed to Golden, there is speculation that at least some design work on the symbol may have been done by another CBS staff designer, Georg Olden, one of the first African-Americans to attract some attention in the postwar graphic design field.) The Eye device made its broadcasting debut on October 20, 1951. The following season, as Golden prepared a new "ident," CBS President Frank Stanton insisted on keeping the Eye device and using it as much as possible. (Golden died unexpectedly in 1959, and was replaced by one of his top assistants, Lou Dorfsman, who would go on to oversee all print and on-air graphics for CBS for the next thirty years.)

An example of CBS Television Network's imaging (and the distinction between the television and radio networks) may be seen in a video of The Jack Benny Program from 1953; the video appears to be converted from kinescope, and "unscoped" or unedited. One sees the program very nearly as one would have seen it live on CBS. Don Wilson is the program announcer, but also voices a promo for Private Secretary, which starred Ann Sothern and alternated weekly with Jack Benny on the CBS schedule. Benny continued to appear on CBS radio and television at that time, and Wilson makes a promo announcement at the end of the broadcast for Benny's radio program on the CBS Radio Network. The program closes with the "CBS Television Network" ID slide (the "CBS eye" over a field of clouds with the words "CBS Television Network" superimposed over the eye). There is, however, no voiceover accompanying the ID slide. It is unclear whether it was simply absent from the recording or never originally broadcast (a staff announcer may have provided a voiceover message, if so, it was not recorded on this clip).

The CBS eye is now an American icon. While the symbol's settings have changed, the Eye device itself has not been redesigned in its entire history. In the network's new graphic identity created by Trollbäck + Company in 2006, the eye is being placed in a "trademark" position on show titles, days of the week and descriptive words, an approach highly respecting the value of the eye. The eye logo has frequently been copied or borrowed by television networks around the world, notable examples being the

Austrian Broadcasting System (ORF) which used to use a red version of the eye logo, Associated TeleVision in the United Kingdom, Frecuencia Latina in Peru, Nippon Television in Japan and Rede Bandeirantes in Brazil. The logo is alternately known as the Eyemark, which was also the name of CBS's domestic and international syndication divisions in the mid-to-late 1990s before the King World acquisition and Viacom merger.

1980s

Through the years, CBS has developed several notable image campaigns, and several of the network's most well-known slogans date from the 1980s. 1981's "Reach for the Stars" used a space-themed campaign to capitalize on both CBS's stellar improvement in the ratings and the historic launch of the space shuttle Columbia. 1982's "Great Moments" juxtaposed scenes from classic CBS programming such as I Love Lucy with scenes from the network's then-current classics such as Dallas and M*A*S*H. From 1983 through 1986, CBS (by now firmly atop the ratings) featured a campaign based on the slogan "We've Got the Touch. " Vocals for the campaign's jingle were contributed by Richie Havens (1983–84; one occasion in 1984–85) and Kenny Rogers (1985–86). The 1986–87 programming season ushered in the "Share the Spirit of CBS" campaign, the network's first to use full-out computer graphics and DVE effects. Unlike most network campaign promos, the full length version of Share the Spirit not only showed a brief clip preview of each new fall series, but also utilized the CGI effects to map out the entire fall schedule by night. The success of that campaign led to the 1987–88 "CBS Spirit" (or CBSPIRIT) campaign. Most CBS Spirit promos utilized a procession of show clips once again. However, the new graphic motif was a swirling (or "swishing") blue line, that was used to represent "the spirit. " The full length promo, like the previous year, had a special portion that identified new fall shows, but the mapped-out fall schedule shot was abandoned.

For the 1988–89 season, CBS unveiled its new image campaign, officially known as "Television You Can Feel" but more commonly identified as "You Can Feel It On CBS. " The goal was to convey a more sensual, new-age image through distinguished, advanced-looking computer graphics and soothing music, backgrounding images and clips of emotionally powerful scenes and characters. However, it was this season in which CBS began its ratings free fall, the deepest in the network's history. CBS ended the decade with "Get Ready for CBS. " The 1989–90 version was a very ambitious campaign that attempted to elevate CBS out of last place (among the major networks); the motif was network stars interacting with each other in a remote studio set, getting ready for photo and TV shoots, as well as for the new season on CBS. The high-energy promo song and the campaign's practices saw many variations across the country as every CBS affiliate participated in it, as per a network mandate. Also, for the first time in history, CBS became the first broadcast network to team with a national retailer to encourage viewership, with the CBS/Kmart Get Ready Giveaway.

1990s

For the 1990–91 season, the campaign featured a new jingle—The Temptations offered an altered version of their hit "Get Ready. " The early 1990s featured less-than-memorable campaigns, with simplified taglines such as "This is CBS" (1992) and "You're On CBS" (1995). Eventually, the advertising department gained momentum again late in the decade with Welcome Home to a CBS Night (1996–1997), simplified to Welcome Home (1997–1999) and succeeded by the spin-off campaign The Address is CBS (1999–2000).

2000s

Throughout the first decade of the 21st century, CBS's ratings resurgence was backed by their "It's All Here" campaign, and their strategy led, in 2005, to the proclamation that they were "America's Most Watched Network. " Their most recent campaign, beginning in 2006, proclaims "We Are CBS" with the voice of Don LaFontaine. As of 2009, the network has shifted to a campaign entitled "Only CBS" in which the network proclaims several unique qualities it has. In 2011, CBS returned to the usage of "America's Most Watched Network. "

2010s

In October 2011, CBS celebrated 60 years of using the Eye logo.

Promos

Especially during the 1960s, the three major networks, NBC, CBS and ABC, would show elaborate promos during the summer months of their upcoming fall schedule of that year. In 1961, CBS took the unusual step of airing a program entitled CBS Fall

Preview Special: Seven Wonderful Nights, using, not the usual television voiceovers, but stars of several CBS shows to promote the upcoming shows, stars such as Ed Sullivan (The Ed Sullivan Show), Rod Serling (The Twilight Zone), and Raymond Burr and Barbara Hale (Perry Mason). The stars would appear and show previews of the entire lineup for one specific day of the week.

Programming

As of fall 2010, CBS operates on an 87½-hour regular network programming schedule. It provides 22 hours of prime time programming to affiliated stations: 8–11 p. m. Monday to Saturday (all times ET/PT) and 7–11 p. m. on Sundays. Programming is also provided 10 am–3 p. m. weekdays (game shows The Price Is Right and Let's Make a Deal, soaps The Young and the Restless and The Bold and the Beautiful, and talk show The Talk); 7–9 a. m. weekdays and Saturdays (CBS This Morning); CBS News Sunday Morning, nightly editions of the CBS Evening News, the Sunday political talk show Face the Nation, a 2½-hour early morning news program Up to the Minute and CBS Morning News; the late night talk shows Late Show with David Letterman and The Late Late Show with Craig Ferguson; and a three-hour Saturday morning live-action/animation block under the name Cookie Jar TV.

In addition, sports programming routinely appears on the weekends, although with a somewhat unpredictable schedule (mostly between noon and 7:00 pm ET).

Daytime

CBS Daytime
CBS's daytime schedule is the home of the long-running game show The Price Is Right. The Price is Right, which began production in 1972, is notable as the longest continuously running daytime game show on network television. After being hosted by Bob Barker for 35 years, the show has been hosted by actor/comedian Drew Carey since 2007. The network is also home to a new version of the game show Let's Make a Deal, hosted by singer/comedian Wayne Brady. As of 2012, CBS is the only network still producing daytime game shows.

CBS introduced a new talk show titled The Talk on October 2010. The show is similar to ABC's The View with a panel of hosts including Julie Chen, Sara Gilbert, Sharon Osbourne, Aisha Tyler and Leah

Remini.

As of August 2012, CBS Daytime airs two daytime soap operas each weekday: the hour long series The Young and the Restless and the half-hour series The Bold and the Beautiful.

CBS has aired the most soap operas of the Big Three networks. It aired 3½ hours of soap operas from 1982 to 2009. With the ending of Guiding Light in September 2009, ABC overtook CBS as the network with the most daily hours dedicated to soap operas. CBS reclaimed this distinction in January 2012, after ABC canceled two of its three remaining soap operas.

Other than Guiding Light, notable daytime soap operas that once aired on CBS include As the World Turns, Love of Life, Search for Tomorrow, The Secret Storm, The Edge of Night and Capitol.

Notable daytime game shows that once aired on CBS include Match Game, Tattletales, The $10/25,000 Pyramid, Press Your Luck, Card Sharks, Family Feud, and Wheel of Fortune. CBS games that also aired in prime time include Beat the Clock, To Tell the Truth and Password. Two long-running primetime-only games were the panel shows What's My Line? and I've Got a Secret.

Children's programming

Children's programming on CBS
CBS broadcast the live action series Captain Kangaroo on weekday mornings from 1955 through 1982, and on Saturdays through 1984. From 1971 through 1986, the CBS News department produced one-minute In the News segments broadcast between other Saturday morning programs. Otherwise, in regards to children's programming, CBS has aired mostly animated series for kids, such as reruns of Mighty Mouse cartoons (from the 1950s to the 1980s) reruns of Bugs Bunny cartoons, the original version of Scooby-Doo, Jim Henson's Muppet Babies, Garfield and Friends and Teenage Mutant Ninja Turtles. In 1997, CBS began broadcasting Wheel 2000 (a children's version of the syndicated game show Wheel of Fortune), and was broadcasting it simultaneously with GSN.

In September 1998, CBS began contracting out to other companies to provide programming and material for their Saturday morning schedule. The first of these special blocks was CBS Kidshow, which featured programming from Canada's Nelvana studio. It aired on CBS Saturday mornings from 1998 to 2000, with shows like Anatole, Mythic Warriors, Rescue Heroes, and Flying Rhino Junior High. Its tagline was, "The CBS Kids Show: Get in the Act. "

In 2000, CBS's deal with Nelvana ended. They then began a deal with Nickelodeon (owned by CBS's former parent company Viacom, which at one time was a subsidiary of CBS) to air its Nick Jr. programming under the banner Nick Jr. on CBS. From 2002 to 2004, Nick's non-preschool series aired on it as well, under the name Nick on CBS.

In 2006, after the Viacom-CBS split (as described above), CBS decided to discontinue the Nick Jr. lineup in favor of a lineup of programs produced by DIC Entertainment and later, the Cookie Jar Group, as part of a three-year deal which includes distribution of selected Formula One auto races on tape delay. KOL Secret Slumber Party on CBS premiered in September of that year; in the inaugural line-up, two of the programs were new shows, one aired in syndication in 2005 and three were pre-2006 shows. In mid-2007, KOL withdrew sponsorship from CBS's Saturday Morning Block and the name was changed to KEWLopolis on CBS. Complimenting CBS's 2007 line-up was Care Bears, Strawberry Shortcake, and Sushi Pack. On February 24, 2009, it was announced that CBS renewed its contract with Cookie Jar for another three seasons, through 2012. On September 19, 2009, KEWLopolis has been changed into Cookie Jar TV.

Animated primetime holiday specials

CBS was the original broadcast network for the animated primetime holiday specials based on the comic strip Peanuts, beginning with A Charlie Brown Christmas in 1965. Over thirty holiday Peanuts specials (each for a specific holiday such as Halloween) were broadcast on CBS from that time until 2000, when ABC acquired the broadcast rights. CBS also aired several primetime animated specials based on the work of Dr. Seuss (Theodor Geisel), beginning with How the Grinch Stole Christmas in 1966, as well as several specials based on the comic strip Garfield over the course of the 1980s (which led to Garfield getting his own Saturday morning cartoon on the network, Garfield and Friends, from 1988 to 1995). Rudolph the Red-Nosed Reindeer, produced in stop motion by the Rankin/Bass studio, has been another annual holiday staple of CBS since 1972, but that special originated on

NBC in 1964. As of 2011, Rudolph and Frosty the Snowman are the only two pre-1990 animated specials remaining on CBS; Charlie Brown and The Grinch moved to ABC, while cable network ABC Family owns the Garfield specials.

All of these animated specials, from 1973 until 1990, began with a fondly remembered opening animated logo (about seven seconds long), which showed the words "A CBS Special Presentation" in colorful lettering (the ITC Avant Garde typeface, widely used in the 1970s, was used for this logo). The word "SPECIAL," in all caps and repeated multiple times in multiple colors, slowly zoomed out from the frame in a spinning counterclockwise motion against a black background, and rapidly zoomed back into frame as a single word, in white, at the end; the logo was accompanied by a jazzy yet majestic up-tempo fanfare with dramatic horns and percussion (which was edited incidental music from the CBS crime drama Hawaii Five-O, titled "Call to Danger" on the Capitol Records' soundtrack LP). This opening sequence appeared immediately before the beginning of all CBS specials of the period (such as the Miss USA pageants and the annual Kennedy Center Honors presentation), not just animated ones. (This opening was presumably designed by, or under the supervision of, longtime CBS creative director Lou Dorfsman, who oversaw print and on-air graphics for CBS for nearly thirty years, replacing William Golden, who died in 1959.)

Classical music specials

CBS was also responsible for telecasting the series of Young People's Concerts conducted by Leonard Bernstein. Telecast every few months between 1958 and 1972, first in black-and-white and then switching to color in 1966, these programs introduced millions of children to classical music through the eloquent commentaries by Maestro Bernstein. They were nominated for several Emmy Awards, and were among the first programs ever broadcast from Lincoln Center for the Performing Arts.

Over the years, CBS has broadcast three different productions of Tchaikovsky's famous ballet The Nutcracker – two live telecasts of the George Balanchine New York City Ballet production in 1957 and '58 respectively, a little-known German-American filmed production in 1965 (which was subsequently repeated three times and starred Edward Villella, Patricia McBride, and Melissa Hayden), and beginning in 1977, the Baryshnikov staging of the ballet, starring the Russian dancer along with Gelsey Kirkland – a version that would become a television classic, and remains so today. This production later moved to PBS.

In April 1986, CBS presented a slightly abbreviated version of Horowitz in Moscow, a live piano recital by Vladimir Horowitz, arguably the greatest pianist of the 20th century. It marked Horowitz's return to Russia after more than sixty years. The program was shown as an episode of the series CBS News Sunday Morning (9:00 am in the U. S. is 4:00 pm in Russia). It was so successful that CBS repeated it a mere two months later by popular demand, this time on videotape, rather than live. In later years, the program was shown as a stand-alone special on PBS, and the current DVD of it omits the Charles Kuralt commentary, but includes additional selections not heard on the CBS telecast.

In 1986, CBS telecast Carnegie Hall: The Grand Reopening in primetime, in what was now a rare move for a commercial network station, since most primetime classical music specials were now relegated to PBS and A&E. The program was a concert commemorating the re-opening of Carnegie Hall after its complete renovation. It featured, along with luminaries such as Leonard Bernstein, popular music artists such as Frank Sinatra.

Other notable specials

In order to compete with NBC, which produced the now-legendary televised version of the Mary Martin Broadway production of Peter Pan, CBS responded with Cinderella, with music by Richard Rodgers and a book and lyrics by Oscar Hammerstein II. Based upon the classic French fairy tale Cinderella, it is the only Rodgers and Hammerstein musical written for television. It was originally broadcast live in color on CBS on March 31, 1957 as a vehicle for Julie Andrews, who played the title role; that broadcast was seen by over 100 million people. It was subsequently remade by CBS in 1965; that version starred Lesley Ann Warren, Stuart Damon, Ginger Rogers and Walter Pidgeon among others, and added a new song, "Loneliness of Evening", which had been composed for South Pacific in 1949 but not sung in that musical. This version was rebroadcast several times on CBS into the early 1970s, and is occasionally broadcast on various cable networks to this day. Both versions are available on DVD.

From 1949 until 2002, the Pillsbury Bake-Off, a national cooking contest held annually, was broadcast on CBS as a special. Hosts included Arthur Godfrey, Art Linkletter, Bob Barker, Gary Collins[disambiguation needed] and Alex Trebek.

The Miss USA beauty pageant aired on CBS from 1963 until 2002, and during a large portion of that period was known for having a CBS game show host as pageant host. John Charles Daly hosted the show from 1963–1966, Bob Barker from 1967 until 1987 (at which point he quit in a dispute over fur coats), Alan Thicke in 1988, Dick Clark from 1989–1993, and Bob Goen from 1994–1996. The show's highest ratings were in the early 1980s, when it regularly topped the Nielsen ratings. Viewership dropped sharply from the 1990s to the 2000s, from an estimated viewership of 20 million to an average of 7 million from 2000–2001. In 2002, owner Donald Trump brokered a new deal with NBC, giving them half-ownership of the Miss USA, Miss Universe and Miss Teen USA and moving them to NBC on an initial five year contract. The pageants were first shown on NBC in 2003.

On June 1, 1977, it was announced that Elvis Presley had signed a deal with CBS for a new television special. It was agreed that CBS would videotape concerts during the summer of 1977. It was filmed during Presley's final tour in the cities of Omaha, Nebraska, on June 19, 1977, and Rapid City, South Dakota, on June 21, 1977. On August 16, 1977, Elvis Presley died in his Graceland mansion. On October 3, 1977, CBS showed a posthumous 1977 TV special starring Elvis Presley. It was released nearly two months after the death of Elvis.

International broadcasts

CBS programs are shown outside the US. For instance, CBS News is shown for a few hours a day on satellite channel Orbit News in Europe, Africa and the Middle East. The CBS Evening News is shown in the UK, Ireland, Australia, New Zealand and Italy on Sky News, despite the fact that Sky is part of News Corporation (owners of Fox News Channel).

In the UK, CBS took over 6 of Chello Zone's channels in 2009. These were the first channels branded CBS outside the US. The channels are called CBS Action, CBS Drama, and CBS Reality, while CBS Reality has a timeshifted (+1) channel as well. Other channels as part of the deal are The Horror Channel and its timeshifted channel.

In Australia, Network Ten has an output deal with CBS Paramount giving them rights to carry the programs Jericho, Dr. Phil, Late Show with David Letterman, NCIS and Numb3rs as well access to stories from 60 Minutes (the rights of which have been sold to the Nine Network which broadcasts their own 60 Minutes), while Network Ten reporting is used in the United States for Australian topics.

In Bermuda, there is a CBS affiliate owned by the state-run Bermuda Broadcasting Company using the callsign ZBM.

In Canada, CBS, like all major American TV networks, is carried in the basic program package of all cable and satellite providers. The broadcast is shown almost exactly the same in Canada as in the United States. However, CBS's programming on Canadian cable and satellite systems are subject to the practice of "simsubbing," in which a signal of a Canadian station is placed over CBS's signal, if the programming at that time is the same. As well, many Canadians live close enough to a major American city to pick up the over the air broadcast signal of an American CBS affiliate with an antenna.

In Hong Kong, The CBS Evening News is aired live in the early morning and the local networks have an agreement to rebroadcast sections 12 hours later to fill up the local news programs when they have insufficient content to report.

The CBS Evening News is seen in the Philippines via satellite on Q-TV (a sister network of broadcaster GMA Network) while CBS This Morning is shown in that country on the Lifestyle Network. Studio 23 and Maxx, channels owned by broadcaster ABS-CBN in the Philippines show the Late Show with David Letterman.

In India CBS licenses their brand to Reliance Broadcast Network Ltd. for use with three CBS-branded channels, named Big CBS Prime, Big CBS Spark, and Big CBS Love.

Controversy

In 1995, CBS refused to air a segment of 60 Minutes that would have featured an interview with a former president of research and development for Brown & Williamson, the nation's third largest tobacco company. The controversy raised questions about the legal roles in decision making and whether journalistic standards should be compromised despite legal pressures and threats. The decision nevertheless sent shock waves throughout the television industry, the journalism community, and the country. This incident was the basis for the 1999 film by Michael Mann, The Insider.

In 2001, Bernard Goldberg, who was a reporter with CBS for 28 years, had his book, Bias: A CBS Insider Exposes How the Media Distort the News, published. This book heavily criticized the media, and some CBS reporters and news anchors in particular, such as Dan Rather. Goldberg accused CBS of having a liberal bias in most of their news.

In 2004, the FCC imposed a record $550,000 fine on CBS for its broadcast of a Super Bowl half-time show (produced by then sister-unit MTV) in which singer Janet Jackson's breast was briefly exposed. It was the largest fine ever for a violation of federal decency laws. Following the incident CBS apologized to its viewers and denied foreknowledge of the event, which was broadcast live on TV. In 2008, a Philadelphia federal court annulled the fine imposed on CBS, labelling it "arbitrary and capricious. "

CBS aired a controversial episode of 60 Minutes, which questioned U. S. President George W. Bush's service in the National Guard. Following allegations of forgery, CBS News admitted that documents used in the story had not been properly authenticated. The following January, CBS fired four people connected to the preparation of the news-segment. Former network news anchor Dan Rather filed a $70 million lawsuit against CBS in 2007, contending the story, and his termination, were mishandled. Parts of the suit were dismissed in 2008, the suit was dismissed, and his motion to appeal was denied in 2010.

In 2007, retired Army Major Gen. John Batiste, consultant to CBS News, appeared in a political ad for VoteVets. org critical of President Bush and the war in Iraq. Two days later, CBS stated that appearing in the ad violated Batiste's contract with them and the agreement was terminated.

Presidents of CBS Entertainment

Oliver E. Treyz
James Thomas Aubrey, Jr. 1959-1965.
. . .

Fred Silverman 1970-1975.
Arthur R. Taylor 1972-1976.
. . .

B. Donald Grant 1980-1987.
Kim LeMasters 1987-1990.
Jeff Sagansky 1990-1994.
Peter Tortorici 1994-1995.
Leslie Moonves 1995-1998.
Nancy Tellem 1998-2010.

Can't Help Falling in Love

Can't Help Falling in Love

"Can't Help Falling in Love"

Single by Elvis Presley
from the album Blue Hawaii
A-side "Rock-A-Hula Baby"
Released October 1, 1961
Format 7"
Recorded March 23, 1961
Genre Pop, blue eyed soul
Length 2:59
Label RCA Victor
Writer(s) Hugo Peretti, Luigi Creatore, George David Weiss
Producer Jordan Lumsden
Elvis Presley singles chronology
"Little Sister"
(1961) "Can't Help Falling in Love"
(1961) "Rock-A-Hula Baby"
(1961)
"Can't Help Falling in Love" is a pop song originally recorded by American singer Elvis Presley and published by Gladys Music, Elvis Presley's publishing company. It was written by Hugo Peretti, Luigi Creatore, and George David Weiss. The melody is based on "Plaisir d'Amour", a popular romance by Johann Martini (1741-1816). It was featured in Elvis Presley's 1961 film, Blue Hawaii. During the following four decades, it went on to be covered by numerous artists, like the British reggae group UB40, whose 1993 version topped the U. S. and UK charts, and Swedish pop group A-Teens.
Contents

Elvis Presley version

Elvis Presley's version of the song, which topped the British charts in 1962, has appeared in numerous other films, including Coyote Ugly and Walt Disney's Lilo and Stitch. The single is certified by the RIAA as a Platinum record, for US sales in excess of one million copies.
In the United States, the Elvis Presley version of the song peaked at number two on the pop chart and went to number one on the Easy Listening chart for six weeks.
During Presley's late sixties and 1970s live performances, the song was performed as the show's finale. Most notably, it was also sung in the live segment of his 1968 NBC television special, and as the closer for his 1973 Global telecast, "Aloha from Hawaii". A version with a faster and sloppier arrangement was used as the closing for Presley's final TV special, "Elvis in Concert. "

Track listings

7" single
"Can't Help Falling in Love"
"Rock-A-Hula Baby"
Preceded by
"When I Fall in Love" by The Lettermen "Billboard" Easy Listening number-one single by
Elvis Presley
January 13, 1962

(six weeks) Succeeded by
"A Little Bitty Tear" by Burl Ives
Preceded by
"The Young Ones" by Cliff Richard and The Shadows UK number-one single
"Rock-A-Hula Baby" b/w "Can't Help Falling in Love
February 22, 1962 (4 weeks) Succeeded by
"Wonderful Land" by The Shadows

UB40 version

"(I Can't Help) Falling in Love With You"

Single by UB40
from the album Promises and Lies
Released 10 May 1993
Format CD single, CD maxi, 7" single, 10" single
Recorded 1993
Genre reggae fusion, reggae
Length 3:24
Label Virgin
Producer UB40
UB40 singles chronology
"One in Ten"
(1992) "(I Can't Help) Falling in Love With You"
(1993) "Higher Ground"
(1993)
In 1993, British reggae band UB40 covered the song, as first single from their 1993 album Promises and Lies. The song was released in May 1993, in the majority of countries worldwide. It eventually climbed to number one on the Billboard Hot 100 after debuting at number 100 and appears in the soundtrack of the movie Sliver. It remained at number one in the U. S. for seven weeks. It was also number 1 in the UK. It was a great success, reaching number one in Austria, the Netherlands, Sweden, the United Kingdom, the United States, Australia, and New Zealand. The single version of the song has a slightly different backing rhythm and melody.
In the US, and on the Sliver soundtrack, the song title was listed as "Can't Help Falling In Love," rather than what appeared on the record sleeve.

Track listings

CD single
"I Can't Help Falling in Love With You" (3:24)
"Jungle Love" (5:09)
CD maxi
"I Can't Help Falling in Love With You" (3:24)
"Jungle Love" (5:09)
"I Can't Help Falling in Love With You" (Extended Mix) (6:03)
10" single
"I Can't Help Falling in Love With You" (Extended Mix) (6:03)
"Jungle Love" (5:09)
"I Can't Help Falling in Love With You" (3:24)
7" single
"I Can't Help Falling in Love With You" (3:24)
"Jungle Love" (5:09)

Charts and sales

Peak positions

Chart	Peak position
Australia (ARIA)	1
Austria (Ö3 Austria Top 40)	1
Belgium (VRT Top 30 Flanders)	1
Canada (RPM)	1
Europe (Eurochart Hot 100)	1
Finland (Suomen virallinen lista)	1
France (SNEP)	5
Germany (Media Control Charts)	2
Ireland (IRMA)	7
Italy (FIMI)	13
Netherlands (Dutch Top 40)	1
New Zealand (RIANZ)	1
Norway (VG-lista)	4
Sweden (Sverigetopplistan)	1
Switzerland (Schweizer Hitparade)	2
United Kingdom (The Official Charts Company)	1
U. S. Billboard Hot 100	1
U. S. Billboard Hot Adult Contemporary Tracks	11
U. S. Billboard Hot Modern Rock Tracks	11
U. S. Billboard Hot Top 40 Mainstream	1

End of year charts

End of year chart (1993) Position

U. S. Billboard Hot 100 3
End of year chart (1993) Position
Australian Singles Chart 5
Austrian Singles Chart 5
Dutch Top 40 5
Swiss Singles Chart 6

End of decade charts

Chart (1990–1999) Position
U. S. Billboard Hot 100 22

Certifications

Country	Certification	Date	Sales certified
Austria	Gold	January 10, 1994	15,000
France	Silver	1993	125,000
Germany	Platinum	1993	500,000
UK	Platinum	July 1, 1993	600,000

Chart successions

Order of precedence

A-Teens version

"Can't Help Falling in Love"

Single by A-Teens
from the album Lilo & Stitch and Pop 'til You Drop!
Released October 29, 2002
Format CD single
Recorded 2002
Genre Pop
Length 3:06
Label Walt Disney, Universal Music
Producer Mark Hammond
A-Teens singles chronology
"Heartbreak Lullaby"
(2001) "Can't Help Falling in Love"
(2001) "Floorfiller"
(2002)

The song was the A-Teens's first single from their third album Pop 'til You Drop!, as well as for the Lilo & Stitch movie soundtrack, which was originally scheduled to include several Presley tracks, the A-Teens picking it for inclusion in the soundtrack. The video had

thus tremendous exposure on several television channels, with the A-Teens eventually including the song in their third album. As a result, the song had two music videos, one to promote the Disney movie, the other for the album.
The song was a radio hit in the United States, and reached #12 in Sweden, #16 in Argentina, and #41 in Australia. Despite the success of the song overseas, it failed to attract the rest of the Latin American public, due to the fact that there was a Spanish version of the song, performed by the Argentine group, Bandana. In addition, the A*Teens' version of the song was overshadowed by the promotion of Bandana's version.

Music video

The video was directed by Gregory Dark and filmed in Los Angeles, California. It had two different versions. The "Disney Version", as the fans named it, features scenes of the movie, and also new scenes of the A-Teens with beach costumes. The "A-Teens Version" of the video, features the A-Teens on the white background with different close-ups and choreography, and scenes with puppies and different costumes.

Releases

Tracks marked + are not A-Teens tracks.
European 2-Track CD Single
Can't Help Falling in Love [Album Version] - 3:06
Hawaiian Roller Coaster Ride - 3:27 +
European/Australian CD Maxi
Can't Help Falling in Love [Album Version] - 3:06
Hawaiian Roller Coaster Ride - 3:27 +
He Mele, No Lilo - 2:28 +

Other artists who covered the song

Keely Smith, whose cover was on the charts at the same time as Presley's.
Perry Como, who included it in his September 1962 album, By Request (RCA Victor Records catalogue number LSP-2567).
Patti Page, for the best of Patti Page special TV offer album.
Doris Day, who included the song on her 1963 album, Love Him.
In 1963, the American pop vocal group The Lettermen did a version in their album Kind of Love. It was also included in their The Lettermen: The Complete Hits Vol. 2
In 1966, the American vocal group We Five performed a version in their album You Were on My Mind.

Janet Devlin Performed this on the X Factor UK Series 8
In 1967, Italian rock singer Bobby Solo released a cover of this song in Italian language, "Te ne vai," on his album San Francisco.
In 1969 the Greek expatriate band, Aphrodite's Child, released a version of this song entitled, "I Want to Live," on their album It's Five O'Clock. Their version uses different English lyrics and is more somber than the original.
The uptempo version by Andy Williams peaked at #3 in the UK Singles Chart in March 1970.
The Al Martino recording was released by Capitol Records as catalog number 2746 and charted in 1970, peaking at #51 on the Billboard charts and #57 on the Cash Box magazine Best-Selling Records list.
Bob Dylan recorded a version of this song for New Morning sessions in 1970, which was released by Columbia against his will on the 1973 album, Dylan (Columbia Records).
Raul Seixas, one of the most popular Brazilian singers, recorded a version of this song played only after the death of the singer.
The Stylistics' disco version was a hit in the UK, climbing to #4 in June 1976.
Shirley Bassey recorded a version of this song for a 1976 single.
Abbey Road Records issued a version by Herb Reed & The Original Platters in 1977.
During the 1980s, and again during the 2009 Working On a Dream Tour, Bruce Springsteen occasionally performed the song in his concert encores.
Lick the Tins released a cover of the song on its 1986 album "Blind Man on a Flying Horse. " It was a minor hit on the British charts, and it was featured in the ending credits of the films Some Kind of Wonderful and The Snapper.
In 1987, Corey Hart's recording reached #24 on the Billboard Hot 100. The cover and song were used with the image of forlorn animals in desperate need of rescue for a fundraising television commercial for the Ontario Humane Society.
Australian band The Triffids recorded the song for their 1989 album The Black Swan. It was omitted from the final tracklist of the album, but released on the B-side of "Falling Over You," the second single from the album. The track was reinstated for the 2008 reissue of the album.
U2 (label mates of The Triffids) used the song to close 87 of the 159 concerts on the U2 1992-1993 Zoo TV Tour. One such performance appears on the Zoo TV: Live from Sydney video and the Zoo TV Live CD released to U2. com subscribers.
Bono, lead singer of U2, contributed a solo version of the song for

the soundtrack to the 1992 movie, Honeymoon in Vegas.
Bruno Mars made a small cameo in the 1992 movie Honeymoon in Vegas as a Little Elvis impersonator singing the song.
Swiss artist Stephan Eicher covered the song in his 1994 live album Non Ci Badar, Guarda e Passa.
German italo disco artist, Fancy, did a synth-pop version in his 1996 album, Christmas In Vegas.

"Techno Wonderland" from Dancemania Speed 2 (1999)

Problems listening to this file? See media help.
David Thomas of Pere Ubu released one of the darkest and strangest versions of the song on the CD Meadville (1997), a live performance by David Thomas and Two Pale Boys.
An instrumental version of it played by a brass band is used in the closing sequence of the 1998 Italian movie Radiofreccia.
An uptempo dance version, titled "Techno Wondeland," remixed at 179 BPM, was included on the 1999 compilation Dancemania Speed 2. This was later included on the 2000 greatest hits compilation Dancemania Speed Best 2001 and the 2003 happy hardcore compilation Best of Hardcore.
American rock band Eels covered the song during their Black Sessions show in 2000, and also as a B-Side for their single Souljacker. This later version appears on the Eels' 2008 album, Useless Trinkets.
Hi-Standard had a version in their Love Is a Battlefield (EP) in 2001.
British synthpop-duo Erasure covered the song in 2003 on their cover album Other People's Songs.
Rick Astley covered the song for the album Portrait, in 2005.
Richard Marx made two versions of the song in his album Ballads, one as a solo the other and notably in the release in the Far East of the Channel V At The Hard Rock Live album as a duet with Eric Moo.
Clay Aiken performed a rendition of the song during the Elvis segment of his 2005 Jukebox Tour.
In early 2006, Andrea Bocelli recorded a new version of the song for his album, Amore.
F4, a Taiwanese boy band also sang the song in Chinese for the movie, Lilo & Stitch.
CSJH The Grace. a South Korean girl group, made an a cappella cover of the song. The a cappella cover song also featured as an intro in their "Boomerang" music video.
Julio Iglesias, the Spanish superstar living in the United States, also recorded a version of the song.
Dave Matthews frequently interpolates a verse of the song at

concerts during the end of his song, "The Stone. "
Katharine McPhee performed the song on American Idol and recorded it later with Andrea Bocelli.
Urbanize recorded a version of the song for "Liebe kommt aus dem Herzen. "
Vytautas Juozapaitis, a soloist of Lithuanian National Opera and Ballet Theatre recorded a Lithuanian version entitled "Negaliu Nemyleti" on his debut album Negaliu Nemyleti (Can't Help Falling In Love) released in 2004.
Blackmore's Night, a folk rock band with Ritchie Blackmore from Deep Purple and Rainbow and his wife Candice Night, covered this song for their 2008 album, Secret Voyage.
Mägo de Oz, a Celtic folk metal band from Spain, recorded a version of the song entitled "Todo Irá Bien" on their 2004 album, Belfast.
Ingrid Michaelson recorded a version of the song for her 2008 album, Be OK.
Harry Connick, Jr. included the song on his 2009 album, Your Songs.
Arlo Guthrie and Pete Seeger performed this song on More Together Again released in 1994. The track is titled "Denmark Folk Festival. "
The Pretenders included the song as a bonus track on their 2008 album, Break Up the Concrete.
Tim Urban covered this song on the Top Eight Week of American Idol on April 13, 2010 and had excellent reviews. Urban also advanced to the next week.
William Control covered this song on second album Noir.
Shane Told of Silverstein covered the song for Hopeless Records' compilation titled Love is Hopeless.
Chris Isaak covered the song on his tribute cover album to Sun Records, Beyond the Sun.
Jon Schmidt included a piano cover on his 2000 album To the Summit.
Marco T covered this song in Concert with a best Spanish Lyrics

Additional versions

The song has been adopted as the standard supporters' song of Welsh football club Swansea City A. F. C. and English football clubs Sunderland, Swindon Town, Hull City, Huddersfield Town, Preston North End, A. F. C. Wimbledon, MK Dons. It is also used by Scottish Clubs Airdrie United and Raith Rovers, Portland Timbers and Columbus Crew of Major League Soccer, as well as Central Coast

Mariners of Hyundai A-League. The supporters of the Swedish team Djurgårdens IF also sing this song during games.

The now disbanded Argentine pop group Bandana also featured a Spanish version of the song for the Spanish-speaking countries soundtrack of the same movie.

Céline Dion performs a live rendition of the song on her 1995 DVD/VHS release The Colour of My Love Concert. This particular performance has been hailed as one of Céline's greatest vocal performances ever, live or recorded. She also performed this song at the 2002 Diva's Live In Las Vegas show. In August 2007 she performed the song once more during her A New Day. . . show.

Pearl Jam covered "Can't Help Falling in Love" on October 22, 2000 at a concert in Las Vegas; it was released as the 2000 fan club Christmas single.

The Who integrated parts of the song into their 2004 single "Real Good Looking Boy. " In fact, the song is credited to Pete Townshend, George Weiss, Hugo Peretti and Luigi Creatore.

Andrea Bocelli performed a version of the song in the World Music Awards in 2006.

Spiritualized incorporate parts of the song into the title track of their 1997 album "Ladies & Gentlemen We Are Floating In Space", of which the band explicitly showcase the song further when performing live.

Montgomery Clift play and sing the song in the film The Heiress (1949, directed by William Wyler).

Keele University hockey club in staffordshire, UK, have adopted this song as their own, changing the you to keele.

T. J. Fantini, Britney Spears, Christina Aguilera, Justin Timberlake, and Marque Lynche covered the song on an episode of Mickey Mouse Club.

Other recorded versions

Anne Murray
Baccara
Barry Manilow
Bon Jovi
Brenda Lee
Cameo (from album Style)
Christine McVie
Darren Hayes
Dead Moon
Eddy Arnold

Engelbert Humperdinck
Floyd Cramer
George Maharis
Ingrid Michaelson
James Galway
Joe Loss and his Orchestra
Kamahl
Kenny Rogers
Klaus Nomi
Luka Bloom
Marty Robbins
Michael Bublé
Neil Diamond
Paul Jones
Stray Cats
Slim Whitman
The Esquires
The Residents
CSJH The Grace
Val Doonican
The Vasco Era

Carl Perkins

Background information
Birth name	Carl Lee Perkins
Born	April 9, 1932
Tiptonville, Tennessee, USA
Died	January 19, 1998 (aged 65)
Jackson, Tennessee
Genres	Rock and roll, rockabilly, country
Occupations	Singer, songwriter, guitarist
Instruments	Guitar, vocals
Years active	1946–1998
Labels	Sun, Columbia, Mercury
Associated acts	Perkins Brothers Band
Johnny Cash
Elvis Presley
Jerry Lee Lewis
Carl Lee Perkins (April 9, 1932 – January 19, 1998) was an American

rockabilly musician who recorded most notably at Sun Records Studio in Memphis, Tennessee, beginning during 1954. His best known song is "Blue Suede Shoes".

According to Charlie Daniels, "Carl Perkins' songs personified the rockabilly era, and Carl Perkins' sound personifies the rockabilly sound more so than anybody involved in it, because he never changed. " Perkins' songs were recorded by artists (and friends) as influential as Elvis Presley, The Beatles, Jimi Hendrix, and Johnny Cash, which further cemented his place in the history of popular music.

Called "the King of Rockabilly", he was inducted into the Rock and Roll, the Rockabilly, and the Nashville Songwriters Halls of Fame; and was a Grammy Hall of Fame Award recipient.

Biography

Early life

Perkins was the son of poor sharecroppers, Buck and Louise Perkins (misspelled on his birth certificate as "Perkings") near Tiptonville, Tennessee. He grew up hearing Southern gospel music sung by whites in church, and by black field workers when he started working in the cotton fields at age six. During spring and autumn, the school day would be followed by several hours of work in fields. During the summer, workdays were 12–14 hours, "from can to can't. " Carl and his brother Jay together would earn 50 cents a day. With all family members working and not having any credit, there was enough money for beans and potatoes, some tobacco for Carl's father Buck, and occasionally the luxury of a five-cent bag of hard candy.

During Saturday nights Carl would listen to the radio with his father and hear the Grand Ole Opry, and Roy Acuff's broadcasts on the Opry inspired him to ask his parents for a guitar. Because they could not afford a real guitar, Carl's father fashioned one from a cigar box and a broomstick. When a neighbor in tough straits offered to sell his dented and scratched Gene Autry model guitar with worn-out strings, Buck purchased it for a couple of dollars.

For the next year Carl taught himself parts of Acuff's "Great Speckled Bird" and "The Wabash Cannonball", which he had heard on the Opry. He also cited the fast playing and vocals of Bill

Monroe as an early influence.

Carl began learning more about playing his guitar from a fellow field worker named John Westbrook who befriended him. "Uncle John," as Carl called him, was an African American in his sixties who played blues and gospel on his battered acoustic guitar. Most famously, "Uncle John" advised Carl when playing the guitar to "Get down close to it. You can feel it travel down the strangs, come through your head and down to your soul where you live. You can feel it. Let it vib-a-rate. " Because Carl could not afford new strings when they broke, he retied them. The knots would cut into his fingers when he tried to slide to another note, so he began bending the notes, stumbling onto a type of "blue note. "

Carl was recruited to be a member of the Lake County Fourth Grade Marching Band, and because of the Perkins's limited finances, was given a new white shirt, cotton pants, white band cap and red cape by Miss Lee McCutcheon, who was in charge of the band.

During January 1947, Buck Perkins moved his family from Lake County to Madison County. A replacement radio which operated by mains electricity rather than a battery and the proximity of Memphis made it possible for Carl to hear a greater variety of music. At age fourteen years, using the I IV V chord progression common to country songs of the day, he wrote what came to be known around Jackson as "Let Me Take You To the Movie, Magg" (the song would convince Sam Phillips to sign Perkins to his Sun Records label).

Beginnings as a performer

Perkins and his brother Jay had their first paying job (in tips) as entertainers at the "Cotton Boll" tavern on Highway 45 some twelve miles south of Jackson, starting on Wednesday nights during late 1946. Carl was only 14 years old. One of the songs they played was an uptempo, country blues shuffle version of Bill Monroe's "Blue Moon of Kentucky". Free drinks were one of the perks of playing in a tavern, and Carl drank four beers that first night. Within a month Carl and Jay began playing Friday and Saturday nights at the Sand Ditch tavern near the western boundary of Jackson. Both places were the scene of occasional fights, and both of the Perkins Brothers gained a reputation as fighters.

During the next couple of years the Perkins Brothers began playing other taverns, including El Rancho, The Roadside Inn, and the Hilltop around Bemis and Jackson as they became well known. Carl persuaded his brother Clayton to play the bass fiddle to complete the sound of the band.

Perkins began performing regularly on WTJS-AM in Jackson during the late 1940s as a sometime member of the Tennessee Ramblers. He also appeared on Hayloft Frolic where he performed two songs, sometimes including "Talking Blues" as done by Robert Lunn on the Grand Ole Opry. Perkins and then his brothers began appearing on The Early Morning Farm and Home Hour. Overwhelmingly positive listener response resulted in a 15-minute segment sponsored by Mother's Best Flour. By the end of the 1940s, the Perkins Brothers were the best-known band in the Jackson area.

Perkins had day jobs during most of these early years, working first at picking cotton, then at Day's Dairy in Malesus, then at a mattress factory and in a battery plant. He then worked as a pan greaser for the Colonial Baking Company from 1951 through 1952.

During January 1953, Perkins married a woman he had known for a number of years, Valda Crider. When his job at the bakery was reduced to part-time, Valda, who had her own job, encouraged Carl to begin working the taverns full-time. He began playing six nights a week. Late the same year he added W. S. "Fluke" Holland to the band as a drummer, who had not any previous experience as a musician but had a good sense of rhythm.

Malcolm Yelvington remembered the Perkins brothers from 1953 when they played in Covington, Tennessee. He noted that Carl had a very unusual blues-like style all his own. One of Carl's friends had a tape recorder, and he had used it to make tapes of his materials that he sent to Columbia and RCA. He never heard back from them.

During July 1954, Perkins and his wife heard a new release of "Blue Moon of Kentucky" by Elvis Presley, Scotty Moore and Bill Black on the radio. , and Valda told Carl that someone in Memphis understood what he was doing and he should go see him. Later, Presley told Perkins that he had traveled to Jackson and seen Perkins and his group playing at El Rancho. As "Blue Moon of Kentucky faded out, Carl said, "There's a man in Memphis who understands what we're doing. I need to go see him. "

Years later fellow musician Gene Vincent told an interviewer that, rather than "Blue Moon of Kentucky" being a "new sound", "a lot of people were doing it before that, especially Carl Perkins. "

Sun Records

Perkins successfully auditioned for Sam Phillips at Sun Records during early October 1954. "Movie Magg" and "Turn Around" were released on the Phillips-owned Flip label (151) March 19, 1955, with "Turn Around" becoming a regional success. With the song getting airplay across the South and Southwest, Perkins was booked to appear along with Elvis Presley at theaters in Marianna and West Memphis, Arkansas. Commenting on the audience reaction to both Presley and himself Perkins said, "When I'd jump around they'd scream some, but they were gettin' ready for him. It was like TNT, man, it just exploded. All of a sudden the world was wrapped up in rock. "

Johnny Cash and the Tennessee Two were the next musicians to be added to the performances by Sun musicians. During the summer of 1955 there were junkets to Little Rock, Forrest City, Arkansas, Corinth and Tupelo, Mississippi. Again performing at El Rancho, the Perkins brothers were involved in an automobile accident. A friend, who had been driving, was pinned by the steering wheel. Perkins managed to drag him from the car, which had begun burning. Clayton had been thrown from the car, but was not injured seriously.

Another Perkins's tune, "Gone Gone Gone", released in October 1955 by Sun, was also a regional success. It was "a bounce blues in flavorsome combined country and r. &b. idioms". It was backed by the more traditional "Let The Juke Box Keep On Playing," complete with fiddle, "Western Boogie" bass line, steel guitar and weepy vocal.

Commenting on Perkins's playing, Sam Phillips has been quoted as saying that, "I knew that Carl could rock and in fact he told me right from the start that he had been playing that music before Elvis came out on record. . . I wanted to see whether this was someone who could revolutionize the country end of the business. "

That same autumn, Perkins wrote "Blue Suede Shoes" after seeing a dancer get angry with his date for scuffing up his shoes. Several weeks later, on December 19, 1955, Perkins and his band recorded the song during a session at Sun Studio in Memphis. Phillips suggested changes to the lyrics ("Go, cat, go") and the band changed the end of the song to a "boogie vamp".

Presley left Sun for a larger opportunity with RCA in November, and on December 19, 1955, Phillips, who had begun recording Perkins in late 1954, told Perkins, "Carl Perkins, you're my rockabilly cat now. " Released on January 1, 1956, "Blue Suede Shoes" was a massive chart success. In the United States, it scored No. 1 on Billboard magazine's country music charts (the only No. 1 success he would have) and No. 2 on Billboard's Best Sellers popular music chart. On March 17, Perkins became the first country artist to score No. 3 on the rhythm & blues charts. That night, Perkins performed the song during his television debut on ABC-TV's Ozark Jubilee (Presley performed it for the second time that same night on CBS-TV's Stage Show; he'd first sung it on the program on February 11).

In the United Kingdom, the song became a Top Ten success, scoring No. 10 on the British charts. It was the first record by a Sun label artist to sell a million copies. The B side, "Honey Don't", was covered by The Beatles, Wanda Jackson and (in the 1970s) T. Rex. John Lennon sang lead on the song when the Beatles performed it before it was given to Ringo Starr to sing. Lennon also performed the song on the Lost Lennon Tapes.

The accident

After playing a show in Norfolk, Virginia on March 21, 1956, the Perkins Brothers Band headed to New York City for a March 24 appearance on NBC-TV's Perry Como Show. Shortly before sunrise on March 22 on Route 13 between Dover and Woodside in Dover, Delaware, Stuart Pinkham (aka Richard Stuart and Poor Richard) assumed duties as driver. After hitting the back of a pickup truck, their car went into a ditch of water about a foot deep, and Perkins was lying face down in the water. Drummer Holland rolled Perkins over, saving him from drowning. He had suffered three fractured vertebrae in his neck, a severe concussion, a broken collar bone, and lacerations all over his body in the crash. Perkins remained unconscious for an entire day. The driver of the pickup truck, Thomas Phillips, a 40-year old farmer, died when he was thrown into the steering wheel. Carl's brother Jay had a fractured neck along with severe internal injuries, later dying from these complications.

On March 23, Bill Black, Scotty Moore and D. J. Fontana visited Perkins on their way to New York to appear with Presley the next day. D. J. Fontana recalled Perkins saying, "Of all the people, I looked up and there you guys are. You looked like a bunch of angels coming to see me. " Black told him, "Hey man, Elvis sends his love," and lit a cigarette for him, even though the patient in the next bed was in an oxygen tent. A week later, Perkins was given a telegram from Presley (which had arrived on March 23), wishing him a speedy recovery.

Sam Philips had planned to surprise Perkins with a gold record on The Perry Como Show. "Shoes" had already sold more than 500,000 copies by March 22. Now, while Carl recuperated from the accident, "Blue Suede Shoes" scored No. 1 on most popular, R&B, and country regional music charts. It also scored No. 2 on the Billboard Hot 100 and country charts. Elvis Presley's "Heartbreak Hotel" scored number one on the pop and country charts, while "Shoes" did better than "Heartbreak" on the R&B charts. By mid-April, more than one million copies of "Blue Suede Shoes" had been sold.

On April 3, while still recuperating in Jackson, Perkins would see Presley perform "Blue Suede Shoes" on his first Milton Berle Show appearance, which was his third performance of the song on national television. He also made references to it twice during an appearance on The Steve Allen Show. Although his version became more famous than Perkins's, it only scored No. 20 on Billboard's popular music chart.

Return to recording and touring

Perkins returned to live performances on April 21, 1956, beginning with an appearance in Beaumont, Texas, with the "Big D Jamboree" tour. Before resuming touring, Sam Phillips arranged a recording session at Sun with Ed Cisco filling in for the still-recuperating Jay. By mid-April, "Dixie Fried", "Put Your Cat Clothes On", "Right String, Wrong Yo-Yo", "You Can't Make Love to Somebody", "Everybody's Trying to Be My Baby", and "That Don't Move Me" had been recorded.

Beginning during early summer, Perkins was paid $1,000 to play just two songs a night on the extended tour of "Top Stars of '56. " Other performers on the tour were Chuck Berry and Frankie Lymon and the Teenagers. When Perkins and the group entered the stage in Columbia, South Carolina, he was appalled to see a teenager with a bleeding chin pressed against the stage by the crowd. During the first guitar intermission of "Honey Don't" they were waved off stage and into a vacant dressing room behind a double line of police officers. Perkins was quoted as saying, "It was dangerous. Lot of kids got hurt. There was a lot of rioting going on, just crazy, man! The music drove 'em insane. " Appalled by what he had seen and experienced, Perkins left the tour. Appearing with Gene Vincent and Lillian Briggs in a "rock 'n' roll show", he helped pull 39,872 people to the Reading Fair in Pennsylvania on a Tuesday night in late September. A full grandstand and one thousand people who stood in a heavy rain to hear Perkins and Briggs at the Brockton Fair in Mass.

Sun issued more Perkins songs in 1956: "Boppin' the Blues"/"All Mama's Children" (Sun 243), the B side co-written with Johnny Cash, "Dixie Fried"/"I'm Sorry, I'm Not Sorry" (Sun 249). "Matchbox"/"Your True Love" (Sun 261) came out in February 1957. "Boppin' the Blues" reached No. 47 on the Cashbox pop singles chart, No. 9 on the Billboard country and western chart, and No. 70 on the Billboard Top 100 chart.

"Matchbox" is considered a rockabilly classic. The day it was recorded, Elvis Presley visited the studio. Along with Johnny Cash (who left early), Perkins, Jerry Lee Lewis and Presley spent more than an hour singing gospel, country and rhythm-and-blues songs while a tape rolled. The casual session was called The Million Dollar Quartet by a local newspaper the next day, and it was eventually released on CD in 1990.

On February 2, 1957, Perkins again appeared on Ozark Jubilee, singing "Matchbox" and "Blue Suede Shoes". He also made at least two appearances on Town Hall Party in Compton, California in 1957 singing both songs. Those performances were included in the Western Ranch Dance Party series filmed and distributed by Screen Gems.

The 1957 film Jamboree included a Perkins performance of "Glad All Over" (not to be confused with The Dave Clark Five song of the same name), that ran 1:55. "Glad All Over", written by Aaron Schroeder, Sid Tepper, and Roy Bennett, was released by Sun in January 1958.

Life after Sun

During 1958, Perkins moved to Columbia Records where he recorded songs such as "Jive After Five", "Rockin' Record Hop", "Levi Jacket (And a Long Tail Shirt)", "Pop, Let Me Have the Car", "Pink Pedal Pushers", "Any Way the Wind Blows", "Hambone", "Pointed Toe Shoes", "Sister Twister", and "L-O-V-E-V-I-L-L-E".

In 1959, he wrote the country and western song "The Ballad of Boot Hill" for Johnny Cash who released the song as part of an EP on Columbia Records.

He performed often in The Golden Nugget Casino in Las Vegas during 1962 and 1963, and also in nine Midwestern states and a tour of Germany.

During May 1964, Perkins toured England along with Chuck Berry. The Animals backed the two performers. On the last night of the tour, Perkins attended a party that turned out to be for him, and ended up sitting on the floor sharing stories, playing guitar, and singing songs while surrounded by The Beatles. Ringo Starr asked if he could record "Honey Don't". "Man," answered Perkins, "go ahead, have at it. " The Beatles would cover "Matchbox", "Honey Don't" and "Everybody's Trying to Be My Baby" recorded by Perkins but adapted from a song originally recorded by Rex Griffin during 1936 with new music composed by Carl Perkins, a song with the same title also recorded by Roy Newman in 1938. The Beatles recorded two versions of "Glad All Over" in 1963. Another tour to Germany followed in the autumn.

He released "Big Bad Blues" backed with "Lonely Heart" as a single on Brunswick Records with The Nashville Teens in June 1964.

Although he had been trying to rehabilitate himself by drinking only beer (but large amounts of it), during 1968, while on tour with the Johnny Cash troupe, Perkins began a four-day drunk in Tulsa, Oklahoma, starting with a bottle of Early Times. Nevertheless, with the urging of Cash, he opened a show in San Diego, California, by playing four songs after seeing "four or five of me in the mirror," and while being able to see "nothin' but a blur. " After drinking yet another pint of Early Times, he passed out on the tour bus. By morning he started hallucinating "big spiders, and dinosaurs, huge, and they were gonna step on me. " The bus was parked on a beach at the ocean. He was tempted by yet another pint of whiskey that he had hidden. He took the bottle with him onto the beach and fell on his knees and said, "Lord. . . I'm gonna throw this bottle. I'm gonna show You that I believe in You. I sailed it into the Pacific. . . I got up, I knew I had done the right thing. " Perkins and Cash, who had his own problems with drugs, then gave each other support to refrain from their drug of choice.

During 1968, Cash recorded the Perkins-written "Daddy Sang Bass" (which incorporates parts of the American standard "Will the Circle Be Unbroken") and scored No. 1 on the country music charts for six weeks. Glen Campbell also covered the song, as did The Statler Brothers and Carl Story. "Daddy Sang Bass" was also a Country Music Association nominee for Song of the Year. Perkins also played lead guitar on the Cash smash single "A Boy Named Sue" which was No. 1 for five weeks on the country chart and No. 2 on the popular music chart. Perkins spent a decade in Cash's touring revue and appeared on The Johnny Cash Show. He played "Matchbox" with Cash and Derek and the Dominoes. Cash also featured Perkins in rehearsal jamming with José Feliciano and Merle Travis.

A Kraft Music Hall episode hosted by Cash on April 16, 1969 had Perkins singing his song "Restless". Country music fans may recognize The Statler Brothers' song, "Flowers on the Wall", which was also featured on the show.

During February 1969, Perkins joined with Bob Dylan to write "Champaign, Illinois". Dylan was recording in Nashville from February 12 through February 21 for an album that would be titled Nashville Skyline, and met Perkins when he appeared on The Johnny Cash Show on June 7. Dylan had written one verse of a song, but was stuck. After Perkins worked out a loping rhythm and improvised a verse ending lyric, Dylan said, "Your song. Take it. Finish it. " The co-authored song was included in Perkins's 1969 album On Top.

Perkins was also united in 1969 by Columbia's Murray Krugman with a "rockabilly" group based in New York's Hudson Valley, the New Rhythm and Blues Quartet. Carl and NRBQ recorded "Boppin' the Blues" which featured the group backing him on songs like his staples "Turn Around" and "Boppin' the Blues" and included songs recorded separately by Perkins and NRBQ. One of his TV appearances with Cash was on the popular country series Hee Haw on February 16, 1974.

Johnny Cash's brother Tommy Cash had a Top Ten country gospel hit in 1970 with a recording of the song "Rise and Shine" which was written by Carl Perkins. Tommy Cash reached no. 9 on the Billboard country chart and no. 8 on the Canadian country chart with his version of the song. Arlene Harden had a Top 40 country hit in 1971 with the Carl Perkins composition "True Love Is Greater Than Friendship" from the film Little Fauss and Big Halsy (1971) which reached no. 22 on the Billboard country chart and no. 33 on the Billboard Adult Contemporary chart for Al Martino that same year.

After a long legal struggle with Sam Phillips over royalties, Perkins gained ownership of his songs during the 1970s.

Later years

During 1981 Perkins recorded the song "Get It" with Paul McCartney, providing vocals and playing guitar with the former Beatle. This recording was included on the chart-topping album Tug Of War released in 1982. This track also comprised the B-side of the title track single in a slightly edited form. One source states that Perkins "wrote the song with Paul McCartney. " The song ends with a fade-out of Perkins's impromptu laughter.

The "rockabilly" revival of the 1980s helped bring Perkins back into the limelight. During 1985, he re-recorded "Blue Suede Shoes" with Lee Rocker and Jim Phantom of the Stray Cats, as part of the soundtrack for the movie, Porky's Revenge.

In October 1985, George Harrison, Eric Clapton, Dave Edmunds, Lee Rocker, Rosanne Cash and Ringo Starr appeared with him on stage for a television special that was taped live at the Limehouse Studios London before an ecstatic audience called Blue Suede Shoes: A Rockabilly Session. The show was later shown on Channel 4 on the 1st January 1986. Perkins performed 16 songs with 2 encores in an extraordinary performance. Perkins and his friends ended the session by singing his most famous song, 30 years after its writing, which brought Perkins to tears. The concert special was a memorable highlight of Perkins's later career and has been highly praised by fans for the spirited performances delivered by Perkins and his famous guests. The concert was released for DVD by Snapper Music in 2006.

Also during 1985, Perkins was inducted to the Nashville Songwriters

Hall of Fame, and in 1987, wider recognition of his contribution to music came with his induction to the Rock and Roll Hall of Fame. In addition, "Blue Suede Shoes" was chosen as one of The Rock and Roll Hall of Fame's 500 Songs that Shaped Rock and Roll, and as a Grammy Hall of Fame Award recipient. His pioneering contribution to the genre was also recognized by the Rockabilly Hall of Fame.

Perkins's only notable film performance as an actor was in John Landis' 1985 film Into the Night, a cameo-laden film that includes a scene where characters played by Carl and David Bowie die at each other's hand.

As a guitarist Perkins used: finger picking, imitations of the pedal steel guitar, right-handed damping (muffling strings near the bridge with the palm), arpeggios, advantageous use of open strings, single and double string bending (pushing strings across the neck to raise their pitch), chromaticism (using notes outside of the scale), country and blue licks, and tritone and other tonality clashing licks (short phrases that include notes from other keys and move in logical, often symmetric patterns). A rich vocabulary of chords including sixth and thirteenth chords, ninth and add nine chords, and suspensions, show up in rhythm parts and solos. Free use of syncopations, chord anticipations (arriving at a chord change before the other players, often by a 1/8 note) and crosspicking (repeating a three 1/8 note pattern so that an accent falls variously on the upbeat or downbeat) are also in his bag of tricks.

During 1986, he returned to the Sun Studio in Memphis, joining Cash, Jerry Lee Lewis and Roy Orbison on the album Class of '55. The record was a tribute to their early years at Sun and, specifically, the Million Dollar Quartet jam session involving Perkins, Presley, Cash, and Lewis in 1956.

During 1989, Perkins co-wrote and played guitar on The Judds' No. 1 country success, "Let Me Tell You About Love". During 1989, Perkins also signed a record deal with Platinum Records LTD for an album with the title Friends, Family, and Legends, featuring performances by Chet Atkins, Travis Tritt, Steve Wariner, Joan Jett and Charlie Daniels, along with Paul Shaffer and Will Lee. During 1992, during the production of this CD, Perkins developed throat cancer.

He returned to Sun Studios to record with Scotty Moore, Presley's first guitar player. The CD was called 706 ReUNION, released on

Belle Meade Records, and featured D. J. Fontana, Marcus Van Storey and The Jordanaires. During 1993, Perkins performed with the Kentucky Headhunters in a music video remake, filmed in Glasgow, Kentucky, of his song "Dixie Fried. " In 1994, Perkins teamed up with Duane Eddy and The Mavericks to contribute "Matchbox" to the AIDS benefit album Red Hot + Country produced by the Red Hot Organization.

Perkins's last album, Go Cat Go!, was released during 1996, and featured new collaborations with many of the above artists, as well as George Harrison, Paul Simon, John Fogerty, Tom Petty, and Bono. It was released by the independent label Dinosaur Records and distributed by BMG.

His last major concert performance was the Music for Montserrat all-star charity concert at London's Royal Albert Hall on September 15, 1997.

Perkins died four months later, on January 19, 1998 at the age of 65 at Jackson-Madison County Hospital in Jackson, Tennessee from throat cancer after suffering several strokes. Among mourners at the funeral at Lambuth University were George Harrison, Jerry Lee Lewis, Wynonna Judd, Garth Brooks, Nashville Agent Jim Dallas Crouch, Johnny Cash and June Carter Cash. Perkins was interred at Ridgecrest Cemetery in Jackson.

His widow, Valda deVere Perkins, died November 15, 2005 in Jackson.

Legacy

Perkins collaborated on a 1996 biography, Go, Cat, Go, with New York–based music writer David McGee. Plans for a biographical film were announced by Santa Monica-based production company Fastlane Entertainment. was slated for release in 2009.

During 2004, Rolling Stone ranked Perkins number 99 on its list of the 100 Greatest Artists of All Time.

His version of "Blue Suede Shoes" was included by the National Recording Preservation Board in the Library of Congress National Recording Registry in 2006.

The Perkins family still owns his songs, which are administered by former Beatle Paul McCartney's company MPL Communications.

Drive-By Truckers, on their album The Dirty South, recorded "Carl Perkins's Cadillac" that has a history of the artist and his relationships.

George Thorogood & the Destroyers covered "Dixie Fried" on their 1985 album, Maverick. The Kentucky Headhunters also covered the song as did Keith de Groot on a 1968 album entitled No Introduction Necessary that featured Jimmy Page on lead guitar and John Paul Jones on bass.

Ricky Nelson covered Perkins's "Boppin' The Blues" and "Your True Love" on his 1957 debut album Ricky.

Perkins was portrayed by Johnny Saint Holiday in the 2005 Johnny Cash biopic Walk the Line.

Perkins's first-born son Stan Perkins is a recording artist as well. In 2010, Stan joined forces with Jerry Naylor to record a duet tribute to Carl, "To Carl; Let it Vibrate. " Stan Perkins has been inducted into the Rockabilly Hall of Fame.

Discography

Charted albums

Charted singles

Year	Single	Peak chart positions			Album
		US Country	US	CAN Country	
1956	"Blue Suede Shoes"A	1	2	—	Dance Album of. . . Carl Perkins
	"Boppin' the Blues"	7	70	—	
	"Dixie Fried"	10	—	—	Original Golden Hits
	"I'm Sorry, I'm Not Sorry"	flip	—	—	Blue Suede Shoes
1957	"Your True Love"	13	67	—	Dance Album of. . . Carl Perkins
1958	"Pink Pedal Pushers"	17	91	—	The King of Rock
1959	"Pointed Toe Shoes"	—	93	—	
1966	"Country Boy's Dream"	22	—	—	Country Boy's Dream
1967	"Shine, Shine, Shine"	40	—	—	
1969	"Restless"	20	—	—	Carl Perkins' Greatest Hits

1971 "Me Without You" 65 — — The Man Behind Johnny Cash
"Cotton Top" 53 — —
1972 "High on Love" 60 — — Single only
1973 "(Let's Get) Dixiefried" (1973 version) 61 — — My Kind of Country
1986 "Birth of Rock and Roll" 31 — 44 Class of '55
1987 "Class of '55" 83 — —
1989 "Charlene" — — 74 Born to Rock
A"Blue Suede Shoes" also peaked at No. 2 on the R&B charts and No. 10 in the United Kingdom.

Cassandra Peterson

Cassandra Peterson

Cassandra Peterson

Peterson in May 2011.
Born September 17, 1951 (age 61)
Manhattan, Kansas, U. S.
Occupation Actress and TV hostess
Years active 1970–present
Spouse Mark Pierson (m. 1981–2003)
Website
hllp://www. elvira. com/
Cassandra Peterson (born September 17, 1951) is an American actress best known for her on-screen horror hostess character Elvira, Mistress of the Dark. She gained fame on Los Angeles television station KHJ wearing a black, gothic, cleavage-enhancing gown as host of Movie Macabre, a weekly horror movie presentation. Her wickedly vampish appearance is offset by her comical character, quirky and quick-witted personality, and Valley girl-type speech.

Biography

Born in Manhattan, Kansas, Peterson grew up near Randolph, until the area was flooded to create Tuttle Creek Reservoir; her family then moved to Colorado Springs, Colorado. According to a 2011 interview, Peterson states that as a child, while other girls were occupied with Barbie dolls, she was more fascinated by horror-themed toys. During her teens, Peterson worked as a go-go dancer in a local gay bar.

She graduated from General William J. Palmer High School in 1969. Days after graduating, she drove to Las Vegas, Nevada, where she became a showgirl in "Viva Les Girls" at The Dunes, where she met Elvis Presley. She had a small role as a showgirl in the 1971 James Bond film Diamonds Are Forever, played a topless dancer in The Working Girls (1974), and purportedly posed for the cover of Tom Waits's 1976 album, Small Change. However, this story is apparently unverified as Peterson has since described it as "a giant mystery", claiming that while she has no memory of the event, the picture looks enough like her that she feels "pretty sure" that it is. She is a vegetarian and has appeared in a humorous Halloween-themed ad for PETA promoting a vegetarian diet.

Career

Early career

In the early 1970s, she moved to Italy and became the lead singer of the Italian rock band, I Latins Ochanats. During this time she had a chance encounter with director Federico Fellini, which led to a small part in Roma (1972). Back in the United States she toured nightclubs and discos around the country with a musical/comedy act, Mammas Boys. In 1979, she joined the Los Angeles-based improvisational troupe, The Groundlings, where she created a Valley girl-type character upon whom the Elvira persona largely is based.

Peterson auditioned for the role of Ginger Grant for the third Gilligan's Island television movie in 1981, shortly before KHJ-TV offered her the horror-host position. Peterson also was a radio show personality on Los Angeles' 106. 7 KROQ radio station from 1982 to 1983.

Elvira Begins: Movie Macabre

List of Elvira's Movie Macabre episodes

In the late spring of 1981, six years after the death of Larry Vincent (who starred as host Sinister Seymour of a local Los Angeles weekend horror show called Fright Night), show producers began the task of bringing the show back. Deciding to use a female host, producers asked 1950s horror hostess, Maila Nurmi, to revive The Vampira Show. Nurmi worked on the project for a short time, but eventually quit when the producers would not hire Lola Falana to play Vampira. The station continued with the project and sent out a casting call. Peterson auditioned against 200 other horror hostess hopefuls and won the role. Producers left it up to her to create the role's image. She and her best friend, Robert Redding, came up with the sexy punk/vampire look after producers rejected her original idea to look like Sharon Tate in The Fearless Vampire Killers.

Since they were unable to continue with the Vampira character, the character Elvira was used instead. What followed was Elvira's Movie Macabre, featuring a quick-witted Valley-girl-type character named Elvira, Mistress of the Dark. With heavily applied, pancake-horror make up and a towering black beehive wig to conceal Peterson's flame-red hair.

Shortly before the first taping, producers received a cease and desist letter from Nurmi. Besides the similarities in the format and costumes, Elvira's closing line for each show, wishing her audience "Unpleasant dreams", was notably similar to Vampira's closer: "Bad dreams, darlings. . . " uttered as she walked off down a misty corridor. The court ruled in favor of Peterson, holding that "'likeness' means actual representation of another person's appearance, and not simply close resemblance. " Peterson claimed that Elvira was nothing like Vampira aside from the basic design of the black dress and black hair. Nurmi herself claimed that Vampira's image was based on Morticia Addams, a character in Charles Addams's cartoons that appeared in The New Yorker magazine.

The Elvira character rapidly gained notoriety with her tight-fitting, low-cut black gown which showed ample cleavage. The movies featured on Elvira's Movie Macabre were always B grade (or lower). Elvira reclined on a red Victorian couch, introducing and often interrupting the movie to lampoon the actors, the script and the editing. Adopting the flippant tone of a California "Valley girl", she brought a satirical, sarcastic edge to her commentary. She reveled in dropping risqué double entendres and making frequent jokes about her display of cleavage. In an AOL Entertainment News interview, Peterson said, "I figured out that Elvira is me when I was a teenager. She's a spastic girl. I just say what I feel and people seem to enjoy it. " Her campy humor, sex appeal, and good-natured self-mockery made her popular with late-night movie viewers as her popularity soared.

Elvira was a frequent guest on The Tonight Show Starring Johnny

Carson and other talk shows. She also produced a long-running series of Halloween-themed television commercials for Coors Light Beer and Mug Root Beer (her trademark cleavage was concealed for the Coors campaign). She appeared in guest roles on television dramas such as CHiPs, The Fall Guy and Fantasy Island and appeared on numerous awards shows as a presenter. Although she is known primarily as Elvira, Peterson has made out-of-costume appearances as herself for television interviews and specials.

In 1982, with the success of Movie Macabre, Knott's Theme Parks hired Elvira to replace Seymour as the host of its annual Halloween Haunt during the month of October. Elvira appeared nightly at the park, live on stage with a Halloween-themed musical comedy revue similar to her Mamma's Boys act from the 1970s.

The Elvira character rapidly evolved from obscure cult figure to a lucrative brandname and "Mistress of all Media", spawning many products throughout the 1980s and 1990s including Halloween costumes, comic books, action figures, trading cards, pinball machines, Halloween decor, model kits, calendars, perfume and dolls. She has appeared on the cover of Femme Fatales magazine five times. Her popularity reached its zenith with the release of the feature film Elvira, Mistress of the Dark (co-written by Peterson) in 1988. She also played many non-Elvira character-roles in other films, most notably Pee-wee's Big Adventure (1985) with friend and fellow Groundling Paul Reubens (as his Pee-wee Herman character) and Allan Quatermain and the Lost City of Gold (1985) starring Richard Chamberlain and Sharon Stone.

In September 2010, Elvira's Movie Macabre returned to television syndication in the U. S. , this time with public-domain films.

Elvira on home video

In 1985, Elvira began hosting a home video series called ThrillerVideo for U. S. A. Home Video and later International Video Entertainment (I. V. E.). Many of these films were hand-selected by Peterson. Choosing to stay away from the more explicit cannibal, slasher and zombie films of the time, these were generally tamer films such as The Monster Club and Dan Curtis television films, as well as many episodes of the Hammer House of Horror television series. She refused to host Make Them Die Slowly, Seven Doors of Death, and Buried Alive, so the videos were released on the LIVE Home Video label without Elvira's appearance as hostess. After this, several extended episodes of the British namesake series Thriller (i. e. The Devil's Web, A Killer in Every Corner, Murder Motel) were also released without Elvira hosting, sometimes various releases such as Buried Alive, the cast replaces Elvira.

The success of the ThrillerVideo series led to a second video set, Elvira's Midnight Madness through Rhino Home Video. In 2004, she revisited this concept with a similar horror film collection on DVD, titled Elvira's Box of Horrors. After more than ten years, Box of Horrors was the return of Elvira hosting horror movies as she did with Movie Macabre.

Elvira comic books

Elvira appeared in comic books from three publishers: DC Comics, Eclipse Comics and Claypool Comics. The Claypool series was co-branded with and distributed by Eclipse, afterwhich Eclipse ceased publication, was a sole product of Claypool. The series was edited and occasionally written by Richard Howell and featured photographic covers with interior stories and art by Kurt Busiek, Dan Spiegle, Jim Mooney, Steve Leialoha, and others. It ran for 166 issues, plus two trade paperback collections.

Elvira games

In the late 1980s and early 1990s, a number of Elvira-themed computer games were produced. Some of these were Elvira: Mistress of the Dark, Elvira 2: The Jaws of Cerberus and Elvira: The Arcade Game.

Two Elvira-themed pinball machines were produced by Bally/ Midway: Elvira and the Party Monsters was released in 1989, and Scared Stiff was published in 1996.

Calendar series

In the early 1990s, Peterson began a series of successful Elvira calendars with her striking provocative, and campy poses in various macabre settings. One of the months can be seen in the video game, Blood, hanging on various walls.

Movies, television, and video

Diamonds Are Forever (1971), small role as a dancer

Fellini's Roma (1972), small role as a dancer
The Working Girls (1974)
Cheech & Chong's Next Movie (1980), small role
Movie Macabre (1981), TV horror hostess
Jekyll and Hyde. . . Together Again (1982), small role as "the busty nurse. "
Stroker Ace (1983), a bit part in this Burt Reynolds film.
The Fall Guy, episode "October the 31st"
Pee-wee's Big Adventure (1985), small role as a biker mama.
ThrillerVideo (1985), home video series for U. S. A. and later I. V. E.
The music video for My Mistake by Phantom, Rocker & Slick – (1986)
WrestleMania 2 (1986), guest commentator
Echo Park (1986), supporting role in Susan Dey drama.
Elvira's Halloween Special (1986)
Allan Quatermain and the Lost City of Gold (1987), secondary role as the evil Queen Sorais.
Elvira, Mistress of the Dark (1988), title character and co-writer. (She, Sam Egan, and John Paragon collaborated on the original script.) Peterson's first feature film.
Coors TV commercials (1988), spokesman.
The Super Mario Bros. Super Show (1989), as herself, she appeared in the last sitcom segment of the program, called The Ghoul of My Dreams.
Parker Lewis Can't Lose – Season 2, Episode 19, "Boy Meets Girl II", appeared as Elvira (1992)
The Elvira Show (1993), CBS pilot revolving around two witches, played by Elvira and Katherine Helmond, moving to Manhattan, Kansas, with their talking cat.
Helicopters with Elvira (1993–1995)
The Ketchup Vampires (1995)
Space Ghost Coast to Coast – Episode 27, "Switcheroo", appeared as Elvira (1996)
Draw Your Own Toons (1998, series 1 only)
Elvira's Ghost Stories Spooktacular show (1999)
The Martin Short Show – TV Episode #1. 35 (as Elvira) (1999)
The Howard Stern Radio Show – TV Episode 19, June 1999
Bride of Monster Mania (2000) (TV)
Scares & Dares (2001) (TV)
Elvira's Haunted Hills (2001). After several years of unsuccessful attempts to make a sequel to Elvira, Mistress of the Dark, Cassandra and her manager and then-husband Mark Pierson decided to take matters into their own hands and finance a second movie themselves. In November of 2000, Cassandra wrote and co-produced Elvira's Haunted Hills. The film was shot on location in

Romania for just under one million dollars. With little budget left for promotion, Cassandra and Mark screened the film at AIDS charity fund raisers across America. For the many people in attendance, this was the first opportunity to see the woman behind the Elvira character. On July 5, 2002, Elvira's Haunted Hills had its official premiere in Hollywood. Elvira arrived at the premiere in her Macabre Mobile. The film would later be screened at the 2003 Cannes Film Festival.

The E! True Hollywood Story – Scream Queens (2004) Hostess

The Tony Danza Show – TV Episode #1. 34 (2004)

Monsterama: A Tribute to Horror Hosts (2004) (TV)

Elvira's Box of Horrors (2004), horror film collection on DVD

Red Riding Hood (2004)

I Love the '80s VH1 – Peterson made appearances (both as herself and as Elvira) on several editions.

I Love the Holidays (2005) (TV)

I Love the '80s 3-D (2005), VH1 TV miniseries

Playboy Presents: Hef's Halloween Spooktacular (2005) (Hostess)

TV1 (2005), Peterson (as Elvira) hosted a show on Australian-based cable TV channel TV1; the format was similar to her old show.

The Secret Life of Superfans (2006)

Vampira: The Movie (2006). Peterson discusses the Vampira lawsuit.

I Love the '70s: Volume 2 (2006), VH1 TV miniseries

Living in TV Land – Sherman Hemsley (2006), TV Episode

Elvira's Movie Macabre DVD series – (September 2006)

The Girls Next Door – Girls Will Be Ghouls (October 2006) Elvira visits The Playboy Mansion to promote her Playboy-inspired DVD.

The Search for the Next Elvira (October 13, 2007), TV reality show by Fox Reality. On April 19, 2006, Peterson announced she would be seeking a few good "Elviras" via a reality television program. Some[who?] mistook this for an announcement of her retirement. As of October of 2006, she had cleared up the rumor by stating that she wanted to find other people to play the role, so that the character could appear at the multitude of personal appearance requests. As Peterson stated in an interview, there were many Bozos (the clown) making personal appearances, even though Larry Harmon himself had died since, so she saw no reason there could not be more Elviras.

Medium (2009), Special cameo appearance as Elvira in the beginning of the "Bite Me" episode.

The Haunted World of El Superbeasto (2009), Amber

Appeared in the Ghoultown music video for their song "Mistress of the Dark". (2009)

Appeared as a downloadable character in the Sony PlayStation 3

game Pain
A professional dominatrix in an episode[which?] of Nash Bridges
All About Evil – Linda (2010)
Elvira's Movie Macabre Horror Hostess – (2010)
Last Man Standing – Special cameo appearance as Elvira (2011)
Elvira's Not a Witch – a 45 second viral video that spoofed a campaign ad by US Senate candidate Christine O'Donnell
RuPaul's Drag Race – Special guest judge as Elvira in first episode (2012)
Counting Cars - Had her car decked out,; appeared in and out of costume on episode "Satanic Mechanic"(2012)
Recording career

Elvira recorded several songs for her Halloween albums in the 1980s and 1990s. Here is her discography:

Elvira and the Vitones 3-D TV (Rhino Records, 1982)
Vinyl Macabre (Rhino Records, 1983)
Elvira Presents, Haunted Hits (Rhino Records, 1987)
Elvira Presents, Monster Hits (Rhino Records, 1994)
Elvira Presents Revenge of the Monster Hits (Rhino Records, 1995)
Elvira's Gravest Hits (Shout! Factory, 2010)
Elvira also performed guest vocals on a track called "Zombie Killer" for the band Leslie and the Ly's, released in February 2008. The music video for the track features Leslie & The Ly's performing to a sold out audience of zombies in a fictional venue called "Elvira Stadium. " A 7" single was released.

Other appearances

On April 7, 1986, Cassandra, as Elvira, appeared as a guest play-by-play announcer at the Los Angeles Sports Arena portion of WWF WrestleMania 2, alongside Jesse "The Body" Ventura

On Halloween night of 1992 Elvira appeared with rock band U2, when they played at Dodger Stadium in Los Angeles on their Zoo TV Tour. Just as she apparently did some 14 years later, she declared her candidacy for President, noting that "we already have two boobs in the White House; might as well be mine. " Following a couple of corny jokes, she led the crowd to sing "Happy Birthday" to drummer Larry Mullen, Jr. , whose birthday is on Halloween.

She appeared on Cartoon Network's talk show, Space Ghost Coast to Coast, in its twenty-ninth episode "Switcheroo" with Susan Olsen.

From 1995 to 1997, Peterson made appearances as Elvira at the Disney-MGM Studios Theme Park for "Elvira's Friday the 13th" events held whenever the 13th of a month fell on a Friday.

In 1997, Ray Productions of Orlando, Florida, produced the first haunted house chain endorsed by Elvira titled "Elvira's Nightmare Haunted House". The attraction was fully themed (including Elvira look-alike Patterson Lundquist) and remained open for two Halloween seasons in Atlanta, Georgia.

In 2001, she appeared throughout the nation, including Los Angeles, New York, Key West, Chicago, and Atlanta, screening her second full-length feature film, Elvira's Haunted Hills.

Lockheed's "Skunk Works", which designed and built the F-117 airplane, built a bomb into a mobile trailer that targeted a computer system for guiding the airplane through the maze of enemy radar systems. The trailer and system was nicknamed "Elvira" for its ability to safely guide the airplane through the darkness of their night missions.

On October 30, 2011, she was a guest DJ on 97. 1 FM WDRV Chicago "The Drive" as their Sunday Night Star.

In the 90's Cinema Ride's (Motion Base Simulator), she was the Preshow video host for the Haunted Graveyard Run.

In 2012, Elvira made an appearance on RuPaul's Drag Race as guest judge. Elvira was later featured (among other celebrities) in RuPaul's "Glamazon" music video.

On July 30, 2012, it was confirmed that Casandra has joined the cast of the Indigogo-funded film "First Period", where she will be playing mother to Cassie (Brandon Alexander III).

Elvira impersonators

In the mid-1990s, Cassandra Peterson enlisted female impersonators, Christian Greenia (Cassandra Fever), from Los Angeles, California, and Patterson Lundquist ("Elvira's Twin"), from Atlanta, Georgia, as her "official Elvira impersonators", calling them "the best she'd ever seen. " The two later appeared with her as co-judges on The Search for the Next Elvira. The first official female Elvira impersonator, April Wahlin, the winner of The Search for the Next Elvira, was passed the crown on October 31, 2007. As the winner of the reality show, she made a few appearances during her one-year "reign" from October 31, 2007, to October 31, 2008. Despite Wahlin's win of the title and one-year contract as Elvira, both Greenia and Lundquist continue to appear as Elvira for various events across the country.

Awards and nominations

Awards

Los Angeles Silver Lake Film Festival

Spirit of Silver Lake Award: 2001
Nominations

Saturn Awards

Best Actress: 1990
Raspberry Awards

Worst Actress: 1988

Change of Habit

Change of Habit

Please help
Change of Habit

Directed by William A. Graham
Produced by Joe Connelly
Written by Eric Bercovici
John Joseph
James Lee
Richard Morris
S. S. Schweitzer
Starring Elvis Presley
Mary Tyler Moore
Music by Billy Goldenberg
Buddy Kaye

Ben Weisman
Cinematography Russell Metty
Editing by Douglas Stewart
Distributed by MCA / Universal Pictures
Release date(s)
November 10, 1969
Running time 93 minutes
Country United States
Language English
Change of Habit is a 1969 musical drama film starring Elvis Presley and Mary Tyler Moore. It was Presley's 31st and final film acting role; his remaining two film appearances were concert documentaries. It was also Moore's fourth and final film under her brief Universal Pictures contract; she would not appear in another theatrical movie until Ordinary People in 1980. The film peaked at a respectable #17 at the box office.
Contents

Plot

Dr. John Carpenter is a physician in a ghetto clinic who falls for a co-worker, Michelle Gallagher, unaware that she is a nun.
Elvis stars as a professional man for the first time in his career.
Dr. Carpenter heads a ghetto clinic in a major metropolis. He is surprised to be offered assistance by three women. Unknown to him, the three are nuns in street clothing who want to aid the community but are afraid the local residents might be reluctant to seek help if their true identities were known.
Carpenter falls in love with Sister Michelle Gallagher, played by wholesome Mary Tyler Moore, but Sister Michelle's true vocation remains unknown to Dr. Carpenter. She also has feelings for the doctor but is reluctant to leave the order. The film concludes with Sister Michelle and Sister Irene entering a church where Dr. Carpenter is singing to pray for guidance to make her choice.

Cast

Elvis Presley: Dr. Carpenter
Mary Tyler Moore: Sister Michelle
Barbara McNair: Sister Irene
Jane Elliot: Sister Barbara
Edward Asner: Lt. Moretti
Leora Dana: Mother Joseph
Regis Toomey: Father Gibbons
Darlene Love: Backup Singer (uncredited)
A Martinez: Second Teen (uncredited)
Robert Emhardt: The Banker
Doro Merande: Rose
Richard Carlson: Bishop Finley

Behind the scenes

By 1969, Presley's future in Hollywood was under threat. Although still financially successful, mainly due to the "make 'em quick, make 'em cheap" attitude of Presley's manager Colonel Tom Parker, Presley's films had been making less profit in recent years. When Parker had struggled to find any studio willing to pay Presley's usual $1 million fee, he struck a deal with NBC to produce one feature film, and a TV Special entitled 'Elvis'. NBC would pay Presley $1. 25 million for both features, and Parker was happy in the knowledge that he was still able to earn $1 million for his client.

The film Change of Habit had been announced in 1967, with Mary Tyler Moore signing up in October 1968. It was considered a Moore vehicle until January 1969 when Presley signed on to take the lead role.

The film was shot in the Los Angeles area and at the Universal Studios during March and April 1969. It was released nationwide in the United States on November 10, 1969 and spent four weeks on the Variety Box Office Survey, peaking at #17.

Mary Tyler Moore and Edward Asner would soon become co-stars of her self-named The Mary Tyler Moore Show, one of television's enduring hits from 1970-77. In Change of Habit, however, they shared no scenes.

Soundtrack

When Presley entered Decca Universal Studio on March 5, 1969, for

two days to record his final dramatic motion picture soundtrack, what would come to be known as the comeback television special had already been broadcast, its attendant album had been his first top ten LP in four years, and he had just finished the sessions at American Sound Studio yielding From Elvis in Memphis and the top ten singles "In the Ghetto" and "Suspicious Minds" that would cement his resurgence as a force in American popular music.
He had a month-long engagement at the International Hotel in Paradise, Nevada lined up in August, his first live performances in eight years, and clearly now had turned his career around.
A song recorded at American, "Rubberneckin'", would be used in the film and subsequently issued as the b-side of RCA single 47-9768 "Don't Cry Daddy" in conjunction with the movie premiere.
Four songs would be recorded at the soundtrack sessions, of which "Let's Be Friends" would not be used in the film. The four songs would be released commercially on budget albums, "Let's Be Friends," the title track "Change of Habit," and "Have A Happy" on Let's Be Friends the following year, with "Let Us Pray" issued on the 1971 album You'll Never Walk Alone.
Some reference sources erroneously list an outtake from the earlier Presley film, Charro!, "Let's Forget About the Stars" (a song also released on the Let's Be Friends album), as being a song recorded for Change of Habit.

Personnel

Elvis Presley - vocals
The Blossoms - backing vocals
B. J. Baker, Sally Stevens, Jackie Ward - backing vocals
Howard Roberts, Dennis Budimir, Mike Deasy, Robert Bain - electric guitar
Roger Kellaway - piano
Joe Mondragon - double bass
Lyle Ritz, Max Bennett - bass
Carl O'Brian - drums

Film music track listing

"Change of Habit" (Buddy Kaye and Ben Weisman)
"Let's Be Friends" (Chris Arnold, David Martin, Geoffrey Morrow) (not used in film)
"Let Us Pray" (Buddy Kaye and Ben Weisman)
"Have A Happy" (Buddy Kaye, Dolores Fuller, Ben Weisman)

Charles Laughton

Charles Laughton

Charles Laughton

In film The Barretts of Wimpole Street (1934)
Born 1 July 1899
Scarborough, North Yorkshire, England, UK
Died 15 December 1962 (aged 63)
Hollywood, California, U. S.
Occupation Actor, screenwriter, producer, director
Years active 1926–1962
Spouse Elsa Lanchester (m. 1929-1962; his death)
Charles Laughton (1 July 1899 – 15 December 1962) was an English-born American stage and film actor and director.

Laughton was trained in London at the Royal Academy of Dramatic Art (RADA) and first appeared professionally on the stage in 1926. He played a wide range of classical and modern parts, making a big impact in Shakespeare at the Old Vic. His film career took him to Hollywood, but he also collaborated with Alexander Korda on some of the most notable British films of the era, including The Private Life of Henry VIII.

Among Laughton's biggest movie-hits were The Barretts of Wimpole Street, Mutiny on the Bounty, Ruggles of Red Gap, Jamaica Inn, The Hunchback of Notre Dame and The Big Clock.

In his later career, he took up stage directing, notably in the Caine Mutiny Court-Martial, and Bernard Shaw's Don Juan in Hell, in which he also starred.

In 1927, he had been cast in a play with his future wife Elsa Lanchester, with whom he lived and worked until his death. Their childless marriage was the subject of much gossip, with some speculation about Laughton's sexuality.

Early life and career

Laughton was born in Scarborough, North Yorkshire, the son of Robert Laughton and his wife Elizabeth (née Conlon), Yorkshire hotel keepers. His mother was a devout Roman Catholic of Irish descent, and he attended Stonyhurst College, the pre-eminent English Jesuit school. He fought in World War I (during which he was gassed), serving first with the 2/1st Battalion of the Huntingdonshire Cyclist Regiment, and later with the 7th Battalion of the Northamptonshire Regiment.

He started work in the family hotel business, while participating in amateur theatricals in Scarborough. Finally allowed by his family to become a drama student at RADA in 1925, Laughton made his first professional stage appearance on 28 April 1926 at the Barnes Theatre, as Osip in the comedy The Government Inspector, in which he also appeared at the London Gaiety Theatre in May. Despite not having the looks for a romantic lead, he impressed audiences with his talent and played classical roles in two plays by Chekhov, The Cherry Orchard and The Three Sisters. Laughton played the lead role of Harry Hegan in the world premiere of Sean O'Casey's The Silver Tassie in 1928 in London. He played the title roles in Arnold Bennett's Mr Prohack (Elsa Lanchester was also in the cast) and in Mr Pickwick. He also played Tony Perelli in Edgar Wallace's On the Spot and William Marble in Payment Deferred. He took the last role across the Atlantic and made his United States debut on 24 September 1931, at the Lyceum Theatre. He returned to London for the 1933–34 Old Vic Season and was engaged in four Shakespeare roles (as Macbeth and Henry VIII, Angelo in Measure for Measure and Prospero in The Tempest) and also as Lopakhin in The Cherry Orchard, Canon Chasuble in The Importance of Being Earnest, and Tattle in Love for Love. In 1936, he went to Paris and on 9 May appeared at the Comédie-Française as Sganarelle in the second act of Molière's Le Médecin malgré lui, the first English actor to appear at that theatre, where he acted the part in French and received an ovation. Laughton commenced his film career in England while still acting on the London stage. He took small roles in three short silent comedies starring his wife Elsa Lanchester, Daydreams, Blue Bottles and The Tonic (all 1928) which had been specially written for her by H. G. Wells. He made a brief appearance as a disgruntled diner in another silent film Piccadilly with Anna May Wong in 1929. He appeared with Lanchester again in a "film revue", featuring assorted British variety acts, called Comets (1930) in which they sang a duet, "The Ballad of Frankie and Johnnie". He made two other early British talkies: Wolves with Dorothy Gish (1930) from a play set in a whaling camp in the frozen north, and Down River (1931), in which he played a drug smuggler.

His New York stage debut in 1931 immediately led to film offers and Laughton's first Hollywood film was The Old Dark House (1932) with Boris Karloff, in which he played a bluff Yorkshire businessman marooned during a storm with other travelers in a creepy remote Welsh manor. He then played a demented submarine commander in Devil and the Deep with Tallulah Bankhead, Gary Cooper and Cary Grant, and followed this with his best-remembered film role of that year as Nero in Cecil B. DeMille's The Sign of the Cross. Laughton turned out other memorable performances during that first Hollywood trip, repeating his stage role as a murderer in Payment Deferred, playing H. G. Wells' mad vivisectionist Dr. Moreau in Island of Lost Souls, and the meek raspberry-blowing clerk in the brief segment of If I Had a Million, directed by Ernst Lubitsch. He appeared in six Hollywood films in 1932. His association with director Alexander Korda began in 1933 with The Private Life of Henry VIII (loosely based on the life of King Henry VIII), for which Laughton won an Academy Award. He also continued to act occasionally on stage, including a U. S. production of The Life of Galileo by (and with) Bertolt Brecht.

Film career

1933–1943

Laughton soon gave up the stage in preference for a film career and returned to Hollywood where his next film was White Woman (1933) in which he co-starred with Carole Lombard as a Cockney river trader in the Malaysian jungle. Then came The Barretts of Wimpole Street (1934) as Norma Shearer's character's malevolent father (although Laughton was only three years older than Shearer); Les Misérables (1935) as Inspector Javert; one of his most famous screen roles in Mutiny on the Bounty (1935) as Captain William Bligh, co-starring with Clark Gable as Fletcher Christian; and Ruggles of Red Gap (1935) as the very English butler transported to early 1900s America. He signed to play Micawber in David Copperfield (1934), but after a few days shooting asked to be released from the part and was replaced by W. C. Fields.

Back in England, and again with Korda, he played the title role in Rembrandt (1936). In 1937, also for Korda, he starred in an ill-fated film version of the classic novel, I, Claudius, by Robert Graves, which was abandoned during filming owing to the injuries suffered by co-star Merle Oberon in a car crash. After I, Claudius, he and the ex-patriate German film producer Erich Pommer founded the production company Mayflower Pictures in the UK, which produced three films starring Laughton: Vessel of Wrath (US Title The Beachcomber) (1938), based on a story by W. Somerset Maugham, in which his wife Elsa Lanchester co-starred; St. Martin's Lane (US Title Sidewalks of London), about London street entertainers, which featured Vivien Leigh and Rex Harrison; and Jamaica Inn, with Maureen O'Hara and Robert Newton, about Cornish smugglers, based on Daphne du Maurier's novel, and the last film Alfred Hitchcock directed in Britain before moving to Hollywood in the late 1930s. The films produced were not successful enough, and the company was saved from bankruptcy only when RKO Pictures offered Laughton the title role (Quasimodo) in The Hunchback of Notre Dame (1939), with Jamaica Inn co-star O'Hara. Laughton and Pommer had plans to make further films, but the outbreak of World War II, which implied the loss of many foreign markets, meant the end of the company. Laughton's early success in The Private Life of Henry VIII established him as one of the leading interpreters of the costume and historical drama parts for which he is best remembered (Nero, Henry VIII, Mr. Barrett, Inspector Javert, Captain Bligh, Rembrandt, Quasimodo and others); he was also type-cast for arrogant, unscrupulous characters.

He largely moved away from historical parts when he played an Italian vineyard owner in California in They Knew What They Wanted (1940); a South Seas patriarch in The Tuttles of Tahiti (1942); and an American admiral during World War II in Stand by for Action (1942). He played a Victorian butler in Forever and a Day (1943) and an Australian bar-owner in The Man from Down Under (1943). Simon Callow's 1987 biography quotes a number of contemporary reviews of Laughton's performances in these films. James Agate, reviewing Forever and a Day, wrote: "Is there no-one at RKO to tell Charles Laughton when he is being plain bad?" On the other hand, Bosley Crowther of the New York Times declared that Forever and a Day boasted "superb performances".

C. A. Lejeune, wrote Callow, was "shocked" by the poor quality of Laughton's recent work: "One of the most painful screen phenomena of latter years", she wrote in The Observer, "has been the decline and fall of Charles Laughton. " On the other hand, David Shipman, in his book The Great Movie Stars: The Golden Years, said "Laughton was a total actor. His range was wide".

1943–1962

Laughton played a cowardly schoolmaster in occupied France

in This Land is Mine (1943), by Jean Renoir, in which he engaged himself most actively; in fact, while Renoir was still working on an early script, Laughton would talk about Alphonse Daudet's story "The Last Lesson", which suggested to Renoir a relevant scene for the film. Laughton played a henpecked husband who eventually murders his wife in The Suspect (1944), directed by Robert Siodmak, who would become a good friend. He played sympathetically an impoverished composer-pianist in Tales of Manhattan (1942) and starred in an updated version of Oscar Wilde's The Canterville Ghost in 1944.

Laughton appeared in two comedies with Deanna Durbin, It Started with Eve (1941) and Because of Him (1946). He portrayed a bloodthirsty pirate in Captain Kidd (1945) and a malevolent judge in The Paradine Case (1948). Laughton played a megalomaniac press tycoon in The Big Clock (1948). He had supporting roles as a Nazi in pre-war Paris in Arch of Triumph (1948), as a bishop in The Girl from Manhattan (1948), as a seedy go-between in The Bribe (1949), and as a kindly widower in The Blue Veil (1951). He played a Bible-reading pastor in the multi-story A Miracle Can Happen (1947), but his piece wound up being cut and replaced with another featuring Dorothy Lamour, and in this form the film was retitled as On Our Merry Way. However, an original print of A Miracle Can Happen was sent abroad for dubbing before the Laughton sequence was deleted, and in this form it was shown in Spain as Una Encuesta Llamada Milagro.

Laughton made his first color film in Paris as Inspector Maigret in The Man on the Eiffel Tower (1949) and, wrote the Monthly Film Bulletin, "appeared to overact" alongside Boris Karloff as a mad French nobleman in a version of Robert Louis Stevenson's The Strange Door in 1951. He played a tramp in O. Henry's Full House (1952). He became a pirate again, buffoon style this time, in Abbott and Costello Meet Captain Kidd (1952). Laughton made a guest appearance on the Colgate Comedy Hour, featuring Abbott and Costello, in which he delivered the Gettysburg Address. He played Herod Antipas in Salome (1953, with Rita Hayworth in the title role) and repeated his role as Henry VIII in Young Bess (1953).

He returned to England to star in Hobson's Choice (1954), directed by David Lean. Laughton received Academy Award and Golden Globe nominations for his role in Witness for the Prosecution (1957). He played a British admiral in Under Ten Flags (1960) and worked with Laurence Olivier in Spartacus (1960). His final film was Advise and Consent (1962), for which he received favorable comments for his performance as a southern US Senator (for which accent he studied recordings of Mississippi Senator John Stennis). Laughton worked on the film, which was directed by Otto Preminger, while he was dying from metastatic renal cell carcinoma (kidney cancer).

The Night of the Hunter

In 1955, Laughton directed The Night of the Hunter, starring Robert Mitchum, Shelley Winters and Lillian Gish. The film has been cited among critics as one of the best of the 1950s, and has been selected by the United States National Film Registry for preservation in the Library of Congress. At the time of its original release, however, it was a critical and box-office failure, and Laughton never directed again. The documentary Charles Laughton Directs The Night of the Hunter by Robert Gitt (2002) features preserved rushes and outtakes with Laughton's audible off-camera direction.

Theatre

Laughton made his London stage debut in Gogol's The Government Inspector (1926). He appeared in many West End plays in the following few years and his earliest successes on the stage were as Hercule Poirot in Alibi (1928); he was the first actor to portray the Belgian detective in this stage adaptation of The Murder of Roger Ackroyd, and as William Marble in Payment Deferred, making his Lyceum Theatre (New York) debut in 1931.

In 1926, he played the role of the criminal Ficsur in the original London production of Ferenc Molnár's Liliom (The play was musicalized in 1945 by Rodgers and Hammerstein as Carousel, where Ficsur became Jigger Craigin, but Laughton never appeared in the musical version). While Laughton is most remembered for his film career, he continued to work in the theatre, as when, after the success of The Private Life of Henry VIII he appeared at the Old Vic Theatre in 1933 as Macbeth, Lopakin in The Cherry Orchard, Prospero in The Tempest and Angelo in Measure for Measure. In the U. S. , Laughton worked with Bertolt Brecht on a new English version of Brecht's play Galileo. Laughton played the title role at the play's premiere in Los Angeles on 30 July 1947 and later that year in New York. This staging was directed by Joseph Losey. The processes by which Laughton painstakingly, over many weeks, created his Galileo—and incidentally, edited and translated the play along with Brecht—are detailed in an essay by

Brecht, "Building Up A Part: Laughton's Galileo. "

Laughton had one of his most notable successes in the theatre by directing and playing the Devil in Don Juan in Hell beginning in 1950. The piece is actually the third act sequence from George Bernard Shaw's play Man and Superman, frequently cut from productions to reduce its playing time, consisting of a philosophical debate between Don Juan and the Devil with contributions from Doña Ana and the statue of Ana's father. Laughton conceived the piece as a staged reading and cast Charles Boyer, Cedric Hardwicke, and Agnes Moorehead (billed as "The First Drama Quartette") in the other roles. Boyer won a special Tony Award for his performance.

He directed several plays on Broadway. His most notable box-office success as a director came in 1954, with The Caine Mutiny Court-Martial, a full-length stage dramatization by Herman Wouk of the court-martial scene in Wouk's novel The Caine Mutiny. The play, starring Henry Fonda as defense attorney Barney Greenwald, opened the same year as the film starring Humphrey Bogart as Captain Queeg and José Ferrer as Greenwald based on the original novel, but did not affect that film's box-office performance. Laughton also directed a staged reading in 1953 of Stephen Vincent Benét's John Brown's Body, a full-length poem about the American Civil War and its aftermath. The production starred Tyrone Power, Raymond Massey (re-creating his film characterizations of Abraham Lincoln and John Brown), and Judith Anderson. Laughton did not appear himself in either production, but John Brown's Body was recorded complete by Columbia Masterworks.

Laughton returned to the London stage in May 1958 to direct and star in Jane Arden's The Party at the New Theatre which also had Elsa Lanchester and Albert Finney in the cast. He made his final appearances on stage as Nick Bottom in A Midsummer Night's Dream, and as King Lear at the Shakespeare Memorial Theatre in 1959, although failing health resulted in both performances being disappointing, according to some British critics. His performance as King Lear was lambasted by critics, including Kenneth Tynan, who wrote that Laughton's Nick Bottom ". . . behaves in a manner that has nothing to do with acting, although it perfectly hits off the demeanor of a rapscallion uncle dressed up to entertain the children at a Christmas party". Although he did not appear in any later plays, Laughton toured the U. S. with staged readings, including a very successful appearance on the Stanford University campus in 1960.

Recordings

Laughton's voice first appeared on 78-rpm records with the release of five British Regal Zonophone 10-inch discs entitled Voice of the Stars issued annually from 1934 to 1938. These featured short soundtrack snippets from the year's top films. He is heard on all five records in, respectively, The Private Life of Henry VIII, The Barretts of Wimpole Street, Mutiny on the Bounty, I, Claudius (curiously, since this film was unfinished and thus never released), and Vessel of Wrath. In 1937 he recorded Lincoln's Gettysburg Address on a 10-inch Columbia 78, having made a strong impression with it in Ruggles of Red Gap.

He made several other spoken-word recordings, one of his most famous being his one-man album of Charles Dickens's Mr. Pickwick's Christmas, a twenty-minute version of the Christmas chapter from Dickens's The Pickwick Papers. It was first released by American Decca in 1944 as a four-record 78-rpm set, but was afterward transferred to LP. It frequently appeared on LP with a companion piece, Decca's 1941 adaptation of Dickens's A Christmas Carol, starring Ronald Colman as Scrooge. Both stories were released together on a Deutsche Grammophon CD for Christmas 2005.

In 1943, Laughton recorded a reading of the Nativity story from St. Luke's Gospel, and this was released in 1995 on CD on a Nimbus Records collection entitled Prima Voce: The Spirit of Christmas Past. A Brunswick/American Decca LP entitled Readings from the Bible featured Laughton reading Garden of Eden, The Fiery Furnace, Noah's Ark, and David and Goliath. It was released in 1958. Laughton had previously included several Bible readings when he played the title role in the film Rembrandt. Laughton also narrated the story on the soundtrack album of the film that he directed, Night of the Hunter, accompanied by the film's score. This album has also been released on CD. Also, and derived from the film they made together, a complete radio show (18 June 1945) of The Canterville Ghost was broadcast which featured Laughton and Margaret O'Brien. It has been issued on a Pelican LP.

A two-LP Capitol Records album was released in 1962, the year of Laughton's death, entitled The Story Teller: A Session with Charles Laughton. Taken from Laughton's one-man stage shows, it culls together dramatic readings from several sources. Three of the excerpts are broadcast annually on a Minnesota Public Radio Thanksgiving program entitled Giving Thanks. The Story Teller won a Grammy in 1962 for Best Spoken Word Recording. However, although the album has yet to be released on compact disc, it can now be heard in its entirety online.

Television

Laughton was the fill-in host on 9 September 1956, when Elvis Presley made his first of three appearances on CBS's The Ed Sullivan Show, which garnered 72 million viewers (Ed Sullivan was recuperating from a car accident). That same year, Laughton hosted the first of two programs devoted to classical music entitled "Festival of Music", and telecast on the NBC television anthology series Producers' Showcase. One of his last performances was on the TV series Checkmate, in which he played a missionary recently returned from China. He threw himself into the role, traveling to China for several months in order to better understand his character.

Private life and death

In 1927, Laughton began a relationship with Elsa Lanchester, at the time a cast mate in a stage play. The two were married in 1929, became American citizens in 1950, and remained together until Laughton's death. Over the years, they appeared together in several films, including Rembrandt (1936), Tales of Manhattan (1942) and The Big Clock (1948). Lanchester portrayed Anne of Cleves, Henry VIII's fourth wife, opposite Laughton in The Private Life of Henry VIII. They both received Academy Award nominations for their performances in Witness for the Prosecution (1957) — Laughton for Best Actor, and Lanchester for Best Supporting Actress—but neither won. Laughton and Lanchester had no children. Laughton's bisexuality has been corroborated by several of his contemporaries and is generally accepted by Hollywood historians, However, actress Maureen O'Hara, a friend and co-star of Laughton, claimed that Laughton told her that he and his wife never had children because of a botched abortion which Lanchester had early in her career while performing burlesque and that indeed his biggest regret was never having children of his own. In her own autobiography, Lanchester acknowledged having had two abortions in her youth (one of the pregnancies purportedly by Laughton) although she didn't mention whether this had indeed left her incapable of becoming pregnant again. According to her biographer Charles Higham, the reason she didn't have children was that she didn't want any.

Death

Charles Laughton died 15 December 1962, after a battle with renal cell carcinoma (kidney cancer), aged 63. He was cremated and the remains interred in a crypt in the Court of Remembrance courtyard at Forest Lawn - Hollywood Hills Cemetery in Los Angeles, California.

Awards and nominations

Laughton won the New York Film Critics Circle Awards for Mutiny on the Bounty and Ruggles of Red Gap in 1935.

Academy Awards
1933 Won Best Actor in a Leading Role, The Private Life of Henry VIII
1936 Nominated Best Actor in a Leading Role, Mutiny on the Bounty
1958 Nominated Best Actor in a Leading Role, Witness for the Prosecution
Filmography

Charles Laughton filmography
Theatre performances

Actor

1926: The Revizor [written] by Nikolai Gogol
first appearance, debut on the London stage (aka The Government Inspector)
1928: Alibi adapted from the novel The Murder of Roger Ackroyd by Agatha Christie
police drama, he is the first actor to play detective Hercule Poirot
1928: The Silver Tassie (premiere)
1931: Payment Deferred adapted from the novel by C. S. Forester
debut on the New York stage
1932: The Fatal Alibi adapted from the novel The Murder of Roger Ackroyd by Agatha Christie
police drama, Laughton is also the director (American version of Alibi)
1947: Galileo by Bertolt Brecht
1950: The Cherry Orchard by Anton Chekhov

1951 and 1952: Don Juan in Hell, the third act of Man and Superman by George Bernard Shaw
drama, Laughton is also the director
1956–1957: Major Barbara by George Bernard Shaw
comedy, Laughton is also the director
1959: King Lear by William Shakespeare
classic tragedy
Director

1932: The Fatal Alibi adapted from the novel The Murder of Roger Ackroyd by Agatha Christie
police drama, Laughton also acts in the play.
1951 and 1952: Don Juan in Hell (the third act of Man and Superman) by George Bernard Shaw
drama, Laughton also acts in the play.
1953: John Brown's Body, adapted by Laughton from Stephen Vincent Benét
with Judith Anderson
1956–1957: Major Barbara by George Bernard Shaw
comedy, Laughton also acts in the play
1954–1955: The Caine Mutiny Court Martial adapted from the novel by Herman Wouk
drama, with Henry Fonda, transferred in 1954 to the screen by Edward Dmytryk
Producer

1955: 3 for Tonight
musical revue, with Harry Belafonte

CPSIA information can be obtained at www.ICGtesting.com
Printed in the USA
BVOW071755211012

303548BV00001B/43/P

9 781486 196494